DAVID SMITH

NORTH AND SOUTH

Britain's Economic, Social and Political Divide

SECOND EDITION

PENGUIN BOOKS

For Richard, Thomas, Emily and Elizabeth

06216596

PENGUIN BOOKS

Published by the Penguin Group
Penguin Books Ltd, 27 Wrights Lane, London W8 5TZ, England
Penguin Books USA Inc., 375 Hudson Street, New York, New York 10014, USA
Penguin Books Australia Ltd, Ringwood, Victoria, Australia
Penguin Books Canada Ltd, 10 Alcorn Avenue, Toronto, Ontario, Canada M4V 3B2
Penguin Books (NZ) Ltd, 182–190 Wairau Road, Auckland 10, New Zealand

Penguin Books Ltd, Registered Offices: Harmondsworth, Middlesex, England

First published in Pelican Books 1989
Second edition published in Penguin Books 1994
1 3 5 7 9 10 8 6 4 2

Typeset by Datix International Limited, Bungay, Suffolk
Printed in England by Clays Ltd, St Ives plc
Set in 10/12 pt Monophoto Times

CONTENTS

ACKNOWLEDGEMENTS

Thanks are due to the many people who helped in the research and writing of this book, and particularly to the many specialists in this field who willingly provided me with their own research. My very special thanks go to my wife Jane and my children Richard, Thomas, Emily and Elizabeth, for their patience and understanding. Jon Riley at Penguin was, as ever, a helpful and encouraging editor.

INTRODUCTION

North and South has endured as a description of many of the important economic, social, cultural and political differences within Britain. It was certainly in common use in the 1850s when Mrs Gaskell wrote a novel of the same name, a title which this book has stolen. And its usage increased during the 1980s, when references to a North–South divide were many and varied.

When the first edition of this book was written in 1988, the existence of significant North–South differences, most of them in the South's favour, was beyond doubt. Unemployment rates in the South were roughly half those in the North. Income levels were higher, and rising fastest, in southern areas. Southerners were also the main beneficiaries of a rising stock market, partly through government privatization offers, and of increasing levels of inheritance. House prices in the south-east were 2½ times levels for comparable properties in Yorkshire and Humberside, the north, the north west and Wales. The great boom for the service industries, including retailing but in particular financial and business services, was in full swing, and benefiting those areas closest to London. The odds appeared stacked firmly in the South's favour.

My purpose in writing North and South was to demonstrate that, ultimately, an over-concentration of wealth and economic activity in the South was both unhealthy and inefficient. Congestion would bring unnecessary costs. The South, I feared, could sink under the weight of its own economic success. The 'unbalanced economy', as I described it, would exacerbate the traditional weaknesses of the British economy, a tendency towards

higher inflation and a chronic balance of payments problem. If
one dominant part of the economy was booming, it would force
governments to adopt macro-economic policies that, while appropriate to conditions there, would also hit the rest. A lack of
economic balance would mean higher unemployment.

What I did not expect was that the unbalanced economy
would come to grief in so rapid and spectacular a way. Moreover, the recession of 1990–92, brought on by a sustained period
of very high interest rates, hit the South far harder than the
North. The recession was, in many ways, the South's comeuppance, a reminder that when the talk is of a modern British
economic miracle, it should be taken with a very large pinch of
salt. Southerners borrowed heavily to participate fully in the
miracle, and were left with a burden of debt that made them
acutely vulnerable to high interest rates. Northerners, in contrast, kept their feet on the ground and suffered far less. Thus,
in terms of unemployment and house prices, to take two highly
visible examples, the North–South gap narrowed sharply as a
result of the recession.

This does not mean, however, that North and South has
ceased to be a topic of interest. Far from it: the recession has
raised key questions about the future course of Britain's economic geography. It has not, nor would it be expected to have,
unwound a century or more in which the South has steadily
gained in economic advantage. On a number of economic measures, and even more dramatically in areas such as voting behaviour, a substantial North–South divide remains. At the time I
wrote the first edition of this book, there was no real debate
about the existence of North–South disparities. The fact that
there now is such a debate, with the balance between North and
South seen by many as standing at a crossroads, has made the
task of writing this new edition both more challenging and more
interesting than its predecessor.

There have been a number of books on different aspects of
North – South differences, for example voting behaviour, employment and regional policy, yet I have not come across a single
text which attempts to pull all these strands together. Part of the
reason for this is that the subject, as one quickly discovers, is a

very broad one. And, while some of its elements are not covered here in as much detail as would be ideal, I hope that the process of distilling a wealth of available material has not resulted in too much of importance being left out. In particular, as one who approaches the subject from an economist's standpoint, I have endeavoured to do justice to the other areas where North–South differences are important. Even if this has not been achieved perfectly, it is a reasonable contention that most North–South differences arise from economic factors.

People who have written on North and South have been criticized either for expounding a viewpoint from the lofty, privileged heights of London and the south east, or for representing an inevitably complaining Northern position. As one who originates from the west midlands, an area which in economic terms first swung into the North during the early 1980s but 'rejoined' the South in the 1980s, before suffering again in the 1990–92 recession, I have tried to avoid any built-in prejudices. Whether this has been achieved may depend partly on the reader's own prejudices in these matters.

Finally, a word on some definitions used in the book. A number of different definitions of the regions of the United Kingdom have been used over the years and some of that choice remains today. Regions can be defined according to the sphere of influence of major cities, or the transmission areas of the independent television companies. Many official statistics are available at the level of the county or town. The approach used in this book has, however, been to use the government's standard regions, as detailed in the appendix and as summarized in Figure 1. Under these definitions, which apart from fairly small boundary changes have been in use over a long period, the United Kingdom is broken down into eleven separate areas – the north, Yorkshire and Humberside, the east midlands, East Anglia, the south east, the south west, the west midlands, the north west, Wales, Scotland and Northern Ireland.

Armed with this regional breakdown, the approach in this book, which has also been followed by many researchers in this field, has been to define the South as consisting of five regions – the south east, East Anglia, the south west, the east midlands and the west midlands. Lower-case letters have been used, where appropriate, to distinguish the component parts of the South from its whole. The North is defined as six regions comprising the north, north west, Yorkshire and Humberside, Scotland, Wales and Northern Ireland.

It would be surprising if the economic, political and other differences between North and South followed a neat line according to the boundaries of the government's standard regions. But it is probably the best we can do. Some parts of the South, as here defined, are economically disadvantaged. One thinks of the old mining areas of Cornwall, in the south west and therefore the South, which were for a long time the target of regional aid. More recently, even parts of the south east have suffered, to the point where they have made a justifiable claim for government regional assistance. Some would doubt the inclusion of the two regions of the Midlands as part of the South. However, the rationale for their inclusion is that, in the case of the east midlands, the region has been a clear beneficiary of spillover activity and prosperity from the south east. The west midlands has been, since the 1930s, part of a zone of prosperity, originally based on manufacturing industry, which stretched from London to Birmingham. This was interrupted in the early 1980s, but it was on its way to being re-established during the latter part of that decade, before the recession struck. In any case, a more narrow definition of the South, to take in just the south east, East Anglia and the eastern half of the south west, would, over the long term, strengthen rather than weaken the appearance of sharp North–South differences in the United Kingdom.

There is a case for refining the breakdown of the United Kingdom beyond the simple North–South division. One approach divides the country into four areas – the highly prosperous south east itself; the areas bordering the south east – East Anglia, parts of the south west and the east midlands; the old industrial heartlands of the west midlands, the north west and Yorkshire and Humberside; and a 'Celtic fringe' of the very north of England, Cornwall, Wales, Scotland and Northern Ireland. Useful though such an approach can be, there is also a danger that, in refining the breakdown too much, one will be unable to see the wood for the trees.

The same is true of the argument that any differences in wealth and prosperity in Britain do not have their base in North–South differences because there have always been prosperous areas and towns in the North, and disadvantaged parts of the South. This is perfectly true. But, again taking the long view, there must have been something about the South which resulted in it having more than its fair share of thriving towns and well-to-do individuals. And it is that which this book sets out to examine.

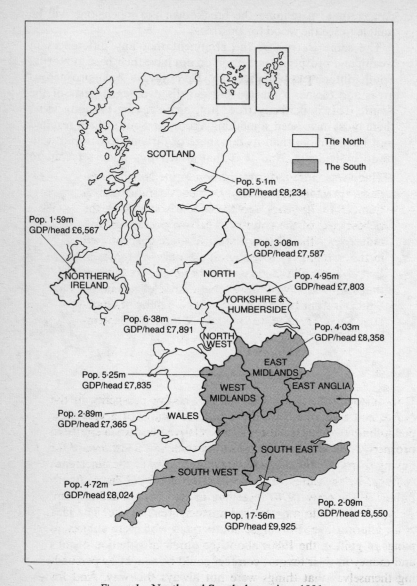

Figure 1   North and South, by region, 1991

Source: Central Statistical Office, *Regional Trends 1993.*

1

THE LONG DIVIDE

There was more industrialization in the North, originally, therefore there has to be more de-industrialization. Until 70 years ago the North was always the richest part of the country. The two present growth industries – the City and tourism – are concentrated in the South. I try to encourage people to go North; that is where all the great country houses are because that's where the wealth was. Now some of it is in the South. It's our turn, that's all. (Lord Young of Graffham, Secretary of State for Trade & Industry, September 1987)

TAKING IT IN TURNS?

Does history tell us that shifts in the relative prosperity of the North and South of Britain are but the swings of a very slow pendulum? In other words, was the relative increase in southern prosperity during much of this century somehow a just reward for having to endure the brash northern successes of the nineteenth century? By the same token, could the bursting of the southern bubble in the early 1990s be telling us that, by the millennium, we will be well into a prolonged northern renaissance? The idea is an alluring one. For those southerners who were subject to pangs of guilt in the 1980s about the unfair distribution of jobs and money in their favour, comfort could be sought by persuading themselves that things were not always this way. And for northerners, not only did the belief that they once had the upper hand over the South provide solace but, by inference, they knew that by hanging around for long enough their turn would come again. And, for Conservative politicians, if the market eventually ensured that everyone got a fair crack of the whip, why interfere? It is an idea, as the above quotation illustrates, that found favour in high places in Margaret Thatcher's Conservative Government in the 1980s. But is it true?

As with most such arguments, it depends on where you start. In the predominantly agricultural society before the industrial revolution, the ownership and productiveness of the land was the key to the distribution of wealth and economic activity. If we go back as far as the Domesday Book, in 1086, we find that Norwich, with a population of 5,000, was the largest town in the records, although the survey did not include London, or Winchester, where the Royal Treasury was located.

LONDON'S DOMINANCE

An important feature of the period from the fourteenth to the seventeenth centuries, immediately before the industrial revolution, was the rapid growth of London, both in size and influence. As far back as the fourteenth century, as the development of the cloth industry produced a more diversified regional economy, benefiting towns such as Leeds, Halifax and Bradford, together with parts of East Anglia and Wales, London was dominant. Its population was over 50,000 and, with a prosperity built upon trade, it acted as a magnet for immigrants from other parts of the South.

In the following centuries, a North–South divide became even more apparent, both in the distribution of wealth and in the quality and character of life. According to G. M. Trevelyan, in his incomparable *English Social History:*

Under the Tudor Kings the life of England north of the Trent bore a character of its own. The constant troubles of the Scottish border, the poverty of the whole region except the clothing valleys and the mining districts, the greater strength of old feudal loyalties and pretensions, and the greater popularity of the monasteries and the old religion differentiated it from the rest of England in the reign of Henry VIII, and to a lesser extent under Elizabeth. (1944, Vol. II, pp. 13–14)

By 1642 and the outbreak of the first Civil War, London's population had swelled to more than half a million and dominated England in a way that was not matched in other European countries. As John Morrill has written in the *Oxford Illustrated History of Britain*:

Paris, the largest town in France, had 350,000 inhabitants in the mid-seventeenth century. The second and third largest were Rouen and Lyons with 80,000–100,000 inhabitants. In Europe, there were only five towns with populations of more than 250,000, but over one hundred with more than 50,000 inhabitants. In England, however, London had well over half a million inhabitants by 1640 or 1660: Newcastle, Bristol and Norwich, which rivalled one another for second place, had barely 25,000 each. London was bigger than the next fifty towns in England combined. It is hard to escape the conclusion that London was growing at the expense of the rest. Its stranglehold on overseas trade, and therefore on most of the early banking and financial activity, was slow to ease; in consequence much of the trade from most of the outports had to be directed via London. In the seventeenth century the major new 're-export' trades (the importation of colonial raw materials such as sugar and tobacco for finishing and dispatch to Europe) were concentrated there. London dominated the governmental, legal and political world . . . By 1640, 10 per cent of all Englishmen lived in the capital and one in six had lived part of their lives there. By 1690 the richest one hundred Londoners were among the richest men in England. No longer was wealth primarily the perquisite of the landed. (1984, pp. 293–4)

London's growth and vitality in this period is underlined by the fact that neither the plague nor the fire had any permanent effect on its expansion. Indeed, the fire had the effect of eradicating slum housing and creating a building boom.

The growth of London had direct implications for the prosperity of agriculture in the South, already favoured over the North for climatic reasons. Kent became the 'garden of England' not because of some innate beauty in the county, as is sometimes thought, but because it provided for the growing appetite of London. At a time when nearly 90 per cent of the population worked on the land, according to Gregory King's estimate for 1688, proximity to the expanding London market was clearly a great advantage, and one primarily enjoyed by the Home Counties and East Anglia. The poorest of all the agricultural classes were the peasants of Scotland, Wales and Ireland.

INDUSTRY IN THE SOUTH

The increasing demand for food from an expanding population together with the agricultural revolution of the seventeenth century, including the enclosures which continued into the eighteenth century, increased the spread of what was by now a more intensive farming throughout the country. Rising food prices and more productive methods of agriculture ensured that there was money to be made out of the land, although this did not necessarily benefit the ordinary agricultural labourer.

Even so, by the time of the industrial revolution of the second half of the eighteenth century, writers could still refer to 'the agricultural South". Not that this necessarily did justice to the South. In the middle of the seventeenth century, by virtue of local iron ore deposits, there were thirty-four iron furnaces in Kent and Sussex, largely devoted to satisfying the strong military demand for cannons. Similarly, the naval shipyards at Chatham, Deptford and Woolwich were major employers. The wars of the eighteenth century had the effect of disproportionately boosting demand and economic activity in the South, anticipating a later uneven regional pattern in military expenditure.

The civil wars themselves, in which the country divided along lines broadly similar to the North and South described in this book, while highly complex in their origins, could be seen as in part directly derived from the new conflict between old money, based on land, and new money, emanating from trade. As George Orwell described it in *The Road to Wigan Pier*, written in 1937:

It was the industrialization of the North that gave the North–South antithesis its peculiar slant. Until comparatively recently the northern part of England was the backward and feudal part, and such industry as existed was concentrated in London and the south east. In the Civil War, for instance, roughly speaking a war of money versus feudalism, the North and West were for the King and the South and East for the Parliament. (1959, p. 113)

Trevelyan, while acknowledging that the civil wars were 'a struggle for London and its appendages against the rural North and West' (1944, Vol. II, p. 99), saw them in somewhat different terms. They were not, in his view, a war between rich and poor, or even the product of a Royalist army forced to fight because of feudal dependence. Rather, people had a relatively free choice based on their own opinions in the 'war of ideas' in Church and State. But certainly, without the wealth and manpower of London, Parliament could not have hoped to secure victory. And yet, ironically, the end of the civil wars produced a relative decline in London's previously dominant position. As Christopher Hill writes in his *Reformation to Industrial Revolution*:

The victory of South and East over North and West in the civil war led, paradoxically, to a reversal of the growing economic dominance of London, against which the outports had been struggling at least since 1604. During the civil war the monarchy could no longer protect the companies, and a period of virtual free trade ensued. (This was one reason why London companies were anxious for an early peace with the King, even if by compromise.) But under the Protectorate the East India Company and the Merchant Adventurers recovered government support, in return for loans. All accounts agree on the flourishing state of London's trade in the early 1650s. Yet the fillip given to colonial trade by the Navigation Acts undoubtedly promoted the prosperity of outports like Exeter, Plymouth, Bristol and Liverpool in the late seventeenth and eighteenth centuries; just as its stimulus to ship-building helped the shipyards of Whitby, Scarborough, Hull and Newcastle. The percentage of English shipping tonnage owned by Londoners was 43·3 in 1702, 29·9 in 1788. (1969, pp. 137–8)

The industrial revolution was not, therefore, a rude shock to London and the South. Although any effective shift of economic power did not come until the nineteenth century, and then relatively briefly, the expansion of activity in the North was apparent by the early part of the eighteenth century.

MUCK AND BRASS

There was no single year or decade in which Britain's industrial revolution can be said to have occurred. Many industrial processes were well-established long before the middle of the eighteenth century, including the blast furnace – in use in the fifteenth and sixteenth centuries. However, most economic historians would put the industrial revolution in the second half of the eighteenth century when, in Professor Walt Rostow's (1960) phrase, 'the take-off into self-sustained growth' occurred.

Peter Mathias, in his book *The First Industrial Nation* (1983), pinpoints such a process at work in the period between the 1740s and the 1780s, when major inventions and innovations occurred. James Watt and Matthew Boulton were building and selling steam engines by 1780. The spinning jenny, water frame and 'mule' all emerged in this period. Perhaps as importantly, inventions developed for use in the coal industry were diffused among a wide range of rapidly developing industries.

By 1780 the industrial revolution was well in train. 'Here came a break with a tradition of economic life, and a pace of change, which had lasted for centuries and which, in certain essential characteristics, had been universal across all countries of the globe up to that time,' writes Mathias (1983, p. 3), reinforcing his point with the observation that if the post-1780 growth rate of Britain was projected back, the economy would not have existed at some point in relatively recent history.

The North, economically disadvantaged in the agricultural economy that Britain had been, now came into its own. It was rich in the natural resources of coal and iron ore on which Britain's industrial development was based. As early as the 1680s, the Durham and Northumberland coalfields were producing a combined total of more than 1·2 million tons of coal a year, out of just under 3 million tons for the country as a whole. The coalfields of the north east were followed in importance by Yorkshire, Lancashire, Cheshire and the Midlands, with a combined annual output of 800,000 tons, Scotland with 475,000 and Wales 200,000.

One hundred years later, in the 1780s, national coal output

had increased to over 10 million tons annually, out of which the north east coalfield produced 3 million, the Yorkshire, Lancashire, Cheshire and Midlands area 4 million, Scotland 1·6 million and Wales 800,000. There was coal mined in significant quantities in other parts of the country, notably the Forest of Dean, Somerset and Devon, but the industry was dominated by the North and the Midlands.

Navigable rivers, particularly the Severn and the Trent, provided transport for raw materials and the products of the new industrial age, an advantage that was extended during the canal age of the late eighteenth century. By 1800, the map of Britain's canal system showed a highly developed network in the centre of the island, at its most intense in the area stretching from Yorkshire and Lancashire down to the south Midlands. Large parts of the South were left untouched by the canal age.

MANCHESTER

As we move into the nineteenth century, the focus of interest, inevitably, switches to Manchester. Manchester, its wealth and strength built upon the Lancashire cotton industry, was the world's first industrial city. This derived not primarily from natural resources – the availability of local coal was a relatively unimportant consideration – but from a combination of entrepreneurship, with cotton kings such as Robert Peel and Richard Arkwright, and proximity to the port of Liverpool, both for the importation of raw material from the southern United States and the West Indies and the export of finished product, much of it to the important colonial markets.

Manchester usurped the traditional position held by York as the capital of the North. More significantly, for much of the nineteenth century it appeared to eclipse London. Its population grew from 40,000 in the late 1780s to more than 140,000 by the census of 1831 – still small in comparison with London but catching up fast. Of equal fascination for visitors, even those accustomed to the poverty and squalor of the London slums, were the social conditions in this unfettered industrial city.

Alexis de Tocqueville, after a visit to Manchester from France in 1835 wrote in his *Journeys to England and Ireland* (quoted in Gary Messinger in his *Manchester in the Victorian Age*, 1985, p. 55):

From this foul drain ... the greatest stream of human industry flows out to fertilise the whole world. From this filthy sewer pure gold flows. Here humanity attains its most complete development and its most brutish; here civilization works its miracles, and civilized man is turned back into a savage.

Just as uncomplimentary was Friedrich Engels, who based *The Condition of the Working Class in England in 1844* on his lengthy period in Manchester. There can be few grimmer scenes than the following, described by Engels in the 1840s:

The view from this bridge, which is fully concealed by a high parapet from all but the tallest mortals, is quite characteristic of the whole district. At the bottom the Irk flows, or rather stagnates. It is a narrow, coal-black, stinking river full of filth and rubbish which it deposits on the more low-lying right bank. In dry weather this bank presents a spectacle of the most revolting blackish-green puddles of slime from the depths of which bubbles of miasmatic gases constantly rise and create a stench which is unbearable even to those standing on a bridge forty or fifty feet above the level of the water. (1973, p. 81)

The rapid industrial development of Manchester, unfettered by local-authority or central-government control, had created an environmentalist's nightmare. Manchester, of course, was not alone in this. In the north east, the west midlands, south Yorkshire, other parts of Lancashire and south Wales, large areas of the country were lost to the dirty, voracious, industrial monster. If Manchester attracted the most attention, it was because it was the biggest. It was also, to visitors accustomed to the idea of a city as a place in which there was diversity and culture, brutal in its devotion to the single aim of making money. It certainly offended the sensibilities of the Poet Laureate Robert Southey, who visited Manchester in 1807:

A place more destitute of all interesting objects than Manchester is not easy to conceive. In size and population it is the second city of the kingdom, containing above fourscore thousand inhabitants. Imagine this multitude crowded together in narrow streets, the houses all built of brick and blackened with smoke: frequent buildings among them as large as convents, without their antiquity, without their beauty, without their holiness, where you hear from within, as you pass along, the everlasting din of machinery; and where the bell rings it is to call wretches to their work instead of their prayers. (quoted in Messinger, 1985, p. 16)

Manchester and the other great industrial cities of the North and Midlands – Leeds, Liverpool, Birmingham, Derby, Sheffield – strove to lift themselves out of these grim conditions. Civic pride was evident in those monuments to the Victorian age, the great town halls. Cities competed to build the largest, and often most gloriously irrelevant, town hall. Manchester was in the forefront of social reform, notably through the work of Dr James Kay and the Manchester Statistical Society. It led the way in freely available primary and secondary education and in the establishment of the country's first public library. Eventually, in 1851, when Manchester put on a northern version of the Great Exhibition, Queen Victoria – after much persuasion – visited the city, although she could not be persuaded to spend the night there.

For Manchester and the other great industrial centres of the Victorian age, the association of industrial wealth with dirt, pollution and congestion was a strong one. 'Where there's muck there is money', the phrase goes, but it also applied in the reverse, in that a necessary by-product of industrial money were the conditions which continued to strike visitors to the industrial North well into the twentieth century, and in some cases still do.

Not that the people who lived and worked in the industrial North necessarily thought that there was anything wrong, or indeed unusual, about this. Engels described a meeting with a Manchester businessman thus:

One day I walked with one of these middle-class gentlemen into Manchester. I spoke to him about the disgraceful unhealthy slums and drew his attention to the disgusting condition of that part of town where the factory workers lived. I declared that I had never seen so badly built a town in my life. He listened patiently and at the corner of the street at which we parted company he remarked: 'And yet there is a great deal of money to be made here. Good morning, Sir.' (quoted in Marcus, 1974, p. 234)

TWO NATIONS

The northern prosperity of the nineteenth century contrasts with the southern prosperity of the twentieth century in several respects. One of the most important lies in the spread of wealth in the two periods. The industrial workers of the nineteenth century did benefit from higher wages and this led on to, for example, higher agricultural wages in the North. But the benefits of the industrial revolution, in wealth and lifestyle, accrued mainly to the entrepreneurs, the factory and mill owners. Although there was some migration from South to North – from Kent to the Lancashire cotton industry for example – the vast majority of the new industrial workers came from the farms in the North, or were immigrants from Ireland. The gulf between the new rich and the poor in the North, the source of Disraeli's observations on the 'two nations' in Britain, was graphically described by a nineteenth-century clergyman, Canon Richard Parkinson:

There is no town in the world where the distance between the rich and the poor is so great, or the barrier between them so difficult to be crossed. I once ventured to designate the town of Manchester the most *aristocratic* town in England; and, in the sense in which the term was used, the expression is not hyperbolical. The separation between the different classes, and the consequent ignorance of each other's habits and condition, are far more complete in this place than in any other country of the older nations of Europe, or in the agricultural parts of our own kingdom. There is far less *personal* communication between the master cotton spinner and his workmen, between the calico printer and his blue-handed boys, between the master tailor and his apprentices, than there is between the Duke of Wellington and the humblest labourer on his estate, or than there is between good old George the Third and the meanest errand-boy about his palace. I mention this not as a matter of blame, but I state it simply as a *fact*. (quoted in Briggs, 1968, p. 114)

If the industrial North held mixed attractions for the working classes, it was both frightening and fascinating for the early Victorian middle and upper classes in the South. They could wonder at, and to a certain extent admire, what was happening up there, but they had no desire to be part of it. Elizabeth Gaskell, in her *North and South*, written in the mid-1850s, describes the situation of the family of a southern clergyman transplanted to the brutality of the industrial North. The gloom engendered by the prospect of such a move is captured in the following passage when the heroine, Margaret Hale, is told by her father that he is both giving up the clergy and taking the family from the rural idyll of Helstone in Hampshire to Milton-Northern (closely based on Manchester):

'Where are we to go to?' said she at last, struck with a fresh wonder as to their future plans, if plans, indeed, her father had.

'To Milton-Northern,' he answered, with a dull indifference, for he had perceived that, although his daughter's love had made her cling to him, and for a moment strive to soothe him with her love, yet the keenness of the pain was as fresh as ever in her mind.

'Milton-Northern! The manufacturing town in Darkshire?'

'Yes,' said he, in the same despondent, indifferent way. (1970, p. 70)

The shock to Margaret Hale's mother was even greater. 'Fancy living in the middle of factories, and factory people!' she declared. (p. 80).

North and South, in which southern sensibilities come up against the harsh, industrial attitudes of a big northern manufacturing town, was, like Mrs Gaskell's *Mary Barton*, based on her own Manchester experiences. It was serialized in Dickens's weekly *Household Words* in 1854 and 1855, having been preceded in that publication by *Hard Times*, written by Dickens himself, in which the typical Northern businessman was represented by the appalling Mr Gradgrind. *North and South* eventually emerges as more sympathetic to the North than *Hard Times* or *Mary Barton*, but the overall picture presented by these and other literary excursions northwards, including those of Disraeli, was to reinforce southern prejudices about the industrial North. There may have been money to be made there, but the drawbacks were many.

THE END OF THE GOLDEN AGE

The golden age of the industrial North, and of the nineteenth-century British economy as a whole, lasted for most of the first three quarters of that century. But by the last thirty to thirty-five years of Victoria's reign, the golden age was looking distinctly tarnished. Britain was still the foremost industrial power. However, in simple terms, Britain was there first and other countries were gaining fast. And in many cases, for example in the fields of scientific education, mass production and research and development, other countries learned to do it better.

The depression of 1873–96 marked a break in Britain's previously rapid development. According to calculations by Matthews, Feinstein and Odling-Smee, in their *British Economic Growth, 1856–1973* (1982), the growth rate of the economy, which had been on a rising trend, slipped from an annual average rate of 2·2 per cent a year in the period 1856–73 to 1·8 per cent a year from 1873–1913. The growth rate of manufacturing fell from 2·6 per cent to 2 per cent, and the rate of expansion of mining production halved. Perhaps as significantly, Germany and the United States embarked on a period of expansion twice as fast as that of Britain after 1870. The newly expanding industrial economies were investing at a rate which allowed them to take advantage of the latest technology, thus reinforcing their advantage. By 1913, Britain, which had pioneered the modern chemical industry, had been left behind, accounting for only 11 per cent of world output, against 34 per cent for the United States and 24 per cent for Germany.

A writer in *Cornhill* magazine in 1881, quoted by the historian Asa Briggs in his *Victorian Cities* (1968, p. 48) captured the fears of Londoners, apparently left behind by the aggressive, industrial North. London, once 'the very focus of national thought and industry, surrounded on every side by the most flourishing parts of the country', had become 'isolated in the midst of the agricultural south'. And, to the same writer, London's loss of relative economic power had been accompanied by an erosion of the capital's influence. 'The existence of a Manchester School or a Birmingham School has only been possible in the last fifty years and has been rendered possible by this comparative isolation . . . The position has largely divorced the feelings of London from the feelings of the industrial centres.'

It was not obvious at the time, but such complaints were starting to become inappropriate. Just as British industry was starting to lose out against countries which had experienced their industrial revolutions later, so the balance was slowly beginning to shift back from North to South. W. D. Rubinstein, writing in the spring 1988 edition of *The Oxford Review of Economic Policy*, using county by county totals of income-tax assessment – which would have picked up the incomes of the professional and middle classes – records a shift back to London in income distribution in the second half of the nineteenth century. There was a rapid decline in the proportion of London incomes in the national total from the early 1800s to the 1850s, followed by an equally rapid increase from around 1860. By the late nineteenth century, London incomes accounted for nearly half of the total – broadly similar to the position a century before. Meanwhile, the young men of the late Victorian/early Edwardian middle classes opted for careers in the civil service or the London-based professions, rather than in manufacturing industry.

As Asa Briggs himself observed:

During the 1890s the pull of London tightened. Local newspapers began to lose ground to national newspapers. National advertising began to increase greatly in scope and scale. The same branded goods began to be offered in shops in all parts of the country. Neither the aesthete nor the expert was as much at home in the provinces as he was in the huge metropolis. Political and economic trends began to depend less on local social and market forces and more on national pressures from the centre. (1968, p. 48)

TWENTIETH-CENTURY DECLINE

In the latter part of the eighteenth century and for much of the nineteenth century there had been a shift in the economic balance in Britain in favour of the North. This did not mean, of course, that the South did not experience a rapid growth of economic activity and prosperity over this period, but rather that such growth was even stronger in the North. Whether this period represented an unusual interlude in the more typical pattern whereby the South enjoyed most of the economic advantages, only time will tell. But the twentieth century has, for the most part, been a time of relative decline for the North in comparison with the South. For most of the time this decline was gentle and, because it occurred within an expanding and more prosperous economy, often imperceptible. But it was punctuated by two periods in which the decline of the North was a sharp one, in both relative and absolute terms. The great depression of the inter-war years and the deep recession of the early 1980s hit the North hard and shifted the balance of the British economy sharply.

The Depression

'The Victorian economy of Britain crashed in ruins between the two world wars,' wrote Eric Hobsbawm in his *Industry and Empire* (1969, p. 207). 'The sun, which, as every schoolboy knew, never set on British territory and British trade, went down below the horizon.' And it was in this crash, and the manner of the recovery from it, that the industrial North suffered and the South benefited.

The depression, which resulted from a combination of world recession, protectionism, and errors in policy, of which Churchill's decision to return to the Gold Standard at an overvalued exchange rate in 1925 ranks high on the list, changed the face of the British economy. At first, immediately after the end of the First World War, little seemed to have changed. The traditional, northern-based industries of coal, iron and steel, textiles and shipbuilding, having had to supply the needs of the military during the war, were met with pent-up demand from peacetime markets when the war ended, and experienced near-boom conditions. But this was short-lived, and few people remembered the good times in the long nightmare that followed.

The causes of the North–South divide of the 1920s and 1930s are well known. The old, staple industries were hardest hit by the loss of world markets and weak domestic demand, and these were principally located in the North. The new expanding lighter industries, satisfying and in some cases creating consumer demand, grew strongly during this period, and these were mainly based, or set up, in the South and the Midlands.

In the coal industry, home demand for coal suffered in the great depression but, by 1937–8, output for the home market, at 185 million tons a year, was broadly equivalent to its pre-First World War level. However, the British coal industry, hit by declining world demand and a loss of competitiveness, suffered a slump in exports. Output per man-shift in Britain's coal mines grew by 10 per cent between 1913 and 1936, compared with 80 per cent in the Ruhr in Germany and nearly 120 per cent in the Netherlands. Coal exports – 100 million tons a year before the First World War – averaged well under 50 million tons in the 1930s. More than half a million coal-mining jobs were lost, employment declining from over 1·2 million in 1920 to 700,000 by 1938.

The iron and steel industry, similarly, was hard hit by a downturn in world demand, only recovering with the rearmament boom later in the 1930s. Between 1929 and 1932 the production of pig iron slumped by 53 per cent, and of steel by 45 per cent. In the depths of the depression, 44 per cent of pig-iron workers and 48 per cent of steel workers were unemployed.

The shipbuilding industry, working to capacity in the latter stages of the 1914–18 war, largely to replace British shipping sunk by Germany, had been forced to turn its attention away from its traditional export markets. As a result, other countries were forced to develop their own shipbuilding capacity and some, most notably the United States, did this so successfully that they never needed to order from the British yards again. As the 1920s progressed, naval demand dried up while the commercial demand for new ships was hit by the sharp downturn in world trade in the early 1930s. In 1933 the number of launchings from British yards fell to just 7 per cent of the pre-1914 level. The closure of the Palmer's yard in Jarrow, the chief source of employment in the town, occurred in that year. Through the process of merger and acquisition, and with the help of a scheme financed by the Bank of England and the clearing banks, one million tons of shipbuilding capacity was scrapped during the 1930s. At its height, unemployment among shipyard workers was over 60 per cent.

The cotton industry, the basis of Manchester's emergence as the first truly industrial city, also declined during this period. Unlike the other staple industries, however, the economic upturn of the later 1930s left the cotton industry virtually untouched. It suffered not only from the competition from cheaper foreign products but also from the emergence of the new, man-made fibres. Production of yarn dropped from 1,982 million lbs in 1912 to 1,047 million lbs by 1930, and was still only 1,070 million lbs in 1938. The manufacture of piece goods declined from 8,050 million square yards in 1912 to 3,500 million in 1930 and further, to 3,126 million, in 1938. India, originally an important market for the Lancashire cotton industry, became an important producer in its own right, quadrupling production of piece goods between 1913 and 1938, in mills equipped, ironically, by Lancashire engineering firms. Employment in the Lancashire cotton industry at the end of the 1930s was roughly half its pre-1914 level, with around 300,000 jobs lost. But the existence of other industries, notably engineering – less hard-hit by the depression and quick to recover after it – at least provided other sources of employment in the area for the fortunate few.

That was, however, a comparatively rare feature of the industrial North in the 1920s and 1930s. Many of those who lost jobs in this period remained on the dole until the Second World War brought with it a sharply increased demand for manpower. Orwell's polemical blast *The Road to Wigan Pier* (1937) can be criticized for not making up its mind whether it is a hymn of praise to northern industrial workers, and the miners in particular, or an outraged cry against the economic injustices of the period and, in passing, a sideswipe at Hampstead socialists. Certainly, Orwell knew what he was looking for in the North. Even so, the grimness of northern industrial life he described – both for those in work and the unemployed – can be challenged only on the degree of misery that existed. For clearly, such misery was both deep and long-lasting.

The Road to Wigan Pier was and is a powerful book, and nowhere more so than in the author's description of the practice among the Wigan unemployed of 'scrambling for the coal' – obtaining coal from among the slag-heap waste, by boarding the train carrying the waste while it was in motion, often at great personal danger. Meanwhile, the wives and children of the unemployed would root among the slag heaps for coal pieces worth taking home for fuel:

We walked up to the top of the slag-heap. The men were shovelling the dirt out of the trucks, while down below their wives and children were kneeling, swiftly scrabbling with their hands in the damp dirt and picking out lumps of coal the size of an egg or smaller. You would see a woman pounce on a tiny fragment of stuff, wipe it on her apron, scrutinize it to make sure it was coal and pop it jealously into her sack.

That scene stays in my mind as one of my pictures of Lancashire: the dumpy, shawled women, with their sacking aprons and their heavy black clogs, kneeling in the cindery mud and the bitter wind, searching eagerly for tiny chips of coal. They are glad enough to do it. In winter they are desperate for fuel; it is more important almost than food. Meanwhile all round, as far as the eye can see, are the slag-heaps and hoisting gear of collieries, and not one of those collieries can sell all the coal it is capable of producing. (1959, pp. 103–5)

The contrast between the performance of the old industries and the new, expanding ones – motors, electrical engineering, rayon, food-processing and a wide range of consumer goods – was striking. So too was the difference in economic conditions in the North and the South in this period.

In the period 1929–36 the unemployment rate as a percentage of the insured population averaged 7·8 per cent in the south west, 8·8 per cent in London, 11·1 per cent in the south east (excluding London) and 15·2 per cent in the Midlands. Taking these areas as representing the South, the (unweighted) average unemployment rate was 11 per cent. Over the same period, the north west had an average unemployment rate of 21·6 per cent, Scotland 21·8 per cent, the north east 22·7 per cent and Wales 30·1 per cent, giving an average rate of 22·8 per cent for 'the North'.

The new industries did not have to be based where there were deposits of coal, iron ore or other materials. They ran on electricity, by that time becoming generally available through the creation of the national grid. The new industries were footloose, and, perhaps because of that, the people who ran them deliberately reacted against the idea of being based in the traditional industrial areas of the North. Even so, the location decisions of that time did not appear to be based on economic logic, as Sidney Pollard, in his book *The Development of the British Economy, 1914–80*, pointed out:

In preferring the south to the north, industrialists moved into areas of higher rents and higher wages; they left areas with well-developed public utilities and plentiful labour for districts in which good roads and other services had still to be laid out, and where labour was scarce, untrained and had to travel long distances to work. Nor was it true that trade unions were more restrictive in the north; in fact, the only clear-cut case in this period of an industry driven out by high wages and trade union power was the printing industry, which migrated out of Central London to such places as St Albans, Cheltenham and Ipswich, largely because of the accident that the London and provincial trade unions of typographers had not amalgamated.

There may have been a few industrialists who consciously preferred the climate or the amenities of the south, and there may have been a few others who worked out the comparative costs in some detail. But largely, industry moved south because the south was expanding and prosperous, and London and the Midlands thus benefited by the same kind of snowball effect which had created the industrial centres of the north and Wales in the past. (1983, pp. 79–80)

Southern Prosperity

The motor industry recorded a five-fold increase in output between 1924 and 1937, raising production from 95,000 to 511,000. At the same time, in a style reflected in later mass-market products, car prices fell, bringing them within the reach of a greater number of people. Even so, car ownership was the privilege of the few, even at the end of the 1930s, although export markets, and particularly the colonial markets, were important. Unlike the commercial vehicle industry, important parts of which were based in the North – Foden and ERF were in the same Cheshire town of Sandbach, Leyland was in the town of Leyland in Lancashire – mass production of cars was exclusively concentrated in the Midlands and the South.

The 1920s and 1930s, as well as being a period of rapid expansion for the motor industry, were also a time of rationalization. By the time of the 1929 crash, three quarters of the mass market was supplied by Austin from Birmingham, Morris from Oxford and Ford from Dagenham in Essex. Ford's original British factory, established before the First World War, was at Old Trafford, Manchester. In the 1920s, Henry Ford wanted to set up a European base in Britain and settled on the Dagenham site, although his representative in England had advised building the plant near the docks in Southampton. The Dagenham plant was originally fuelled partly by the burning of London's rubbish and drew upon the supply of unskilled labour on the overspill Becontree estate, to where people had been moved from inner London. In the 1930s, other firms were claiming a significant share of the market – Vauxhall in Luton, Triumph, Singer, Hillman and Jaguar from Coventry, and so on – but this did nothing to change the southern and Midlands bias of the industry.

With the development of the electricity-supply industry and the national grid, so came a growing market for electrical consumer goods, supplied from factories such as that of Hoover, in Perivale, west London. The number of electricity consumers increased from just over 700,000 in 1920 to nearly three million by 1929 and more than eight million by 1938. Electric cookers, radios, gramophones (and huge, clumsy-looking radiograms, which combined the two), refrigerators, vacuum cleaners and washing machines, typically manufactured in the new industrial hub of the south east, developed into mass-market products. Britain led the way in Europe with the development of television, through collaboration between the principal manufacturer, EMI (Electrical and Musical Industries) and the broadcaster, the British Broadcasting Corporation.

Monuments to this new type of industry sprang up along the

Great West Road out of London. As well as Hoover's Perivale factory, Smith's Crisps, Macleans, the toothpaste manufacturer, Firestone tyres, Gillette, and Curry's cycles and radios, all had factories along London's main western artery. It was a development which J. B. Priestley, used to the dirty, smoky factories of the North, found remarkable, as in his *English Journey* of 1934:

After the familiar muddle of West London, the Great West Road looked very odd. Being new, it did not look English. We might suddenly have rolled into California. Or, for that matter, into one of the main avenues of the old exhibitions like the Franco-British Exhibition of my boyhood. These decorative little buildings, all glass and concrete and chromium plate, seem to my barbaric mind to be merely playing at being factories. You could go up to any one of the charming little fellows, I feel, and safely order an ice-cream or select a few picture postcards. But as for industry . . . I cannot believe them capable of it. (1984, pp. 9–10)

Television was first broadcast in 1936, although it was not until well after the Second World War that it offered serious competition to the staple leisure industry of the inter-war years – the cinema. Studios were built all around London – at Elstree, Croydon, Denham, Merton Park, Pinewood, Ealing, Cricklewood, Fulham and other suburban locations – drawing on the ready supply of talent from the West End theatre. In the 1920s, legislation had been passed requiring cinemas to show a quota of British-made films. And the cinema was an industry, controlled from the South, which found a ready market in the North. Even in the most depressed industrial areas, cinemas of impressive grandeur sprung up.

By the mid-1930s, the battle for the consumer's shillings had become an intense one. National newspapers, based in London, enjoyed a period of unprecedented advertising riches and joined in circulation battles of ferocious proportions. For the cigarette smoker, untroubled by post-war concerns about the health risks associated with smoking, it was a period of wide choice. The author Roald Dahl described the 1930s as a golden age in confectionery manufacture, a period when many of the types of chocolate, such as Mars Bars and Kit Kats, that survive and prosper to this day first appeared. It was also a period of major expansion and change in retailing. Woolworth, then owned and run by the American parent company, embarked on a rapid expansion of its outlets, selling cheap and accessible goods to the new mass market. Boots, based in Nottingham, increased the number of its shops from 200 in 1900 to nearly 1,200 by 1938, offering among other things low-cost cosmetics for the factory, office and shop girl, as well as its own lending library.

Priestley, again, captured the mood of this new consumer society, built upon the spending power of the South:

If the fog had lifted, I knew that I should have seen this England all around me at the northern entrance to London, where the smooth wide road passes between miles of semi-detached bungalows, all with their little garages, their wireless sets, their periodicals about film stars, their swimming costumes and tennis rackets and dancing shoes ... You need money in this England, but you do not need much money. It is a large scale, mass-production job, with cut prices. You could almost accept Woolworth's as its symbol. (1984, pp. 300–301)

Looked at with the benefit of hindsight, the inter-war years do not appear to have been the period of unalloyed gloom that they are normally characterized as. Between 1924 and 1935, for example, overall industrial output in Britain rose by more than 30 per cent. The new and modified products of the period brought many formerly luxury goods into the domain of the ordinary consumer.

But it was also a period when the balance of economic power shifted dramatically between North and South. In 1923, the Ministry of Labour's four southern divisions – London, the south east, the south west and the Midlands – accounted for 46·6 per cent of the insured working population, and the rest of the country 53·4 per cent. By 1938 the position had reversed itself, with the South accounting for 53·9 per cent of the insured population and the North 46·1 per cent.

The old industrial areas suffered a steady decline in their relative economic performance over the period, punctuated by the years of absolute decline. In 1924 the old industrial areas (Lancashire and Cheshire, the West Riding of Yorkshire, Northumberland and Durham, South Wales and Monmouthshire and

West Central Scotland) accounted for 49·6 per cent of net industrial output in Britain, well above the 28·7 per cent in the new industrial areas (principally the south east and the west midlands) and the 21·7 per cent share for the rest of the country. By 1930, the old areas' share had dropped to 42·2 per cent, compared with 33·4 per cent for the new areas and 24·2 per cent for the rest. In 1935, the old areas accounted for only 37·6 per cent of total output, only just ahead of the 37·1 per cent for the new areas, with 25·3 per cent for the rest.

For the old industrial North there had been a radical change. The areas which had come to prominence in the industrial revolution now had to take second place to the new, consumer-based industries of the South. As late as the mid-1920s they had accounted for virtually half of Britain's industrial output. By the time of the outbreak of the Second World War their share was down to little more than a third. As Eric Hobsbawm put it, in *Industry and Empire*:

The discovery of the mass market was not new. Certain industries and industrial areas – notably the Midlands – had always concentrated on the domestic consumer, and had done well by this policy. What was new was the visible contrast between the flourishing home market industries and the despairing exporters, symbolized in the contrast between an expanding Midlands and south east, and a depressed north and west. In a broad belt stretching between the Birmingham and London regions, industry grew: the new motor manufacture was virtually confined to this zone. The new consumer-goods factories multiplied along the Great West Road out of London, while emigrants from Wales and the north moved to Coventry and Slough. Industrially, Britain was turning into two nations. (1969, pp. 218–19)

The relative decline of the industrial North was halted during the years of the Second World War, although certain aspects of that decline, notably a steady fall in coal production, continued through the war years. The steel industry did well during the 1939–45 war, as did engineering and chemicals. But in no way was the industrial shift to the South reversed in the war years. The factories producing consumer goods were easily turned over to wartime use, most notably with the conversion of car factories to aircraft manufacture. There was also a deliberate boost to agricultural output, to provide Britain with self-sufficiency in food.

Post-War Recovery and Recessions

When we come on to the post-war period, we are into the area of regional policy, which is considered in detail later in the book. Suffice it to say here that economic policy, both in its general and regional aspects, had an underlying philosophy for most of the post-war period. This was that the experience of the inter-war years, both in its overall impact on the economy and, as importantly, in the regional divisions it threw up, should never be allowed to happen again. Although unemployment consistently remained higher in the North during the 1950s and 1960s, it was a time of expansion and, although it did not always seem so at the time, of optimism. Regional accents became fashionable, northern authors and actors balanced the traditional dominance of the London set. Liverpool, largely thanks to the Beatles, became a centre for popular culture.

The consensus economics of the 1950s and 1960s, in which both Conservative and Labour governments undertook active Keynesian policies of demand management, or, more unkindly, 'stop-go', and assigned a key role to regional policy, was irrevocably damaged in the recession which followed the 1973–4 oil crisis. It was willingly abandoned by Margaret Thatcher's Conservative Government, elected in 1979. The relative decline of the North, held in check by policies deliberately designed to direct economic activity to the regions, could not survive the abandonment of such policies in the name of greater economic efficiency, or an overall economic policy stance which had as an important side-effect a second body blow to Britain's traditional staple industries. A North–South divide, every bit as bad in its relative if not its absolute effects, was the natural result.

So, is what we have seen for most of the twentieth century merely the South getting its just deserts, after earlier northern prosperity, as the quotation from Lord Young suggested? Few would deny that the North had a period of considerable prosperity for much of the nineteeth century, even if it was unevenly distributed among the population. The industrial revolution transformed the North. De-industrialization in the present century transformed it again and, in terms of prosperity and wealth, for the worse. But it is hard to see the industrial revolution as an example of the economic pendulum on its slow, regular swing, favouring the North, having been there before. It was, in every respect, a unique period, an interlude of northern prosperity, which should not have been used to justify a subsequent disproportionate concentration of wealth and economic activity in the South.

Now, however, the economic landscape has changed again. The recession that began in mid-1990, and which the economy was only beginning to shake off nearly three years later, undid many of the sharp gains in employment, income and wealth that the South recorded in the 1980s, while the North lagged behind. The southern boom was followed by a spectacular bust. Those regions that had soared highest during the Thatcher years dived precipitately in the recession that became her legacy. In the popular mind, the recession that began in 1990 not only narrowed the North–South gap but left the North with net advantages over the South. The South's relative advance, which had lasted for more than a century, had apparently been wiped out in a single, dramatic recession. The slowly swinging pendulum had jerked suddenly, and decisively, in the North's favour. Does the popular image fit the facts? And, if the North has not yet regained the economic dominance it enjoyed for much of the nineteenth century, is it with set to do so as we move into the twenty-first century? It is with these questions that the rest of this book will concern itself.

2

PERCEPTIONS OF NORTH AND SOUTH

When you go into the industrial North, you are entering a strange country. This is partly because of certain real differences which do exist, but still more because of the North–South antithesis which has been rubbed into us for such a long time past. There exists in England a curious cult of Northernness, a sort of Northern snobbishness. A Yorkshireman in the South will always take care to let you know that he regards you as an inferior. If you ask why, he will explain that it is only in the North that life is 'real' life, that the industrial work done in the North is the only 'real' work, that the North is inhabited by 'real' people. The South merely by rentiers and their parasites. (George Orwell, *The Road to Wigan Pier*)

> Bright and fierce and fickle is the South.
> And dark and true and tender is the North.
> (Alfred, Lord Tennyson, *The Princess*)

Perceptions of the North and South of Britain as being different, if not irrevocably divided, are as strong in the late twentieth century as they have ever been. Indeed, the economic boom of the second half of the 1980s, and the subsequent recession, has merely strengthened such perceptions. It was in the South, predominantly, that people lost their heads during the boom years, over-borrowing and over-spending and getting deeper in debt. And it was southerners who suffered most of the consequences when the bubble burst. Northerners, meanwhile, kept their feet firmly on the ground. If this meant missing out on some of the excesses of the boom years, then fine, as long as the downside was also limited. The analogy that springs to mind is that of the hare and the tortoise.

Thus, to the extent that the recession has narrowed economic differences between North and South, as it clearly has, it has also emphasized social and behavioural differences. Not that the broad North–South categorization can possibly hope to pick up all the subtleties of regional and local disparities. Yorkshire people may behave more like Lancastrians than Londoners do, but they still would see themselves as very different from one another. There is no frontier between North and South on either side of which everyone votes and behaves differently and experiences changed economic circumstances.

WHY NORTH AND SOUTH?

That said, North and South remains a powerful and enduring framework within which to examine Britain, for four main reasons. The first is that, at least until the recession of the early 1990s, a fuzzy line drawn between the Severn and the Wash showed, on a wide range of economic measures, marked and widening differences between those regions above and below the line.

Secondly, even if the economic gap has narrowed, the political map of Britain – at least as far as representation in the House of Commons is concerned – shows two nations. Even after nearly two years of recession, the April 1992 General Election showed Conservative support strongest, indeed dominant, in the South, with support for Labour concentrated in the North.

Thirdly, social differences, even in an age of national television, remain important. Everyone has encountered the modern equivalent of George Orwell's Yorkshireman, even though *The Road to Wigan Pier* was written more than half a century ago. Some of these social differences have their roots in long-standing economic distinctions, not just to do with relative prosperity but also related to the structure of industry and the spread of occupations between white-collar and blue-collar jobs.

Finally, North and South is important if enough people believe it to be so, and the indications are that they do. It may be that, when the South was prospering most, there was some great equalizing process at work, perhaps the invisible hand of the market, whereby what southerners gained on the swings of higher income and better job opportunities, they lost on the roundabouts of congestion, punishingly high housing costs and the miseries of commuting. Many northerners have long taken the view that, in terms of lifestyle, they would never exchange their lot for that of southerners, even if they have regularly complained about the South's economic advantages. If true, then the North's gain as a result of the recession of the early 1990s has been even greater than the bald economic data would suggest. Not only are southerners stuck with their overcrowded, unsatisfactory lifestyles, but the compensations are far fewer. Attitudes change slowly, particularly those ingrained over a very long period. North–South attitudes will persist.

THE UNHEALTHY NORTH

Perhaps most fundamental among such differences is that in the North, harsh as it sounds, people die younger and are more subject to cancer and heart disease. If the North is less stressful because of all that congestion in the South, it certainly does not show through in the health statistics.

Official mortality statistics for 1990, adjusted for the age structure of the population in each region, showed that for men, the highest death rate – at 1,290 per 100,000 population – was in Scotland, followed by Northern Ireland (1,258), the north (1,243), the north west (1,227), Yorkshire and Humberside (1,164) and Wales (1,159). Adjusted death rates in the south east, south west and East Anglia were well below these levels, at between 1,001 and 1,026 per 100,000 population.

A similar picture emerged for women, with Scotland again holding the unenviable top position, with 1,271 deaths per 100,000 population in 1990, again followed by Northern Ireland (1,246), the north (1,236) and the north west (1,209). The south east, south west and East Anglia were again the places where the grim reaper was least likely to strike, with adjusted death rates ranging from 1,019 to 1,032 per 100,000 population.

Although these figures relate to one year, 1990, they do not represent an isolated example. Death rates in the North have been substantially higher than those in the South over a long period. Improved nutrition and health care has, of course, brought about a steady reduction in death rates and greater longevity across the whole country, but it has failed to eliminate the North–South gap.

A study commissioned by the British Heart Foundation and carried out by Professor Gerald Shaper of the Royal Free Hospital found that the incidence of high blood pressure was much greater in industrial towns in the northern half of the country than in the rest. The study, published in May 1988, recorded high blood pressure in a third of men aged 40–59 in towns such as Dunfermline and Dewsbury, compared with rates as low as 11 per cent in Guildford.

The important distinction here appeared to be between industrial and other towns – the position in Harrogate in Yorkshire was, for example, only slightly worse than that in Guildford. But, with a higher proportion of people in the North living in industrial towns, and a higher proportion of men engaged in manual work – apparently more susceptible to high blood pressure than their non-manual counterparts – the net result was that men in the North were more likely to suffer from high blood pressure, and therefore heart disease and strokes, than those in the South.

This indeed is a point which applies more generally in the North–South debate. There are leafy villages and spa towns in the North that, over a very long period, have been just as attractive and prosperous as those in the South. But a higher proportion of people in the North live in the old industrial conurbations, in which many of the problems of late twentieth-century Britain – and many of the shortcomings in the quality of life – appear to be concentrated.

The Health Divide by Margaret Whitehead and her colleagues, the final report of the Health Education Council before its abolition in March 1987, echoed the 1980 *Report of the Working*

Group on Inequalities in Health (known as the Black Report after its chairman, Sir Douglas Black) in noting major regional differences in health:

Striking regional disparities can still be observed. Death rates were highest in Scotland, followed by the north and north west regions of England, and were lowest in the south east of England and East Anglia, confirming the long established North–South gradient. What is becoming increasingly clear from fresh evidence, though, is the great inequalities which exist between communities living side by side in the same region. Numerous studies at the level of local authority wards have pinpointed pockets of very poor health corresponding to areas of social and material deprivation. Alongside them, areas with much better health profiles can be detected and these exhibit more affluent characteristics. Although such deprived areas can be found throughout the country, the North has a higher concentration of them than the south and south east. (Townsend, Davidson and Whitehead, 1988, p. 352)

There seems little doubt that serious illnesses are more prevalent and average life expectancy lower in the North. The highest death rates from heart disease among both men and women are in Northern Ireland, Scotland, the north, the north west and Yorkshire and Humberside. Rates are significantly lower in the southern half of the country.

Similar, although less marked, regional differences also exist in the distribution of death rates from cancer, with the north, the north west and Scotland standing out as being significantly above the rest of the country. Northern Ireland, however, has a relatively low death rate from cancer.

North–South differences in mortality rates and the incidence of diseases which kill have been the subject of intense argument. In stark form, the debate has come down to two basic propositions. One is that health is a product of environment and economic circumstances, over which individuals have little control. Thus, it is argued, the old industrial towns in the North remain less healthy places to live, in spite of legislation to limit pollution and clean up the atmosphere. And, while stress-related diseases are associated in the popular mind with the overworked, coronary-bound executive, they are more likely to be experienced by a low-paid manual worker worried about his job, or by the unemployed and their families. In addition, health and fitness are seen as luxury goods and, as with all luxury goods, greater prosperity brings them within the reach of more people – witness the fitness boom in the United States, which has had significant effects on death rates from heart disease.

There is a substantial body of evidence, both academic and anecdotal, linking poverty, unemployment and the threat of redundancy to ill health and premature death. At its most extreme, unemployment leads to actual or more often attempted suicide. The provost of Dunfermline, responding to the British Heart Foundation study on blood pressure, attributed his town's poor showing to worries over unemployment: 'I suppose if you have a lot of men worried about whether they are going to keep their jobs, then that leads to stress. Apart from that, I can't see why we should be worse than anywhere else. We are not particularly hard drinking or unhealthy' (Jenkins, 1988).

Both *The Health Divide* and the Black Report found strong links between wealth, poverty, social class and health. Those in manual occupations were found to be less healthy than their counterparts in white-collar jobs, and less likely to avail themselves of preventive medicine. Worst of all was the position of the unemployed, according to *The Health Divide*:

The unemployed and their families have considerably worse physical and mental health than those in work. Until recently, however, direct evidence that unemployment caused this poorer health was not available. Now there is a substantial body of evidence of unemployment causing a deterioration in mental health, with improvements observed on re-employment. (Townsend, Davidson and Whitehead, 1988, p. 352)

The fact that the recession of the early 1990s has produced greater regional equality of unemployment should, on this view, also even out health differences. But such effects should not be expected quickly. For one thing, the impact of unemployment on health is likely to be greatest where people have given up hope of re-employment, and this, in turn, will most probably be in those regions where there is a long tradition of high unemployment, and a limited choice of alternative occupations. For another, unemployment is only one factor among many contributing to health differences.

A study prepared for the North Regional Health Authority by Bristol University in 1986 attributed premature death, permanent sickness and low birth weights in the region to poverty and unemployment. And it was in response to this that Edwina Currie, a junior health minister in the Thatcher Government with a gift for creating controversy – a gift which later led to her departure from the Government over her allegations that most eggs produced in Britain were infected with salmonella – launched a vigorous exposition of the other main argument about North–South health differences. They were due, she said, principally to unhealthy eating and living habits in the North which, with education, could be changed.

'We have problems here of high smoking and alcoholism,' she told a conference in Newcastle in September 1986:

Some of these problems are things we can tackle by impressing on people the need to look after themselves better. That is something which is taken more seriously down south. There is no reason why it can't be taken more seriously here and then we will end up with better health for everyone.

I honestly don't think the problem has anything to do with poverty. My family grew up in Liverpool and they didn't have two beans but as a result of good food, good family and good rest, they grew up fit and well. The problem very often for people is, I think, just ignorance and failing to realize that they do have some control over their lives. I recognize that this is easy for me to say. My problem is to encourage all our good people here to help get that message across. Health care is what you get when things go wrong in society. But in most advanced societies, people are taking much more interest in making sure that as far as possible things don't go wrong.

The remarks were indeed controversial, probably deliberately so, and produced an outcry in the North, particularly the inference of ignorance and the claim that the South, with its record on health, was somehow a more advanced society.

However, as with most overstated arguments, it contained important kernels of truth. Within a general fall in cigarette smoking in the country – from 45 per cent in the mid-1970s to 30 per cent by 1990 – the north, north west, Yorkshire and Humberside, Wales and Scotland retained the highest proportion of smokers. The Scots spend about a third more than the national average on cigarettes, followed by Northern Ireland, the north and the north west.

Households in the northern regions allocate a greater proportion of weekly expenditure to alcohol. And, in spite of lower incomes and outgoings, and lower prices for alcohol, people in Scotland, the north, the north west, Wales and the east midlands spend more in absolute terms on alcohol than the national average. Here too, the Scots appeared to be taking most risks with their health – and not, as in the popular myth, because they are a nation of hardened whisky drinkers. Rather, vodka drinking north of the border is significantly above the average for Britain, although wine-drinking has failed to develop as strongly as in the South.

Mintel, the market research company, reported in its *Regional Lifestyles 1992* that eating patterns did vary by region. In the south east and south meat-eating was least prevalent, and the tendency to buy low-fat products the greatest. The further north, the less the concern for healthy eating, with Scotland said to stand out as 'a maverick nation', ignoring many modern dietary trends. The report also found a greater tendency in the South to take part in fitness-related leisure activities. And, it said:

The notion of the supposed 'real' man downing several pints of beer only holds true for a minority in the more responsible 1990s but still has some sway in the south west, Wales and the North, especially the north west. In the South, 'real' men are an endangered species and more likely to be found drinking at home rather than at a pub. Northerners, especially in Yorkshire and the north east, are more likely to enjoy a night out at the pub and to go there for company and socializing as much as for drinking. (1992)

Northerners clearly do themselves no favours by maintaining relatively high levels of alcohol and tobacco consumption, and by their tendency towards less healthy eating. And the idea that the relatively poor health of northerners was largely due to poor diet and unhealthy living, as well as an unwillingness to use available preventive medical services, was understandably attractive to Conservative ministers. It is much easier, and cheaper, to run an advertising campaign promoting healthy living than to tackle the root causes of health disparities. But when the overwhelming body of evidence points to deep-seated health differences between North and South, and firmly establishes the cause of such disparities as different social conditions, the unhealthy living argument is at best a distraction and at worst an attempt to paint over a very serious problem. Lower levels of cigarette smoking and alcohol consumption, together with unhealthy eating patterns, might reduce the health gap a little, but they would come nowhere near to eliminating it.

In the first edition of this book I asked the question whether increasing congestion in the South, together with the increasing pace of life, would take its toll on the health of southerners. The recession has done nothing to ease congestion as defined by living space, although it has made life somewhat more bearable for commuters. A different set of questions may now arise, such as whether worries about redundancy, business failures and home repossessions will produce a significant increase in stress-related illnesses in the South. Anecdotal evidence, based on the experience of individuals, would suggest that it will, although, as with the health problems caused by actual unemployment touched on above, the effects are likely to be slow to show through in regional comparisons. North–South differences, we should remember, are long-standing and will not easily disappear.

Some of these differences, it would seem, are all too visible. A hospital consultant who moved up from Kent to Barnsley found that his new patients had aged beyond their years. Paul Bryant, an orthopaedic consultant, was reported in 1987 as saying: 'I was disturbed to find I was regularly over-estimating the age of my patients over 40 by 10 or 15 years. There is no doubt that social hardship exacts a heavy toll.' His comments brought an immediate explanation from a Barnsley councillor. 'It's fairly obvious why we look older,' he said. 'We work a damn sight harder. Miners have always been old men at 40. Up here we have always carried the affluent South on our backs' (Willsher, 1987).

One explanation for the aged appearance of northern men, not necessarily based on scientific evidence, is that men in the North have less hair than their counterparts in the South. Under the headline 'Horrible Secret of Northern Baldies!' the *Sun* reported that 'more than two thirds of baldies live in the North'. This startling conclusion was based on the client list of a Harley Street hair specialist, Neagle Cathcart, who was apparently persuaded to say: 'There is no doubt the North–South parting is getting wider.' The conclusion was based on the fact that 71 per cent of the clinic's patients came from the North, suggesting either that there really were significant differences in the incidence of baldness, or that men in the North were more vain and prepared to do something about it. His own explanation was based on the Viking ancestry of many northerners – with the Vikings apparently famous for early hair loss – and partly on social conditions and stress.

Baldness, curiously, comes up in other North–South surveys. One, conducted in 1992 by Pantron, manufacturers of hair restorer, found that men in Newcastle were unworried by hair loss, convinced that it would not affect their personality. But a third of Londoners thought that it would. But 44 per cent of women in the South found bald heads attractive, and 72 per cent would go out with a bald man, while none of the women surveyed in the North were attracted by baldness in their men, and only 13 per cent would go out with one. If true, even if employment has faded as a factor encouraging southward migration, bald northerners could have another reason to move to the South.

Another physical difference, which emerged from a survey of 10,000 women in 1990 by *Looks* magazine, is that northern women have larger breasts. The survey suggested that, while the average bra size nationally was 34B, 61 per cent of women in Scotland take a 36-inch bra, with half of them having a 'C' cup. In the south east, a third of women took an 'A' or 'AA' cup. The survey's organizers concluded that the North–South difference was largely due to a greater emphasis on weight loss and physical fitness among southern women, rather than in-bred variations in shape.

A COOLER MORAL CLIMATE

Are northerners somehow more moral and fairer-minded than their faster and looser counterparts in the South? Most surveys on attitudes suggest this to be the case. A series of surveys carried out by Market and Opinion Research International (MORI) during the 1980s suggested that people in the North, while more likely to smoke cigarettes, were less likely to use cannabis or harder drugs. This is supported by the official data for drug offences, showing by far the highest concentration of drug offences in the south east. In 1990, 124 people per 100,000 population were convicted or cautioned for drug offences in the south east, four times the rate, for the north. But the north west, with 81 offences per 100,000 population, came second to the south east.

As for sex, northern men are more disapproving of adultery, with a consistently higher proportion taking the view that affairs with other men's wives are wrong. However, according to a 1986 MORI survey on 'modern man', men in the North claimed a more active sex life than those in the South. Presumably this was also true for northern women. The survey showed that 71 per cent of northern men had sex more than once a week, against 61 per cent in the South. At the other end of the scale, 17 per cent of men in the North had sex less than once a week or never, against 33 per cent in the South.

In 1990, a Today/TV-am survey of the British male, based on more than 2,000 interviews, suggested the North–South differences among men increase with age. Among 18–25-year-olds, there were virtually no differences in leisure behaviour or in attitudes towards women and sex. Most in this group thought it vital that their girlfriend or wife remained faithful but that a little straying on their own part was forgivable. At 30-plus, northern men were found to be more preoccupied with sex than their southern counterparts, with the latter more obsessed with work. For the 40-plus category, perhaps surprisingly, southern men were less tolerant of women colleagues, and did not believe in special concessions for working mothers.

With the exception of Northern Ireland, which has a very low divorce rate for religious reasons, no clear North–South patterns appear in the statistics for divorce and remarriage. The highest proportions of marriages where one or both partners have been previously married, around 30 per cent in 1990, were in the south west and East Anglia. But the rate for the south east, at just over 25 per cent, was below the national average.

The crime statistics suggest not that moral standards are higher in the North, but rather the reverse. In recent years, the highest rates of recorded crime have been in the north, the north west and Scotland. In 1990, for example, official figures show that there were 11,892 notifiable offences per 100,000 population in the north, almost double the rate in East Anglia, more than 33 per cent above the south east and, interestingly, three times the rate in Northern Ireland.

In the north, the north west and Yorkshire and Humberside, burglary, theft, handling stolen goods and criminal damage were significantly above the national average and well above levels in the South. Apart from persistently high unemployment breeding crime, the main factor in these statistics was probably the greater proportion of people living in industrial conurbations in the most crime-affected regions. But the figures are an antidote to repeated suggestions that northerners, while they may not be so affluent, enjoy a better quality of life. The threat of being a victim of burglary or other crimes would be a significant factor in most people's assessment of the quality of life.

Every so often a crime takes place that is so horrific, and receives such widespread attention, that it rises above the specific and appears to convey a general message. In February 1993, such an event occurred. A two-year-old boy, James Bulger, was abducted from a shopping centre in Bootle on Merseyside, and brutally murdered. Worse still, two 10-year-old boys were charged with his murder. The case, which received worldwide attention, appeared to sum up Britain's malaise, and particularly that of cities such as Liverpool, where unemployment has become a way of life for generations and where, particularly among the young, respect for law and order is a rare commodity. Such an event could, of course, have happened in many other large conurbations in Britain. The North, however, has more of them and, as the figures show, it has a persistently worse crime record.

Conurbation factors – the tendency for there to be a higher crime rate in areas where population is heavily concentrated – together with varying proportions of the population from different ethnic backgrounds, probably explain why the north west, the north and Yorkshire and Humberside have the highest rate of births outside marriage in Britain. In the ten years from 1980, the proportion of births to unmarried mothers increased sharply over the country as a whole, from one in eight to more than a quarter. By 1990, over 34 per cent of births fell into this category, compared with 24 per cent in the south west and a national average of 28 per cent.

NORTH–SOUTH STEREOTYPES

In 1992, BBC 2 ran a special evening of programmes, under the title Granadaland, to celebrate the thirty-fifth anniversary of Granada, the Manchester-based commercial television station. It included an early episode of *Coronation Street*, the long-running northern soap opera. One of the characters was looking wistfully at photographs of some ideal home in the South. 'Eh,' she said, 'look at all them drying cupboards and a spin drier! I can just see myself sitting on that porch, knitting and eating chocolates and listening to a transistor radio.' *Coronation Street*, the most influential British soap of them all, dates from the early 1960s and was based on the gritty northern reality of the time. According to Nancy Banks-Smith, writing in the *Guardian*:

Derek Granger, the producer, said that in *Coronation Street* Tony Warren created the most famous set of characters outside Dickens. Warren had climbed on a filing cabinet and refused to come down until they let him write about what he knew. From the cabinet he could see row on row of Coronation Streets. (1992)

The evening featured a section on northern stereotypes, as depicted in Granada's own programmes. The images were of back-to-back terraced houses; clogs; cloth caps; powerful, brassy women; 'real' men; the rituals of tea-drinking; and a social life centred around the pub. Such stereotypes, while used for entertainment, may have had the effect of inhibiting economic development in the North. According to Dr Fred Robinson of the University of Newcastle, in a report entitled *The Great North?*, they reinforce perceived divisions between North and South:

Tension and mistrust between North and South evidently has a long history. In part, it is based on deep-rooted antagonisms – between the centre and the provinces, and between a supposed affluent middle-class South and deprived working-class North. Legendary conflicts and misconceptions made the North an easy subject for music-hall jokes or, latterly, a place and a people easily lampooned in the television sitcom. And inaccurate perceptions are further reinforced by powerful representations of the North in the past – the setting of *When the Boat Comes In* or Catherine Cookson's Tyneside of the 1920s. The rapidly expanding heritage industry – of Beamish, steam railways and other industrial relics – has added to the sense of a region living for the past and even living *in* the past: a backward area. Small wonder, then, that southerners may have images of the North which are outdated, a landscape of pits, shipyards and steelworks, complete with Andy Capp and his whippets. (1990, p. 3)

The trouble is that people not only believe the stereotypes but, often, mould their attitudes to fit them. Desmond Albrow, a Yorkshireman writing in the *Daily Telegraph* in 1990, noted that northern resentment towards the South had increased with the latter's economic success in the 1980s. It would be easier, he suggested, to create a united Europe than heal Britain's North–South divide: 'Give the North a child to the age of 12 and it has got it for life.' He added:

I was taught that Yorkshire was the best and the biggest and, in parts, the most beautiful county in England. Its textile industries were the envy of the world. It had produced, among others, the Brontës, Delius, the Sitwells, Henry Moore, Barbara Hepworth and J. B. Priestley. There was muck and, despite much unemployment, lots of brass. There was then a confidence that is missing in today's two-nation England ... Small dents are being made in the war of prejudice but the war smoulders on, fanned by the Auberon Waughs on one hand and Hattersleys and Parkinsons on the other. What we need is a truce, a period of silence while the North recaptures its old pride and dismantles its prejudices. The South would accept the olive branch because its heart has never really been in the scrap. (1990)

The new North that the marketing men would want us to take as a model is that of the vast and successful Gateshead Metro and Sheffield Meadowhall shopping centres. It is that part identified by Saffery Champness, a firm of accountants specializing in handling the financial affairs of wealthy individuals, as the 'golden triangle'. According to Saffery Champness, the area bounded by York, Wetherby and Harrogate has more super-rich people, with a minimum net worth of £20 million, than any other part of the country except London's Belgravia and Mayfair. And the triangle, which includes Marston Moor – where Cromwell defeated the forces of the King in 1644 – could be stretching wider. Saffery Champness suggested that its boundaries could be drawn within a wide area bounded by Liverpool, Newcastle and Grimsby, to take in the full extent of personal wealth in northern England. Darras Hall in Newcastle was identified in a BBC documentary as having a bigger proportion of managerial and professional people (90 per cent) than anywhere in the country save for a few isolated areas in the south east.

John Dyson, of the Huddersfield-based stockbroker BWD Rensburg, identified what he described as the 'northern playground' late in 1991, a group of attractive, prosperous, low-unemployment towns, with diversified local economies. He wrote:

Currently, Britain's most prosperous area stretches from the Lake District across the Pennines to York. This is the 'northern playground', encompassing as it does areas of outstanding natural beauty and

historical interest. Within easy reach of all the main conurbations of
the north east, north west and Yorkshire, it is not an area dependent on
a seasonal trade; visitors go to it throughout the year. Overall, the area
has been little affected by rising unemployment: Windermere, for example, now has the lowest unemployment rate on the UK mainland. Most
other areas in the country with an unemployment rate below 4 per cent
are also in this area. They are Kendal, Keswick, Penrith, Settle, Harrogate, Ripon, Malton, Northallerton and Pickering. Small places in
themselves, but when put together it forms a coherent area and suggests
something significant is happening. Indeed, before the end of the year it
is likely that North Yorkshire will have overtaken Surrey, West Sussex
and Berkshire as the county with the lowest unemployment rate in the
country. (1991)

Pockets, even swathes of prosperity, let alone golden triangles,
however, can hardly be said to represent the norm in the North.
As Dyson noted: 'One should not overestimate the changes that
are taking place and pretend that all the North's many structural
and historical problems have been solved overnight.' Prosperous
northern areas existed even as the North–South gap was
widening in the 1980s, and they will continue to exist, and
expand, in a more prosperous North. But grim reality has a
nasty habit of intruding, such as with the riots on the down-
trodden Meadow Well estate in North Shields in 1991, where
unemployment was more than 80 per cent and petty burglary is
a way of life. It was in Newcastle that ram-raiding, smashing
stolen cars into shop-fronts and looting the contents, began.
Ghettos of affluence are one thing, but for much larger numbers
in the North life is lived on 'sink' estates, the more traditional
ghettos of poverty.

Les Smith, a playwright and Labour candidate in Bolton,
could describe, in 1991, scenes that were every bit as grim as
those described by Orwell in *The Road to Wigan Pier*. He wrote:

A chip shop on the Top O'the Brow estate in Bolton. Here the
unemployment is phenomenal, the alsatians are half crazy and the kids
are playing on the streets in the drizzle at 10 at night. The lunch-time
queue stretches outside the chip shop. One by one fat mothers, 24 years
old going on 45, two toddlers draped around them, a third baby

squatting in the buggy, get to the counter and order – chips with gravy, chips with scraps (bits of fried batter that have fallen from the fish) and chips with pea soup (the water that the dried peas have been soaked and cooked in). Chips. Not with everything. With anything that's free or cheap. Few can afford fish. Not even on Giro day. My ears are itching as I listen to conversations of who's in jail now, who's living with whom, who's getting one over on the DSS. The rules of civil society simply do not apply here. (1991)

This is not necessarily typical of all of the North. Nor is Manchester's Moss Side, with its drug wars that are, in virtually all respects including the widespread use of knives and guns, as bad as those to be found in any American city. But they are indicative of the legacy of years of high, morale-sapping unemployment, of living on social security, of deep-seated misery. This is the slack that a northern recovery has to take up, and to whom the existence of a millionaire set in North Yorkshire is quite meaningless.

THE SOUTHERN CONSUMER AT BAY

New consumer products, and in particular consumer durables, tend to be taken up more quickly in the South, probably because of greater affluence, and then trickle up to the North. The North typically lags behind in the early stages of new consumer durables becoming available to the market. However, for most well-established consumer durables there is no strong evidence of regional disparities in ownership. In the early 1990s, the regions with the highest proportions of households having washing machines, 90 per cent, were the north, the east midlands and Scotland. The south east, at 84 per cent, had one of the lowest proportions (only Northern Ireland was lower). But the south east's low rating was because of the concentration of launderette-using single-person households in Greater London. For dishwashers, a relatively new mass-market development in Britain, the biggest proportion of owners was in the South. The proportion of households owning dishwashers in the south east in 1990, 17 per cent, was $2\frac{1}{2}$ times the level in the north, Yorkshire and Humberside and Wales. Virtually every household

in the country has a fridge, with no significant regional variations, although ownership of deep freezers, surely only partly
related to differences in climate, was greater in the South.

As for home entertainment, the household without a television
set is now a rarity, with only 2 per cent across the country
without a set (this probably includes some who have a television
but choose not to pay the licence fee). In 1990, 93 per cent of
households had colour TVs, with no significant regional variations. Ownership of videos perfectly illustrates the point outlined
above about the spread of durables ownership from the South.
In 1984–5, on the official Family Expenditure Survey figures, the
highest proportion of households owing or renting video players
was 32 per cent in the south east, and the average for the United
Kingdom as a whole was 28 per cent. By 1990, the national
figure had climbed to 62 per cent and in most regions the figure
was above 60 per cent.

Does this sort of figure, based on what might be regarded as
measures of prosperity, suggest that the North–South divide is
non-existent? After all, households in straitened circumstances
are not likely to have a video player in the house. Or are they?
Just as it used to be the case that people who could not meet
their hire purchase commitments would give up the furniture
before the television set, so the video may have achieved similar
status. Satellite television, taken by some two million households,
has achieved its biggest inroads into the market among lower-
income families. Certainly, video rental has proved highly popular in areas of high unemployment. And, for the majority of
consumer durables, there is a period after their introduction
when prices are high, which is followed by a fall. The fact that
the North rarely gets in on the ground floor when new 'big
ticket' items of household expenditure become available suggests
that price acts as more of a constraint in the North, which fits in
with observed regional variations in income and wealth.

Other measures of prosperity suggest that the South is well
ahead. In 1990, on official data, there were between 396 and 420
cars per 1,000 population in the south east, East Anglia and the
south west. In Scotland and the north, the figures were 294 and
295 respectively, a significant difference. The proportion of

households with telephones was similarly higher in the three most prosperous regions in the South, although not as markedly so as with cars.

As the southern-led consumer boom of the 1980s gave way to the high-street recession of the early 1990s, however, the pattern changed. While London's Oxford Street and Brent Cross in north London were crying out for customers, centres such as Meadowhall in Sheffield and the Metro Centre in Gateshead continued to report good business. One of the saddest examples of the shift in fortunes was the Tobacco Dock development, a stone's throw from my office in London's Docklands. Built as 'London's second Covent Garden', and opened at the tail end of the boom of the 1980s, its up-market shops were intended to attract an up-market 'yuppie' (young upwardly mobile professionals) clientele, rich on big earnings in the City. Tobacco Dock opened, however, when the City yuppies were finding that there was an inverse relationship between earnings and job security. The development was soon in receivership and, while still functioning at time of writing, albeit with at least half its premises unoccupied and the rest struggling, it stands as a monument to the overblown ambitions of the boom years.

The shift in fortunes had some surprising aspects. Nilgin Yusuf, writing in the *Guardian* in 1991, recorded the fact that the high-fashion shops of London's South Molton Street and Beauchamp Place had run into hard times. 'When there's less money, fashion is the first luxury to go,' said one disgruntled shop-owner. But in the North, conditions were very different. Pollyanna in Barnsley, a fashion store selling lines by Azzedine Alaia, Romeo Gigli, Jean Muir and Jasper Conran, could report a rising level of business selling to local women professionals – doctors, solicitors and accountants. 'In the north, we have learnt to cope with difficult times,' said Rita Britton of Pollyanna. 'Remember the miners' strike and pit closures were here. I think the recession took everyone by surprise in London.' Two Glasgow fashion shops, Ichi Ni San and Saxs, the latter with struggling shops in Brighton, could also report good business. 'Here, young people are the ones with money,' said Linda Lawrence, a director of Ichi Ni San in Glasgow. 'They are not tied down with mortgages or cars.' The yuppie, always thinner on the ground in the North compared with the South, appeared to have better staying power up there.

THE NORTH'S ENTERPRISE GAP

Robin Wight, an advertising man and unsuccessful Conservative candidate in the north east in the June 1987 general election, had little doubt that the North suffered from a lack of entrepreneurial spirit. Writing in *The Times* shortly after the election, he said:

The anti-entrepreneurial culture of the North has kept private capital at bay. Worse, the whole process of setting up a business is alien to a part of Britain that has been in either public-sector employment (coal, steel, railways, etc.) or public-sector unemployment. The torch of capitalism in the north east has barely flickered since Robert Stephenson struck a match under his rocket in the last century. In the rest of Britain today there is a waiting list to get on to the Enterprise Allowance Scheme, which helps people to set up their own business, but in the north east there is a shortage of applicants. (Wight, 1987)

The notion that the North has an 'employment culture', with a particular emphasis on public sector employment, rather than an 'enterprise culture', is a powerful one. Robert MacDonald of Durham University, in a study of business start-ups by young entrepreneurs in Cleveland, found that only 10 per cent were successful. The entrepreneurs were hampered by their youth, class and locality, and by competition from larger established firms, from the black economy, and from other participants in government schemes. 'For the clear majority of youth,' he concluded, 'enterprise means neither glorious success nor gory failure but a twilight world of hard work, low pay, casual labour and insecurity' (Smith, 1992b, p. 6).

Self-employment grew strongly during the 1980s, in all regions. The increases were, however, far bigger in the South than the North. In the 1979–90 period self-employment increased by between 73 per cent (for the west midlands) and 110 per cent (the south west) in the five regions of the South. This compared with a national rise of 76 per cent. Overall, self-employment in the South increased by 991,000, or 87 per cent. In the North, the increases were typically around 50 per cent over the period, although Yorkshire and Humberside managed a large 102 per cent rise. In Northern Ireland, self-employment rose by only 19 per cent. Overall, for the North, 460,000 more people became self-employed over the 1979–90 period, an increase of 59 per cent.

The distinction was even more marked in the growth of new businesses. Net new business registrations increased by 26 per cent in the country as a whole during the long 1982–90 economic upswing. The biggest increase, by far, was in the south east, where the number of businesses rose by 38 per cent, followed by East Anglia and the south west, with 27 per cent. Overall, the number of businesses in the South rose by 32 per cent over the period. By contrast, none of the regions of the North achieved an increase of more than 18 per cent (this again was recorded by Yorkshire and Humberside, which could lay claim to be the most enterprising region in the North). The total number of businesses in the North rose by 16 per cent, half the increase achieved in the South. The distinction is still clearer when we look at the number of new businesses created. The South accounted for more than three quarters (76 per cent) of the national total.

The Thatcherite enterprise economy of the 1980s was, therefore, largely a southern phenomenon. But it would be unfair to conclude on the basis of this that this indicates a lack of initiative and entrepreneurial drive among northerners. Enterprise feeds upon economic growth and, in the case of small businesses, on growth in consumer spending and housing-market activity. There were other factors supporting small-business formation in the South, as Ron Martin and Peter Tyler explained in 'The Regional Policy Legacy of the Thatcher Years':

To the extent that an enterprise revolution has occurred, it has been concentrated in the South and East. This is hardly surprising: both the formation and survival of new businesses are shaped in large part by local economic conditions, not only the relative buoyancy of demand but also the scale and quality of business support infrastructures, including access to finance. In all these respects the northern regions of Britain, including the Development Areas, have been disadvantaged relative to the southern part of the country. The regional components of the Government's Enterprise Initiative have failed to rectify this disparity. (1991, p. 16)

In the 1980s, small-business growth was a symptom of a healthy, vibrant, enterprise economy that, according to supporters of the Conservative strategy of Mrs Thatcher, was here to stay. The recession of the early 1990s underlined the downside of an enterprise economy that owed much to unsustainable demand growth. Small businesses proved to be particularly vulnerable in the recession. Indeed, the downturn in the economy and in the housing market interacted in a particularly cruel way for southern small businessmen. Many, encouraged by the banks, had over-borrowed, against the security of the family home. When the business encountered problems, and the bank called in the loan, not only was their home at risk but, often, its market value had dropped well below the level required to meet the bank's demands. The South's enterprise advantage was transformed into a major disadvantage. Employment was risky enough in the recession, but self-employment even more so.

BRIDGING THE GAP

Northerners remain northerners, even when in the South. When the first edition of this book was published, I took part in a radio phone-in programme covering much of southern Britain. The majority of the calls were from northerners, some of them resident in the South for 30 years, bemoaning the fact that, compared with home, their neighbours were cold and unfriendly. Desmond Albrow, the Yorkshireman quoted earlier in this chapter, confessed that, after years of living in the South, 'northern atavism still triumphs,' adding, 'When I hear the affected voices of some middle-class southerners, I reach for my northern gun. The semi-detached complacency of suburbia still amuses me.'

In the 1980s, southerners found it difficult to accept that the North was economically disadvantaged and, to the extent that they did, many believed the fault lay with northerners themselves. Liverpool's problems, it was often argued, were due to the bloody-mindedness of Liverpudlians: it became the classic example of a city where bad industrial relations and high unemployment went hand-in-hand, with the former seen as contributing to the latter. In the 1980s, where the enterprise economy was very largely a southern phenomenon, northerners were often seen from the South as having deliberately opted for a quieter life, even choosing unemployment rather than uprooting in search of work. The most common argument was that, what the South gained in higher incomes, wealth and employment, it lost in house prices, congestion and the miseries of commuting. The fact that the latter were products of the former largely escaped notice. And few southerners would admit to an inferior quality of life compared with their northern counterparts.

In January 1987, the *Sunday Times* ran a feature highlighting the fact that there were areas of prosperity in the North, and accompanied it with a leading article headed 'The Nonsense of North–South' (*Sunday Times*, 1987a). As is so often the case, to the eternal regret of journalists, the response it elicited was perhaps more interesting than the original feature. One letter, from a woman reader in Sutton in Surrey, perfectly encapsulated the hard-line southern view. It said:

Thank you for bringing some balance, and truth, to the great North–South divide myth. Last summer, I found that northerners as usual seemed to comprise the majority of English tourists abroad. I met one woman panicking over a lost handbag containing a £2,000 ring and a man with a spectacular sports car 'joost coming back from a rally in Geneva'.

One does not begrudge these people and one does not diminish the problems for the English northern unemployed, but let us have an end to this constant barrage of less than honest, loaded propaganda which appears to be aimed at eventually getting money out of southern pockets for the north of England, when there are still some very well-lined pockets up there.

After all, they have to pay a lot less for their houses than we do. (*Sunday Times*, 1987b)

It was balanced by a letter from a reader in Birkenhead, who criticized the paper for missing the point about the difference between North and South:

It does not lie in inferior housing conditions nor even shopping facilities, as you correctly state, but mainly in terms of jobs.

In Birkenhead I have never met anyone living in squalor. And as for supermarkets and stores there are more than enough already. Levels of unemployment however are some 60 per cent higher in the North as a whole than in the South, and not only in the worst affected areas, while job vacancies are less than half as numerous.

The North–South divide may not be a precise definition, but there is no doubt in my mind and the minds of many others that it does exist. (*Sunday Times*, 1987b)

It may be that so deeply entrenched are North–South attitudes that breaking them down is well-nigh impossible. But successful attempts have been made to improve understanding. The Granada *World in Action* programme invited Matthew Parris, then a Conservative MP, to spend a week on social security in Newcastle. He tried and failed to live within the amount of money available to him and found the experience a deeply affecting one. 'I understood how deprived unemployed people felt,' he said later. 'I'd never before lived in an area of high and hopeless unemployment, or realized what a deep loathing there is for the Conservative Party. There is an enormous credibility gap: I don't think most Conservatives realize what it's like' (Woffinden, 1988).

In January 1988, Yorkshire Television's *First Tuesday* programme conducted a more ambitious experiment called 'The Swap'. It transplanted the family of a man employed as a skilled worker in Winchester to the situation of an unemployed man's family in Middlesbrough, and vice versa. The man from Middlesbrough, Dave Pugh – unemployed for four years – took on the job of his Winchester swap, Dave Hogan, for a week, while the Hogans took on the life of being jobless in Middlesbrough for a week.

Even in that short time, there was a perceptible shift in attitudes. The Hogans from Winchester, exposed to the misery of unemployment, softened noticeably towards the problems of the unemployed and experienced a greater realization of their own good fortune. The Pughs from Middlesbrough, while understandably regarding their week in two-car, dishwasher prosperity somewhat as a child experiences being let loose in a toy shop, also shifted their attitudes. In particular, Dave Pugh, a strong union man, found that he could work unexploited in a principally non-union factory.

Active town councils have long sought twinning arrangements, notably with other, similar towns in Europe. In the late 1980s, a brief fashion emerged for North–South twinning, proof, if it were needed, of Britain's two nations. In one example, Crowborough in East Sussex advertised for a northern twin and found one in the railway town of Horwich in Lancashire. For Crowborough, according to the town clerk's secretary, the motive was clear: 'Our council felt it wanted to know a little bit more about what lies north of the Watford gap.' The visitors from the north were impressed. 'When we spent a day down there, everything seemed so clean, fresh and new,' said Lena Smith, town clerk. 'We hope our exchange will foster cultural, sporting and social links and give both towns a better understanding of life in different parts of the country.' But if the southern town thought it was playing Lady Bountiful to its hard-hit northern twin, a rude shock lay ahead. At the time of the inaugural meeting of the two councils in 1990, Lancashire's unemployment rate, at 5.5 per cent, was low by the standards of the North, but above East Sussex's 4 per cent rate. By 1993, Lancashire had a 9.3 per cent unemployment rate, compared with 12.6 per cent for East Sussex. On the definition used by the Birkenhead *Sunday Times* reader quoted above, the North–South divide had not just disappeared but, in this example, had actually shifted in the North's favour. But, as we shall see, things may be a little more complicated than that.

3

A POLITICAL DIVIDE

> Two nations between whom there is no intercourse
> and no sympathy; who are as ignorant of each other's
> thoughts and feelings, as if they were dwellers in
> different zones or inhabitants of different planets.
> (Benjamin Disraeli, *Sybil*, 1845)

> There are grave dangers in a Britain increasingly
> divided into two nations, a confident South and an
> angry and resentful North. (William Rodgers, 1981)

It was the night of Thursday 9 April 1992, general election
night. At ten o'clock, both the BBC and ITN began their all-
night election programmes with exit-poll results suggesting that
no party would come out with an overall majority, but that the
most likely outcome, after thirteen years of Conservative rule,
was a minority Labour administration. Labour, having lost the
1987 election by a margin of 147 seats (the Conservative majority
over all other parties was 102 seats), had led in the opinion polls
before and during the 1992 election campaign. Although Labour
had slipped during the final few days of the campaign, the party
still appeared to be on course to end up, at the very least, with
the most seats in a hung parliament.

But then, at 11.23, the cameras switched to Basildon, the
locale of the archetypal 'Essex man', the new working-class
Conservative voter who, under Margaret Thatcher, had deserted
Labour. Essex man had done well in the boom of the late 1980s.
He was in work, and his wages had risen strongly. His house,
perhaps a former council property he had bought under the

Conservatives' 'right-to-buy' legislation, had shot up in value. He may have belonged to a trade union in the past, but he approved of the successful reining back of trade-union power under Thatcher. Essex man had, however, fallen on hard times in the recession. High interest rates and falling house prices meant that home-ownership had become a poisoned chalice. Even if he was still in work, he knew plenty of people who had lost their jobs, and he was worried about his own. Around him, the talk was no longer of an economic boom, but of failing businesses and prolonged recession. Basildon, importantly, was a marginal seat, one of the southern target seats that Labour had to win if it was to stand any chance of victory. But, when the Basildon result was declared, the sitting Conservative MP David Amess holding on with 44·9 per cent of the vote (against 42·2 per cent for the Labour candidate), it was clear that things were not going according to plan. At that point, the Labour leader Neil Kinnock said later, he realized he had lost the election.

The Conservative victory with a 21-seat majority, predicted by John Major, but believed by few even among his own party and media supporters, was a tribute to his own impromptu campaigning skills, which included the use of a soapbox and the apparently unfashionable rejection of, among other things, a move towards Scottish devolution. More than that, however, it reinforced the deep North–South voting divisions in Britain. For those who claimed the disappearance of a North–South economic divide, there was little doubt that the hard evidence of the election strongly supported the view that there were continuing political divisions in the country. The south east, East Anglia and the south west made up a sea of Conservative blue, broken only by a small number of lonely islands of Labour and Liberal Democrat support. The North, meanwhile – including Scotland and Wales – did not show the same uniformity of support for the opposition parties, but the election result confirmed that, for Labour in particular, the North contained a solid base of support long missing for the party in the South.

For potential Labour MPs, parts of the South have been regarded as barren electoral territory for many years – the type of constituency where they have to suffer defeat in serving their political apprenticeship on their way to a winnable seat. The same is true for Conservatives in most industrial constituencies in northern England, Scotland and Wales, where, as a physical attack on a Conservative candidate in the north east during the 1987 election proved, the political dangers can be compounded by physical ones.

The high point of Conservative dominance in the South was achieved by Margaret Thatcher in her 1983 and 1987 general election victories. The April 1992 election showed some modest erosion of that position, as Table 3.1 shows. But the fact that the erosion was so modest, at a time when economic conditions had turned against the South, merely underlined the fundamental nature of regional differences in party support. The development of a solidly Conservative South and a mainly Labour North has been under way at least since the first Thatcher election victory in 1979. The present regional divide between the voting strength of the two main parties has been traced back to trends which started in the mid-1950s, although there is nothing new about the Conservative Party being stronger in the South than in the North. In 1885, for example, the Conservatives won 54 per cent of the vote in the south east, but only 42 per cent in northern England. In 1910, the Conservative share of the vote in the south east was 57 per cent, and again only 42 per cent in the northern regions of England.

It is possible, of course, to look at this development in one of two ways. Until the 1992 election, it could be argued that voting behaviour under the Conservatives reflected the effects of the party's management of the economy, and its impact on the regions. The South became more solidly Conservative because it benefited directly from the policies of the incumbent party. Meanwhile, the relative, and in some cases absolute, decline of regions in the North sharply reduced Conservative support there. The 1992 election showed, however, that the party's support in the South was strong enough to withstand the effects of policies which could almost have been designed to hit Conservative voters hardest.

The other side of the same coin, leaving aside the role of the

Liberal Democrats, is the decline of Labour support in London, the Midlands and in those parts of southern England where it was formerly strong, to the point where some observers have seriously questioned whether Labour can now be considered to be a national party.

In truth, neither Labour nor the Conservative Party are national parties in the sense of enjoying broadly uniform support across the whole country. Disraeli's two nations, 'the privileged and the people' were the rich and the poor, notably in the manufacturing towns of the North. But the present-day regional distribution of Conservative support is a long way from his vision of his party as 'the national party; it is the really democratic party of England'.

This chapter will not be a detailed, constituency-by-constituency analysis of voting behaviour in Britain, owing to the constraints of space and the fact that this ground has already been comprehensively covered elsewhere, notably in *A Nation Dividing?* by Johnston, Pattie and Allsop, and in a series of later papers by the same authors, and also, although it is less concerned with regional voting patterns, in *The British General Election of 1992*, by Butler and Kavanagh. Instead, the aim is twofold. It is to examine the extent to which the pattern of electoral support in Britain is directly related to economic differences between North and South. In other words, if there is a permanent shift in the North's favour, which began in the recession of the early 1990s, will voting patterns catch up? Could Conservative voters in the South come to realize that, in continuing to support the party in the 1992 election, they were voting against their own self-interest? The alternative argument, a depressing one for Labour, is that the economic recovery of the later 1990s will result in a rippling out of Conservative support from the South (where, on this view, the Conservatives are unassailable even in difficult economic circumstances), as growth and prosperity is enjoyed by the North. Before coming on to these questions, however, it is necessary to set the scene with some basic statistics on political support in Britain.

BRITAIN'S POLITICAL GEOGRAPHY

In Table 3.1, the numbers of seats won by the Conservatives, Labour and the Liberal Democrats (the Alliance in 1983 and 1987 and the Liberal Party alone in 1979) are given for the standard regions of Britain. Northern Ireland is excluded from the analysis because of the very different political framework there. The results for 1979, as in Johnston, Pattie and Allsop's *A Nation Dividing?*, are those derived by a research team for the BBC and ITN. The team reworked the actual results for 1979 to fit the constituencies introduced prior to the 1983 election. Thus, the 1979, 1983, 1987 and 1992 results are on a consistent basis.

The dominance of the Conservative Party by 1987 in the three most southerly regions of the country, leaving aside Greater London, was staggering, and it remained so, in spite of some overall losses in these areas, in 1992. After the April 1992 election, the Conservatives held no less than 106 out of the 109 seats in the south east excluding Greater London, Labour holding or winning only Oxford East, Southampton Itchen and Thurrock (the party's sole success in capturing Essex man's support). In the south west, the Conservatives had 38 out of 48 Parliamentary seats, and in East Anglia 17 out of 20. Thus, in these three areas, the Conservative Party held 91 per cent of the seats in the House of Commons. Taking the definition of the South used in this book, the Conservatives faded in Greater London and, in particular, in the west midlands. From a position of having 58 Greater London seats in 1987, to Labour's 23, the Conservatives under John Major slipped to 48, with Labour rising to 35. Even after the April 1992 election, the Conservatives had twice as many seats as Labour in the east midlands but could only equal Labour (at 29 seats each) in the west midlands, having lost seven seats there.

Even so, Conservative dominance of the South remained a remarkable feature of Britain's political landscape in the 1992 election. Despite losing a total of 28 southern seats, the Conservative Party still held 266 out of 361, or 74 per cent, of the South's seats in the House of Commons. The 266 southern Conservative

Table 3.1 Seats won by region, 1979–92

	Conservative				Labour				Liberal Democrat			
	1979	1983	1987	1992	1979	1983	1987	1992	1979	1983	1987	1992
South East	147	162	165	154	44	27	24	38	1	3	3	1
of which Greater London	48	56	58	48	36	26	23	35	0	3	3	1
South West	42	44	44	38	5	1	1	1	1	3	3	6
East Anglia	17	18	19	17	2	1	1	3	0	1	0	0
East Midlands	23	33	30	28	18	8	11	14	0	0	0	0
West Midlands	33	36	36	29	25	22	22	29	0	0	0	0
The South	262	293	294	266	94	59	59	88	3	7	6	7
Yorks & Humberside	19	24	22	20	34	28	33	34	0	2	0	0
North West	37	36	34	27	35	35	36	44	1	2	3	2
North	7	9	8	6	30	26	27	29	1	2	1	1
Scotland	23	21	10	11	44	41	50	49	3	8	9	9
Wales	12	14	8	6	23	20	24	27	1	1	3	1
The North	98	104	82	70	166	150	170	183	6	16	16	13
Total	360	397	376	336	260	209	229	271	9	23	22	20

Sources: R. J. Johnston, C. J. Pattie and J. G. Allsop, *A Nation Dividing?*; D. Butler and D. Kavanagh, *The British General Election of 1992.*

seats represented 79 per cent of the party's strength in the House of Commons.

In the North, the position was reversed, with Labour continuing to hold the majority of seats in all five regions. In the three regions of the north of England, the Conservatives lost a total of nine seats between 1987 and 1992, and in each case Labour comfortably held the most seats following the April 1992 election. Indeed, one of Labour's few successes was its record in winning north west marginal constituencies. Over the period 1979–92, the Conservatives lost most support in Wales (down from 12 to 6 seats) and Scotland (down from 23 to 11), although the latter, one up on 1987, was greeted as a minor triumph. Before the election, some pundits predicted that, so unpopular were the Conservatives north of the border, they would struggle to have enough MPs to staff the Scottish Office with ministers. The Scottish and Welsh figures exclude seats won by the two nationalist parties. In the case of Scotland, three seats were held by the Scottish National Party (SNP) in April 1992, while in Wales Plaid Cymru won four seats.

For the North as a whole, the Conservatives won 70 out of 273 seats, or just over a quarter of the total, while Labour had 183, or 67 per cent. Of Labour's 271 House of Commons representatives after the April 1992 general election, 68 per cent were in the North, its strength there not quite a mirror image of Conservative strength in the South.

Another way of looking at the same phenomenon is on the basis of share-of-the-vote statistics, summarized in Figure 2 opposite. This shows clearly the strength of Conservative support in southern England, with its share of the April 1992 general election vote averaging more than 50 per cent in the south east, excluding Greater London, and in East Anglia. For much of the rest of England, including outer London, the south west, the east and west midlands, and parts of Yorkshire and Humberside and the north west, the Conservative share is 40 to 49·9 per cent, generally enough to win a seat in a three- or four-way parliamentary contest. In inner London, and further away from southern England, the rural north, the area around Greater Manchester, rural Wales and north-east

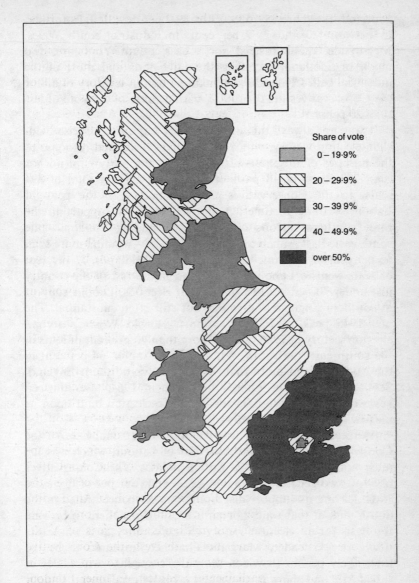

Figure 2 Regional Conservative strength, 1992

Source: D. Butler and D. Kavanagh, *The British General Election of 1992*.

Scotland, the share averages 30 to 39·9 per cent. It falls further, to between 20 and 29·9 per cent, in industrial south Wales, Merseyside, the industrial north east, South Yorkshire, and much of Scotland, including the Highlands and most of the industrial belt. Clydeside was the most barren territory of all for the Conservatives in April 1992, with a share of the vote of less than 20 per cent.

It was not always this way. In 1945, Labour's surprise land-slide election victory, which was perhaps a delayed response to the miseries of the inter-war years, saw the party gain no less than 203 seats, in all parts of the country, for a total of 394 seats, to the Conservatives' 210. In that year, the peak of Labour's voting fortunes, it enjoyed majority support in the three southern regions of England, including London – the south east, East Anglia and the south west – winning more than 55 per cent of Parliamentary seats. In the Midlands, 71 per cent of seats went to Labour in 1945, and in the rest of the country just under 70 per cent. In subsequent elections, Labour support in southern England was lower, but still often substantial. The post-1945 peak of Labour support, Harold Wilson's second election victory in 1966, gave it more than 40 per cent of seats in the south east, the south west and East Anglia, 64 per cent in the Midlands and more than 70 per cent in northern England, Scotland and Wales. Labour had won in 1964, after thirteen years of Conservative rule, and the 1966 election built upon its narrow majority significantly.

As recently as 1975, it was the narrow regional base of the Conservative Party, rather than that of Labour, which was the most noteworthy feature of British politics. The Conservatives had lost two general elections in 1974, and four out of five since 1964, leaving its support disproportionately concentrated in the South and, at that time, not sufficiently strong there to provide the basis for an election victory in the country as a whole. Its newly elected leader, Margaret Thatcher, appeared to be the least likely person to widen the party's appeal, particularly in the North, and she was up against a highly experienced Labour leader in Harold Wilson. But Wilson resigned in 1976 and his successor, James Callaghan, made the mistake of not calling a general election in the autumn of 1978, which Labour would almost certainly have won.

The present (post-April 1992) Conservative dominance of the South is enough to give the party 266 seats, just 60 short (on seats in the South alone) of that required for an overall House of Commons majority. The Conservatives, in other words can continue to do badly in the North without necessarily losing power. But the party's position has become more fragile. If it loses as many seats in the North at the next election as it did between June 1987 and April 1992 (12 in all, with its strength down from 82 to 70), then its majority would disappear. If it loses as many in the South (40), then Labour would romp home.

According to Pattie, Johnston and Fieldhouse, in a paper 'Plus ça change? The Changing Electoral Geography of Great Britain, 1979-92', the Conservatives' success in April 1992 was due to the cushion of southern support built up in the 1980s. However, there were warning signs for the Government in the 1992 result. They wrote:

The Conservatives had a lucky escape in 1992. Before the election, the Labour party's prospects were better than at any election since 1979, but they still lost. For the Government, things looked bleak in the run-up to the campaign. But, despite a deep recession which was affecting its 'core region' most and a run of poor opinion polls, it managed to retain a working majority. There are many reasons for that, including residual fears over Labour's fitness to govern. But the Conservatives were certainly helped back into power by the electoral geography of the 1980s. The regional polarization of that decade gave them a very large cushion of very safe seats in the south of the country. The recession of the late 1980s and early 1990s did lead to a drop in Conservative fortunes in the hardest-hit regions, especially in the south. But, severe as the recession was, it did not erode Conservative votes enough to lose the party large numbers of seats in its southern heartland. That said, there are crumbs of comfort for Labour, and there are signs of possible future dangers for the Government. Labour in 1992 continued its slow recovery from the abyss of 1983, and now has a smaller mountain to climb at the next election. Crucially, it is starting to regain ground in the key regions of the English Midlands, and is even picking up in the south of England, both of which it must do to win office again. For the Conservatives, however, every silver lining has its cloud!

The party's southern cushions, while substantial, have been eroded. It will take a smaller (though still sizeable) push next time for the opposition to win those seats. Unless the Government can take action to remedy the recession in the south of the country, it runs the risk of further alienating its core support. (1993)

Labour's Achilles' heel, particularly in the south east, was the pledge by John Smith, then the shadow Chancellor, to remove the ceiling for employee National Insurance contributions. This meant that the marginal tax rate (the contributions, like income tax, are a direct tax on income) would rise by 9 per cent for everyone earning more than £21,060 in the 1992–3 financial year if Labour was elected. Since £21,060 was below the level of average earnings in many parts of the South, the implication was clear – a Labour victory would mean higher taxes. A further tax pledge, to increase the top rate of income tax from 40 to 50 per cent on gross incomes of around £40,000 and above, also had a damaging influence on Labour support, although less so than was the case for National Insurance contributions (NICs).

There are, however, good reasons to believe that Labour's problem on this front will not be so great next time. For one thing the party, with Smith having succeeded Neil Kinnock as leader, has learned the lesson of the 1992 defeat. For another, the re-elected Conservative Government also proved that it was a party of higher taxation. In his March 1993 Budget, Chancellor Norman Lamont announced an increase in the rate of NICs from 9 to 10 per cent, with effect from April 1994. He also announced an extension of value added tax to domestic gas and electricity bills.

If a shift in regional economic fortunes is occurring, with the North benefiting at the expense of the South, then the Conservatives could replace lost southern seats with gains in northern constituencies. The Conservative Party tends to be stronger in rural areas than in industrial areas. But, as a more detailed regional breakdown of Britain into twenty-four separate regions, used by Butler and Kavanagh, shows, any shift in the regional economic balance that had occurred by the time of the April 1992 election was not reflected in northern rural gains for the Conservatives. Table 3.2 provides a summary.

Table 3.2 Party gains and losses, by detailed region

	Conservative			Labour		
	1987 seats	1992 seats	Gain/ Loss	1987 seats	1992 seats	Gain/ Loss
Inner London	13	8	−5	13	20	+7
Outer London	45	40	−5	10	15	+5
Outer Metropolitan Area	57	56	−1	0	1	+1
Outer south east	50	50	0	1	2	+1
Devon and Cornwall	14	12	−2	0	1	+1
Rest of south west	30	26	−4	1	3	+2
East Anglia	19	17	−2	1	3	+2
East midlands	31	28	−3	11	14	+3
West midlands Metropolitan	14	10	−4	17	21	+4
Rest of west midlands	22	19	−3	5	8	+3
South Yorks Metropolitan	1	1	0	14	14	0
West Yorks Metropolitan	9	9	0	14	14	0
Rest of Yorks/Humberside	21	20	−1	33	34	+1
Greater Manchester	10	9	−1	19	20	+1
Merseyside	4	4	0	11	12	+1
Rest of north west	20	14	−6	6	12	+6
Tyne & Wear	1	1	0	12	12	0
Rest of north	7	5	−2	15	17	+2
Industrial Wales	4	3	−1	20	21	+1
Rural Wales	4	3	−1	4	6	+2
Central Clydeside	1	1	0	23	23	0
Rest of industrial belt	4	4	0	22	22	0
Highlands	0	0	0	1	1	0
Rest of Scotland	5	6	+1	4	3	−1

Source: D. Butler and D. Kavanagh, *The British General Election of 1992*, pp. 286–7.

Only one result in April 1992, the Conservative gain from Labour in Aberdeen South, supports the theory that the party could win seats to replace those lost in its traditional southern heartlands. The Aberdeen South result, in an area which admittedly had undergone a second economic resurgence as a result of increased North Sea activity (unemployment in the Grampian region was below 5 per cent in 1992), was untypical. Average incomes in Aberdeen were also high and would have been hit by Labour's tax plans.

WHO VOTES FOR WHOM?

Johnston, Pattie and Allsop, in their book *A Nation Dividing?* followed a slightly different route by breaking the country's Parliamentary constituencies down into thirty-one 'functional' regions, according to the main occupations of the people living there, prosperity, the proportion of immigrants, and so on. Thus, all thirty-one constituencies defined as 'very high status' – with the highest concentration of professional and managerial occupations and owner-occupation – were Conservative in the 1979, 1983 and 1987 elections, as might be expected, and these included Altrincham and Sale, Beverley, Cheadle, Crosby and Wirral West, all in the North. All remained Conservative in April 1992. Conservative support also tended to be strong, but declining, in so-called 'conurbation white collar' areas (including Aberdeen South, Cardiff Central, Edinburgh South, Leeds North West, Manchester Withington, Newcastle upon Tyne Central and Sheffield Hallam). Of the northern constituencies in this category, Cardiff Central, Edinburgh South, Manchester Withington and Newcastle Central were all won or held by Labour in April 1992. Conservative support in resorts and retirement areas has traditionally been strong, with the party holding Blackpool North, Blackpool South, Clwyd North West, Scarborough and Southport (all the northern towns in this category) in 1992. The Conservatives have also traditionally done well in so-called 'prosperous towns with little industry' including Conwy, Fylde, Harrogate and Hexham, and in agricultural areas in England and Wales.

There are a large number of constituencies in the South which have long been considered so safely Conservative that, as the saying goes, the party could put up a chimpanzee as candidate and still be sure of winning (though the loss of Newbury and Christchurch in by-elections in 1993 knocked this view). The same is generally true for Labour in many of the old industrial areas of the North. What is also true, however, is that there are a significant number of safe Conservative seats in the rural areas and the more prosperous, generally non-industrial, towns in the North. The electoral success of the Conservatives has been based on maintaining its hold on such constituencies, while achieving almost blanket coverage in parts of the South.

This in turn raises the question of whether there is a true political North–South divide. There are clearly important regional differences in the voting strength of the parties, but is this because similar people in different regions vote differently or, rather, because the North and the South differ according to the proportion of affluent and poor in the population? In other words, is the solicitor or banker as likely to vote Conservative whether he lives in Wigan or Woking? And, will the unskilled labourer living in council accommodation support Labour whether his constituency is Dulwich or Darlington?

LOCATION AND VOTING

One contention of this book is that the distinction between North and South has become more important than the old class differences in Britain. For this to be true in the context of voting behaviour, itself traditionally thought of as one of the best demonstrations of class attitudes, it is necessary to show that where people live is a more important determinant of how they vote than their social position. Fortunately, there is substantial evidence that supports this case and that regional variations in voting behaviour have grown rather than diminished.

The traditional Conservative voter can be thought of as in a white-collar job, owning his house and car, educated to at least 'A' level standard and philosophically opposed to excessive state intervention and trade unionism. The hard core Labour voter is in skilled or unskilled manual work, left school early, belongs to a trade union, lives in a rented council house, and believes in both redistribution and wider economic intervention by the state. If people in Britain fitted neatly into these two categories then analysing regional voting behaviour would be relatively easy. And when they do, voting behaviour is not necessarily predictable. Much academic attention was devoted to the small but solid proportion of Conservative working-class voters in the 1950s and 1960s.

A. Heath, R. Jowell and J. Curtice, in *How Britain Votes*

(1985) used five class definitions to examine voting behaviour. Based on the 1983 election results, the strongest support for the Conservatives was among the so-called petty bourgeoisie – farmers, self-employed manual workers and owners of small businesses – where 71 per cent voted Conservative, 12 per cent Labour and 17 per cent Liberal Democrat (then the Alliance). The strongest support for Labour was among the working class –described as rank-and-file manual workers – in which grouping 49 per cent voted Labour, 30 per cent Conservative, 20 per cent Alliance and 1 per cent for other parties. In between these two groups were the 'salariat' – managers, administrators, supervisors of white-collar staff and professionals and semi-professionals – 54 per cent Conservative; foremen and technicians, 48 per cent Conservative; and routine non-manual workers, 46 per cent Conservative.

The blurring of class differences has increased as the twentieth century has advanced. To take some recent examples, the Conservative policy of selling council houses to their tenants has created a new category of owner-occupier, among households which would probably not have made the transition from tenancy to owner-occupation under any other circumstances. Similarly, the policy of privatizing state-owned industries by share sales aimed at the general public has created a new breed of small investor and, arguably, reduced public support for state ownership of industry. Trade unionism has long extended beyond manual occupations and into white-collar work and the professions. The task of separating class and regional influences in voting behaviour is therefore by no means an easy one.

In spite of this, it is necessary to have some model of party support, whether it be by occupation, education; type of tenure or background, in order to assess whether regional influences on voting behaviour are important. In his 1977 book *Electoral Dynamics*, W. L. Miller took two core classes of Labour and Conservative support, with a managerial core class supporting the Conservatives and a working-class core support for Labour. Within this framework, he argued, variations in party support between constituencies occurred, not only because of differing proportions of the two core classes among the electorate, but also because the minority class in each constituency tended to be influenced by the voting behaviour of the majority. Thus, in a constituency with a majority of core Conservative voters, the actual support level for the Conservative candidate will be even greater than indicated by the proportion of natural Conservative voters because a significant number of voters in the other class will switch allegiance. The opposite effect occurs in Labour constituencies with a high proportion of core Labour working-class voters.

There are a number of reasons why this can be expected to occur. One may be that people prefer to vote for a winning party, almost irrespective of what that party is. Thus, working-class core voters in a safe Conservative constituency may prefer to support the sitting MP rather than, as they might see it, waste their vote on the Labour candidate. Working-class voters living in predominantly middle-class constituencies may wish to distance themselves from colleagues living in other areas by voting Conservative. They are perhaps more likely to be upwardly mobile and identify with and seek to emulate their near neighbours, and perhaps the easiest way of doing this is to vote Conservative. The opposite effects can clearly occur with natural Conservative voters living in Labour strongholds.

This type of model appears to offer a good working explanation of voting behaviour in the 1979, 1983, 1987 and, only to a slightly lesser extent, 1992 general elections. Its main shortcoming is that the core classes of voters make up only a small proportion of the electorate – between a third and a half of voters are not in any occupation at all, being housewives, students or retired – and so it is necessary to provide further distinctions, apart from occupation, in order to predict election results on the basis of social classes within a constituency.

Ian McAllister and Richard Rose, in their book on the 1983 general election, *The Nationwide Competition for Votes*, found that the Conservatives did 5 per cent better in their share of the vote in southern England, excluding London, than was predicted on the basis of social structure. In the north of England, they underperformed by 3 per cent. Labour, meanwhile, did 7 per cent worse than they should have done on the basis of social structure in southern England, and 3 per cent better in northern England.

The 'party strength' theory of voting behaviour is consistent with, and can be much improved upon, by building into the analysis the important additional factor of regional variation in voting behavior. It is this approach that has been developed by Johnston and Pattie, for example in their paper 'Voting in Britain since 1979: A Growing North–South Divide?' to the January 1988 Institute of British Geographers Conference, and built upon in the Johnston, Pattie and Allsop book *A Nation Dividing*?

Detailed voting statistics are available for six classes of occupation – professionals, administrative and managerial, routine non-manual, skilled manual, semi-skilled manual and unskilled manual workers. For the country as a whole, support for the Conservative Party was strongest among those in administrative and managerial occupations. National average support for the Conservatives among people in these occupations was 50 per cent in 1979, 48·8 per cent in 1983 and 49·7 per cent in 1987. This proportion is higher than it appears – in all three cases, between 20 and 25 per cent of people in this class did not vote for any party. But the range of support in this occupational class was wide, reaching more than 60 per cent in 1987 in a scattering of constituencies in southern England and the Midlands, but typically averaging between 45 and 60 per cent in these areas. However, in many constituencies in northern England, Scotland and Wales, Conservative support dropped to between 30 and 45 per cent, and in a significant number of seats in these areas it was as low as 15 to 30 per cent. Overall, the range of support for the Conservatives in 1987 in this occupational group was 12 to 62 per cent.

This range of support for the Conservatives among managers and administrators was mirrored in support for Labour among its core supporters, the unskilled manual workers. In 1987, Labour enjoyed 32·5 per cent support within this group (which contained the highest proportion, nearly 35 per cent, of non-voters). But its support varied widely, typically averaging 40 to 50 per cent in the majority of constituencies in the North but

Table 3.3 Party support by region, April 1992 (percentage of those voting)

	ABC1		C2DE	
	Conservative	Labour	Conservative	Labour
South East	56	20	42	37
South West	50	17	37	33
East Anglia	63	16	50	30
East Midlands	61	22	39	47
West Midlands	60	20	35	46
Yorks & Humberside	53	25	35	50
North West	51	31	30	54
North	49	31	24	60
Wales	51	26	27	53
Scotland	38	28	18	47

Source: Market and Opinion Research International.

dropping to as low as 20 per cent in most of the South. Labour's range of support among unskilled manual workers was 6 to 60 per cent. Its strongest support among its core class of voters was in South Wales, Merseyside, South Yorkshire, Tyneside and Scotland.

The April 1992 general election, which saw a loss of Conservative support among its core supporters in the South, will almost certainly have resulted in a narrowing of regional voting differences among the various classes of electors, although proof of this awaits detailed survey data. One can see intuitively why this should be the case. Skilled workers in the South, who moved towards the Conservatives under Mrs Thatcher, discovered in the recession of the early 1990s the downside of their new party's policies. However, as the Basildon result demonstrated, not enough of them were then willing to switch to Labour. Nor did the Liberal Democrats have a strong enough base to take advantage of the Government's difficulties. Their best showing in Essex, for example, was 30 per cent of the vote. Southern Conservative supporters among managers and professionals, hit hard by the recession, will have tended to move closer, in voting behaviour, to their northern counterparts.

Even so, regional variations in party support within particular social groupings can be expected to persist. Market and Opinion Research International (MORI) data for April 1992 shows that, within the broad ABC1 socio-economic grouping, support for the Conservatives ranged from 38 per cent to 63 per cent. In the C2DE grouping, the range of support for the Conservatives was 18 to 50 per cent. The results are summarized in Table 3.3.

NATIONALISM

If regional factors are an important determinant of voting behaviour, why have the nationalist parties not fared better? A nationalist vote is, after all, the most forthright way for the electorate in Wales and Scotland to express regional preferences. In the April 1992 general election, the Scottish Nationalist Party emerged with 21·5 per cent of the vote in Scotland (7·4 percentage points up on 1987) but only three parliamentary seats out of the Scottish total of 72. This was a particularly disappointing result for the SNP, being one seat down on the party's pre-election position, when large gains had been predicted. Plaid Cymru in Wales did better by concentrating its support in the seats where it was strongest. Although its share of the Welsh vote was just 8·8 per cent (1·6 percentage points up on 1987), it emerged with four seats out of the 38 in Wales. Plaid Cymru's representation was one up on 1987. Even so, in both cases the nationalist parties had failed to capitalize on thirteen years of often unpopular Conservative rule from London. In both Wales and Scotland, the Labour Party, and to a lesser extent the Liberal Democrats (the third party in Wales but only the fourth in Scotland), claimed the lion's share of the protest vote.

The poor performance of the nationalist parties under Mrs Thatcher's prime ministership owed much to their demoralized state following the 1979 referenda on limited devolution, held just before the May 1979 general election. In Wales, the devolution proposals were roundly rejected, with only 20 per cent of those voting and only a tenth of the total electorate in favour. In Scotland, 52 per cent of those who voted in the referendum were in favour of limited devolution, but the terms of the poll required that a majority of the electorate be in favour, and the 52 per cent which voted in favour comprised just 33 per cent of the electorate.

Thus the nationalists began the 1980s widely perceived as single-issue parties but with their single issue no longer on the political agenda. Support for Plaid Cymru in Wales, notwithstanding Gwynfor Evans' 1966 by-election breakthrough in Carmarthen, and subsequent victories, had in any case always been patchy. Plaid Cymru was strongest in Welsh-speaking rural North and mid-Wales, but weak in English-speaking industrial South Wales.

The Scottish Nationalist Party, not being associated with language to the same degree as Plaid Cymru, enjoyed a broader base of support but it too was badly affected by the disillusionment which followed the 1979 devolution referenda. The victories by Winifred Ewing in Hamilton in November 1967 and by Margo MacDonald at Glasgow Govan in November 1973 had paved the way for a strong rise in SNP support and a strong push for devolution in the 1970s. The SNP's share of the Scottish vote, 5 per cent or less in general elections between 1945 and 1966, surged to 30·4 per cent in the October 1974 general election. Under Mrs Thatcher, while Conservative support in Scotland declined, Labour rather than the SNP was the main beneficiary. The SNP share of the Scottish vote, 17·8 per cent in May 1979, slumped to 11·8 per cent in June 1983, before picking up slightly to 14 per cent in June 1987.

For much of the period between the 1987 and 1992 general elections it looked as if nationalist support, particularly in Scotland, was about to emerge as a much bigger factor in the electoral equation. In November 1988 a by-election was held at Glasgow Govan. The result, as is often the case in by-elections, was extraordinary. Jim Sillars, a former Labour MP turned SNP candidate, overturned a 19,500 Labour majority in the same constituency where his wife, Margo MacDonald, had triumphed fifteen years earlier. He won the seat for the SNP with a majority of 3,500 and a swing in his favour of more than 33 per cent. Immediately, the issues of nationalism and devolution were thrust back on the political agenda.

Although the Govan result was seen as an electoral disaster for Labour in one of its safest seats, it was of little comfort for the Conservatives. A primary reason for the SNP victory was that Labour was not seen to be conducting its task of opposition to the Conservatives effectively. In particular, the SNP favoured a policy of non-payment of the Government's community charge (the poll tax), while Labour's leadership had instructed its Scottish candidates not to espouse a policy of breaking the law through non-payment of the charge. What was also new, however, was the vision offered by the successful SNP candidate, Jim Sillars, of Scotland's role in the 1990s. He argued that the further integration of the European Community in 1992 created the opportunity for Scotland to become a state within an increasingly federal Europe. This was rather different from the SNP's ideas in the 1970s, when the risk was that devolution and eventual independence would leave Scotland out on a limb as a small, isolated country. Sillars also called upon Labour, with its forty-nine Scottish MPs, to join the SNP in a Scottish anti-Thatcher alliance. As late as January 1992, just three months before the election, a poll conducted for the *Scotsman* and ITN showed 50 per cent support for the SNP's version of Scottish independence. Even the *Scottish Sun*, sister paper to Rupert Murdoch's pro-Conservative tabloid, supported the SNP, declaring on its front page on 23 January 1992, 'Rise up and be a nation again.' While making clear that it did not approve of everything the party stood for, the newspaper repeated its endorsement on election day, saying, 'The *Scottish Sun* speaks its mind. Enough said. Vote SNP.' The result proved that, whatever the influence of the tabloid newspapers nationally, north of the border they were not a deciding factor.

For a while under Margaret Thatcher, the Conservatives appeared bent on a course of political extinction in Scotland. The introduction of the unpopular poll tax in April 1989 was at best clumsy, and was interpreted by many Scots as evidence of the Thatcher Government's cavalier attitude towards them. Also in 1989, the determinedly Thatcherite Michael Forsyth was made chairman of the Scottish Conservative Party, and set to work explaining his vision of a more Thatcherite Scotland, with fewer public-sector workers and council houses. Thatcher, meanwhile, remained particularly unpopular in Scotland.

John Major, when he succeeded Margaret Thatcher in November 1990, offered a softer style of Conservative rule. He soon replaced Forsyth as Scottish chairman of the party. But he still seemed destined for an embarrassing result in Scotland. Even if the Conservatives succeeded in holding on nationally, the general view was that the party would be all but wiped out in Scotland. Neil Kinnock, the Labour leader, appeared to open the door towards greater independence for Scotland. But Major took a gamble by standing out firmly against any form of independence. In an election rally a few days before polling day, he said:

If I could summon up all the authority of this office, I would put it into this single warning – the United Kingdom is in danger. Wake up my fellow countrymen! Wake up before it is too late!

Against the odds, it worked. Soft Conservative voters rallied to the party, more concerned about what they saw as the dangers of independence than registering a protest vote against the Government. As described earlier, the Conservatives gained a seat (with their overall representation up from 10 to 11) in Scotland. For the SNP, the 1992 election failure, despite a sharp increase in the party's share of the vote, was an object lesson in the waste of support that can emerge when votes are not concentrated in winnable seats. The party even suffered the indignity of losing the Glasgow Govan seat (to Labour), the winning of which in 1988 had lifted so many nationalist hopes. The SNP can regard its 1992 vote as a platform on which to build in the future. Even so, in every seat where the SNP is the main challenger to Labour, it has a mountain to climb. Labour's lead in such seats is in every case more than 10 per cent of the vote.

POLITICS AND ECONOMIC CHANGE

There are many factors which determine how people vote. Support for one party may reflect not voter satisfaction with that party but weakness and disarray among its political opponents. Some would say that this characterized Mrs Thatcher's second election victory, and certainly the extent of that victory, in 1983. Particular aspects of a party's policy may prove unacceptable, even among a substantial proportion of its core supporters – an example of this in the 1980s was Labour's policy of unilateral nuclear disarmament – leading to a protest vote for one of the other parties.

Inevitably, though, the major influence on voting behaviour, certainly in recent years, has been what could broadly be characterized as economic wellbeing. Economists, particularly in the United States, have charted the 'misery index' (the sum of inflation and unemployment rates) and charted the electoral success of governments according to that index. The electoral cycle has been a familiar post-war feature of the British economy, whereby governments endeavour to administer any necessary harsh economic medicine far enough ahead of elections to allow time to then generate boom conditions, or at least a return to rising prosperity, by the time they have to face the electorate. Sir Geoffrey Howe's 'hairshirt' Budget of 1981 was halfway between the 1979 and 1983 elections. His successor, Nigel Lawson, first undertook a squeeze on public expenditure – immediately after the June 1983 election – and then, in 1984–5, a forced period of high interest rates. In 1988, Lawson embarked on a period of high interest rates in order to generate a sharp, inter-election slowdown in the economy, although the subsequent prolonged recession, still in force at the time of the April 1992 election, proved that such things are not open to precise calculation.

The role of economic wellbeing in determining voting behaviour is not a new phenomenon. In the 1950s, when inflation and unemployment were both problems of much smaller magnitude than in the 1970s and 1980s, the electoral rewards arising from producing conditions where people could genuinely believe that they had never had it so good were well known. Iain Macleod, the founder of the 'One Nation' group of Conservatives, explained some of the 1959 electoral success of his party in these terms in an interview with Anthony Sampson for *The Anatomy of Britain* in the early 1960s:

The Conservative Party is associated, and always has been, with the land and with property. But I've always defined property in much wider terms than this. I define it nowadays in terms, not only of estates, but in terms of cars, and houses, the holding of shares, and even refrigerators and washing machines. And this is a form of property which is spreading very fast indeed, and whose owners are becoming, as I think we've seen for some time, increasingly Conservative. Now this is the reason why against all the prognostications of the psephologists and all the other eggheads like myself, we swept the new towns in 1959. Now this is very strange indeed. You would have thought that here is a community of people, obviously not connected with privilege or with inherited wealth, most of them with young families and their way to make in the world, and you would think that here, if anywhere, the Labour and Liberal and radical philosophies would make a great appeal. In fact it is the Conservative philosophy that made an appeal there, because I think the modern Conservative appeal has, within it, a great deal of the radical. (1962, pp. 90–91)

And if all that sounds very familiar when read today, so too does the Labour response, by Hugh Gaitskell from the same source:

During that period we have had a bad economic record in comparison with other industrial countries – indeed, it is really the worst of them all; but nevertheless, it has not been so bad as to cause a great deal of disturbance and indignation at home. The standard of living has risen somewhat and it has risen in ways that especially affect people's homes – television, kitchen gadgets, etc. This may be one reason why people nowadays are more family- and less community-conscious than they used to be. On top of that the Government deliberately encouraged, especially before the election, complacency, a materialistic outlook and the idea of getting on better for yourself never mind what is happening to other people. All that has created a different atmosphere for Britain. Of course, it has been done very professionally – getting at the subconscious as if you were selling detergents or toothpaste. (p. 108)

In that period, the differences between the Labour and Conservative parties were less than in more recent times. And so too were the regional variations in the economy, partly because manufacturing industry was participating in the boom, and partly because regional policy was given a greater role, although the 1950s have been characterized as wasted years in the development of such policy. Thus, it was possible to see Conservative electoral success as clearly related to individual prosperity but, although there were plenty of people during the thirteen years of Conservative Government (1951–64) who doubted whether Labour could ever win again, it was also possible to see Labour as a viable alternative, even in the South.

The emergence of wide regional economic differences in the 1980s, particularly in terms of unemployment, means that the misery index approach can be used as an explanation of regional voting patterns. One part of the index, the inflation rate, can be taken as constant across the whole country at any one time. Although there are clearly regional variations in inflation – arising for example from differential rates of increase in house prices between regions – there is probably much less awareness of variations in general inflation, partly because no official figures are produced for regional inflation rates. We can therefore take the inflation element of the index – the inflation rate at the time of the election for all regions – as 10·3 per cent at the time of the May 1979 election, 3·7 per cent for the June 1983 poll, 4·2 per cent for June 1987 and 4·3 per cent in April 1992.

We can then add on to these national inflation rates the regional unemployment rates, to produce a misery index by region, as in Table 3.4.

Crude though the misery index clearly is, it has the virtue of incorporating inflation into a measure of economic wellbeing. The difficulty with any such index, apart from the fact that it can at best only be a very rough shorthand for a wide variety of economic influences, is that the weight accorded to its components will vary among voters over time and, possibly, by region. In other words, unemployment will be more of a concern in areas of high unemployment and inflation less so, and vice versa. Despite these obvious shortcomings, the index performs reasonably well when set against regional voting patterns, although it is far from clear that the Conservatives won the 1983 election on the basis of their economic success. Non-economic influences, and the fact that, in electoral terms at least, there was no alternative, may have played a more important part in Mrs Thatcher's second election victory.

Table 3.4 The Misery Index*, by region

	May 1979	June 1983	June 1987	April 1992
South East	13·0	11·4	11·8	13·3
South West	14·5	12·6	13·0	13·2
East Anglia	13·6	12·0	12·2	11·7
East Midlands	13·8	13·5	13·9	12·9
West Midlands	14·5	16·9	16·1	14·7
Yorks & Humberside	14·7	15·5	16·2	14·0
North West	15·7	17·3	17·6	14·7
North	17·2	18·7	19·0	15·4
Wales	16·1	17·0	17·2	13·8
Scotland	16·4	16·3	17·9	13·6
Northern Ireland	18·3	19·5	22·5	18·6
United Kingdom	14·6	14·5	14·9	13·8

* The sum of inflation and unemployment rates.
Source: Derived from Department of Employment data.

But the misery index helps explain the increase in Conservative support in the three southern regions – the south east, south west and East Anglia – between 1979 and 1983, after which strongly rising real personal disposable incomes may have taken over as the main economic influence on voting behaviour. It is also consistent with the fact that Conservative support in Scotland, certainly in terms of seats won, held up well between 1979 and 1983, before falling sharply in the four years to 1987, as the misery index rose with the collapse of the oil boom, and the Conservatives did their bit to lose political popularity north of the border with preparatory moves for the early introduction of the Community Charge in Scotland.

The enigma, particularly in 1983, was the voting behaviour of the west midlands. The 1979–81 recession, in reversing previous prosperity and in its devastating effect on manufacturing industry, was arguably felt harder in the west midlands region than in any other part of the country. The misery index increased sharply between 1979 and 1983, while the manifestations of that misery, in factory closures, a loss of confidence for the region and a general air of gloom, were plain enough to see. And yet the Conservatives increased their Parliamentary support in the 1983 election, and Labour's failure there was probably more damaging to the party's overall fortunes than anywhere else in the country.

So why did the Conservatives do well? There were the non-economic explanations for their 1983 success, notably the disarray within the Labour Party and the effect of the 'Falklands Factor' – the benefits to the Government of the military victory over Argentina in 1982 – although its role in securing a second election victory for Mrs Thatcher has been questioned. In any case, there is no obvious reason why these factors should have particularly benefited the Conservatives in the west midlands. More important may have been the fact that, in spite of the devastation caused by the recession in the area, there may have been more of a tendency there to believe the Government's optimism about economic recovery, because of the area's prosperous past. And, while the strength of the Conservative vote in the west midlands in 1983 appeared illogical at the time, the period from 1983 to 1987 was one in which the area, helped by assisted-area status, albeit within a general downgrading of regional policy, 'rejoined the South', having been – in economic terms – a part of the North between 1979 and 1983.

This view receives support from opinion-poll data. At the time of the 1983 election, the west midlands had one of the highest proportions of respondents in the whole country who thought that their personal economic situation had deteriorated over the previous twelve months. But the electorate in Birmingham and the Black Country, according to BBC/Gallup data, was also among the most optimistic about prospects both for their own and the national economic situation over the next twelve months.

Looking at the economic explanations of North–South voting differences from 1983 to 1987, it appears to be the case that the Conservatives did enough – in halting the rise in unemployment – and in the period immediately before the June 1987 election reducing it, to consolidate and in some cases build on their support in the South, while ensuring sufficient representation in the North. Even had the Scottish experience been typical of the North, the Conservatives would have been left with a substantial Parliamentary majority in 1987.

Table 3.5 Employment growth and Conservative strength, 1983–7

	Employment growth 1983–7 (%)	Conservative share 1987 (%)	Change on 1983	Conservative lead over Labour
South East	+ 5·1	52·2	+ 1·7	29·9
East Anglia	+ 15·7	52·1	+ 1·1	30·4
South West	+ 5·1	50·6	− 0·8	34·7
West Midlands	+ 5·7	45·5	+ 0·5	12·2
East Midlands	+ 7·2	48·6	+ 1·4	18·6
Yorks & Humberside	+ 1·7	37·4	− 1·2	− 3·2
North West	− 1·7	38·0	− 2·0	− 3·2
North	+ 3·2	32·3	− 2·3	− 14·1
Wales	− 2·6	29·5	− 1·5	− 15·6
Scotland	− 0·7	24·0	− 4·3	− 18·4

Source: D. Butler and D. Kavanagh, *The British General Election of 1987*, p. 284.

By 1992, the boom and subsequent recession had succeeded in producing a greater equality of misery across regions. In only two regions, the south east and the south west, was the misery index higher in April 1992 than in June 1987. The fact that the Conservatives did not do better in those regions where the index fell sharply between the two elections is probably explained by the Government's failure to synchronize the economic and electoral cycles. Thus, unemployment fell sharply everywhere for more than half of the Parliament (from June 1987 to March 1990), but rose equally sharply during the remainder. And it was the latter that was fresh in people's memories.

In Table 3.5, the counterpart of the unemployment element of the misery index, growth in employment, is set against the Conservative share of the vote in the June 1987 election, and its change compared with 1983 (as in the other economic explanations of voting behaviour, the incumbent party is assumed to benefit in electoral terms from economic success, and vice versa for the opposition). The table shows that the Conservatives increased their share of the vote in areas where employment growth was strongest, with the exception of the south west, although in that region its lead over Labour was bigger than in any other part of the country. In areas of weak growth or declining employment, the Conservatives lost ground and, in all cases, were well behind Labour in voting

Table 3.6 Employment growth and Conservative strength, 1987–92

	Employment growth 1987–92* (%)	Conservative share 1992 (%)	Change on 1987	Conservative lead over Labour
South East	− 4·7	51·2	− 1·0	24·6
East Anglia	− 1·5	51·0	− 1·1	23·0
South West	+ 6·5	47·6	− 3·0	28·4
West Midlands	− 5·1	44·8	− 0·8	6·0
East Midlands	+ 0·7	46·6	− 2·0	9·2
Yorks & Humberside	+ 2·1	37·9	+ 0·5	− 6·5
North West	+ 3·5	37·8	− 0·2	− 7·1
North	− 0·9	33·4	+ 1·0	− 17·2
Wales	+ 10·1	28·6	− 1·0	− 20·9
Scotland	+ 4·7	25·7	+ 1·7	− 13·3

* 1987 employment statistics are for June, 1992 for March.
Sources: Department of Employment Gazette, various issues; D. Butler and D. Kavanagh, *The British General Election of 1992*, pp. 286–7.

support. A marked North–South difference in employment growth and Conservative support is evident from the table.

I have repeated this exercise for the period 1987–92, with the results summarized in Table 3.6. As it shows, the Conservatives did not, in general, gain support even in areas where employment was higher than in 1987. The south west is the most dramatic example of this, where the three percentage point drop in Conservative support was the biggest in the South, despite a 6·5 per cent employment increase. Again, the fact that employment growth was concentrated in the early part of the Parliament, and was followed by a fall, probably explains this apparent lack of gratitude among the voters. Scotland, where a rise in employment went alongside an increase in Conservative support, was the only part of Britain where success in generating employment, measured across the full Parliamentary term, paid obvious political dividends.

There are other economic influences on voting behaviour. As mentioned above, strong growth in voters' real incomes probably played an important role in the 1983–7 period, perhaps more so than employment and unemployment, and the strongest growth in incomes, for those in work, was in the South. Sir Geoffrey Howe had cut both the basic and higher rates of income tax in the June 1979 Budget, but in the following six budgets the only personal tax-cutting element was the less visible one of raising allowances by more than the rate of inflation, a measure which is more even in its effects up and down the income scale. In 1986, the Conservatives resorted to cuts in income tax rates – first reducing the basic rate from 30 to 29 per cent and then in 1987, three months before the election, from 29 to 27 per cent, thus further boosting already strong growth in real incomes.

In 1983, most of the electorate was unsure about whether Mrs Thatcher's economic policies had done any good, certainly in terms of individual wellbeing. The exceptions were the south east, excluding London, and to a lesser extent East Anglia. By 1987, perhaps because of the recent tax cuts, there was a much higher level of optimism across the whole country. The biggest proportion of those who thought their situation had improved in the twelve months prior to the election was in East Anglia, and there were also high proportions in the south east, south west, east and west midlands, together with rural areas in northern England, Wales and Scotland. The exceptions were to be found in the industrial areas of the North – with the majority of respondents saying that their situation had deteriorated, although even there there was quite a high degree of optimism over the likely course of the economy and their personal situation over the following year, albeit nothing like as high as in the South. This suggests that Labour may have done better than it is usually given credit for in 1987, by just consolidating its position in the North.

The point is often made that the influence of unemployment on voting behaviour will always be more muted than might be expected because, even during the recent peaks of UK unemployment, at least 85 per cent of the workforce was in work. This may have been more the case in periods of stable or falling unemployment than when it was rising strongly, as between 1979 and 1983, and when the threat of unemployment extended over a much wider range of the population than those who were actually out of work. This was also the case in the recession of the early 1990s, when, as we shall see, a large number of 'safe' service-industry occupations in the South became subject to large-scale redundancies, fear of which held back economic activity. The influence of the housing market, with falling prices and sharply rising repossessions, also came to the fore, as will be examined later in this book.

Any North–South, or South–North, shifts in economic activity have to be set against other important changes taking place. Often, North–South voting differences have been compounded and in some cases complicated by urban and rural differences. Just as rural areas fared better than the old industrial conurbations under Mrs Thatcher, and to a lesser extent under Mr Major, so this has influenced support for the Conservatives, in some cases independently of North–South differences.

The new factor, which dominated the latter part of the 1987–92 Parliament, was the pendulum of economic advantage swinging back towards the North and away from the recession-hit South. To be accurate, all parts of the country experienced recession, but its effects were relatively more severe in the South. If sustained, this should produce a shift in the political divide between North and South. For the Conservatives the question would be whether the party can stack up enough extra votes in the North to replace those lost in the South. For Labour, the key concern is the size of the southern mountain the party has to climb. It is conceivable that the extra support the party could gain in the South as a result of a changed economic landscape will not mean much in terms of additional Parliamentary representation, while it suffers an erosion of support in the North. Alternatively, the political divide may be permanent. The Conservatives dominated the South in April 1992, in spite of having to call a general election during a period in which many supporters, in economic terms, were on their knees. If it can deliver an economic improvement for its southern supporters by the next general election in 1996 or 1997, then it should gain support, reinforcing the long-standing regional pattern of party support. It is to this question, the permanence of the political divide, that I now turn.

A PERMANENT POLITICAL DIVIDE?

Much has been written and said about the apparent hopelessness of Labour's task in overturning the present Conservative dominance of British politics as long as its appeal is unevenly concentrated in the industrial areas of the North. Writing after the 1983 general election, McAllister and Rose, in their book *The Nationwide Competition for Votes*, observed:

The only way in which the Labour opposition can gain control of the next House of Commons is by winning more than 70 Conservative-held seats in London, the Midlands and the South of England. A Labour strategy of mobilizing support in its territorial bastions distant from London might increase Labour's vote, but it would doom Labour to opposition in the next Parliament. Of the seats that Labour needs to win a majority in the next Parliament, 39 per cent are in the South of England or London, and 64 per cent are between the English Channel and the Mersey. (1984, p. 205)

It was a tall order, which few people, including the authors, expected Labour to achieve. And Labour's achievement between 1983 and 1987, whether deliberate or not, was to win back support in areas of its traditional strength, without making inroads into the Conservative heartland of the South.

The position outlined after the 1983 election by McAllister and Rose remained intact after the 1987 election. The moderate Labour MP Austin Mitchell wrote after Mrs Thatcher's third victory: 'We face a difficult struggle in those huge southern areas we need to win in: the Worcesters, Plymouths, Readings, Harlows and Basildons, because we have already squeezed most of what is possible from Scotland, the North and everywhere in fact except the West and East Midlands.' Mitchell, along with many other Labour MPs, sees the party's only real prospect of success in the South as being in broadening its appeal through substantial shifts in policy.

Johnston, Pattie and Allsop concluded their *A Nation Dividing?*, written after the 1987 general election, with the following:

For Labour, the retreat into the relatively deprived regions of the north creates problems of how to win enough seats to regain power . . . And for the government, while it could sustain itself in power simply by continuing to win in the southern, affluent regions, its loss of support in other areas is not just a blow to its pride but also potentially a threat to the legitimacy of the economic, social and political systems it seeks to defend.

If Conservative policies are generally successful, Labour could be the major loser, since its chances of winning many seats in the south are already remote. It may lose relatively few in the north, because of its large majorities in many seats there, but its relative decline could be matched by a resurgence of Alliance support in the south – if the restructured party is successfully launched. The facts of British electoral geography appear to be stacked against Labour at present; it could become the 'class party' of a shrinking, deprived north. (1988, p. 328)

In some ways history repeated itself in the 1980s when, as in the period following Labour's third successive election defeat in 1959, the Conservatives had a Parliamentary majority of 100 and Labour's narrow appeal was seen as a guarantee of its continuing electoral failure. In 1975, the Conservatives appeared to be doomed to a long period in opposition, this time because they had retreated to their traditional support base in southern England. The pendulum swings.

Had Labour won the 1992 general election, as many expected, it would have been proof of the fact that nothing in politics, including the permanence of a North–South voting divide, can be taken for granted (although Labour could not have hoped, in its wildest dreams, to overtake the Conservatives as the largest party in the South). There is a view, as described above, that the Conservatives, having held on to most of their southern vote in spite of alienating their supporters, cannot be dislodged. The 1992 election was an opportunity for Labour that, barring a repeat of the economic mismanagement of the 1987–92 period, will not easily happen again. Paradoxically, the recession could have reinforced support for the Government among some voters, on the grounds that however bad things were already they could get a lot worse if a new government, committed to policy changes (including higher taxation), was elected. The Conservative Party played successfully on such fears.

The 1992 result has, I would argue, left the North–South political divide more or less intact. Conservative support in the South, it is true, did not remain at the high levels of the Thatcher election victories of 1983 and 1987, but the party remained dominant. Labour succeeded in broadening its regional appeal, but not by enough. As Johnston and Pattie concluded, in a paper entitled 'Is the Seesaw Tipping Back? The End of Thatcherism and Changing Voting Patterns in Great Britain 1979-92':

Against expectations, the Government was re-elected, albeit with a substantially reduced majority. Much of the reason for this must lie in the geography of voting. The Government was indeed punished in its heartland – the geography of recession in the early 1990s did damage the Conservative cause – whilst it was able to regain some lost ground in the North, especially Scotland. The opposite was true for Labour, with in general a better performance in the recession-struck South than in the North. But those reversals of fortune for two of the three main parties were insufficient to offset the polarization that characterized the electoral geography of Britain in 1983 and 1987. Great Britain was less polarized after the 1992 election than it was in 1987, but it remains more divided than was the case when Thatcherism was first implemented in 1979. The Conservatives, despite losing some ground, were still too far ahead in key southern constituencies in 1992 and the opposition parties still had too large a gap to close for sufficient seats to change hands to force a change of government. Herein lies the answer to the major puzzle of 1992: how could the Conservatives win, given that they were defending their record during a deep recession? They won not because of their record, but despite it, because of the large reservoir of support which they had built up over the previous thirteen years: their record over the 1987–92 period depleted that reservoir, but did not drain it and so – to revert to the earlier analogy – the seesaw tipped back, but it has not yet levelled out. (1992a, p. 1504).

One of the curiosities of the 1992 election was that Labour ran the Conservatives close in terms of seats won, but was well behind in its share of the popular vote. Excluding Northern Ireland, the Conservatives had 42·8 per cent of the total votes cast (on a 77·9 per cent turnout), compared with 35·2 per cent for Labour, and 18·3 per cent for the Liberal Democrats. It was this that led Butler and Kavanagh to conclude *The British General Election of 1992* with the following:

> Over four general elections, the Conservatives have averaged only 42 per cent of the vote. That could be a base or a ceiling, but in three-party politics it has proved enough to be decisive. It is the party's substantial lead over Labour in the four elections, 7·6 per cent, 14·8 per cent, 11·5 per cent and 7·6 per cent that is significant. 1992 echoed the earlier elections and confirmed the Conservative dominance over Labour and the imbalance in the British party system. (1992, p. 283)

Against this, proponents of the 'one more push' school of thought for Labour would point to the party's success in concentrating its vote in those seats where it mattered most, the marginals. An increase in Labour support, coupled with a repeat of that success, would thrust the party into power. At least thirty Conservative-held marginals would fall to Labour with a swing of 2·5 per cent or less. They include Bristol North-West; Luton South; Slough; City of Chester; Langbaurgh; Amber Valley; Basildon; Harlow; Erith & Crayford; Enfield; Eltham; Hillingdon, Hayes & Harlington; Hounslow, Brentford & Isleworth; Merton, Mitcham & Morden; Bolton North-East; Bolton West; Bury South; Southampton Test; Dover; Blackpool South; Leicestershire North-West; Lincoln; Norwich North; Corby; Tynemouth; Coventry South-West; Batley & Spen; Swindon; Vale of Glamorgan; Stirling; Aberdeen South; and Ayr.

Labour has pledged to review its taxation policy, which turned out to be an electoral own goal in 1992. The party can also point to the Conservatives' broken tax pledges, following Norman Lamont's decision to extend VAT and increase National Insurance contributions in his 1993 Budget. Labour may also gain as a result of the abolition of the poll tax, which was thought to have persuaded a number of its potential supporters to remove themselves from the electoral register. However, Labour may lose out, by between fourteen and twenty seats, as a result of changes in electoral boundaries. One of the first acts of John Major's re-elected Conservative Government was to place a bill before Parliament requiring the boundary commissions to report before the end of 1994.

Ultimately, however, the outlook for the two main parties will be bound up both in the general outlook for the economy and its regional dimension. If 1992 was the low point of the South's fortunes, then it is difficult to see the Conservatives being toppled in 1996 or 1997 or, for that matter, beyond then. But a period of prolonged economic difficulty for the country, and disproportionate difficulty for the South would leave the Labour Party, which by then will have worked to broaden its appeal, in a strong position.

The central message of this chapter is that, in the four elections since 1979, the North–South dimension in British politics has been a crucial factor. Conservative dominance of the South was eroded in 1992 but not sufficiently to produce an election defeat. The Government, above all, requires a regionally balanced economy in the 1990s. If the South was to re-establish quickly its economic dominance of the 1980s, then northern frustration with a government which looked after its own political heartlands would grow. But if the North prospers and the South lags behind, there are plenty of marginal and not-so-marginal southern seats up for grabs. As a result of the 1992 election, there is everything to play for.

This was underlined in May 1993, when local election results, and a by-election in the constituency of Newbury gave the Conservatives, in the words of John Major, 'a bloody nose'. In Newbury, the Liberal Democrats overturned a Conservative general-election majority of 12,000 to win the seat with a spectacular 22,000 majority. In the shire counties across the South, the Conservatives lost 16 of the 17 councils they controlled, to be left with only Buckinghamshire. Nationally, elections left the Conservatives controlling only 15 out of 127 councils in Britain: one county (Buckinghamshire); one metropolitan authority and 13 London boroughs. The anti-government vote, which many had expected in the April 1992 general election, had finally come to pass. The results, which gave Labour 41 per cent of the vote, the Conservatives 31 per cent and the Liberal Democrats 24 per cent, would have been enough, if repeated in a general election, to give Labour a House of Commons majority of 95 seats. There had, of course, been large setbacks for the Conservatives before. But the scale of the Government's defeat suggested that Britain's political geography was more open than it had ever been in the 1980s.

4

THE DECLINE OF REGIONAL POLICY

> It is no part of our policy to direct where people
> shall live or where firms set up or expand. If we try
> to discourage development and economic growth in
> large parts of the South of England in the hope that
> it will happen in the large cities of the North, we risk
> losing them altogether. (Margaret Thatcher, July
> 1985)

Regional policy – intervention by governments in the location
of industry and people to ensure a more even distribution of
economic activity – first emerged in Britain in the inter-war
years and continues, although in a very different form, to this
day. Its very existence denotes a recognition by governments
that a regional problem exists in the British economy and that
policy can do something to correct it – or at least that the
politicians have to be *seen* to be trying to do something about
it.

There has, however, been a distinct change of attitude towards the role and effectiveness of regional policy. Until the
1970s, the policy was operated with a combination of the
'carrot' and the 'stick'. The carrot was in the form of grants
and other financial incentives to encourage firms to move to
the depressed regions, and for those already there to stay there.
The stick was in planning controls, strictly applied, which prevented companies from setting up or expanding in areas that
were deemed to be prosperous enough already. In the 1980s,
the key change, apart from a general downgrading of the role

of regional policy, has been largely to dispense with the stick, on the argument that discouraging firms from setting up or expanding in any part of the country, even in the overcrowded south east, runs the risk that they will be put off from doing so at all. The carrot of incentives remains in place, albeit in a sharply reduced form, but this policy shift occurred during a period when regional divisions in Britain – perhaps partly because of the change in the nature and scope of the policy – grew sharply wider.

WHY REGIONAL POLICY?

The theoretical and practical basis for regional policy begins from the point at which various regional problems can be identified. Economists have tended to split these into three types of problem. There is, firstly, the *underdeveloped* region, which has perhaps never been a location for industry and has suffered from, say, the relative decline of agriculture. Into this category one could place, for example, mid-Wales. Secondly, there is the problem of the *depressed* region, which has had its share of industrial activity in the past, but has suffered from a depression in its industries. At various times many of the traditional industrial areas of the North have fallen into this category as, in the early 1980s, did the west midlands. Thirdly, and to demonstrate that not all regional problems are those associated with a lack of activity, the problem of the *congested* region has also been identified. The basis of this is that there are congestion costs associated with over-concentration of activity. The cost per head of providing public services, for example, will initially fall with the growth of population in a region. But diseconomies of scale may then set in, as demand for those services reaches breaking point and the cost of adding to them is disproportionately large. Congested roads add to everyone's costs. The south east remains the best long-running example of a congested region, although others have also fallen into this category. The west midlands was regarded as a congested region in the 1950s and 1960s.

Within this classification, two reasons for regional inequalities are usually put forward. The first reason is purely locational. A region may be situated too far away from main markets to be an attractive location for industry and it may not be well-served by transport and communication links. The locational factor can be important even in a small country like Britain, with a well-developed motorway network and every part of the country just a short distance from the sea. However, the second reason, the structural explanation, is also important in any analysis of Britain's regional inequalities. Thus, areas of the country which have a high proportion of declining industries – for example the traditional, staple industries of the North – will suffer from difficulties.

Regional policy can act on both the locational and structural causes of such inequalities. Clearly, far-flung regions cannot be physically moved to more favourable locations. But links between these areas and the rest of the country can be improved. The Severn Bridge was one successful example of how a region, in this case South Wales, could be assisted by the improvement of transport links. The Humber Bridge, intended to benefit the Hull area, was a less successful example. And, if the locational disadvantages of regions cannot be successfully tackled, the disadvantages facing individuals in such regions can be eased, by offering them incentives to move to places where work is more freely available.

Where the problem is structural, policy can act by encouraging the development of new industries and other forms of economic activity, to provide work for those displaced from declining industries. In some cases, this policy will involve assisting the process of decline in some industries in order to provide an additional spur for the development of new industries. A major thrust of regional policy has been to alleviate structural problems.

The emphasis placed on regional policy by governments will depend on their overall economic goals. Economic policy can focus on a number of different areas, typically:

- Ensuring that the resources available in the economy, including labour, are used fully and efficiently

- Seeking to achieve a favourable allocation of such resources between different economic sectors
- Maintaining an adequate rate of growth
- Preventing excessive inflation
- Avoiding disequilibria on the balance of payments
- Establishing a distribution of income that is reasonably equitable.

It is fair to say that for much of the post-war period, until the 1970s, economic policy attempted to steer a line between these different objectives, not always an easy task. The contribution of regional policy was to prevent the under-utilization of resources by, for example, having large numbers of unemployed people in the North, at a time of labour shortages in the South. In this way, and by its influence on the type and location of economic activity that was encouraged, it was also seen to be contributing to a faster rate of growth for the economy as a whole. The main influence on the distribution of income in the country was the tax system. But regional policy also affected the distribution of income between different parts of the country, and helped to limit North–South inequalities.

Regional policy, on the face of it, had little to say about the control of inflation and the balance of payments, although we will come on to the links between regional inequalities and these problems in the next chapter. Regional policy was dealt two body-blows in the 1970s and early 1980s. The first came with the shift of the policy emphasis towards the control of inflation, firstly with the burst of inflation which followed the 1973–4 oil crisis, and secondly the deliberate emphasis on controlling inflation by the Thatcher Government elected in 1979. Increasingly, regional policy came to be regarded as at best a sideshow, at worst an expensive and outdated instrument, at a time when ways were being sought to economize on public spending. And then, after the economy had been through the traumas of stagflation, and the 1979–81 recession, any type of economic recovery was welcome, whether it was based in the North or in the South. Policies which attempted to influence the location of activity were seen both as risky, because of the fear that such activity would be discouraged altogether, and as a luxury that the economy could ill afford. Whether this argued for a temporary rather than a permanent downgrading of regional policy is a key question, to which we can return later. But first let us examine some of the paraphernalia of regional policy and look at some of the evidence on its effectiveness.

THE POLICY IN PRACTICE

Much of the history of regional policy is concerned with the minutiae of regional development grants, assisted areas and industrial development certificates. But attempts by governments to provide assistance to the regions have had their lighter moments. One of these came with the appointment, in January 1963, of the present Lord Hailsham as unofficial 'Minister for the north east'.

Harold Macmillan, then in his last days as Prime Minister, and heavily influenced by his own observations of unemployment in the north east in the 1930s, was also keenly aware that the Conservative Government, after twelve years of continuous rule, was electorally very weak in the area. Lord Hailsham was given the responsibility for advising the Cabinet on reviving industrial activity in the region and creating more jobs. This was in addition to his other responsibilities as Lord President of the Council, Minister for Sport, Leader of the House of Lords and Minister for Science.

Lord Hailsham's multiplicity of roles produced the criticism from Douglas Jay, Labour's front-bench Treasury spokesman, that the appointment was 'largely political sleight of hand'. It also produced a letter in *The Times* from a scientist, concerned both about the implied diminution of his existing roles and doubting whether a job which was to take up a fifth of his time could be seriously intended: 'As a scientist I am insulted. If I were unemployed in the north east, I should be incensed,' the writer concluded.

The new unofficial minister did, however, go about his job in a workmanlike way, even if he did not pursue a proposal that he should take up residence in a semi-detached council house in the new town of Peterlee, County Durham, to get to know the area better. In February 1963, on a visit to Darlington, he donned a cloth cap to get into the spirit of things, but this failed to prevent a noisy demonstration when he announced that he could do nothing to save the town's rail workshops from closure. A month later, he disappointed his audience at a '30 shilling a head roast beef lunch' at the Tyneside Chamber of Commerce, by failing to give details of the expected development plan for the north east.

Three months later, Lord Hailsham was back with something more concrete, although far from specific, which had as its basis the attraction of new investment from outside the region, the improvement of the area's road links with the rest of the country and other public investment in the local infrastructure. The appointment of a minister to tackle the problems of one particular region was, however, the exception to the regional policy rule of the post-war years. For a start, other depressed regions felt hard done by. Merseyside, for example, complained that it had as much right to Cabinet representation as the north east. The norm, therefore, was for regional policy to be generally applied. Indeed, one persistent criticism of post-war regional policy was that it was not selective enough in its approach.

CREATING A REGIONAL POLICY FRAMEWORK

The history of regional policy in Britain can be traced back to 1928 and the establishment by the Ministry of Labour of an Industrial Transfer Board. The Board operated the industrial transfer and juvenile transfer schemes, and provided assisted migration for unemployed workers and their families, in particular for former miners from the old industrial areas to the South and Midlands. The scheme was not, however, a great success, partly because migration was occurring anyway and the additional impact of the schemes was negligible. Most people assisted with moves under the schemes returned to their home towns within a few years.

The transfer schemes were the earliest example of an attempt to tackle the regional problem by taking workers to the work.

They were supplemented in the 1930s by the more usual form of regional policy in Britain, that of taking work to the workers. Some of the most serious areas of unemployment in the mid-1930s were the mining areas – there were unemployment rates of 74 per cent in Brynmawr, 73 per cent in Dowlais and 69 per cent in Merthyr Tydfil, all in South Wales. Thus, mining areas featured prominently in the Special Areas (Development and Improvement) Act of 1934. Under the Act, four areas – South Wales and Monmouthshire, West Cumberland, Tyneside and parts of Durham, and parts of Scotland – were designated as 'special' and, supplemented by further Acts in 1936 and 1937, a policy was evolved of providing assistance for the establishment of new industries, to provide employment opportunities in place of the old, declining industries.

The logic of the special-areas approach was that moving workers to the work was wasteful in that the old industrial regions were already supplied with housing and infrastructure. In addition, evacuating families and communities, leaving ghost towns where there had once been bustle and prosperity, was seen as socially undesirable. The special-areas approach was hardly up and running before the Second World War intervened, but it did provide the basis for much of post-war regional policy. A Royal Commission on the Geographical Distribution of the Industrial Population published its report in 1940 – the Barlow report – and urged a further extension of regional policy. The rationale was simple: incentives had to be provided to compensate for the attractions for industrialists of the South and the Midlands, and in the existing large cities. These incentives could be purely financial, or they could involve the setting up of industrial estates with new factory units and low rates and rents.

Clement Attlee's Labour Government of 1945–51, partly motivated by the strong feeling that the effects of the depression on the North should never be repeated, partly by the success of wartime economic planning, strengthened the machinery of regional policy. The Distribution of Industry Acts of 1945 and 1950 built on the special-areas legislation of the 1930s, with the areas eligible for assistance enlarged and renamed 'development areas'. Under the Acts, the Board of Trade was able to build and equip factory sites, provide finance for trading estates, reclaim derelict land and make grants and loans to firms. This was the 'carrot' in operation. Policy also continued along the "workers to the work" route, with the 1946 Resettlement Scheme, which offered assistance with migration to all unemployed workers, whatever their region.

The immediate post-war period also saw the application of the 'stick' in regional policy, with the 1947 Town and Country Planning Act, an element of which was the introduction of Industrial Development Certificates. Under this legislation all new manufacturing operations or extensions to existing operations over an area of 5,000 square feet required an IDC. The IDCs could be and were used to direct industry away from those areas in which industry was already concentrated. The requirement for development certificates for manufacturing establishments was augmented in 1965 by the Control of Office and Industrial Development Act, under which new Office Development Certificates were required for office building and expansion in London and Birmingham. The 'stick' of development certificates was used with considerable effect. At its peak in the mid-1960s, more than a quarter of applications for industrial development certificates in the Midlands and the South were refused.

It is difficult to say whether this element of the planning process had the intended effect of directing industrial and commercial development to the areas which needed it most, or whether such development, having run up against a planning brick wall in the chosen area, was simply shelved. Certainly, development certificates – a legacy of the planned economy of the war years – were anathema to the newly elected Conservative Government of Mrs Thatcher in 1979. Office-development certificates were quickly abolished. IDCs soon followed although, with only 2 per cent of applications in the Midlands and the South refused in 1979–80, they were already falling into disuse.

Labour governments tended to introduce most of the regional policy legislation in Britain, while Conservative governments, even before Mrs Thatcher, either tolerated it or attempted to pare it back, not always successfully. Apart from the 1945–51

Attlee Government, Harold Wilson's Labour Government of 1964–70 was the most ambitious in the area of regional policy. This included the setting up, in 1964, of regional economic planning councils and boards, under the auspices of George Brown's Department of Economic Affairs and the short-lived experiment with peacetime economic planning in the mid-1960s. The economic planning councils, which had little more than an advisory role, survived longer than the attempt at economic planning. As regional economic development councils they were still in existence until 1980, when they were abolished by the Thatcher Government.

Regional incentives had traditionally been in the form of grants, loans, accelerated depreciation allowances and other inducements to encourage industrialists to invest. They were criticized for their bias towards capital investment, on the grounds that, in theory, such incentives could provide for labour-saving capital investment, when the whole purpose of the exercise was to create more jobs in the regions.

The Wilson Government responded to this in two ways. The first was the introduction by the Chancellor of the Exchequer, James Callaghan, of Selective Employment Tax, or SET. SET was levied at a rate of 15 per cent on the payrolls of service-industry employers, and partly redistributed to manufacturing industry, in which firms were entitled to a 'selective employment premium' of seven shillings and sixpence (37·5p) per employee per week. The aim was clear, if hardly fair. It was to penalize allegedly unproductive service industries in order to boost employment in productive manufacturing industry, although its net effect was to produce lower productivity and higher unit wage and salary costs in manufacturing. But SET also had an important North–South dimension, in that it penalized those regions which had the highest proportion of service-sector activity, and vice versa.

SET was supplemented in the following year, 1967, with a more direct labour subsidy for the regions. The regional employment premium – a refund payable to manufacturing firms in development areas – provided for payments of the equivalent of £1·50 a week for men, 75p a week for women and 47·5p for 'girls'. Originally intended to last until 1974, the rates were actually doubled in that year, before the premium was phased out, under pressure from the European Commission, in 1977. The premium suffered from the same drawbacks as much of post-war regional policy. Capital incentives could be criticized because they did not discriminate between that investment which would have taken place anyway and that where the existence of incentives actually tipped the balance in its favour. Labour subsidies suffered from the same problem, because they were available on all employment in manufacturing in the development areas, and not just marginal employment. The premium also encouraged overmanning. Interestingly, Nicholas Kaldor, the economic adviser to Harold Wilson, wanted to refine the regional employment premium at the time of its introduction, so that within firms it would apply only to those workers engaged in the production process and not office workers and other employees. But he was overruled by the Treasury, which pointed out that this would just lead to a large-scale reclassification by firms of cleaners and clerks into craftsmen.

Post-war regional policy was varied, both in the type of approach adopted, and in the effectiveness of the individual measures adopted. It was a highly changeable policy, although with three lasting elements – grants and other incentives to encourage capital investment; planning controls to limit development in congested regions; and financial incentives for individuals to migrate to where work was more freely available, in roughly that order of importance. Readers are referred to the excellent Employment Institute pamphlet, *Regional Policy: The Way Forward*, by Harvey Armstrong and Jim Taylor, for a full chronology of British regional policy.

This account has not covered the creation of the Scottish and Welsh Development Agencies during the 1970s, both of which have done much useful work in attracting firms and encouraging development. It has also steered clear of the refinement of the assisted areas into development areas, special development areas and intermediate areas (a new tier which emerged in the 1960s) – of great importance to the areas themselves but tedious in the telling.

Suffice it to say that by 1979 there was a complex array of regional policy legislation and machinery in place, further complicated by the wide range of European Community assistance available, most notably through the European Regional Development Fund, set up in 1975. Anyone designing regional policy from scratch would not have come up with the system that was in place by the end of the 1970s. As with all policies which owe their existence to piecemeal legislation, regional policy was cumbersome, contained important elements of wasted resources and inconsistencies, and was a minefield for the businessman trying to find out the best part of the country in which to set up. But some things which appear to have been badly designed happen to work quite well, and this is the key question to ask of regional policy. Did it work?

THE EFFECTIVENESS OF REGIONAL POLICY

Apart from its unwieldy nature, the two most frequent criticisms of the operation of post-war regional policy are firstly, that it did not achieve its stated aim of creating and preserving jobs in the depressed regions and secondly, when it did so it was only at a prohibitively high cost. On top of this there has been the more general criticism that, by interfering with the market mechanism, and subsidizing the regions, the policy contributed to the decline in the relative efficiency of the British economy.

There are serious difficulties involved in assessing the effectiveness of regional policy. As with all empirical work in economics, it is not possible to have a 'control' against which to assess the success of any experiment. Thus, some of the changes attributed to regional policy may have happened anyway.

It is important to bear in mind that the main focus of the policy has been on manufacturing industry and, in particular, on employment in manufacturing. And, on this basis, contrary to the general perception, the experience of much of the post-war period was good. Manufacturing employment was around 7·3 million in the immediate post-war period (1948) on official figures from the Department of Employment. It increased to just under 8·1 million by the end of the 1950s and further, to just below 8·6 million by 1966, a time when regional policy was being used actively. Subsequently there has been a sharp decline in employment in manufacturing, to 7·1 million by 1979 and – the sharpest decline of any period – to 5 million by 1988, and further, to 4·4 million by 1993.

This suggests that, at least until the 1970s, regional policy did more than just move manufacturing employment between regions. Rather, it operated within a period in which the number of such jobs was increasing. The effectiveness of regional policy in encouraging the shift of manufacturing was shown by R. S. Howard, in an official paper *The Movement of Manufacturing Industry in the United Kingdom, 1945–65*, updated to 1981 by Armstrong and Taylor, which showed that, of those firms which moved and survived in their new location, there was indeed a large net loss over the period for the south east and the west midlands, as intended, while all other regions gained. Thus, from 1945 to 1981, the south east lost 1,647 manufacturing establishments and the west midlands 334. Meanwhile, there were gains of 586 for Wales, 365 for the north, 354 for East Anglia, 316 for the south west, 61 for the east midlands, 18 for the north west and 6 for Yorkshire and Humberside.

The figures show that it was not just the old industrial areas which benefited from the outflow from the south east and the west midlands – there were substantial net gains for parts of the South, notably East Anglia, the south west and, to a lesser extent, the east midlands – over the period. But Wales, Scotland and the north also did well out of regional policy. At its peak in the late 1960s, the number of manufacturing jobs flowing out of the south east and the west midlands to other areas was around 25,000 a year.

The number of new jobs created in the assisted areas by regional policy was significant. A paper, *The Effects of Government Regional Economic Policy*, by Moore, Rhodes and Tyler, published by the Department of Trade and Industry in 1986, estimated that 784,000 jobs were created in the assisted areas over the period 1960 to 1981. For most of this period the assisted areas (intermediate, development and special development areas) covered Cornwall and parts of Devon, Wales, and the whole of northern Britain above the Midlands. Of the jobs created, just over a quarter came from firms which had relocated to the assisted areas from other regions, with the implication that such relocation was due to the existence of regional policy. The remainder, nearly three quarters, or around 570,000 jobs, were due to expansion by firms already based in the assisted areas, together with business start-ups. The estimates, which attempted to separate the effects of regional policy from what might be termed the natural growth in employment in the assisted areas, also suggest that the jobs created were durable ones. In 1981, even after the recession of the mid-1970s, and well into the major employment shake-out of the early 1980s, 600,000 of the jobs created by regional policy were found to be surviving.

The success of regional policy has to be assessed, of course, not just in the number of firms persuaded to move, or in the total of jobs created, but also in the cost of that policy in relation to competing public-expenditure claims. In some cases the cost per job was very high indeed. Regional-policy assistance for the Sullom Voe oil terminal in the Shetlands, for example, worked out at a cost of £125,000 a job. More generally, the Department of Trade and Industry's 1984 white paper *Regional Industrial Development* estimated a regional policy cost per job in the 1960s and 1970s of £35,000, in 1984 prices.

There are two important points to be made about such estimates. The first is that they make no allowance for the fact that people who gain employment through the operation of regional policy will begin to pay income tax and generate income and employment for others through their spending. They may also come off the unemployment register, reducing government expenditure in another section of the public accounts. Earlier estimates by Moore and Rhodes, based on regional policy in the two decades to the mid-1970s, suggested that, after taking such factors into account, the net as opposed to the gross cost per job was much smaller and in some cases non-existent. But, to the extent that regional policy did in part involve the transfer of people who were already in jobs to other parts of the country, the question of cost is a legitimate one. The second point is that employment is a long-term investment and, as the 1986 Moore,

Rhodes and Tyler estimates suggest, the jobs created by regional policy tended to be long-lasting. If an unemployed person gains a job through the operation of regional policy then not only does that person gain a potential stream of income (and tax payments) for many years ahead but the overall quality of the labour force is enhanced by the training and work experience he or she obtains.

The cost of each job created or maintained by regional policy was undoubtedly swelled by its lack of selectivity. The majority of regional incentives and subsidies were available to all employers, or at least all manufacturing employers, in the assisted areas. Assistance therefore subsidized jobs that were in place anyway, or which were perfectly safe without a subsidy. The blanket approach of the policy meant that the cost of those jobs for which regional policy was responsible had to be spread over a much larger number of recipients. Not that refining the application of regional policy was an easy task. Suppose that the policy was to provide investment grants or labour subsidies only for new entrants to an assisted area. The situation could arise whereby two firms producing identical products operated side by side in a development area. One, the newcomer to the region, would be eligible for grants and subsidies, lowering costs relative to the existing firm. Not only would such a situation be unfair, but the entry of a lower-cost competitor could put the existing firm out of business, taking us back to square one.

RECESSION AND REGIONAL POLICY

In the period from 1950 to 1970, unemployment in Britain ranged from a low of just over 200,000 to a peak of less than 700,000, and the unemployment rate was typically between 1 and 3 per cent. Significant regional variations in unemployment rates persisted – if they had not there would have been little justification for continuing with regional policy. These variations, however, were within an overall picture in which unemployment was generally low. The south east and the west midlands, often with unemployment rates of less than 1 per cent, could hardly complain about a policy designed to redirect employment to other areas. Indeed, the last thing that firms working in these areas wanted was for new firms to come along and bid up the price of already scarce labour.

The first intimations of what was to be a period of prolonged high unemployment in Britain came in the early 1970s. The peaks of unemployment had moved steadily higher during the 1950s and 1960s. This was partly because, increasingly, the balance of payments acted as a constraint on the economy. In 1971, the Conservative Government of Edward Heath, elected in the previous year, faced a new and more worrying problem – not only was unemployment increasing sharply, but it was accompanied by significantly higher inflation. At the end of 1970, unemployment rates ranged from 1·6 per cent in the south east to 4·4 per cent in both the north and Scotland and 6·7 per cent in Northern Ireland. By early 1972, as the unemployment total neared one million, the rates ranged from 2·2 per cent in the south east to 6·4 per cent in the north, 6·6 per cent in Scotland and 7·5 per cent in Northern Ireland.

Regional inequalities in unemployment remained as the jobless total increased, preserving the argument for regional policy. But at the same time, unemployment in some regions in which development had previously been discouraged was approaching a level at which the policy of directing activity away from those regions could begin to be called into question. This may not have been true for the south east, but the rise in the west midlands' unemployment rate to 3·8 per cent early in 1972 (from 2 per cent at the end of 1970) took it above the national average. Was it appropriate to continue with a policy of directing firms away from such an area?

As it turned out, the policy response was twofold. The first was to embark on a general expansion of the economy through both fiscal and monetary policy (culminating in the Barber boom), and the second was to strengthen regional policy. The Industry Act of 1972, which contained major changes in government support for industry – including help for what opponents of the policy called 'lame ducks' – also included a return to investment grants in the assisted areas (abolished in favour of accelerated depreciation allowances in 1970), as well as other

types of assistance. Grants equivalent to 22 per cent of the cost
of new buildings, plant and machinery in special development
areas (the Glasgow area, the Firth of Tay, Glenrothes, Living-
ston, the industrial north east, Greater Merseyside, Skelmers-
dale, Falmouth-Camborne, Anglesey, East Flintshire, and most
of the south Wales mining valleys) and 20 per cent in development areas (larger areas which typically adjoined the special
development areas).

The charge of unfairness was avoided by the fact that assistance to industry in general was increased, notably through
investment allowances. And, within this increase in assistance
there was recognition of, and a response to, the special problems
of the high-unemployment regions. The effect of these policy
changes, and the rapid expansion of the economy which accompanied them, was a sharp fall in national unemployment – from a
rate of 3·2 per cent for Great Britain early in 1972 to 1·7 per
cent late in 1973. There was also some narrowing in regional
unemployment differences. The south east continued to have the
lowest unemployment rate, and other parts of the South were
also at or below the national average. But the range, from 1·5
per cent in the south east to 3·8 per cent in Scotland and 3·9 per
cent in the north was smaller, and even Northern Ireland had an
unemployment rate of less than 5 per cent by the end of 1973.

It was destined to end in tears, however, when the Barber
boom ran into the 1973–4 oil crisis. The problems faced by the
Labour Government under Harold Wilson, elected in 1974,
were similar in nature to those faced by the Heath administration
in 1971, but writ much larger.

This time unemployment did break through the one million
barrier, alongside the highest inflation rate in Britain's recent
history. The rate of inflation was above 20 per cent for a period
stretching from March 1975 to March 1976, and reached a peak
of 26·9 per cent in August 1975. No part of the country was
immune from the rise in unemployment. In 1976, the unemployment rate reached 3·5 per cent in the south east, a level which, if
it had existed nationally in the 1950s and 1960s, would have
been regarded as catastrophic. Unemployment rates remained far
higher in the North, although one effect of the spread of misery in

this period, and in the 1980s, was the narrowing of the unemployment gap. Excluding Northern Ireland, the north had the highest unemployment rate, but in the mid-1970s this was typically less than twice the rate in the south east. As recently as the early years of the Heath Government, unemployment rates in the North in general had been three times those prevailing in the south east.

Again, the response to a general recession and a rise in unemployment in all regions was, far from the abandonment of regional policy, a vigorous use of it and, in some cases, an expansion of the policy. The regional employment premium was doubled in 1974 (although it was subsequently abolished at the insistence of the European Commission in 1977) and the Scottish and Welsh Development Agencies were established in 1976. In addition, those elements of regional policy carried out by the European Commission became available in Britain and were expanded during this period. The radical review of public expenditure priorities at the insistence of the International Monetary Fund in 1976 had the effect of reducing expenditure on regional policy, but it left the existing framework in place.

THE 1979 RESPONSE

The recession of 1979–81 was more severe than anything the economy had experienced since the inter-war years. A second sharp rise in oil prices, in combination with the newly elected Thatcher Government's high-interest-rate policy, resulted in an over-valuation for sterling of greater magnitude than in the 1920s, when Churchill made the mistake of returning to the Gold Standard at the pre-First World War exchange rate of $4.80. The result of sterling's later over-valuation was a collapse of large parts of manufacturing industry, with manufacturing output slumping by a fifth between the middle of 1979 and early 1981. During the winter of 1980–81, as the headlines told of large-scale redundancies affecting every industrial town and city, unemployment rose by 100,000 a month. Nationally, unemployment rose from 1·2 million in mid-1979 to more than 2 million by the end of 1980 and 3 million in the autumn of 1982. Unemployment rates of between 5 and 10 per cent were soon recorded in the South, while in the North regional rates moved up into the 10 to 20 per cent range, but with some towns experiencing far higher rates of unemployment. The choice facing the Thatcher Government was similar to that faced by Edward Heath in 1971–2 and Harold Wilson in 1974–5, except the scale of the problem was more serious. But the response was different.

The difference came, not merely because the regional problems thrown up by the 1979–81 recession were more severe than anything in the post-war period, but also because of the change in philosophy that had occurred in the Conservative Party under Mrs Thatcher's leadership. To many in the party, regional policy carried undesirable connotations of excessive state intervention, subsidies that preserved inefficiency and overmanning, which, far from helping the regions, actually inhibited their development.

A Conservative Research Department Paper, *A North–South Divide? Some Reflections on Regional Policy*, by Ian Stewart, summarized such views:

Despite the huge sums of public money directed to regional policy, there is no doubt that the policies of the 1960s and 1970s failed to live up to expectations. Jobs were created, but at a great cost to the taxpayer. More importantly, regional policy in those decades appears to have created distortions in the operation of markets which have militated against essential restructuring and have hampered competitiveness. Unemployment in the regions has remained persistently high and there is little evidence that traditional regional policy has furnished the assisted areas with the basis for self-sustaining growth. (1988, p. 99)

Rodney Atkinson, in the paper 'A Return to the Regions' published by the Bow Group within the Conservative Party, also took the view that regional policy had left industry in the North more vulnerable to the forces of recession: 'It was inevitable that having relied on government subsidy of outdated assets, the poorer regions of the UK would suffer a more dramatic collapse than those regions which had not received such extensive support' (1988, p. 8).

To supporters of regional policy, using the experience of 1979–81 and its aftermath to demonstrate the failings of regional policy is rather like saying that umbrellas are no good because they fail to keep you dry in a monsoon. The freak economic conditions of the early 1980s were, it is argued, no excuse for running down a whole policy.

Thus, as Harvey Armstrong and Jim Taylor wrote in their Employment Institute pamphlet *Regional Policy: The Way Forward*:

As regional unemployment disparities have widened, policy makers appear to have become increasingly disillusioned with regional policy. This disillusionment with regional policy stems largely from the fact that, in spite of many years of effort in trying to reduce regional disparities in job opportunities, the sudden and substantial increase in regional unemployment disparities in the 1980s suggests that regional policy has failed – and failed miserably. In our view, this conclusion is contradicted by the facts and must be firmly rejected. (1987, p. 17)

Nor is it the case that the aim of regional policy, during periods of lower unemployment, was simply to spread an existing amount of economic activity more evenly among the regions. Its proponents and practitioners saw regional policy as an important element in a strategy designed to speed economic growth, as Sir Leo Pliatsky, former senior civil servant at the Treasury responsible for public expenditure and and later Permanent Secretary at the Department of Industry, recalled. Describing the process leading to the introduction of the regional employment premium in 1967, in his book *Getting and Spending*, he wrote:

The underlying thesis ... was that, with the uneven distribution of employment in the country, attempts to run the economy at a high level of activity led to overheating in the areas of high employment while unemployment was still relatively high in the Development Areas. By producing a shift in demand and output from the former to the latter, the regional premium would make possible a higher but more evenly spread total demand, thus increasing net output and resources without the inflationary chain reaction which usually resulted from attempts to expand the economy. (1982, pp. 74–5)

THE DECLINE OF REGIONAL POLICY

The principal reason why the widening of the North–South divide in the 1980s cannot be regarded as a failure of regional policy – although this is not to imply that the policy, as applied, was anywhere near perfect – is that it was accompanied by a progressive dismantling of, and reduction in expenditure on, the policy. This was for three principal reasons.

The first was the change in economic conditions themselves. Regional policy in the 1950s and 1960s had been to do with shuffling employment in the direction of the poorest regions. In the 1980s it looked to be more a strategy for shuffling *un*employment, particularly in those years when, in addition to a large rise in unemployment, the supply of new jobs everywhere dried up. Sir Leo Pliatsky's rationale for regional policy in the 1960s, that it prevented overheating in a near full-employment economy, looked inappropriate in the period of high and rising unemployment of the early 1980s. Even after the recovery began – in the spring of 1981 – it took five years before unemployment turned down. And it was only then, in 1986, that the recovery began to take on a robust look. Prior to that (and indeed subsequently to that) jobs were desperately needed anywhere. The argument was that regional policy of the obstructive kind (the 'stick') ran the serious risk of preventing job creation from occurring at all.

The result was that insurance companies and other financial service companies who were moving some of their administrative functions out of London were able to choose other parts of the South as a location. Bristol, for example, was a major beneficiary. In 1988, when Barclays chose where to site a new computer centre, it was at Coventry in the west midlands – previously a town subject to development restrictions. The Bank of England selected Gloucester as an out-of-London location for its Registrar's Department in the same year.

The second reason was associated with the control of public expenditure. 'The Government is determined not merely to halt the growth of public spending but progressively to reduce it,' the Treasury said in its 1980 Public Expenditure White Paper. The aim was to achieve a real reduction in all public expenditure of 4 per cent between 1979–80 and 1983–4. As it turned out, there was no overall reduction in spending, but a real increase of 7·5 per cent. Regional-policy expenditure too rose initially but by the end of the period was one of the few areas in which the Government achieved real spending reductions.

The third and probably most important reason was, however, the fact that regional policy did not fit in with the new Conservative philosophy. As described above, it was seen as cosseting the inefficient and preserving overmanning, while interfering with the workings of the market mechanism. Perhaps more cynically, the main beneficiaries of regional policy were in those areas from which the Conservative Party did not draw much electoral support.

Ron Martin and Peter Tyler, in their paper 'The Regional Legacy of the Thatcher Years', usefully described the Thatcher approach:

The new regional policy model developed under the Thatcher governments can be summarized in three ways. First, it involved a distinct shift from a demand-side to a supply-side approach. Second, the rate and scale of regional support was dramatically reduced, both as measured by annual spending on regional assistance and in terms of the abandonment of what had previously been the main regional policy instruments (IDCs and RDGs). Third, the thrust of policy was shifted away from relatively large-scale capital investment in the regions to the promotion of indigenous enterprise, small firms and market competition in the depressed areas. (1991, p. 11)

Mrs Thatcher's first term saw a radical pruning of regional policy. The 'sticks' of office development permits and industrial development certificates were abolished. From then on, while incentives to locate in the assisted areas continued, those firms which wanted to set up or expand in what had been forbidden territory were no longer prevented from doing so.

Eligibility for regional assistance was sharply reduced. Under the regional policy map inherited by Mrs Thatcher's Government, the whole of northern England, Scotland, Wales, Cornwall and parts of Devon had assisted-area status. Northern Ireland was treated throughout as a special case. By 1982 the percentage of the working population covered by regional assistance had been cut from 47 to 28 per cent, as the map was redrawn. Much of eastern Scotland, a belt stretching up the centre of northern England and southern Scotland, and most of rural Wales, lost assisted-area status over this period. There was one gain – the area around the recession-hit steel town of Corby in Northamptonshire.

Regional development grants were maintained at 22 per cent in special development areas, but cut from 20 to 15 per cent in development areas and abolished in intermediate areas. The regional economic development councils, a relic of George Brown's 1964–5 planning experiment, were disbanded. The one policy initiative in the general area of regional policy, although it was not presented as such, was the creation of 'enterprise zones' in which firms setting up would be entitled to 100 per cent capital allowances, exemption from rates (for ten years) and from development land tax, freedom from certain government controls, speedier processing of official documents and reduced requirements to supply the government with information for the compilation of official statistics. The first eleven were established in Belfast, Clydebank, Corby, Dudley, Hartlepool, the Isle of Dogs in East London, the Lower Swansea Valley, Newcastle/Gateshead, Salford/Trafford, Speke and Wakefield. Their record has been mixed. Some have been highly successful, notably the Isle of Dogs, but others appear to have benefited mainly at the expense of neighbouring areas, with little net benefit for the region in which they are located. By 1988 there were twenty-five zones in operation and the experiment was brought towards a close with the announcement from the Environment Secretary Nicholas Ridley that no further zones would be created in England. The zones had created a net 35,000 jobs. The cost per job in the enterprise zones, it appeared, was no lower and in many cases far higher, than traditional regional policy.

In Mrs Thatcher's second term, there was a further rationalization of regional policy. In November 1984, the Department of Trade and Industry published a White Paper, *Regional Industrial Development*, which included another redrawing of the regional policy map. The old special development areas now became development areas, along with some parts of the country previously designated as such. Overall, the new development areas were to cover 15 per cent of the working population, against 22 per cent for the old development areas and special development areas combined.

In the new development areas regional development grants

were available, but only at 15 per cent, compared with 22 per cent in the former special areas. And they were subject to tighter conditions. A cost per job limit of £10,000 was imposed, except in the case of smaller projects costing up to £500,000 and involving fewer than 200 workers. Alternatively, firms could opt for grants of £3,000 per job created. Some service industries – banking, insurance, finance, business services and industrial research and development – became eligible for grants for the first time.

The most significant change was, however, in the second tier of the new two-tier regional policy – the intermediate areas. In these, no automatic grants were available but selective assistance could be provided. The intermediate areas covered 20 per cent of the working population thanks to, and this was the significant part, the inclusion of the west midlands. An area which had been the focus of regional policy only in the negative sense of attempting to direct development away from it, was now to become eligible for assistance, admittedly on a selective basis. This was testimony indeed to the severity of the manufacturing decline of the first half of the 1980s. Birmingham, Coventry, and the Black Country towns of Wolverhampton, Dudley, Walsall and West Bromwich, once congested, could now claim help from the government in attracting industry.

The 1984 changes in regional policy were presented by Norman Lamont, then an industry minister, as establishing regional aid on a more effective basis. 'The most important feature of our policy is that money will now be spent in the areas with the worst problems and that, in terms of new jobs per pound of expenditure, the new policy will be far more effective than the old' (DTI, 1984). But there was also a substantial reduction in regional policy expenditure implied in the changes. The aim was to cut expenditure by 1987–8 by £300 million a year, relative to the cost of the policy in its previous form.

The process of cutting back on regional policy continued in 1988, with the January 1988 White Paper *DTI – The Department for Enterprise*. Under the changes announced then, automatic eligibility for regional development grants – since 1984 available only in the development areas – came to an end. From 31 March 1988, firms had to prove that without such grants the project would be unable to proceed.

There were changes to encourage the development of small businesses and to allow firms based in the assisted areas to market themselves more effectively. Small firms employing fewer than 25 people became entitled to 15 per cent investment grants (to a maximum of £15,000) and 50 per cent innovation grants (to a maximum of £25,000). Two thirds of the cost of using the services of marketing, design, systems and quality management consultants could be claimed back by firms employing up to 500 people in the assisted areas (compared with 50 per cent for the rest of the country).

The changes were presented by Secretary of State for Trade and Industry Lord Young of Graffham, a man with a penchant for marketing, as part of a policy of 'working with private enterprise in encouraging management to develop their skills'. The intention was to provide as much in selective assistance as had been provided under the more restricted regional development grants since 1984. But critics of the changes saw the switch from automatic to selective assistance as a further downgrading of the role of regional policy.

The Thatcher Government's approach to regional policy was never quite as pure as it was made out to be. Successive Secretaries of State for Wales, notably Nicholas Edwards and Peter Walker, continued to pursue an active regional policy approach, largely through the Welsh Development Agency, in the Principality. Considerable success was achieved in generating new service-sector and manufacturing jobs to replace those lost in the declining coal and steel industries.

The Conservatives were also keen to attract inward investment from Japan, the United States and other European countries, even if this meant offering attractive long-term subsidies. Nigel Lawson, in his book *The View from Number 11*, described one example of this approach. Under the terms of his 1984 Budget, 100 per cent capital allowances were to be phased out. But, it was discovered, this would create a problem. He wrote:

My decision to phase out first-year capital allowances did cause one hiccup just before the Budget. In 1981, Norman Tebbit, while Minister of State at the Department of Industry, had announced that Nissan, the Japanese car manufacturer, would establish an assembly plant in County Durham. Among the factors they had taken into consideration was the prospect of enjoying the 100 per cent first-year capital allowance, and the Chairman of Nissan had a letter from Margaret (Thatcher) alluding to this carrot. But by the time they came to build the plant these allowances would have disappeared under my Budget plans. If nothing had been done, Nissan might well have gone ahead anyway, and certainly the new tax regime brought a considerable amount of new inward investment by overseas companies attracted by the low Corporation Tax rate. But there would have been loud and embarrassing allegations of bad faith which it would have been hard to gainsay. (1992, p. 354)

Fortunately for the Government, a solution was found, as Lawson explained:

We therefore had to devise a general alteration to the Bill that would have the effect of exempting Nissan, while exempting as little else as practicable. This took the form of exempting investment allowances in development areas, provided that they had already been firmly announced. Fortunately in this context, the language in which Finance Bills are drafted is so arcane as to bear little resemblance to the English language, and no one spotted what this particular clause was really about. Had they done so, there might well have been an outcry, and certainly the battery of claims for special treatment I received from industries that felt particularly hard hit by it would have intensified. Meanwhile our Ambassador in Tokyo was able to assure the Nissan Board that its 100 per cent capital allowance was safe, irrespective of the 1984 Finance Act. Nissan was suitably discreet. (p. 355)

REGIONAL POLICY AND THE NORTH-SOUTH DIVIDE

Some of the changes in regional policy in the 1980s were perfectly sensible. A move from blanket aid to more selective help, long advocated in the 1960s and 1970s, was overdue. The problem was that this occurred within the framework of a substantial cut in the regional policy budget, at a time when the economic disadvantages faced by the North were greater than at any time since the 1930s. The rundown of regional policy was not, of course, the primary cause of widening North–South differences in employment opportunities – although the macro-economic policies pursued by the Government were a major factor in creating such differences. Rather, when the problem became bigger, and there was a strong case for stepping up regional policy, the opposite course was pursued.

Britain has benefited from European Community regional aid, but the enlargement of the Community to its present twelve members, and in particular the entry of Spain and Portugal, together with the unification of Germany, is likely to cut the amount received by Britain's poorest regions. The Department of Trade and Industry has warned that EC regional aid to Britain could be cut from more than £300 million a year to less than £100 million.

Even in its own terms, the Conservative Government's approach to regional policy has been flawed and inconsistent. The North's problems were explained by ministers as the inevitable consequence of a shake-out in manufacturing employment, itself exacerbated by the earlier overmanning within British industry. But little has been done to encourage the development of services in the regions to replace falling manufacturing employment. As John McEnery, a former Under Secretary at the Department of Trade and Industry, writing in the *Financial Times* pointed out:

The preponderance of the south east in service employment has existed since at least 1965. Yet, until 1985, successive governments perversely sought to correct national imbalance by subsidizing new manufacturing plant in the assisted areas. Inevitably they failed as they were addressing the wrong problem. Moreover during that time, as in all advanced societies, employment in manufacturing processes was falling while that in services was soaring. By 1984, Britain's economic divide was worse and regional policy discredited.

Only in late 1984 did Conservative ministers find the courage to blow the whistle. Capital-intensive regional development grants for manufacturing plant were phased out and the importance of service jobs for the assisted areas was at last recognized. This was, however, more the abandonment of sin rather than the dawn of new virtue. (1988)

McEnery's particular complaint was that the Government had failed to protect and encourage service employment in the regions in another key respect. One of the central reasons for the North–South divide has been the increased concentration of company head offices and associated support services in London and the south east. Initially, the Government appeared to be aware of this problem, accepting a 1982 Monopolies Commission recommendation that bids for the Royal Bank of Scotland by both the Standard Chartered Bank and the Hong Kong and Shanghai Banking Corporation be rejected on the grounds of the damage that it would do to the regional economy of Scotland. But by 1985 any regional element in competition policy had been removed. Guidelines adopted in that year, when Norman Tebbit was Secretary of State for Trade and Industry, established the only condition for the referral of a bid to the Monopolies Commission as a reduction in competition.

The subsequent Guinness takeover of Scotland's Distillers company, Nestlé's successful acquisition of York-based Rowntree, and the bid for the brewers Scottish and Newcastle by the Australian firm Elders IXL were unopposed by the Government.

It was always obvious that much of the basis of regional policy as it existed in 1979 was anathema to Mrs Thatcher's Conservatives. Industrial development certificates and office development permits smacked of authoritarianism, while regional development grants were against the philosophy that industry, as it became leaner and fitter, also had to learn to fend for itself. What was surprising was that no serious attempt was made, at least in Mrs Thatcher's first two terms, to recast regional policy along market lines, by aiding the mobility of labour and ensuring that differences in labour-market conditions between regions were reflected in wage differentials. Such a policy would have been unpopular, not least in the regions with the biggest unemployment problems. But it would have shown a determination by the Government to do something about the North–South divide. The rundown of regional policy during the 1980s conveyed the strong impression that it was content to do nothing.

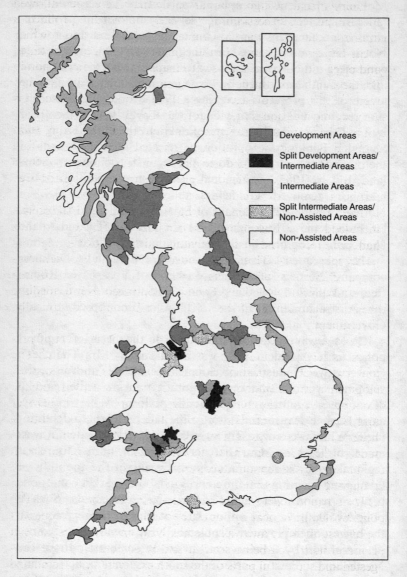

Figure 3 Assisted Areas as defined by the Department of Trade
and Industry at 1 August 1993

Unimportant though regional policy may have been allowed to become, the recession of the early 1990s did produce a dramatic change in the Government's judgement about which areas required assistance. In the summer of 1993, after detailed and often difficult discussions with the European Commission in Brussels, the Department of Trade and Industry produced a new regional policy map (see Figure 3). Out went places such as Accrington in Lancashire; Bradford; Corby in Northamptonshire; Darlington; Scunthorpe; parts of Wrexham, Shotton, Flint and Rhyl in North Wales; parts of Newport and Cardiff in South Wales, and several other places – all parts of the North as defined in this book, which had previously enjoyed assisted-area status.

The newcomers, judged by the history of regional policy, included some surprise names. The candidacy of the west midlands had been recognized in the previous redrawing of the regional policy map in 1984. This was extended in 1993, with Wolverhampton and the City of Birmingham given full development-area status. Walsall, Dudley and Sandwell continued as intermediate areas. The workshop of the world, after limping economically, had been provided with some new crutches.

More dramatic was the conquering of the last bastion of pre-recession economic supremacy in Britain, the south east. The new map included part of the area around Heathrow airport; several parts of London (the Lea Valley, Park Royal and the London end of the East Thames corridor); Clacton; Dover and Deal; Folkestone; Hastings; the Isle of Wight; and Sittingbourne and Sheerness. This was a momentous change, a statement by the Government to the effect that, even if the south east stages a full economic recovery, pockets of deprivation will remain.

It also appeared to signal a change in the ambitions of policy. Previously, firms locating out of the south east had been encouraged to look as far away as possible. Now, inward investment in London itself was being sought, and relocators from the congested and successful parts of the south east were being reminded that there were plenty of 'infill' opportunities relatively close to home. There was no better example of the shift in perceptions about Britain's economic geography, and no better excuse for opponents of regional policy to argue that the whole exercise, ultimately, was pointless.

5

MRS THATCHER'S UNBALANCED ECONOMY

To found a great empire for the sole purpose of raising up a people of customers, may at first sight appear a project fit only for a nation of shopkeepers. It is, however, a project altogether unfit for a nation of shopkeepers; but extremely fit for a nation that is governed by shopkeepers. (Adam Smith, *The Wealth of Nations*)

In economics, and in particular in that branch of the subject known as welfare economics, the textbook trade-off is between *efficiency* and *equity*. Suppose that it was possible to devise a system of taxation and benefits which resulted in everyone receiving the same net income, regardless of their job, or indeed whether they have a job, and the part of the country in which they live. Such arrangements would obviously be equitable. The difficulty is that they would not be at all efficient. There would be no monetary incentive for people to work and there would be no point in anyone developing and producing new products, starting up businesses and so on. Equity would have been achieved but at a high cost to efficiency.

The taxation policy followed by the Thatcher Government in the 1980s, culminating in the reduction in the highest marginal rate of income tax to 40 per cent in the 1988 Budget (from 83 per cent in May 1979) and in the standard rate to 25 per cent (from 33 per cent in May 1979), in combination with a reduction in the value of benefits relative to earnings, was one of making the tax and benefits system less equitable. Inequalities were deliberately built into the system in order to boost incentives and thereby increase efficiency.

A similar development occurred with policy towards the regions, albeit less explicitly. The rundown of regional policy during the 1980s, described in detail in the preceding chapter, was partly to save money, but it also had the aim of improving efficiency even at the expense of reducing equity between the regions. The best example of how this might occur is with a firm that wants to expand its operations in the south east but is prevented from doing so by the refusal of an industrial development certificate. In this situation, some companies will inevitably decide that the alternative, of moving to an assisted area and expanding there, is not acceptable. There is therefore a net loss to the economy. New productive investment does not materialize and there is a resultant loss of growth.

The experience of the 1980s appeared initially to lend support to the view that policies which are deliberately inequitable – or at least policies which result in a loss of equity even if this was not their prime intention – can be associated with a higher rate of economic growth and greater efficiency. In 1987 and 1988, for example, the British economy grew at 4 to 5 per cent a year. Manufacturing productivity was rising at 7 to 8 per cent a year and, while part of this reflected the position of the economy at the top of the business cycle, the consensus was that productivity growth had embarked on a new, stronger phase. Output per head in UK manufacturing industry had, for most of the 1980s, grown at a faster rate than in other major industrial countries, although comparisons that included the recession of 1979–81 were far less favourable. And productivity growth for the whole economy, as distinct from manufacturing industry alone, was less impressive when compared with the experience of most of the post-war period. Even so, there was an improvement in the performance of the 'supply-side' of the economy. The Confederation of British Industry, reporting at the height of the boom in the summer of 1988 that capacity utilization was running at a higher level than at any time since the organization had begun to monitor it in the mid-1950s, made the point that industry was using its available capacity more efficiently than before.

The implication was that imbalances in the spread of economic activity between regions, and in the distribution of income, while undoubtedly unfair, helped to boost efficiency and growth. Had more equitable policies been pursued, the available cake would have been smaller. The relative position of the poorest in the population and the worst-off regions might have been better, but their absolute position might well have been worse.

This argument is, more than ever, open to challenge. We simply do not know how much, if at all, the Conservative Government's taxation policy and the rundown of regional policy contributed to an improvement in the economy's sustainable growth rate. There is a strong body of evidence which suggests that the incentive effects of tax cuts are relatively insignificant. And, against those firms which were allowed to expand in the south east and would have been prevented from doing so under a stricter regional policy regime, has to be set the loss of firms in the North – and by no means all of them lame ducks – during and after the 1979–81 recession. It may be that a better policy could have combined an easing of restrictions on expansion in the south east with a much greater amount of temporary support for those firms in the North which were hit hard by the recession but which could have survived and prospered in the longer term.

Even if one accepted the efficiency argument, the central question remained: will an economy which is unbalanced between regions be one that can continue to grow in an efficient way in the future? And the answer, as the recession of the early 1990s shows (and as was predicted in the first edition of this book) is no. As long as there was a surplus of both labour and capital in *all* regions – as was the case for much of the 1980s – then the concentration of growth in certain parts of the country, while unfair, does not damage the economy's overall growth performance. It creates social problems, sure enough, and it involves an enormous waste of productive resources in those regions not favoured with rapidly expanding economic activity.

The difficulties arise, however, and the problems created by a North–South divide are only really tested, when capacity limits start to be reached in the South, while there are plenty of available resources in the North. In this situation, when firms in the South are reporting shortages of labour and when available plant capacity is stretched to the limit, the North–South divide, far from spurring additional efficiency, will begin to act as a constraint on growth.

Precisely such a situation developed in 1987 and 1988. Conditions of 'overheating' in the labour market had emerged, particularly in the south east, while unemployment nationally was still well over two million and unemployment rates in many northern areas were, by any standards, unacceptably high. Inflation and balance of payments problems arose, eventually leading to action on the part of the then Chancellor of the Exchequer, Nigel Lawson, to slow the economy. This action, a prolonged period of very high interest rates, which was continued by John Major and Norman Lamont, his successors at the Treasury, led inevitably to the recession that took hold of the economy in the middle of 1990 when, to quote Alan Budd, later the Government's Chief Economic Adviser, the economy fell off a cliff.

It is the argument of this chapter that these problems were inextricably linked with the fact that the regional imbalances in the British economy had been allowed to develop in an uncontrolled way. And, leading on from this, an economy in which imbalances remain will always run up against capacity limits sooner, and be forced to tolerate a permanently higher level of unemployment, than one in which the distribution of activity is more even. The effects of the early 1990s' recession, one of which has been to produce spare capacity in all regions, mean that the constraint imposed by regional imbalances will not bite again for a considerable time, as we will see in the next chapter. But before examining this in detail, let us look at the extent to which North–South imbalances were allowed to develop in Britain.

THE STATISTICS OF THE DIVIDE

The South, defined for the purposes of this book as the south east, East Anglia, the south west and the east and west midlands, covers approximately 38 per cent of the land area of the United Kingdom, while the North (Yorkshire and Humberside, the north west, the north, Wales, Scotland and Northern Ireland) has the remaining 62 per cent.

When it comes to the distribution of population, though, the position is very different. At present, around 58 per cent of the population is in the South and 42 per cent is in the North. Thus, while there is a 60/40 split in land area in favour of the North, the position is virtually reversed when it comes to population. The proportion of the population living in the South has increased steadily during the twentieth century, during which time there has been an overall increase in the UK population of around 60 per cent. In other words, although all regions are now more heavily populated than they were, population growth in the South has been far stronger. In the early part of this century the population split between North and South was roughly 50/50. At the end of the Second World War, the North was down to around 47 per cent of the population of the UK and by the early 1960s about 45 per cent. Thus, the relative shift of population to the South has been a long-term trend.

The shift in the distribution of economic activity in favour of the South is, if anything, more marked than the pattern of population. Although very long-term data on the regional composition of gross domestic product is not available, the importance of the industrial north during the nineteenth century would tend to suggest that at the start of the present century the North accounted for at least 50 per cent of GDP. The figures in Table 5.1 underline how different the position had become during the 1980s.

Even more than the distribution of population, economic activity was, by 1990, concentrated in the South. The figures, it will be noted, exclude the GDP of the North Sea oil and gas fields on the Continental Shelf. This is because, despite frequent claims that it is Scotland's oil (and mostly Scotland's gas), the

Table 5.1 GDP by region (as percentage of total)

	1966	1976	1987	1990
North	5·1	5·4	4·8	4·7
Yorks & Humberside	8·4	8·2	8·0	8·0
East Midlands	5·8	6·4	6·7	6·9
East Anglia	2·8	3·1	3·5	3·7
South East	35·8	33·9	35·8	36·0
South West	6·1	6·9	7·6	7·7
West Midlands	9·8	9·0	8·4	8·4
North West	11·7	11·2	10·3	10·1
Wales	4·2	4·5	4·3	4·3
Scotland	8·5	9·1	8·4	8·3
Northern Ireland	1·7	2·2	2·1	2·1
*United Kingdom**	100·0	100·0	100·0	100·0
The South	60·3	59·3	62·0	62·7
The North	39·7	40.7	38·0	37.3

* Excluding Continental Shelf. (The profits and surpluses from North Sea oil and gas output comprise the GDP of the Continental Shelf. These are not apportioned to any single region of the UK.) Pre-1974 figures are not directly comparable because of boundary changes, although the differences are small.
Source: Central Statistical Office, *Regional Trends*, various editions.

GDP of the Continental Shelf – which consists of the profits and surpluses earned there – is regarded as belonging to the whole country and so, if there was any regional division of Continental Shelf GDP, it would have to be shared out among all regions, presumably on the basis of population. This does not mean that the figures understate Scotland's share of gross domestic product. Oil support operations around Aberdeen and in other parts of Scotland (and to a lesser extent Eastern England) will have the effect of adding to GDP in the relevant region, as will the earnings of workers employed on North Sea rigs and platforms but with their permanent residence on the mainland. The GDP of the Continental Shelf is assumed to be solely profits and surpluses earned there, less stock appreciation.

Another way of looking at the distribution of activity is to examine the share of GDP by region, relative to that region's population. In 1990 the South accounted for 62·7 per cent of GDP and 58 per cent of population. It therefore has a greater share of economic activity than was warranted on population

Table 5.2   GDP per head, by region (UK = 100)

	1966	1976	1987	1990
North	91·0	95·6	89·2	86·9
Yorks & Humberside	97·8	94·0	92·4	91·1
East Midlands	99·6	96·0	97·5	97·1
East Anglia	98·0	94·7	99·4	101·3
South East	108·4	112·2	117·7	118·3
South West	98·1	90·8	94·3	94·8
West Midlands	101·7	98·1	92·0	93·3
North West	94·5	96·4	92·1	90·8
Wales	95·1	89·6	86·1	85·5
Scotland	91·5	98·6	93·9	94·2
Northern Ireland	84·9	81·0	76·9	77·3
The North*	93·5	94·4	90·4	89·5
The South*	104·5	104·0	106·9	107·5

* Averages of regions in the North and the South, weighted according to population. Pre-1974 figures are not directly comparable because of boundary changes.
Source: Central Statistical Office, Regional Trends, various editions.

grounds alone. This is most dramatically the case for the south east. Some 30·5 per cent of the population is squeezed into the south east corner of Britain, in an area which covers just 11·2 per cent of the United Kingdom. And yet this small corner accounted for 36 per cent of UK GDP in 1990. Figures for gross domestic product per head, relative to the UK average, are reproduced in Table 5.2 and underline the growing advantage the South in general, and the south east in particular, enjoyed.

Several points stand out from Table 5.2. The first is the fact that by 1990 the south east had moved to a position far in advance of the rest of the country in terms of GDP per head, and that this dominance had grown over a very long period (and been particularly reinforced in the 1980s). It was true both of Greater London, which had an index value of 125·8 in 1987, and of the rest of the south east ('Roseland' in the jargon), which had an index of 113·5. The figures also illustrate that differences between North and South are long-standing, but if we take the period between 1966 and 1976, such differences narrowed slightly, possibly because of the influence of larger expenditures on regional policy, or perhaps because the recession which followed the 1973–4 oil crisis did not discriminate as much between regions as that of 1979–81. The widening of the North–South divide in the 1980s is unmistakable. Alongside the increasing dominance of the south east there is also strong evidence of an improvement for those regions bordering the south east – notably East Anglia and the south west.

The South's higher GDP per head can also be expressed in cash terms. In 1990, for example, the south east had a level of GDP per head of £9,730 – 18·3 per cent above the national average and around 30 per cent higher than most regions in the North, and more in the case of others. It also translates directly into higher levels of personal disposable income per head. In 1990, income per head after tax in the south east was £7,650 – 29 per cent more than the £5,920 level in the northern region.

These comparisons at a regional level underline the extent to which, during the 1980s, the South had developed a growing economic advantage over the North. They also show, however, that there are wide variations, even at a regional level, within what we have defined as the North and the South for the purposes of this book. A common criticism of the idea that there were important North–South economic differences in Britain was based on the argument, indeed the observed fact, that there were (and are) very large disparities within regions, so that robust economic good health and prosperity existed in parts of the North, and economic disadvantage lived on in areas of the South. Thus, there was every difference between parts of Dorset and Wiltshire, which benefit from commuters' incomes and the spread of south east prosperity, and the old tin-mining areas of Cornwall, long affected by high unemployment and many of the disadvantages (distance from London, lack of alternative employment opportunities) faced by the North. And yet these areas are all in the south west. By the same token, some of the industrial towns of the south east, such as Chatham with its redundant dockyards, are within commuting distance of London but were (and are) well below the south east average on any measure of prosperity. There was, of course, nothing new about this argument, which has a habit of coming round at times when economic differences between North and South are becoming an embarrassment. It was advanced in the 1930s and it was advanced again in the 1980s.

It is answered in three ways. The first is the fact that, because the South was on the whole more prosperous and responsible for a greater proportion of economic activity than the North, it follows that the North could not have as many prosperous and booming towns as a proportion of its total, as the South. If not, then the regional averages would have been wrong.

The second response is based on the argument about efficiency and equity rehearsed earlier in this chapter. Just as 1980s' growth was accompanied by, even if it was not directly due to, a greater degree of inequality nationally, so the same was likely to be true in microcosm within the regions. In other words, inequalities within regions are to be expected irrespective of whether those regions are growing rapidly or slowly, although it may be the case that the tensions created by rapid growth throw up more intra-regional inequalities than conditions of slow growth or steady decline.

Thirdly, the serious research that was done on North–South differences at a local level (as opposed to the rather spurious 'quality of life' surveys) showed that, even after allowing for areas of prosperity in the North and economically disadvantaged parts of the South, significant North–South differences remained.

Tony Champion of the University of Newcastle and Anne Green of the Institute for Employment Research at Warwick University produced a paper, 'In Search of Britain's Booming Towns', in 1985, updated and expanded it in 1988 with a paper called *Local Prosperity and the North–South Divide*, and further updated it in 1990 with *The Spread of Prosperity and the North–South Divide: Local Economics Performance in Britain during the Late Eighties*. The methodology used in all three papers was similar, but the specific aim of the third paper in the series was to discover the extent to which there was a 'ripple effect' at work, in the form of southern prosperity spreading out and benefiting the North.

In their 1990 paper they ranked 280 towns or local labour-market areas (excluding Northern Ireland), according to a range of ten measures of prosperity, divided into 'static' and 'change' variables, using data that, in most cases, applied to 1989. The static measures were the unemployment rate, the average length of unemployment, the proportion of people employed in traditional industries, the proportion employed in certain service and high-technology industries and the average house price. The change variables were the recent change in unemployment, the change in total employment, the change in employment in selected service and high-technology industries, population change and house price trends.

On this basis, it was possible to derive an index of prosperity for each of the 280 local labour-market areas and thereby rank every town in Britain. The same towns did not necessarily perform best on each of the ten components making up the Champion–Green amalgamated index of prosperity. But, significantly, all ten best performers were in the area defined as the South in this book, and all ten worst performers were in the North. A summary of Champion and Green's top and bottom twenty 'winners and losers', based on their amalgamated index, is contained in Table 5.3. In each case, the maximum score obtainable for any of the ten components of the index is 0·1, and the maximum total score is 1·0. It will be noted that the top twenty were all from the South (and the majority from the south east), and the bottom twenty from the North. The highest performing northern town was Harrogate, which ranked 37.

The Champion–Green analysis underlined the extent of the South's economic advantage, on a comprehensive range of measures, by the late 1980s. The picture was reinforced by taking the median scores for each region, as shown in Table 5.4. This table is interesting in that it shows that the Lawson boom of the late 1980s did achieve a spread of prosperity from the south east, but that the main beneficiaries (those that caught up most with the south east) were the other regions in the South – East Anglia, the south west, and the east and west midlands – and to a lesser extent Yorkshire and Humberside and Wales.

It may be thought that the Champion–Green amalgamated measure, by including static elements such as house prices and unemployment levels, will have inevitably failed to pick up on the fact that some northern areas recovered rapidly during the

Table 5.3 Winners and losers

Top 20			Bottom 20		
Town	Index score	Position	Town	Index score	Position
Horsham	0·796	1	Mansfield	0·322	261
Newbury	0·788	2	Llanelli	0·320	262
Milton Keynes	0·713	3	South Shields	0·319	263
Haywards Heath	0·708	4	Dunfermline	0·317	264
Bishop's Stortford	0·704	5	Bishop Auckland		
Tunbridge Wells	0·700	6	& Aycliffe	0·315	265
Bracknell	0·698	7	Peterhead	0·313·	266
Reigate/Redhill	0·696	8	Ayr & Prestwick	0·302	267
Reading	0·695	9	Alloa	0·299	268
Stratford-on-Avon	0·690	10	Mexborough	0·298	269
St Albans	0·685	11	Stranraer	0·294	270
Andover	0·675	12	Thurso	0·294	271
Dereham	0·673	13	St Helens	0·293	272
Bournemouth	0·667	14	Paisley	0·293	273
Woking/Weybridge	0·667	15	Liverpool	0·292	274
Winchester	0·666	16	Sunderland	0·283	275
Guildford	0·666	17	Castleford &		
Basingstoke	0·661	18	Pontefract	0·282	276
Maidenhead	0·661	19	Kirkcaldy	0·281	277
Northampton	0·660	20	Kilmarnock	0·274	278
			Peterlee	0·271	279
			Greenock	0·253	280

Source: T. Champion and A. Green, *The Spread of Prosperity and the North–South Divide.*

1980s. But, when only the 'change' elements of the index are included, the picture is little different. The top ten on this basis were Newbury, Dereham, Milton Keynes, Horsham, Wellingborough, Deal, Redditch, Northampton, Bishop's Stortford and Corby. And the bottom ten were Liverpool, Elgin, Peterlee, Kirkcaldy, Banff & Buckie, Castleford & Pontefract, Aberdeen, Paisley, Greenock and Thurso.

The study found that there were indeed wide variations in prosperity within regions and that such variations were particularly large in the south east. However, even the worst-performing towns in the south east scored higher than a substantial proportion of those in, say, Yorkshire and Humberside. The results supported the view that it was better for a town to do badly in the South than in the North.

Table 5.4   Regional prosperity

1989			1987		
Region	Median score	Rank	Region	Median score	Rank
South East	0·608	1	South East	0·613	1
East Anglia	0·578	2	East Anglia	0·522	2
South West	0·545	3	South West	0·501	3
East Midlands	0·492	4	East Midlands	0·461	4
West Midlands	0·483	5	West Midlands	0·433	5
Yorks			North West	0·426	6
& Humberside	0·432	6	Yorks		
Wales	0·427	7	& Humberside	0·398	7
North West	0·409	8	North	0·391	8
North	0·389	9	Scotland	0·377	9
Scotland	0·351	10	Wales	0·375	10
National median	0·485			0·441	

Source: T. Champion and A. Green, *The Spread of Prosperity and the North–South Divide.*

Champion and Green's conclusion was that, far from destroying the idea that there is a North–South divide, their detailed analysis at the town level reinforced it. But, encouragingly for some regions, there was evidence that southern prosperity was rippling out, although not quickly enough to be of benefit to those regions furthest from the south east. They concluded:

Thus, while the North–South divide seems as fundamental as it was earlier in the 1980s, this latest analysis reflects the subsequent peaking of the south east's economic recovery and the outward spread of development and prosperity into adjacent regions. By the end of the decade, this process appears to have reached as far as Wales and the west midlands on the western side of Britain and Yorkshire and Humberside on the eastern side. However, as the performance of these regions has improved, so has the position of the regions further north deteriorated in relative terms. (1990, p. 32)

But, they added:

Yes, there are clear signs of an outward ripple of economic growth from London and the south east, but these developments have so far been limited in both numerical scale and geographical coverage and have in most respects served to reinforce the broad contrast between South and North rather than reduce it. (p. 40)

And, with the storm clouds gathering over the economy, they were already concerned that this process was about to come to an end:

> If the 'ripple' is part of the general process of recovery, then it could be expected that this recovery will continue to run its course and benefit the remoter parts of the country. The chief problem in this context, however, is that owing to the long time lag between the onset of recovery in London and its arrival in the far North – over five years – the national economic situation is vastly changed, with high interest rates and faltering economic growth serving to damp down the positive effects associated with the recovery process as it reaches the end of the line. (p. 42)

Looking back on the late 1980s from the perspective of 1993, its images are, if anything, harder to conjure up than those of the 1970s or 1960s, so rapid has been the transformation of Britain's economic circumstances. The boom, with the South leading it, was portrayed as an economic miracle by ministers who also claimed, astonishingly, that the North–South economic divide, which had never been wider, did not exist. In the first edition of *North and South*, written at the height of the boom, and two years before the onset of recession, I wrote:

> After an initial phase of growth, an unbalanced economy will run up against constraints sooner than one which is balanced. There are also potential inflationary dangers of an uneven distribution of activity. The greater the congestion within a region, the greater the upward pressure on costs and prices, as a result both of crowding and the strength of demand. And, when wage levels set in the most rapidly growing regions become national norms, pay starts to rise at a faster rate than is justified. Finally, the British economy in the late 1980s has become one with an increasingly vulnerable balance of payments position.

With hindsight, the main fault in that analysis was a failure to see how quickly, and how dramatically, these problems would exert themselves, to the detriment of the economy in general and the overheated South in particular. It may be that we will never again see such a combination of unsustainable boom and regional imbalances. Even so, the dangers of allowing North–South disparities to develop in the way that they did are worth setting out.

CONSTRAINTS ON GROWTH

There are several reasons why a regionally unbalanced economy will run into constraints at a lower level of activity and a higher level of unemployment than one where regional distribution is more even. If we look at the three factors of production – land, labour and capital – each has its part to play in the explanation. The overall supply of land is obviously fixed, although the supply of land for office or industrial use can be varied, depending on planning constraints, the pressure from alternative uses, and so on. In the extreme, an over-concentration of activity in one area of the country will mean that additional land for productive use can only be obtained by squeezing out another productive use, for example agriculture, or by eating into residential areas.

No one would suggest for a moment that all available land for industrial development or other business uses is near to being exhausted. In practice, the land constraint begins to bite much earlier than this through sharply rising land values or rentals. In this situation, according to the Conservative Government view of the 1980s, the response of business will be to expand in those areas where land is more plentiful, and rents and land values lower. The difficulty with this kind of market-determined regional policy is that it falls into similar problems to those singled out by the same Conservative critics of traditional regional policy. And these, in the main, are that while some businesses will undoubtedly read the signals from the market and expand in the North if faced with a land constraint in the South, others will not expand at all. In the end, it may make a little difference whether it is a civil servant or a land agent who seeks to direct the business elsewhere in the country. And this situation arises directly from the fact that a belief had been allowed to develop, reinforced by actual practice over a long period, that it was better to locate in the South and that a northern location was second best.

The second constraint is that of labour. The Lawson boom succeeded in pushing the national unemployment rate down from 11·1 per cent in 1986 to 5·7 per cent by early 1990. In East

Anglia the rate dropped to 3·3 per cent – 3 per cent is regarded by economists as equivalent to 'full' employment. In the south east and south west, unemployment was 4 per cent or below. The national average was pushed up by high unemployment rates in the north (8·8 per cent), north west (7·7 per cent), Scotland (8·4 per cent) and Northern Ireland (13·7 per cent).

Regional labour constraints arose, not just from the South's move towards full employment, but from a mismatch between available skills and the requirement of business. And shortages of skilled workers existed even in northern areas of high unemployment. During the second half of the 1980s, the Confederation of British Industry identified shortages of skilled labour as a factor limiting business expansion in most areas of the country.

This may be thought of as a simple reflection of Britain's training gap relative to other industrial countries, as identified by the National Institute for Economic and Social Research and others. But it also had an important North–South dimension. The training record of British industry in comparison with, say, Germany, has long left much to be desired. Until the manufacturing recession of 1979–81, however, there was throughout industry a formalized training system in place, notably through apprenticeships. Much of this system has been dismantled during the 1980s, for two principal reasons. The first was the shake-out in manufacturing employment itself, which left employers questioning whether they would be able to continue paying their existing skilled workers, let alone train new ones. That and the fact that many companies which had undertaken extensive worker training programmes in the past went out of business, meant a sharp reduction in skills training.

The second reason was that apprenticeships operated as an important source of power for the trade unions. Union insistence that new entrants to an industry undergo a five-year training period ensured a limited supply of workers to that industry and, therefore, higher wages. The problem was that, in the general attack on union restrictive practices in the 1980s, many useful apprenticeship training programmes were also lost. The baby was to a large extent thrown out with the bathwater.

The southern-based economic expansion of the 1980s could, for a time, suck in those skills which were still appropriate (the industrial changes of the period meant that many skills became redundant along with their possessors). Skilled workers and professionals are more mobile than unskilled workers – both because they are more likely to be owner-occupiers with a property to sell, rather than council tenants, and also because they are better at obtaining information about available jobs elsewhere – and moved more readily to the South to work. But the ad hoc approach to training in the 1980s, while on the face of it providing more freedoms and flexibility, carried a fundamental drawback. Companies which continued to pursue extensive programmes in providing their employees with skills, and improving those skills, ran the risk that, at the end of the process, those workers would be tempted away by the lure of higher pay to other employers who were less diligent about training. In the trade-off between the high cost of training and that of paying slightly higher wages, training could all too easily lose out. The ad hoc approach to training could mean a lowest common denominator outcome.

David Finegold and David Soskice, in the *Oxford Review of Economic Policy* of autumn 1988, identified this 'free rider' problem as one reason for Britain's poor training record. They also cited the role of the Government and the shift in the composition of industry from manufacturing to services, itself a characteristic of the North–South shift in the British economy.

Skill shortages can arise from a number of sources. Failings in the educational system are undoubtedly one. A smaller but significant factor may also be the loss of key people to other countries through the 'brain drain'. This was a reason given by the Chancellor of the Exchequer Nigel Lawson for the large cuts in the higher rates of income tax in the March 1988 Budget. The Government also responded by a gradual shift in the emphasis of its own employment schemes towards training, although the training element involved in such schemes was the cause of bitter dispute between it and the Trades Union Congress, culminating in the TUC's decision in September 1988, later relaxed, to boycott the Government's Employment Training programme for the long-term unemployed. And critics were to argue that the new emphasis on training was simply an attempt by the Government to undo the damage it caused by allowing the collapse of the apprenticeship system and dismantling the industrial training boards in the 1980s.

Much of the blame also lay with business itself, which was either too concerned that the 1980s recovery would peter out, or too worried about short-term profit goals, to invest enough in training. This is another reason why the distinction had to be made between short- and long-term efficiency gains in the British economic recovery in the 1980s, and why a recovery based in the South was bound to run up against labour constraints even at high levels of national unemployment.

The same was true for investment, if in a slightly different way. Like land, most capital is fixed in its location. This is true for public-sector investment, in roads, hospitals and other types of 'social' capital, and it is true for the majority of private-sector investment – factories, plant and equipment.

Any shift in economic activity and population from North to South creates a major problem for public-sector investment decisions. Schools, hospitals and roads are likely to be underused in the North, but in short supply in the South. The difficulty is that, if the Government responds to such a shift by increasing infrastructural investment in the South at the expense of the North, then this has the effect of reinforcing the North–South divide, both in the direct employment opportunities it creates and in removing potential constraints on southern expansion.

For most of the 1980s, public-sector investment – defined as gross fixed capital formation by government – was split roughly 50/50 between North and South, admittedly within the context of lower overall public investment in real terms. In other words, the North had more public investment per head of population than the South. Not all of this reflected the policy of the Conservative Government – some of the investment carried out over this period was on the basis of decisions taken much earlier. But the result was spare infrastructure capacity in the North and overused capacity in the South.

The M25 orbital motorway around London was a case in

point. After years of wrangling, the process of building the M25 began in the 1970s (by way of a long series of bitter planning inquiries) and was not completed until well into the 1980s. But the motorway, when built, quickly proved inadequate for the traffic using it. A study by the consultants Brian Colquhoun and Partners found that the traffic using the south-western stretch of the motorway exceeded projections by nearly 75 per cent, largely owing to the use of the motorway for short journeys by commuters. Serious traffic jams on the M25 soon became both frequent and legendary, and almost as soon as the orbital ring was completed the job began of widening that stretch of the road, at the cost of further delays. Meanwhile, local authorities seeking to attract industrial development to the North could justifiably use pictures of empty motorways in their advertisements.

The South has had a larger share of private-sector industrial investment during the 1980s – averaging 55 to 60 per cent of the total (excluding the North Sea). Thus, to a greater extent than for public-sector investment, private investment by industry reflected the pattern of economic activity. Private investment capacity is more easily scrapped than infrastructural investment, and this occurred in the North during and after the 1979–81 manufacturing recession.

Britain's investment record, however, remained generally poor during the 1980s. Industrial investment received a short-term boost in 1984 following changes in the system of corporation tax and capital allowances. But it was not until 1988 that industry could start to talk of an investment boom, and this after several years of strong growth in profits. And the sharp rise in interest rates in the autum of 1988 threatened (and eventually did) push this boom into sharp reverse.

Some of the rapidly expanding southern-based industries invested aggressively. The 'Big Bang' changes in the Stock Exchange dealing system of 1986 were preceded by a wave of investment in computer capacity and other high-technology capital. This was followed by a boom in London office building, including the development of the giant Canary Wharf project, later to feature as one of the recession's spectacular failures, deep in Docklands. But in other industries the shift in the structure and location of industry was not accompanied by a large enough shift in investment. The Confederation of British Industry reported record levels of capacity utilization during 1988 and warned that if planned investment was shelved, serious capacity constraints would emerge.

NORTH–SOUTH AND INFLATION

The constraints described above had direct implications for inflation. If land in the South is scarce and land prices high, then – in the absence of a shift to the cheaper land areas of the North – these costs will be passed on by producers in the form of higher prices. An offset was available because of the fact that northern-based firms were able to take advantage of lower rentals to keep their prices down. But, with the majority of economic activity concentrated in the South, this compensating factor was limited in its effects.

Congestion costs and the pressure on the infrastructure also directly added to inflation. The southern-based firm paid for its service engineers or salesmen to sit in traffic jams on the M25 or in central London. With competition for employees intense, it had to subsidize its long-distance commuters by interest-free season-ticket loans or, in some cases, by providing employees with tickets as a perk. The cost in the form of direct subsidies of moving commuters into and out of central London every day was estimated at £500 million a year, while the cost of traffic jams in the South was far higher.

A study, *The Cost of Congestion*, by the British Road Federation, estimated that traffic delays in London and its conurbation produced a £1·45 billion annual addition to vehicle operating costs. This was nearly half of congestion costs in conurbations for the whole of Britain. The study also cited the case of one seven-mile stretch of the M1, between Hemel Hempstead and Luton. The congestion costs resulting from the fact that 100,000 vehicles a day used this section, compared with an upper design threshold of 79,000, were estimated at £1 million a year, and such situations were repeated throughout the South. This is not to say that the North is a traffic-free paradise – congestion costs in Greater Manchester were estimated at £500 million a year and there are well-known motorway troublespots throughout the country. But the most serious bottlenecks were in the south east.

The most important route from the unbalanced economy to higher inflation was, however, through the labour market. I described above the situation of skill shortages. In the rapidly growing high-technology and financial-service industries of the South, these became acute as the 1980s progressed. In this situation, wages and salaries are bid up as firms compete against one another for relatively scarce skilled personnel.

Even without the specific problem of skill shortages, the existence of large regional differences in employment, if not eradicated by worker migration, will mean that labour markets in some parts of the country are subject to pressure, and this pressure will have the effect of pushing up wages in that region. Estimates by Olympia Bover, John Muellbauer and Anthony Murphy, in the Centre for Economic Policy Research paper 'Housing, Wages and UK Labour Markets', suggested that there was a direct link from the housing market to higher wage levels. High house prices in the South prevented workers from moving there, where work was more freely available, creating a 'mobility trap'. The result of this, they estimated, was to push up manual wages in Britain by 4·4 percentage points between 1984 and 1988.

The Bank of England, in an article in the Bank's August 1988 *Quarterly Bulletin*, recognized the potential dangers of this situation:

The disparity of economic performance between regions of Great Britain is a potential source of concern because the absence of adjustment can lead to a situation where there is greater than average upward pressure on prices in some regions co-existing with less than full utilization of resources in other regions ... Such a situation implies an inefficient use of resources, and it is for this reason that successive governments have attempted to reduce the disparities in resource utilization through various regional policies. (1988, p. 374)

The Bank's research, surprisingly, found no relationship between house prices and earnings for different regions. Instead, it concluded, the variation came through differences in unemployment rates between areas of the country. This is what one would expect given the nature of the labour market in Britain, with a high proportion of pay set nationally, and national pay increases largely reflecting labour-market pressures in those parts of the country in which unemployment is lowest and the pressure greatest.

If high wages in the South were balanced by low wages in the North, then the implication of regional imbalances for inflation would be less serious. The fact is that wages will tend to be determined by the high-growth, prosperous areas, suggesting that national pay pressures will always be out of line with national unemployment levels as long as large regional disparities in unemployment are allowed to persist. There has been considerable resistance to attempts by employers to 'regionalize' pay. In September 1988, Post Office workers all over the country went on strike over an attempt to introduce recruitment bonuses in areas where the Post Office was encountering staffing difficulties, notably the south east. The growth of earnings in Britain failed to come down in line with lower inflation in the first half of the 1980s. The boom eventually pushed average earnings growth, nationally, to 10 per cent a year.

The contribution of the North–South divide to inflation was tacitly admitted by the Chancellor of the Exchequer, Nigel Lawson, during the latter part of 1988. Interest rates were raised sharply, from a base rate of 7·5 per cent in June to 12 per cent by August, and further to 13 per cent in November (eventually reaching 15 per cent by the end of 1989), in an attempt to cool the economy in response to rising inflation, which reached more than 6 per cent in the autumn of that year, and subsequently rose to almost 11 per cent. Lawson asserted, correctly, that the move would hit the booming south east harder than the rest of the country. John Major, then Chief Secretary to the Treasury, referred specifically to the deliberate attempt that was being made to slow the housing market. And yet this was at a time when, in large areas of the North, in both the housing and labour markets, conditions were a long way from overheating. Inflation was being driven higher by the pace and concentration

of economic activity, and in particular spending power – itself
derived partly from sharply rising house prices – in the South.
Sure enough, the early effects of this tightening policy were to
rein back consumer spending in parts of the South rather more
sharply than in the North, because of the greater vulnerability
of southerners, with their larger mortgages, to high interest
rates. But there was much worse to come.

THE BALANCE OF PAYMENTS PROBLEM

The Achilles' heel of the British economy for much of the post-
war period has been the balance of payments. During the 1950s
and 1960s, the current-account position – typically in small
deficit or surplus – largely determined the stance of government
economic policy, during the infamous 'stop-go' period. In the
1970s, under the impact of the first world oil crisis and the
associated sharp rise in oil prices, the current-account deficit
widened dramatically, reaching a peak of £3·32 billion, or 4 per
cent of gross domestic product, in 1974. In the early 1980s,
North Sea oil transformed Britain's balance-of-payments position into one of large current-account surplus. At its peak in
1981 – with imports restricted by the depressed state of the
economy – the current-account surplus reached £6·3 billion, or
nearly 2·5 per cent of GDP.

The collapse in world oil prices in the mid-1980s, and the
beginnings of a decline in North Sea oil output, had the effect of
exposing the fundamental weakness of Britain's balance of payments. Import penetration was high and rising for a wide range
of products, and the non-oil visible trade deficit had been
deteriorating steadily.

In 1987 and 1988, as consumer spending grew strongly, partly
under the impact of tax reductions, a weak current-account
position turned into a huge and rapidly widening deficit, which
required policy action. In both July and October 1988, the
monthly current-account deficit exceeded £2 billion. The deficit
was running at more than 3 per cent of GDP and looked likely
at best to stay around this level for some time, at worst to
deteriorate further. The 1988 deficit was £16·2 billion (4 per cent

Table 5.5 The balance of payments (£ billion)

	1982	1983	1984	1985	1986	1987	1988	1989
Non-oil exports	44·7	48·2	55·4	61·8	64·4	70·7	74·4	86·3
Non-oil imports	47·4	56·7	67·7	73·3	78·1	86·5	98·6	112·2
Non-oil trade balance	−2·7	−8·5	−12·3	−11·4	−13·6	−15·7	−24·2	−25·9
Oil trade balance	4·6	7·0	6·9	8·1	4·1	4·2	2·8	1·3
Trade balance	1·9	−1·5	−5·3	−3·3	−9·6	−11·6	−21·5	−24·7
Invisibles* balance	2·7	5·3	7·1	6·1	9·6	7·1	5·3	3·0
Current account	4·6	3·8	1·8	2·8	0·1	−4·5	−16·2	−21·7

* Services, transfers, interest, profits and dividends.
Source: Central Statistical Office, *Economic Trends*, December 1992. Differences are due to rounding.

of GDP), rising to £21·7 billion (4·9 per cent of GDP) in 1989, before moving lower in response to the economy's slowdown.

How much was this imbalance related to the regional imbalances which had been allowed to develop in Britain? They were linked in two important respects. The first was the change in the structure of British industry, and in particular the reduced role of manufacturing, which had been largely responsible for the emergence of wider North–South economic differences. The second was the nature of the consumer spending boom in itself, and the extent to which a Southern-led boom was more likely to leak into imports than one which was more evenly spread.

The most important shift within a deteriorating balance of payments in the 1980s was in the performance of manufacturing industry. In 1980, Britain had a trade surplus on manufactured goods of £5·5 billion; £4·1 billion on finished manufactures and £1·4 billion on semi-manufactures (largely components). By 1985, manufacturing trade was in deficit by £3·1 billion, a £3·2 billion deficit on finished manufactures only partly offset by a small (£0·1 billion) surplus on semi-manufactures. In 1990, the position had worsened dramatically, with an overall deficit on manufactured trade of £13·7 billion, £10 billion on finished manufactures and £3·7 billion on semi-manufactures. Import penetration, particularly in manufactured goods, rose strongly during the 1980s. In simple terms, Britain's manufacturing base was exposed as being far too small in relation to the level of domestic demand. Imports of goods and services as a percentage of total final expenditure (domestic demand plus exports) rose from 20 per cent in 1980 to 25·3 per cent in 1990. By the late 1980s, with the exception of oil – and this position could be expected to change with declining North Sea output – Britain had a deficit on all visible trade categories, from raw materials through to finished products. It can be argued, of course, that the changes in the structure of British industry in the 1980s – which were part of the widening North–South divide – would have produced this trade deterioration even if the new industries had been more evenly spread throughout the regions. This may or may not be true, although it is plain that the country needed not just a redistribution of those new industries which replaced the old, but more of them.

The Government was guilty of ignoring warnings about Britain's emerging manufacturing trade problem. In 1985, the House of Lords Select Committee on Overseas Trade, chaired by Lord Aldington, warned of the dangers in the Government's neglect of manufacturing industry. Taking evidence from, among others, Sir John Harvey-Jones, then chairman of ICI, and Lord Weinstock, managing director of GEC, the Committee warned that the country could rely neither on a permanent trade surplus in oil nor on service industries filling the trade gap left by a declining manufacturing sector. Many service industries, it pointed out, were themselves dependent upon a healthy manufacturing industry. Sir Hector Laing, then chairman of United Biscuits, told the Committee that 'The present Government has in effect made a virtue of not having a vision of the future of British industry and a positive policy of distancing the state from the industrial sector. I think the Government should acknowledge that the nation does have an industrial problem in which it has a serious policy interest' (quoted in Johnson, 1991, p. 215).

The Government's attitude was confirmed by Nigel Lawson, in his Mansion House speech in October 1985. 'The Government,' he said, 'wholly rejects the mixture of special pleading dressed up as analysis and assertion masquerading as evidence which leads the Committee to its doom-laden conclusion.' But the Committee was right to be doom-laden. In the event, the deterioration in Britain's manufacturing trade position was even worse than it had feared.

It was also the case that the fast-growing high-technology and service industries of the South were themselves bigger importers than their predecessors, either of components and other semi-manufactures – where there was a shift into deficit – or, in the area of computers and other data processing equipment, finished products. One feature of the early 1980s manufacturing recession was the necessary shake-out of inefficient firms. But another, equally important development was the loss of many companies, often northern-based, which supplied capital equipment to industry. The combination of low demand at home for capital equipment – because of the manufacturing recession itself – and the loss of export markets because of the high value of sterling, drove many firms out of business. The result was that when investment rose strongly in the late 1980s, a large proportion of the capital equipment needed had to be imported from abroad. The surge in imports of consumer goods caught the eye in 1987 and 1988, but there was an accompanying rise in imports of capital goods. A similar problem arose for components. Higher output by all sectors of British industry during the boom resulted in a disproportionate rise in imports, as Christopher Johnson explained in his book *The Economy Under Mrs Thatcher, 1979–90*:

The main weakness was in industrial inputs, such as semi-manufactures, and in intermediate manufactured goods. Because of the closure of large parts of manufacturing industry in the 1980–81 recession, in the 1987–9 boom the UK lacked the capacity to supply demand for a wide range of materials and components of the kind provided by small and medium-sized engineering and contracting companies. (1991, p. 213)

One offsetting factor, in the South's favour, was that Britain continued to run a surplus on the 'invisibles' side of the current account – services, interest, profit and dividends, and transfers. A high proportion of these earnings originated in the South, notably from the City of London. The invisibles surplus rose from £1·77 billion in 1980 to a peak of £9·63 billion in 1985. However, the improvement in the invisibles surplus was not sufficient to compensate for the worsening visible-trade position. And the late 1980s saw the the beginnings of a decline in the invisibles surplus, with a shift into substantial deficit on the tourism account and a decline in the City's earnings overseas, partly because of the October 1987 stock-market crash, but also because of increased competition, which had the effect of driving down the fees charged for City services. By 1990 the invisibles surplus had shrunk to just £1·78 billion, equivalent to its level in cash terms in 1980, but far smaller after allowing for inflation.

A key element in Britain's worsening trade position was the consumer spending boom of the 1980s, which was accompanied by a rising tendency among consumers to buy imported goods – a rising marginal propensity to consume imports. There are two reasons why the South can be said to have been responsible for the lion's share of Britain's deteriorating position on trade in consumer goods. The first is that not only was the biggest share of consumer spending concentrated in the South (60 per cent or more) but also the fastest growth in spending has been in the southern half of Britain. The second reason, supported by anecdotal if not hard evidence, is that for many products consumers are less concerned about 'buying British' if they are in areas in which manufacturing has not traditionally been the mainstay of the local economy.

Between 1981, the trough of the first Thatcher recession, and 1989, there was a 110 per cent growth in consumer spending in the United Kingdom in money terms. The fastest growth rates were recorded in East Anglia (135 per cent), the south west (123 per cent) and the south east (116 per cent). They were followed, perhaps surprisingly, by Northern Ireland (112 per cent) and the east midlands (also 112 per cent). But in all other regions the increases lagged well behind, ranging from 92 per cent for the north to 108 per cent for Yorkshire and Humberside.

The faster the growth in consumer spending, the more that such spending goes beyond the basic necessities of food, fuel and housing, and on to clothing, footwear, cars and consumer durables. And, even if there were no regional variations in preferences for domestically produced as against imported goods, faster spending growth in the South would be expected to result in consumer expenditure with a higher import content.

Car ownership, as noted in Chapter Two, is at a higher level in relation to population in the South. It follows that, even allowing for broad regional similarities in the frequency with which people replace their cars (there are variations but they do not follow any North–South pattern) new car purchases will be disproportionately concentrated in the South. One consequence of this is that, since the new car market has been characterized by a rising import propensity, the South will inevitably be responsible for the greater part of the deficit on cars, which was more than £4 billion in 1988.

In addition – for all consumer products – when demand is growing strongly in the South, it is as easy, certainly in terms of distance, for that demand to be satisfied from the Continent as from northern Britain. With the completion of the European Community's internal market at the end of 1992, and the opening of the Channel Tunnel in 1994, it may become even easier.

CONCLUSION

The boom of the late 1980s was associated with a marked widening of the North–South economic divide. Any boom, when the expansion of domestic demand rises substantially above growth in the economy's productive potential, is ultimately unsustainable. The North–South dimension of the 1980s made the Lawson boom particularly unsustainable. Eventually, an unbalanced economy becomes an inefficient one, in that it is doomed to operate at a higher level of unemployment and a lower rate of growth than one in which economic activity is more evenly distributed. Regional imbalances exacerbate balance-of-payments and inflation problems. There has been a tendency to regard the North–South divide as unfair but not necessarily harmful to the economy. The recession that followed the Lawson boom, which was both deep and prolonged,

under lined the dangers of allowing the economy to become
unbalanced. And it is this recession, and its impact on North–
South differences, that I will now examine.

6

MR MAJOR'S RECESSION

> If it isn't hurting, it isn't working. (John Major, on
> taking over as Chancellor of the Exchequer, October
> 1989)

The severe recession that began in Britain in the summer of
1990 differed from its recent predecessors (notably 1974–5 and
1980–81) in several respects. It was not prompted by an international event outside the Government's control, such as the
OPEC (Organization of Petroleum Exporting Countries) oil
price hikes, that had done so much damage in the mid-1970s
and early 1980s. Iraq's invasion of Kuwait in August 1990
and the subsequent Gulf war briefly pushed world oil prices
higher, but only after Britain's recession was underway. This
recession was the direct product of deliberate policy actions to
reduce inflation, in an economy that had been allowed to
embark on an unsustainable boom. The recession of the early
1990s was a direct consequence of the policy errors of the
1980s.

It differed from its predecessors, too, in that it had not come
after a change in government, as was the case for Labour in
1974–5 and for the Conservatives in 1980–81. Denis Healey
described the economic situation he inherited from Anthony
Barber, Chancellor of the Exchequer in the 1970–74 Heath
Government, as 'practically beyond repair'. It was, he said,
'like the Augean stables'. Sir Geoffrey Howe, who in 1979
inherited the economy after Healey's five-year Chancellorship,
following Margaret Thatcher's election victory, could argue that

he too was faced with the task of clearing up after his predecessor. Howe had less cause to do so, given that the monetarist policy he pursued was basically that adopted by Healey in 1976. But such is the game of politics. And in other areas, most notably the strength of trade-union power and the size of the public sector, the 1979 Conservatives took the view that they had acquired control of an economy that needed major surgery. In 1990, however, the Conservatives could not blame Labour, any more than they could blame world events. The mistakes had come from their own side. Major, who succeeded Thatcher as Prime Minister in November 1990, having spent just over a year as Chancellor, later referred to his difficult inheritance. However, having been Chief Secretary to the Treasury for two years after the June 1987 general election, when most of the policy errors were committed, Major could not pretend to be an innocent victim of circumstances.

Perhaps the most notable feature of the recession, however, was that it hit hardest those parts of the economy where the boom of the 1980s had been most pronounced. It was, in almost every respect, proof of the old adage that the bigger they are, the harder they fall. The more that individuals and companies had borrowed to enjoy the fruits of the new prosperity of the Thatcher years, the more that they were exposed when high interest rates were used as the principal tool for cooling, and eventually freezing, an overheated economy. The bigger the surge in house prices, as the race to lock into inflated property values took on the feel of a modern gold rush, the more dramatic was the downside. The recession produced a phenomenon that was new to modern Britain – falling, and in some cases collapsing, house prices. Above all, the recession produced an immediate unwinding of the sharp North–South economic disparities of the 1980s. In 1988, on measures ranging from house-price differentials, through incomes, wealth and employment, the North–South divide had never been wider. Under the impact of recession, the divisions of the 1980s began to dissolve. Southerners had borrowed most heavily, and their house prices had risen to unthinkable levels, with associated connotations of a substantial and sustainable increase in wealth. I shall examine this unplanned shift back towards a more balanced economic geography for Britain, and attempt to assess the extent to which the widening divide of the 1980s has been bridged in the early 1990s. First, however, it is necessary to set the scene with a brief account of how Mrs Thatcher's booming, unbalanced economy turned, under Mr Major, into the longest, and arguably the most painful, recession in the post-war period.

THE DESCENT FROM BOOM TO BUST 1988–92

How did the booming economy of the late Thatcher years turn into a deep and lasting recession under John Major? The economic policy battles and mistakes of the period are a book in themselves, and readers are referred to my *From Boom to Bust* (Penguin) for the full story. But the broad outline can be simply told. Three factors are central to the economy's development during the boom and subsequent recession. The first was the Conservative belief, rapidly put into practice, in a financial system that, as far as possible, operated on the basis of price rather than direct rationing. Less than six months after Thatcher came to power in May 1979, in October 1979 to be precise, her Chancellor Sir Geoffrey Howe announced the removal of all Britain's exchange controls. This dramatic step was followed, in the middle of 1980, by the removal of the 'corset' controls on the banking system, which during the 1970s had been used to limit the growth in bank lending. The corset, which applied to the British banks, had in any case been made redundant by the abolition of exchange controls, which opened up a new source of borrowing to British residents and companies – they could perfectly legally obtain funds directly from foreign banks, or from overseas subsidiaries of British banks.

The new freedom enjoyed by the banks had a particular impact on one sector of the economy, the housing market, previously monopolized by the building societies (who themselves were later given the opportunity to extend their lending activities, notably to general consumer finance). The liberalization of the banks' lending activities fitted in with another strand of Conservative policy, encouraging home-ownership, including the sale of council properties to their tenants. The building societies, limited by the availability of savers' funds, had operated an effective mortgage rationing system. But, from the early 1980s, rationing was no more. There were other measures. Hire-purchase controls, used by post-war chancellors to limit consumer credit and spending, were removed in July 1982. These and other steps to deregulate the financial system were the sleeping giant that only fully awoke in the second half of the 1980s, when falling unemployment had the effect of persuading consumers that restraint was no longer necessary and when a combination of low interest rates and (temporarily) low inflation created the impression that the good times were there to stay.

In the boom years, borrowing by individuals soared. In 1987, personal-sector borrowing was £39·4 billion, rising to £53·9 billion in 1988, and remaining high at £48·7 billion in 1989 and, even in 1990, £41 billion. The growth of borrowing easily outstripped the rise in incomes, so that the ratio of personal debt to income increased sharply, rising from under 60 per cent in 1980 to 115 per cent by 1991. This increase in gearing by individuals (a similar, but less dramatic rise occurred in respect of company borrowing) meant that the economy was highly sensitive to interest rates. In particular, a rise in interest rates in a heavily indebted economy could be expected to hit investment and spending hard. Individuals reined back sharply on new borrowing. In 1991, for example, the net increase in consumer credit was just a third of its 1989 level. Later, consumers began to reduce their indebtedness by paying back, in net terms, outstanding credit. But the process was a painfully slow one.

The second significant factor was the Government's attitude towards taxation and, in particular, towards the timing of tax reductions. The post-war Keynesian consensus had been based on the understanding that both fiscal (taxation and public spending) policy and monetary policy would be used as short-term weapons for controlling the economy. Under the philosophy developed under Thatcher, most notably during Nigel Lawson's 1983–9 Chancellorship, taxation policy took on a very different role. Taxation policy was essentially *microeconomic* in character, being used to improve incentives and thus improve the supply-side of the economy. Lawson summed up the philosophy in his 1984 Mais Lecture at the City University in London, when he said:

It is the conquest of inflation, and not the pursuit of growth and employment, which is or should be the objective of macroeconomic policy. And it is the creation of conditions conducive to growth and employment, and not the suppression of price rises, which is or should be the objective of microeconomic policy. (1984)

If taxation policy, subject to the constraint of the public sector borrowing requirement, was part of microeconomic policy, then there was no need to raise taxes when the economy was growing, even if it was growing too strongly, and cut them during slow-downs. Tax changes were made independently of the economy's position in the economic cycle. This meant that, in the three budgets of March 1986, 1987 and 1988, the basic rate of income tax was cut, in stages, from 30 to 25 per cent. In the last budget in the sequence, the top rate was also reduced sharply, from 60 to 40 per cent. The 1986 changes could be justified on the old demand-management rules. There was no evidence then that the economy had embarked on an unsustainable boom. But those of 1987 and in particular 1988 were introduced at a time when the economy was already booming. The 1987–8 tax cuts reinforced the impression that a new era of growth and prosperity was here to stay. They also had the direct effect of boosting the level of post-tax income against which new borrowing could be taken on. The combination of tax cuts and very low interest rates in 1988, against the backdrop of a boom in the housing market and in consumer spending, was enough to tempt even a saint. For the south east, with easily the biggest share of higher-rate taxpayers, the effect was particularly dramatic.

The third factor, touched on briefly above, was that, for a relatively short but highly damaging period, the main weapon of macroeconomic control, monetary policy (and within it, interest rates) lost sight of its basic objective, the control of inflation.

Lawson, in essence, allowed himself to be distracted from his own 1984 dictum. The distraction came from the European Monetary System (EMS) and, in particular, from the system's exchange rate mechanism (ERM). In 1985, after experiencing two unsettling bouts of sterling weakness during the two years since he had become Chancellor, Lawson became attracted to the idea of taking sterling into the ERM, the semi-fixed currency system which had been operating since 1979. Thatcher, however, remained wedded to the Conservatives' original view of formal exchange rate systems, which were that they interfered with a market which, as she was later to observe memorably, 'you cannot buck'.

In the autumn of 1985, Lawson, backed by several senior members of the Cabinet, including Sir Goeffrey Howe, his predecessor at the Treasury, put up a strong proposal to take the pound into the ERM. Thatcher, however, would have none of it, agreeing only to reconsider the question at a later date. Lawson, however, was convinced that Thatcher was wrong, and determined to prove it. The opportunity came early in 1987 when, after a year in which the pound had been allowed to fall (producing another mini sterling crisis in October 1986), international moves to stabilize exchange rates came to fruition. The Group of Seven (the United States, Japan, Germany, Britain, France, Italy and Canada) agreed at a Paris meeting to attempt to hold the dollar at the level at which an earlier successful example of international currency cooperation (the September 1985 Plaza agreement) had succeeded in bringing it down to. The Paris agreement, known as the Louvre accord, had as its main element the fixing, within broad target ranges, of the dollar's value against the Deutschmark and Japanese yen. A logical extension of the accord, which appealed to a Chancellor who wanted to demonstrate the virtues of currency stability, was to attempt to restrict sterling's fluctuations. And since the Deutschmark was the ERM's anchor currency, it was the natural choice for a sterling target.

There followed the period of shadowing the Deutschmark, the setting of an informal target range for the pound against the German currency, which was eventually followed, in 1990, by formal membership of the ERM. For almost six years, from early 1987 until September 1992 (when sterling was ignominiously forced out of the ERM), the main determinant of British interest-rate policy was the pound's level against the Deutschmark. And, since throughout the period Britain's economic experience was markedly different from that of the other European Community countries, the quest for exchange-rate stability resulted in a loss of control over interest rates. Thus, during the course of 1988, bank base rates were reduced to a ten-year low of 7·5 per cent but within six months were up to 13 per cent. In 1989, sterling weakness forced rates up to a punitive 15 per cent, a level they were to remain at for a full year, as Major, who had succeeded Lawson as Chancellor in October 1989, prepared the ground for the pound's formal entry into the ERM. Rates were cut to 14 per cent on entry in October 1990, but subsequent reductions were painfully slow, constrained by the need to preserve sterling's ERM parity. By 16 September 1992, with the recession more than two years old, base rates were at 10 per cent, 2·5 percentage points above the low-point of 1988, a year when the economy was at the height of perhaps the most powerful boom of the post-war period. (The Barber boom of the early 1970s produced the strongest growth performance of any single year, when gross domestic product rose by a staggering 7·4 per cent in 1973, before sinking immediately into recession. However, growth over the 1986–8 period, a cumulative 13·2 per cent, exceeded that over the 1971–3 period, when it was 12·3 per cent.)

Interest-rate policy, or rather the sublimation of that policy to the needs of the exchange rate, therefore contributed to the excesses of the boom years, while significantly adding to the scale and duration of the subsequent recession. The combination of all three factors, the ready availability of credit, substantial tax reductions and, during the boom, low interest rates, represented a very heady brew. Had a group of economists sat down and planned for a runaway boom, it is doubtful that they could have come up with a better set of conditions. And, once interest rates had been raised to very high levels, both to slow the boom and support the exchange rate, the combination of these and very high levels of indebtedness (built up courtesy of the liberal-ized banking system) could only result in severe recession. It remains to be seen to what extent the partial unwinding of the tax cuts of the 1980s will lock the economy into a period of subdued growth. Norman Lamont, who succeeded Major as Chancellor on the latter's elevation to Prime Minister in Novem-ber 1990, announced in his March 1993 Budget that, with effect from April 1994, indirect taxes would be increased (through the extension of VAT to domestic fuel and power) as would direct taxes (employee National Insurance contributions were to be raised from 9 to 10 per cent of income).

THE SOUTH'S RECESSION

If the economic conditions of the second half of the 1980s could have been designed to produce a powerful economic boom, they were also ideally fashioned to ensure the South's disproportion-ate share of that boom. The role of income-tax reductions, and in particular the impact of sharp cuts in the higher rates of tax on the above-average earnings of southerners, has already been touched upon. But there were other factors. The housing boom of the 1980s began in the south-east and gradually rippled out to the rest of the country. When interest rates were reduced in 1987 and 1988, they added fuel to an already roaring housing-market fire in the South, with prices rising by as much as 50 per cent a year in parts of the south-east and East Anglia. The North, by comparison, lagged well behind. Financial liberalization brought with it a new freedom to borrow, but it also produced a sharp increase in employment in financial services, much of it in the South. Employment in the banking, finance and insur-ance sectors rose from 1·7 million in 1980 to 2·7 million by 1990.

By contrast, the method used to slow the economy, and eventually to plunge it into recession, was, intentionally or otherwise, particularly well-targeted towards southerners. The doubling of interest rates between May 1988 (when they were 7·5 per cent) and October 1989 (15 per cent) was a swift and harsh lesson to those who had borrowed at the height of the boom. According to the 1992 *Regional Economic Outlook*, produced by Oxford Economic Forecasting and the Northern Ireland Economic Research Centre:

The sustained period of high interest rates, 15 per cent from October 1989 to October 1990, reversed the house-price spiral which played such a large role in feeding the debt-driven expansion of the credit boom years. The subsequent downturn in the housing market has itself fuelled the recession. House prices have declined in nominal terms, reducing wealth and undermining consumer confidence, and house sales have been flat since 1989. The 1980s' house-price boom had a distinct regional pattern which is now well known. House prices grew fastest and have subsequently fallen furthest in the south east and its contiguous regions of East Anglia and the south west. Not surprisingly, the unravelling of the house-price boom has had its most severe impact on these regions. (1992, p. 2)

Even before it became clear, from the middle of 1990 onwards, that the economy had embarked on a full-scale recession, it was evident that something significant was happening to the regional make-up of Britain's economy. House prices in London and the south east, having led the boom, stopped rising during 1989. And, underlining the speculative nature of many housing transactions during this period, when house prices levelled out they removed an important argument for buying – the prospect of an automatic capital gain. House prices in the South had risen sharply because people thought they would carry on rising. It was silly to be left out of the game, even if it meant borrowing much more, in relation to income, than would have been considered wise in the past. But when as a result of high mortgage rates the process paused, people saw the Emperor's new clothes for what they were. The only silly thing about the housing market in the South was the level of prices. The North was eventually to catch a housing chill (albeit a much milder strain), but the South succumbed first and suffered most. Comparing 1990 to 1989, for example, average house prices in East Anglia fell by more than 10 per cent, by 6 per cent in the south east and by nearly 10 per cent in the south west. In Yorkshire and Humberside, the north, the north west and Scotland, however, prices carried on rising, by between 9 and 15 per cent. High

Table 6.1   The housing recession: debt and equity

	Average outstanding mortgage, 1989	Mortgage as % of average earnings, 1989	House price change 1989–91	House price change as % of income
South East	£27,499	191·9	− £8,374	− 42·2
Greater London	£30,833	191·4	− £4,861	− 22·8
Rest of South East	£25,717	202·4	− £10,939	− 58·0
East Anglia	£22,452	197·6	− £7,300	− 40·9
South West	£21,398	185·6	− £8,241	− 45·9
East Midlands	£18,562	172·4	− £939	− 5·3
West Midlands	£19,176	171·7	£1,146	6.8
Yorks & Humberside	£15,786	142·7	£5,603	33.0
North West	£18,202	158·1	£7,077	48.7
North	£14,266	129·4	£5,045	30.6
Wales	£13,200	119·8	£903	5.4
Scotland	£17,648	155·1	£7,600	42.4

Source: Oxford Economic Forecasting/Northern Ireland Economic Research Centre, *Regional Economic Outlook*, August 1992, p. 8.

mortgage rates and falling house prices, the former largely responsible for the latter, hit the South disproportionately hard, as Table 6.1 shows.

The North–South differences in housing-market performance were striking. In the heavily indebted South, falling prices implied a loss of net wealth over the 1989–91 period equivalent, in the worst case, to nearly 60 per cent of per capita annual income (this was the fall in the south east excluding Greater London). Thus, just as positive wealth effects, emanating from rising housing prices, had boosted consumption in the boom years (even if people did not borrow against the value of their house they felt better off), so the opposite occurred when sharply falling prices produced negative wealth effects. In the less indebted North, however, positive wealth effects continued. Indeed, as Table 6.1 shows, these were as powerful in many northern regions as the negative wealth effects were in the South. The main constraint on consumer spending in the North, therefore, was the direct one of high interest rates.

The effect was dramatic. The conversational stand-by at

London dinner parties changed abruptly from discussion of the house-price explosion, gazumping, and all the other characteristics of a runaway boom, to depressing assessments of the new situation of property-market stagnation. Ian Jack, writing in the *Independent*, captured the spirit of the times:

That was perhaps Mrs Thatcher's greatest achievement. She made moralists – the 'people who droned and drivelled that they cared' – seem like humbugs. People in the middle class who raised a protest ('the chattering classes') had to be prepared for the finger that pointed out their own good fortune – the new car, the country cottage, the private school – which was her achievement as well as theirs. I think this infected almost everyone; it certainly infected me. Later in the decade when I left London on stories I would often find myself standing outside estate agent's windows, computing the number of local villas one could buy for the price of a terraced house in London. Home-owners began to use estate agents as therapy, to cheer themselves up. They would have their homes valued on a regular basis. How much ... £250,000? Wonderful, that's up £10,000 in the past month ... And then the age of her miracle passed. (1990)

Many, particularly in the South, could not survive high interest rates and the downturn in the housing market. As will be discussed in more detail in Chapter Eight, housing repossessions (or possessions as the building societies prefer to call them), reached record levels. Possession orders in England and Wales totalled 73,859 in 1991, of which 32,961, or 45 per cent, were in the south east. In 1992, after action by the Treasury to limit the number of repossessions, possession orders fell to 58,752. The lion's share, 25,742 or 44 per cent, continued to be in the south east.

Estate agents, highly visible symbols of the boom years, had succeeded, by their ostentation, in giving mobile phones and BMW cars a bad name. But they were now the new victims of the most dramatic housing recession of the post-war period. Insurance companies, banks and building societies, who had competed to buy up chains of estate agents at the height of the boom, were left with egg on their faces. Impressive corporate logos and luxuriously appointed offices could not compensate for a collapse of business in the previously booming

South. In some cases, estate agencies were sold back to their original owners for a fraction of the purchase price. In others, estate agents joined the queue of service-sector redundancies.

Retailing, which boomed in the South in the second half of the 1980s, turned into another graveyard of overblown hopes. So aggressive were some retailing groups in buying up available city-centre and out-of-town properties that they were christened the 'space bandits'. Every decent-sized town that had any pretensions had a Laura Ashley. Even those with few pretensions acquired a branch of Next. My local high street, by no means an important shopping centre, had two. Trade, it appeared, would automatically follow the opening-up of a new branch. For a while, when retail sales were climbing, in volume, by 5 or 6 per cent a year, it worked. But then the customers stopped coming, at least in the South. While Brent Cross, in north London, struggled, the Gateshead Metro Centre boomed. The John Lewis Partnership, with department stores in most parts of the country, told in its weekly sales statistics of the contrast between depressed business in its southern branches, and continuing brisk trade elsewhere. But the resilience of sales in the North was insufficient to prevent a serious retailing downturn. Retailing employment standing at 2·24 million in mid-1990, had dropped by 200,000 by September 1992. The position may have been even worse than these bald figures suggest. Companies also responded to the downturn in demand by switching a greater proportion of their retailing employees to part-time work.

Small businesses, the living example of the 'enterprise culture' of the Thatcher years, were particularly hard hit by the recession. Again, a phenomenon that had been one of the South's strengths during the good years, turned into a major disadvantage when the going got tough. The south west, with nearly 20 per cent of households dependent upon a self-employed head, was particularly vulnerable, as were the south east and East Anglia, both with more than 16 per cent of families reliant mainly on income from self-employment. Business failures soared in the recession. Company liquidations, on official data, soared by 140 per cent between 1989 and 1992. Personal bankruptcies quadrupled over the same period. When, in the summer of 1991, the *Sunday Times* ran a campaign calling for fairer treatment of small businesses by the banks, it was inundated with cries for help, the vast majority from southern-based companies. For the owner of a business, even a one-man operation, failure was, in many respects, worse than unemployment. Many new small businesses had borrowed heavily to set up and expand. Some later complained that they had been encouraged by the banks to take out larger loans or overdrafts than they themselves considered prudent. And, by convention, much of this finance was against the security of the family home. Thus, when the business folded, many owner-managers lost more than their livelihood, they also had to give up the family home. And, in a falling housing market, there was no guarantee that the sale of that home would raise enough to pay off what the bank was owed. For many, particularly in the South (where there was a bigger proportion of small businesses and where the housing market was weakest), the enterprise dream turned into a nightmare.

All the boom sectors of the 1980s suffered in the early 1990s. And, since the booming service industries were very largely a southern phenomenon, it was there that the pain was felt. The first edition of this book came in time to catch the announcement, by the merchant bank Morgan Grenfell, that it was closing its securities-trading business, with the loss of 450 City jobs. But this was but the first of many such announcements, some large-scale, many others more discreet, with one or two salesmen, traders or analysts 'let go' at the end of the week. Stephen Lewis, a City economist, predicted long before the City shake-out that 50,000 jobs would be lost in the Square Mile, and was ridiculed for doing so. Before long, however, he was well on the way to being proved right. Like estate agents, the striped-shirt, Porsche-driving yuppies of the City's dealing rooms, epitomized the 1980s and underlined the opportunities available in a booming, free-for-all economy. Even Margaret Thatcher, the City's patron saint, was said to be embarrassed by six-figure salaries for the best-paid analysts and dealers, many of them in their twenties, although it should be emphasized that not everyone who worked in the City fitted the tabloid-newspaper image. But even Britain's staid banks and building societies, who in the 1980s had fretted about not being able to attract new employees in the 1990s, when Britain's 'demographic time-bomb' would mean a fall in the number of young people entering the labour market, embarked on savage programmes of branch closures and redundancies. Employment in banking, insurance and finance, 2·71 million in mid-1990, fell by more than 100,000 in the following two years, with more job losses yet to come.

The extent of the North–South shift in unemployment will be examined in more detail in the next chapter. It is, however, central to Britain's changed economic geography. In 1990, unemployment in the south east averaged 371,800, slightly higher than in 1989. By December 1992, it had risen to 941,100, an increase of 569,300 or 153 per cent. Nationally, unemployment rose by 1·31 million by the end of 1992, compared with its 1990 average. The rise in unemployment in the south east thus accounted for 43 per cent of the national increase. The results for other regions, confirming the strong southern bias in the rise in unemployment, are contained in Table 6.2.

The North clearly did not escape the employment effects of what was, after all, a deep and prolonged national recession. The regional differences summarized in Table 6.2 are, however, striking. In 1990, unemployment in the five regions of the South totalled 758,300, 145,700 less than in the six regions of the North. By the end of 1992, southern unemployment had leap-frogged the North – at 1·73 million it was 488,300 above the northern total. This was a dramatic and unprecented shift. As far as jobs were concerned, the recession overturned every preconception about Britain's North–South divide. The biggest increases were in the south east, East Anglia and the south west, the three boom regions of the 1980s which, during the boom, had come close to running out of available workers. These three together accounted for almost 60 per cent of the rise in unemployment, the South as a whole nearly three quarters. By contrast, the best places to be in the recession were in the United Kingdom's peripheral regions, Scotland and Northern Ireland.

Table 6.2   Regional unemployment

	Unemployment 1990	Unemployment December 1992	Percentage change	Percentage of UK rise
South East	371,800	941,100	153	43·4
East Anglia	37,400	85,700	129	3·7
South West	97,200	225,400	132	9·8
East Midlands	99,300	188,500	90	6·8
West Midlands	152,600	290,200	90	10·5
The South	758,300	1,730,900	128	74·2
Yorks & Humberside	161,100	250,600	56	6·8
North West	234,700	333,500	42	7·5
North	122,700	168,500	37	3·5
Wales	86,200	133,500	55	3·6
Scotland	202,100	249,600	24	3·7
Northern Ireland	97,200	106,900	10	0·7
The North	904,000	1,242,600	37	25·8
United Kingdom	1,662,300	2,973,500	79	100·0

Source: Department of Employment, *Employment Gazette*, February 1993.

DID THE RECESSION ELIMINATE THE DIVIDE?

The recession of the early 1990s, in a number of respects, impacted most heavily on the South. After years of watching southerners gain the spoils as the apparent economic miracle under Margaret Thatcher seemed to have lifted Britain out of its cycle of post-war decline, now northerners could stand back and watch the South suffer. Not that the North escaped the recession. But no longer were they under pressure to migrate southwards in search of the highly paid jobs that were ten a penny in London and its hinterland. No longer did they have to listen to smug southerners telling them that a two-bedroomed terraced house in Islington was worth more than an eight-bedroomed mansion in North Yorkshire. The recession of the early 1990s was the South's retribution for believing too much in the Thatcher miracle. It was a lesson, only later learned by John Major, that economies cannot survive without making things that other countries want to buy. In the easy-money 1980s, it was thought unfashionable in the extreme to say that manufacturing mattered. By the early 1990s, it was unfashionable to say otherwise. But, during the period when a City dealer could make more in an afternoon by trading paper than the average industrial worker could earn in a year, those who kept their noses to the grindstone were not only relatively impoverished, they appeared to belong to a different era. The South was the new Britain, living out a British version of the American dream of two-car households, second homes for weekends or holidays in the country or in France, and all based on ownership of an asset, the family home, which could only increase in value. The North was the old Britain, stuck in a low-tech rut from which there was no obvious escape.

Nor was this assumption of superiority confined to a high-earning southern elite. The playwright Les Smith, quoted in Chapter Two, observed:

I have seen London soccer fans, safe in well-policed pens, wave £10 notes at the home support. I have heard their chants of 'We've All Got Jobs'. I have seen the pictures of Metropolitan policemen flashing their weighty overtime-laden pay slips at miners' pickets . . . What is the view from Tunbridge Wells? Do you see only the smart shops, the Porsche salerooms and the estate agents' windows? (1991)

Northern *schadenfreude* at the South's difficulties is one thing, but to what extent did the recession close the divide? The evidence, in the housing market and in employment, is compelling, although as I will discuss later the picture is somewhat more complex than the surface statistics suggest. The one important thing to bear in mind, however, is that underlying economic differences, built up over a very long period of time, are not quickly and easily eliminated. At the time of writing, the latest official regional accounts were for 1991, the year in which the economy in general, and the South in particular, suffered the greatest recessionary drop (with a post-war record fall of 2·5 per cent in gross domestic product). Gross domestic product per capita, one measure of relative regional prosperity, is listed in Table 6.4 (any region which had a per capita GDP equivalent to the UK average would have a score of 100. Those above 100 are above the average and vice versa for those below). The message is plain. The peak of southern economic superiority over the

Table 6.3   GDP per head, by region (UK excluding North Sea = 100)

	1981	1985	1989	1990	1991
South East	116·6	116·4	119·0	118·3	116·5
East Anglia	96·6	100·7	101·0	101·3	100·4
South West	93·4	94·3	94·5	94·8	94·2
East Midlands	97·1	97·4	97·0	97·1	98·0
West Midlands	90·9	92·5	92·3	93·3	92·0
The South*	107·1	107·5	109·0	108·7	107·4
Yorks & Humberside	92·3	92·8	91·1	91·1	91·6
North West	94·5	93·1	90·9	90·8	92·7
North	93·9	90·6	87·8	86·9	89·1
Wales	83·8	83·4	85·6	85·5	86·5
Scotland	96·7	95·6	92·7	94·2	96·7
Northern Ireland	78·7	79·6	77·3	77·3	77·1
The North*	92·5	91·5	89·6	89·8	91·3

* Author's calculations, weighted according to GDP shares in each year.
Source: Central Statistical Office, *Economic Trends*, December 1992, p. 118.

North, and in particular the dominance of the south east, was in 1989. In 1990, and in particular in 1991, the North closed the gap. But how far did it do so? In 1981, per capita GDP in the five southern regions averaged 15·8 per cent more than in the North. By 1985 the gap had widened to 17·5 per cent and, at the peak in 1989, to 21·7 per cent. The closing of the gap saw the South's lead pulled back to 21 per cent in 1990 and 17·6 per cent in 1991.

In broad terms, therefore, the recession had, by the end of 1991, brought the South's lead over the North on this measure back to its position of the mid-1980s, but still significantly above its 1981 position. The South's continuing difficulties in 1992, and beyond, suggest that, when the figures become available, a further closing of what remains a very substantial gap will have occurred. This, in itself, is not particularly surprising. In the first edition of this book I suggested that, since the North-to-South shift of economic activity had gone well beyond its long-run trend in the 1980s, a period of catching up by the North was likely. What was surprising was the dramatic way in which it has occurred. The 1991 rankings of per capita GDP throw up some interesting shifts. In 1989, at the peak of southern dominance, all five southern regions had per capita GDP that exceeded any of the six constituent parts of the North. In 1991, the South still had the top three areas in terms of per capita GDP (the south east, East Anglia and the east midlands). But Scotland, which escaped the recession relatively unscathed, had jumped into fourth place and the north west was ahead of the west midlands. The west midlands, indeed, found itself to be in an uncomfortable pivotal position between North and South. As in 1980–81, the later recession hit west midlands' manufacturing hard. The region, which had struggled to hold on to the coat-tails of the prosperous South in the 1980s, found that, unlike many northern areas, it could not escape the worst effects of the downturn. The contrast between the experiences of the east and west midlands was considerable.

A more direct means of assessing the extent to which the divide was bridged is to examine regional rates of growth (or decline). Unfortunately, no official figures are produced for regional GDP on an inflation-adjusted basis. This is because, although the information is available to do so, successive governments have chosen not to publish statistics for regional inflation rates. Unofficial estimates are, however, available, and Table 6.4 reproduces inflation-adjusted regional GDP estimates made by the National Westminster Bank. These suggest that the boom of the second half of the 1980s was strongest in the south east excluding Greater London (the rest of the south east, or 'Roseland' in the jargon), East Anglia and the east midlands, where growth rates were 4 per cent or more a year. The north, north west, Scotland and Northern Ireland, in contrast, grew by 3 per cent a year or less over this period. The South (annual average growth 4 per cent a year) thus drew well ahead of the North (3·1 per cent average growth) during the boom years. But in 1991, when the South declined by 2·1 per cent relative to the North, and 1992, when the relative decline was 1·1 per cent (and the North was stagnant rather than in recession), the position was reversed. One can think of the fable of the tortoise and the hare. The South raced away during the boom years, to the point where, in 1990, its cumulative growth from the beginning of 1986 exceeded that of the North by 5·2 percentage points. By the end of 1992, however,

Table 6.4   GDP growth, by region

	1980–89	1986–90	1991	1992
South East	2·4	4·0	−4·0	−1·3
Greater London	1·4	3·5	−4·0	−1·5
Rest of South East	3·2	4·3	−4·0	−1·2
South West	3·3	3·9	−2·4	−1·0
East Anglia	4·1	4·3	−2·3	−1·2
East Midlands	2·9	4·0	−1·5	−0·3
West Midlands	1·8	3·8	−3·8	−0·7
*The South**	2·6	4·0	−3·4	−1·1
North	1·8	2·5	−0·2	−0·1
Yorks & Humberside	2·1	3·3	−2·3	0·1
North West	1·4	3·0	−1·2	0·0
Wales	2·8	4·5	−1·8	0·2
Scotland	1·9	2·8	−0·4	0·0
Northern Ireland	2·5	2·8	−3·4	0·1
*The North**	1·9	3·1	−1·3	0·0
UK (excluding North Sea oil and gas)	2·3	3·6	−2·6	−0·6
UK	2·3	3·1	−2·5	−0·5

* Author's estimates, regional GDP growth rates weighted according to regional shares of 1990 GDP.
Source: National Westminster Bank, *Economic and Financial Outlook*, April 1993.

the recession had pushed the South's cumulative lead down to just 1·2 percentage points. The 1990–92 recession had not, in other words, quite unwound the effects of the 1986–90 boom period, let alone the relative advantage gained by the South during the earlier part of the 1980s.

Is it better to be a tortoise or a hare? Northerners, scarred by the 1980–81 recession, never fully took on board the Thatcher miracle of the 1980s. Although mortgages and consumer credit were freely available, even people in secure jobs were more cautious than their southern counterparts in taking on new borrowing. At the same time, the structural changes in Britain's economy, with a reduced role for manufacturing and, in particular, for basic industries such as mining and shipbuilding, continued for much of the decade. Now the boot is on the other foot. The recession of the early 1990s has scarred the South badly, and the big programmes of rationalization

are in sectors such as banking, traditionally one of the main-
stays of the southern economy. There is also the question, which
will be answered in more detail at the end of the book, as to
whether the 1990s promises to be a more industry-friendly
decade, as a result both of circumstance and deliberate acts of
government policy. If so, this should also work broadly in the
North's favour.

RECESSION AND REGIONAL ECONOMIC STRUCTURE

Before leaving this overview of Mr Major's recession, and its
impact on Britain's economic geography, it is necessary to
tackle one puzzle. Why was it that a recession that produced a
sharp fall in manufacturing output, albeit a drop that was not
on the scale of the early 1980s, hit the South so hard? From its
peak in April 1990, manufacturing output dropped by 8·7 per
cent until hitting its cyclical low-point in January 1992. Output
of the service industries peaked in the first quarter of 1990
and appeared to have reached a trough in the third quarter of
1992, by which time it had fallen by just 2·6 per cent. On this
basis, the recession should have been more severe in the
manufacturing-dominated North than the more diversified regional economies of the South. The south east's strength in the
1980s, after all, emanated in part from having a good spread of
economic activity.

This is confirmed in Table 6.5. It shows that, with between 25
and 30 per cent of their local economy consisting of manufacturing, the north, north west, east and west midlands and Wales
should have fared worse than elsewhere. The west midlands
performed according to this rule, but the others did not, or at
least not as much as they should have done. And why, on this
basis, did the south east do so badly?

There are four contributory factors. The first is that, within
manufacturing, certain industries have suffered more than
others. In particular, the end of the Cold War meant a period of
rationalization for defence-related industries. And these, by tradition, were in the South. In addition, companies faced with
extreme financial pressures and needing to cut back took the axe

first to their highest-cost operations. And, again, these tended to be their southern-based factories. The South may also have suffered from relocation decisions taken during the boom years. Companies who took the decision to head northwards because of high costs or the difficulties of obtaining skilled labour did not cancel these strategic moves because the recession had eliminated part of the problem, although the incentive for planning new moves disappeared.

Secondly, financial and business services, accounting for 29 per cent of the economy of the south east for example, were hit particularly hard during the recession, more so than other service industries. Even before adjusting for inflation, the value of the output of financial and business services in the south east fell by 3 per cent between 1990 and 1991. After inflation, the fall was probably 8 per cent or more. Just as the success of this sector had a disproportionate effect in boosting the south east in the 1980s, so its difficulties acted as a drag on the region in the early 1990s.

Thirdly, for many service industries, output exists on the basis of local demand. Such industries cannot survive in a vacuum. Thus, retailing, hotels, garages and other service-providers suffered more in the South, because demand was hit hardest by the Government's high-interest squeeze on the economy. This was also true of financial and business services, which continued to expand, albeit at a slower rate than before, in many northern regions.

Finally, some of the recession's impact on the North was offset by a continued increase in government spending. The traditional, pre-Thatcher role of government was to act in a counter-cyclical way by maintaining or increasing spending to offset a decline in private-sector activity. It follows that, the more important government spending is to the local economy, the greater the scope for such action, whether intended or not, to ameliorate the impact of the downturn. This factor appears to have been important in certain parts of the North, and most notably in Scotland and Northern Ireland. Table 6.5 shows that the proportion of economic activity deriving from public administration, defence, education and health is significantly higher in

Table 6.5 Regional economic structure (sectoral contributions to regional GDP, per cent)

	South East	East Anglia	South West	East Midlands	West Midlands	Yorks & Humberside	North West	North	Wales	Scotland	Northern Ireland
Agriculture	0.7	5.1	3.4	2.5	2.0	2.0	0.9	1.9	2.1	2.6	4.2
Energy & water supply	3.3	1.4	4.6	6.3	3.8	6.7	4.5	6.8	6.2	5.9	4.9
Manufacturing	15.1	21.4	18.7	26.9	29.4	24.9	27.3	28.0	25.5	19.9	17.5
Construction	6.7	7.7	7.8	6.9	6.4	6.7	6.2	7.6	6.4	7.3	6.7
Distribution, hotels, catering & repairs	14.6	16.0	16.3	15.9	13.8	16.6	14.9	13.0	13.6	14.9	13.5
Transport & communication	8.3	8.5	5.6	5.9	5.8	6.6	6.9	6.2	6.0	7.2	4.7
Financial & business services	26.1	13.2	16.2	12.7	13.3	12.1	14.7	10.5	12.7	14.4	11.1
Ownership of dwellings	8.1	7.4	8.1	6.9	7.9	5.9	6.9	6.1	6.0	4.1	4.9
Public administration & defence	7.0	6.6	9.6	6.4	6.0	6.1	5.7	6.3	8.2	8.3	13.5
Education & health	9.1	10.4	9.5	8.8	10.2	10.4	10.1	11.3	11.4	12.8	14.6
Total, including others	100.0	100.0	100.0	100.0	100.0	100.0	100.0	100.0	100.0	100.0	100.0

Source: Central Statistical Office, Economic Trends, December 1992, pp. 120–21. Figures are based on 1991 GDP.

these parts of the UK. Thus the very factor that was supposed to be a disadvantage for these areas in the 1980s, a stubborn refusal to give up their reliance on the state, stood them in good stead in the recession. Again, decisions to relocate government functions away from the south east in the 1980s were a helpful factor for the recipient regions when the downturn came.

The Thatcher years saw a widening of the North–South economic divide to record proportions. The Major years, so far at least, have seen a narrowing of the gap. It remains to be seen whether this has been just the temporary effect of an unusual recession or the beginnings of a lasting change in Britain's economic geography. Before coming on to that, it is necessary to look in more detail at other aspects of the North–South question.

7

A JOBS DIVIDE?

> Work gives them the comfortable illusion of existing,
> even of being important. If they stopped working,
> they'd realize they simply weren't there at all, most
> of them. Just holes in the air, that's all. (Aldous
> Huxley, *Point Counter Point*)

The most basic economic and social need, for the majority of
adults in Britain, is a job. Employment brings with it necessary
income, but it also provides a route to social acceptance, to a
feeling of purpose and to a whole raft of other things which
distinguish those with a job from the involuntarily unemployed.
The importance of regional differences in unemployment rates
cannot be overstated. They provided the spur, from the 1920s
onwards, for the creation and development of regional policy.
From the Jarrow march through to the Toxteth riots, high
unemployment in the regions was seen as the economy's dark
side, present as the unwelcome guest at the feast when times
were good, but exploding in an outburst of anger and frustration
during recessions and slumps. Regional economic analysis began
with North–South differences in unemployment rates, and
often went no further, for the nature of the problem was plain
to see. The rules were straightforward enough. During economic
upturns, the unemployment gap between North and South narrowed. In recession it widened. But it always existed.

The 1990–92 recession, and the boom that preceded it, broke
those long-standing rules. Regional unemployment differences
widened during the growth years of the 1980s, but narrowed

Table 7.1 Regional unemployment rates (per cent), 1965–89

	1965–9	1970–74	1975–9	1980–84	1985–9
South East	1·3	1·4	2·8	6·0	6·6
East Anglia	1·7	2·3	3·3	6·6	6·6
South West	2·2	2·8	4·3	7·3	7·6
East Midlands	1·4	2·4	3·3	7·8	8·3
West Midlands	1·4	2·4	3·9	10·5	10·6
The South *	1·5	1·9	3·3	7·1	7·6
Yorks & Humberside	1·8	3·1	3·8	9·4	10·6
North West	2·0	3·5	4·9	11·0	11·9
North	3·5	4·8	5·6	12·4	13·4
Wales	3·4	3·8	5·2	11·0	11·4
Scotland	3·3	4·8	5·2	9·9	12·0
Northern Ireland	6·6	5·4	7·2	13·4	16·4
The North *	2·9	4·0	5·0	10·8	12·1
United Kingdom	2·0	2·4	4·0	8·7	9·4

* Averages weighted by population.
Source: Central Statistical Office, *Economic Trends, Annual Supplement*, 1992, pp. 120–21.

sharply in the subsequent recession. Anyone looking for North –South economic differences and using as their standing point 1993 unemployment statistics would conclude that there was not a problem. Table 7.1 summarizes the long-term nature of the unemployment differential. Table 7.2, using more recent data, provides the contrast.

Three general conclusions emerge from Table 7.1. The first is that, over a long period stretching from the mid-1960s to the late 1980s, unemployment in the South was lower than in the North. The average southern unemployment rate over the period, 4·3 per cent, compared with an average of 7 per cent for the North. Average unemployment rates across the South were, therefore, generally only between one half and two thirds of those in the North. The second general point is the success of the south east, as the lowest unemployment region in the country for the entire period (sharing that position with East Anglia in the most recent five-year period). Thirdly, with the exception of the west midlands, which jostled for position with Yorkshire and Humberside, every region of the South had unemployment below the rates prevailing in the northern regions. Close competition between the west midlands, generally the worst performing region in my definition of the South, and Yorkshire & Humberside, the best performing northern region, is a feature that shows through in many of the statistics. Many authors, indeed, include the east midlands but not the west midlands as part of the South. Had I done so in this book, then, as Table 7.1 indicates, the South's advantage would have been yet greater.

A long-term employment advantage for the South, and a tight labour market in the south east – often giving rise to labour shortages – has, then, been a basic building-block for students of Britain's North–South divide. Through recovery and recession, the gap remained. Sometimes it narrowed, sometimes it widened, but it was always there. But has it survived the 1990–92 recession?

Never before, in boom or slump, can the differences in unemployment experience between regions have been so marked. By early 1993, unemployment in the south east had virtually doubled since 1988. In all other parts of the South it had risen strongly. But in Scotland and Northern Ireland unemployment was down on its 1988 level, and in Wales, the north and the north west it had barely increased. Greater London's fall from grace was astonishing. In 1990, only the south east as a whole, East Anglia and the south west had lower unemployment rates. Less than three years later, the Greater London unemployment rate, at 11·7 per cent, was exceeded in only two regions, the north and Northern Ireland. Pulled higher by the Greater London unemployment problem, the south east lost its position as the region with the lowest proportion of people unemployed. By 1993, unemployment in the south east was higher than in East Anglia, the south west, east midlands and, most surprising of all, Wales and Scotland.

The special problem of London unemployment, indeed, is central to the change in the jobs divide in the early 1990s. Without it, four areas – the rest of the south east (Roseland), the south west, East Anglia and the east midlands – would have held on to unemployment rates of below 10 per cent. This, of

Table 7.2   Regional unemployment rates (per cent), 1988–93

	1988	1989	1990	1991	1992	1993
South East	5·4	3·9	4·0	7·0	9·4	10·4
of which Greater London	6·8	5·1	5·0	8·2	10·6	11·7
East Anglia	5·4	3·6	3·7	5·8	7·6	8·5
South West	6·2	4·5	4·4	7·1	9·1	9·8
East Midlands	7·1	5·4	5·1	7·2	8·9	9·5
West Midlands	8·9	6·6	5·9	8·6	10·7	11·4
*The South**	6·3	4·6	4·5	7·2	9·4	10·2
Yorks & Humberside	9·3	7·4	6·7	8·7	9·9	10·5
North West	10·4	8·5	7·7	9·4	10·5	10·8
North	11·9	9·9	8·7	10·4	11·3	12·2
Wales	9·8	7·3	6·6	8·7	9·8	10·2
Scotland	11·2	9·3	8·1	8·7	9·5	9·9
Northern Ireland	15·6	14·6	13·4	13·8	14·5	14·7
*The North**	10·8	8·9	8·0	9·4	11·2	10·9
United Kingdom	8·1	6·3	5·8	8·1	9·8	10·5

* Weighted averages, by population. 1993 figures are for February.
Source: Department of Employment, *Employment Gazette*, April 1993.

course, was the swathe of prosperity identified by Champion and Green in Chapter Five. The recession ate away at the relative prosperity of such areas, but had not removed it entirely. However, to exclude Greater London from the south east for the purposes of analysis is to perpetrate a cheat. London's success provided the basis of the south east's prosperity. Its problems are also the south east's problems.

Analysis at the county, or sub-regional, level, provides a further insight into the changing nature of the unemployment problem. Table 7.3 provides county unemployment rates at two points, October 1987 and December 1992, for the purposes of comparison.

In 1987 the ten counties with the lowest unemployment rates in Britain were all in the South. They were West Sussex (4·6 per cent), Berkshire (4·7 per cent), Oxfordshire (4·7 per cent), Hertfordshire (5·1 per cent), Buckinghamshire (5·2 per cent), Suffolk (6·7 per cent), Northamptonshire (7·4 per cent), Gloucestershire (7·4 per cent), Hampshire (7·6 per cent) and Cambridgeshire (7·6

Table 7.3 Unemployment rates by county (per cent)

	1987	1992		1987	1992
South East			Yorks & Humberside		
Bedfordshire	7·7	10·0	Humberside	13·4	11·6
Berkshire	4·7	7·3	North Yorkshire	8·7	6·7
Buckinghamshire	5·2	8·1	South Yorkshire	16·4	13·4
East Sussex	8·5	12·4	West Yorkshire	11·3	9·9
Essex	8·6	11·5	North West		
Greater London	8·8	11·6	Cheshire	11·3	8·5
Hampshire	7·6	9·6	Greater Manchester	13·2	10·6
Hertfordshire	5·1	8·9	Lancashire	11·5	9·0
Isle of Wight	11·6	14·2	Merseyside	19·2	15·3
Kent	9·0	11·0	North		
Oxfordshire	4·7	6·9	Cleveland	18·6	15·0
Surrey*	–	–	Cumbria	9·2	7·9
West Sussex	4·6	7·7	Durham	15·4	11·7
East Anglia			Northumberland	13·4	11·2
Cambridgeshire	7·6	8·2	Tyne & Wear	16·5	13·4
Norfolk	9·6	9·5	Wales		
Suffolk	6·7	7·6	Clwyd	14·1	9·2
South West			Dyfed	15·7	10·0
Avon	8·7	9·7	Gwent	14·1	10·7
Cornwall	15·0	13·8	Gwynedd	16·5	12·2
Devon	11·2	11·0	Mid-Glamorgan	15·9	12·5
Dorset	8·3	10·7	Powys	10·5	6·4
Gloucestershire	7·4	8·3	South Glamorgan	11·7	9·6
Somerset	8·1	9·0	West Glamorgan	14·8	10·0
Wiltshire	9·6	8·3	Scotland		
East Midlands			Borders	8·2	6·5
Derbyshire	11·3	10·0	Central	15·5	9·8
Leicestershire	7·7	8·3	Dumfries & Galloway	11·9	8·6
Lincolnshire	10·9	11·5	Fife	14·9	11·6
Northamptonshire	7·4	8·6	Grampian	8·5	5·2
Nottinghamshire	11·3	11·0	Highland	13·7	11·1
West Midlands			Lothian	12·0	8·6
Hereford &			Strathclyde	17·3	11·9
Worcester	9·6	9·6	Tayside	13·6	9·0
Shropshire	11·6	9·0	Islands	13·7	10·7
Staffordshire	10·3	10·0			
Warwickshire	9·0	9·1			
West Mids. County	13·7	13·0			

* Surrey is not considered to be a self-contained labour market, so no county-level unemployment rate is produced. Unemployment rates are not available at county level in Northern Ireland.

Sources: Central Statistical Office, *Regional Trends* 1988 edition, pp. 40–41; Department of Employment, *Employment Gazette*, February 1993, pp. S31–3.

per cent). By the end of 1992, only half of the lowest ten counties for unemployment were from the South. The lowest unemployment rate in Britain was in Grampian, followed by Powys in Wales, the Borders in Scotland, and North Yorkshire. The lowest ten in December 1992 were: Grampian (5·2 per cent), Powys (6·4 per cent), Borders (6·5 per cent), North Yorkshire (6·7 per cent), Oxfordshire (6·9 per cent), Berkshire (7·3 per cent), Suffolk (7·6 per cent), West Sussex (7·7 per cent), Cumbria (7·9 per cent) and Cambridgeshire (8·2 per cent).

Before moving on, it is worth noting another feature of the county-level unemployment data. This is the existence of very wide variations within regions. Thus, at the end of 1992, unemployment in the south east ranged from 6·9 per cent in Oxfordshire to 12·4 per cent in East Sussex and 14·2 per cent on the Isle of Wight. In the south west, Gloucestershire and Wiltshire had 8·3 per cent unemployment rates but Cornwall 13·8 per cent. In Yorkshire and Humberside, North Yorkshire's 6·7 per cent rate (the lowest in England) contrasted with South Yorkshire's 13·4 per cent. In the north, Cumbria's 7·9 per cent rate was little more than half of Cleveland's 15 per cent. Powys, with 6·4 per cent, was the jewel in the Welsh crown, but Mid-Glamorgan had 12·5 per cent. This has led commentators to suggest, with some justification, that the most serious economic differences in Britain are within, rather than between, regions. In general, though there are clear exceptions such as Cornwall, predominantly rural counties tend to have lower unemployment rates than mostly urban counties. The worst ten counties (excluding Northern Ireland) for unemployment in 1987 – Merseyside (19·2 per cent), Cleveland (18·6 per cent), Strathclyde (17·3 per cent), Tyne and Wear (16·5 per cent), Gwynedd (16·5 per cent), South Yorkshire (16·4 per cent), Mid-Glamorgan (15·9 per cent) Dyfed (15·7 per cent), Central Scotland (15·5 per cent) and Durham (15·4 per cent) – were all in the North. By contrast, by the end of 1992, southern names featured in the list of the worst ten. The worst-hit counties were: Merseyside (15·3 per cent), Cleveland (15 per cent), Isle of Wight (14·2 per cent), Cornwall (13·8 per cent), Tyne & Wear (13·4 per cent), South Yorkshire (13·4 per cent), West Midlands Metropolitan County (13 per cent),

Mid-Glamorgan (12·5 per cent), East Sussex (12·4 per cent), and Gwynedd (12·2 per cent).

The 1990–92 recession therefore produced a substantial evening-out of the misery of unemployment across Britain. This is true both at the regional level and at sub-regional, or county, level. As we saw in the previous chapter, there were big differences in employment experience between regions during the recession. Later in this chapter I shall examine some other facets of regional employment differences, to see how deeply this equalization of unemployment goes, and whether it is likely to be sustained. But first it is necessary to reflect on some of the history of regional employment differences.

UNEMPLOYMENT AND MANUFACTURING DECLINE

In the 1930s, areas which were heavily reliant on the former staple industries of coal, cotton, iron and shipbuilding were most heavily affected by the depression. As Eric Hobsbawm pointed out in his book '*Industry and Empire*':

The real tragedy was that of areas and towns relying on a single industry, prosperous in 1913, ruined between the wars. In 1913–14 about 3 per cent of the workers in Wales had been unemployed – rather less than the national average. In 1934 – after recovery had begun – 37 per cent of the labour force in Glamorgan, 36 per cent of that in Monmouth, were out of work. Two thirds of the men of Ferndale, three quarters of those in Brynmawr, Dowlais and Blaina, 70 per cent of those in Merthyr, had nothing to do except stand at street corners and curse the system which put them there. The people of Jarrow, in Durham, lived by the Palmers' shipyard. When it closed in 1933 Jarrow was derelict, with eight out of ten of its workers jobless, and having like as not lost all their savings in the crash of the yard, which had so long been their harsh and noisy universe. (1969, p. 208)

The recession of the early 1980s was, if anything, less discriminating in its effects. The Lancashire of the 1930s partly compensated for the devastation of its cotton industry through the performance of other manufacturing industries. But when manufacturing output slumped by nearly a fifth from the middle of 1979 to the first quarter of 1981, even the most diversified manufacturing town was hit. And the fall in manufacturing employment from 7·1 million in 1979 to less than 5 million by 1988 ensured that the employment consequences of the manufacturing shake-out were both persistent and severe.

ICI, Britain's biggest industrial company, cut its UK workforce from 89,400 in 1979 to 61,800 by 1983, and further to 55,800 by 1987. GKN, in the 1930s Britain's biggest manufacturing company, slashed the number of its UK employees between 1979 and 1983. By 1987 it had just 19,140 employees in Britain, less than 30 per cent of the 1979 total. Lucas, manufacturer of automotive and aerospace products, had nearly 70,000 UK employees in 1979. By 1983 the workforce had fallen by over 20,000; and by 1987 by nearly 30,000. These examples, while dramatic, come from companies which survived the recession. Others disappeared completely, often with devastating consequences for individual towns.

On top of this, as in the 1930s, there was a dramatic rationalization of activity and employment in those staple industries which remained heavily regional in their structure – industries such as coal, steel and shipbuilding. When the British Steel Corporation closed its steelworks in Consett, County Durham in the summer of 1980, the effect on the local economy was devastating. The closure resulted in 3,700 job losses, to add to more than 400 lost in the closure of the plateworks in the previous winter. That summer, there were only eight job vacancies in the town for 1,400 school leavers. As Adrian Sinfield wrote in his book *What Unemployment Means*, 'The blow was all the greater because the steelworks had dominated the local economy for 140 years. In a classic company town, the Consett Iron Company had owned the shops, the houses and the collieries as well as the steelworks' (1981, p. 65).

The emergence of sharp regional differences in employment and unemployment was guaranteed. In 1980 and 1981 together, there were over one million confirmed redundancies, and nearly 70 per cent of them in the traditional industrial areas of the west midlands, the north west, Yorkshire and Humberside, the north, Scotland and Wales.

There are several striking features about the pattern of

Table 7.4 Manufacturing employment by region

	1971 (000)	1979 (000)	1992* (000)	Change, 1971/79 (per cent)	Change, 1979/92 (per cent)
South East	2,207	1,871	1,101	−15·2	−41·2
East Anglia	192	206	162	7·3	−21·4
South West	423	439	317	3·8	−28·8
West Midlands	1,107	985	556	−11·0	−43·6
East Midlands	599	606	442	1·2	−27·1
Yorks & Humberside	780	708	455	−9·2	−35·7
North West	1,155	971	560	−15·9	−42·3
North	444	410	253	−7·7	−38·3
Wales	324	315	220	−2·8	−30·2
Scotland	676	604	361	−10·7	−40·2
Great Britain	7,890	7,113	4,426	−9.8	−37.8

* September data.
Sources: Department of Employment, *Employment Gazette*, Historical Supplement, February 1987; *Employment Gazette*, February 1993.

manufacturing employment over the 20 years or so from 1971, as summarized in Table 7.4. The first is the extent of the fall, nearly 45 per cent, in national manufacturing employment over the period. Some of this fall was due to a reclassification of manufacturing jobs, for example when companies contracted out work previously done by their own employees, for example cleaning and maintenance, to outside service firms. But most of it was genuine. The second, and perhaps most surprising, is that the south east is easily the major area of manufacturing employment in Britain and, in consequence, has suffered a very substantial decline in employment in this sector. In both the first (1971–9) and second periods (1979–92), the decline in manufacturing employment in the south east was substantial, exceeding the national average fall. There are, indeed, important differences within the latter period. From 1979 until about 1987 the sharpest shake-out in manufacturing jobs was in the North. Manufacturing employment in the south west, East Anglia and the east midlands increased over this period. Since then, the balance has shifted, with far slower rates of decline in the North and, in the case of Yorkshire and Humberside and Wales, higher manufacturing employment in 1992 than in 1987.

The south east, despite having long had the biggest number of manufacturing employees, also traditionally had the benefit of a more diversified economy. In 1979, the proportion of employees engaged in manufacturing by region ranged from 25·1 per cent in the south east to 44 per cent in the west midlands. By 1992, the same two regions occupied top and bottom positions, but the range had shifted downwards and varied between 16 per cent in the south east and 29·4 per cent in the west midlands. There are, of course, two components to such shifts. The first is the decline in manufacturing employment itself which, while individual regional rates differed, no area escaped over the 1979–92 period. The other is the rate of growth of alternative employment. There is clearly a different quality to a fall in the share of manufacturing employment which occurs in an environment of fast-expanding employment in financial and business services, retailing, administration and the leisure industries, from one in which manufacturing employment has fallen and everything else has been stagnant. Although the above description over-simplifies the distinction, the former was closest to the 1980s experience of the South and the latter to that of the North.

BOOM AND BUST IN SERVICE INDUSTRIES

Had the sharp fall in industrial employment during the 1980s been matched by a similar decline in other sectors, the picture, grim enough as it was, would have been even blacker. But there were compensations, and the biggest of these was the growth of employment in service industries. Here, the 1970s and 1980s differed significantly. In the earlier period, the growth of employment in public services provided the main counterweight to industrial redundancies, even if there was no precise match between the two. The redundant steelworker would probably not take on a job as a hospital porter, but his wife might find herself employed as a medical ancillary. In the 1980s, as private services took up the running from the much less rapidly expanding public sector, she was more likely to find a job on a supermarket check-out.

There were different impetuses behind the growth in private

service industries. On one side there were those occupations, notably in retailing and other distribution work, whose expansion was related to local demand and therefore to regional prosperity. On the other were those service industries which typically catered for outside demand, into which category would fall tourism and, perhaps the best example of all, the financial services industry centred on the City of London.

In both categories, the traditional industrial areas hardest hit by the industrial recession were poorly placed. Large-scale redundancies and uncertain employment prospects for those remaining in work had a depressing effect on spending power in whole regions. The budding entrepreneur with a consumer service ready to supply to the public would hardly choose such areas in which to develop his idea. Business services such as accountancy, marketing and public relations could hardly expand rapidly in an environment of industrial retrenchment. Similarly, the old industrial heartlands were, on the face of it, barren ground on which to attempt to base a tourist industry. Eric Hobsbawm's observation, again from *Industry and Empire*, relates to the 1930s but it captures the flavour of the problem as it was seen in the early 1980s:

The grimy, roaring, bleak industrial areas of the nineteenth century – in northern England, Scotland and Wales – had never been very beautiful or comfortable, but they had been active and prosperous. Now all that remained was the grime, the bleakness, and the terrible silence of the factories and mines which did not work, the shipyards which were closed. (1969, p. 208)

During the 1980s, and subsequently, there has been a considerable effort to develop a significant industry built upon Britain's industrial heritage, and this should not be belittled. But in terms of employment, such projects have scarcely offered any compensation for the loss of the original industries on which they are based.

The traditional industrial regions were also poorly placed to take full advantage of the financial services revolution. The financial services industry, based on the City of London, has undergone some regional diversification during the 1980s. But typically this has involved the movement of administrative offices from London to other parts of the South, notably the south west and East Anglia. Only in the later 1980s did the North, and in particular Yorkshire and Humberside, begin to attract significant new financial services' operations. Despite this, the great expansion of financial services, in particular in the run-up to the Stock Exchange 'Big Bang' of October 1986, was of greatest benefit to the south east. In 1979, less than 11 per cent of the region's employment was in banking, finance, insurance, business services and leasing. By 1987, the proportion was more than 15 per cent, roughly twice that of the northern regions, and of Wales and Scotland.

Allowing for all this, it must be said that the growth of employment in service industries in the traditional industrial regions was a key compensating factor in preventing regional employment imbalances from growing even wider than they have done. An analysis by Cambridge Econometrics, in their 1987 edition of *Regional Economic Prospects*, suggested that, after allowing for differences in population growth and special factors such as the south east's dominance of financial services, most of the northern regions performed reasonably well in terms of employment in service occupations, and that their relative performance improved as the 1980s progressed.

In the period 1979–83, against a national average expansion of 1·3 per cent a year employment in private services, the south west recorded an annual average growth rate of 3·3 per cent, followed by 2·2 per cent in East Anglia, 2 per cent in the east midlands, 1·8 per cent in the west midlands and Yorkshire and Humberside, 1·5 per cent in the south east, 1·1 per cent in Northern Ireland, 0·5 per cent in the north, 0·3 per cent in Wales, 0·1 per cent in the north west, and an annual average fall of 0·4 per cent in Scotland.

Over the period 1983 to 1986, within a faster national average growth rate of 3·9 per cent a year, the league table was headed by East Anglia and Yorkshire and Humberside with 5·5 per cent, followed by the west midlands with 4·9 per cent, Wales 4·8 per cent, the north 4·7 per cent, the south east 4·5 per cent, the south west and the east midlands 3·4 per cent,

Table 7.5 Service-sector employment, by region, 1979–92

	1971 (000)	1989 (000)	1992 (000)	Change, 1971–89 (%)	Change, 1979–92 (%)
South East	4,544	5,803	5,391	27·7	−7·1
East Anglia	316	535	541	69·3	1·1
South West	741	1,230	1,247	66·0	1·4
East Midlands	559	932	956	66·7	2·6
West Midlands	908	1,253	1,209	38·0	−3·5
Yorks & Humberside	855	1,218	1,219	42·5	0·1
North West	1,332	1,595	1,597	19·7	0·1
North	584	714	704	22·3	−1·4
Wales	472	649	644	37·5	−0·7
Scotland	1,053	1,344	1,410	27·6	4·9
Great Britain	11,364	15,273	14,918	34·4	−2·3

Sources: Department of Employment, *Employment Gazette*, Historical Supplement No. 1, February 1987; *Employment Gazette*, February 1993.

Scotland and the north west 2·7 per cent and Northern Ireland 1·1 per cent.

While manufacturing employment has been a story of almost continual decline since the early 1970s, this has clearly not been the case for service industries. The 1980s was a boom-time for many service industries just as, for most sectors of manufacturing, it was a struggle for survival. Overall, service-sector employment grew by two million in the 1970s, and by a further two million in the 1980s. It was the uneven distribution of these new service-industry jobs that shaped Britain's North–South jobs divide. And it has been the subsequent decline in such jobs that has helped even out regional differences in unemployment. In the 1980s, in particular, when banking, insurance and finance jobs grew by a million, the South was favoured. But as that expansion has unwound, the South, and most particularly the south east, has suffered.

Table 7.5 shows this effect at work. The three regions bordering the south east – East Anglia, the south west and the east midlands – easily outperformed the rest of the country in growth in service-sector employment. Even the 1990–92 recession did not seriously tarnish the record of these three regions. Employment in services by the autumn of 1992 was higher than in 1989, if only marginally. The financial services' sector was the south east's great success story, but overall employment growth in services in the region over the 1970s and 1980s was below the national average. Only two regions, the north west and north, recorded a noticeably worse employment increase. Scotland's expansion was similar to that of the south east. The south east's strength in services was due not to rapid growth in employment but rather to the fact that a relatively modest expansion started from such a high employment base. By the same token, however, the fact that the south east registered the biggest decline in services employment over the 1989–92 period meant a lot of job losses (410,000).

Combining the period of expansion of the 1970s and 1980s with the consolidation or retrenchment of the early 1990s produces some very interesting results. East Anglia (71·2 per cent overall employment growth) tops the list, as might be expected, and is followed closely by the east midlands (71 per cent) and the south west (68·3 per cent). But the next highest growth rates are all in the North. They are: Yorkshire and Humberside (42·6 per cent), Wales (36·4 per cent) and Scotland (33·9 per cent). Next is the west midlands (33·1 per cent), followed by two northern regions, the north (20·5 per cent) and the north west (19·9 per cent). Bringing up the rear, its relatively modest growth rate of the 1970s and 1980s cut down to size by the recession, was the south east, with an increase of 18·6 per cent, well under 1 per cent a year, over the 1971–92 period.

AN EMPLOYMENT DIVIDE?

Combining these manufacturing and service-sector trends with the growth in self-employment in all regions since 1979, allows some broader judgements to be made about differences in labour-market performance between regions. Table 7.6 shows the growth (or decline) in the employed labour force by region.

The different experiences of manufacturing and service-sector employment between the regions in the 1980s were part of a wider difference in the growth and availability of jobs. Thus, from 1979 to 1987 there was a small, 1·5 per cent fall in the

Table 7.6 Employment growth by region

	June 79 (000)	June 87 (000)	Autumn 92 (000)	Change 1979–87 (%)	Change 1979–92 (%)
South East					
Employees in employment	7,473	7,443	6,834	−0·4	−8·6
Self-employed	651	1,032	1,080	58·5	65·9
Employed labour force*	8,124	8,475	8,041	4·3	−1·0
East Anglia					
Employees in employment	702	796	819	13·4	16·7
Self-employed	79	127	132	60·8	67·1
Employed labour force	781	923	970	18·2	24·2
South West					
Employees in employment	1,598	1,593	1,757	−0·3	9·9
Self-employed	146	278	349	90·4	139.0
Employed labour force	1,744	1,871	2,144	7·3	22·9
West Midlands					
Employees in employment	2,241	2,051	1,965	−8·5	−12·3
Self-employed	141	209	270	48·2	91·5
Employed labour force	2,382	2,260	2,290	−5·1	−3·9
East Midlands					
Employees in employment	1,555	1,529	1,643	−1·7	5·7
Self-employed	116	189	209	62·9	80·2
Employed labour force	1,671	1,718	1,893	2·8	13·3
Yorks & Humberside					
Employees in employment	2,011	1,802	1,915	−10·4	−4·8
Self-employed	134	236	244	76·1	82·1
Employed labour force	2,145	2,038	2,219	−5·0	3·4
North West					
Employees in employment	2,676	2,262	2,357	−15·5	−11·9
Self-employed	214	279	316	30·4	47·7
Employed labour force	2,890	2,541	2,730	−12·1	−5·5
North					
Employees in employment	1,248	1,090	1,119	−12·7	−10·3
Self-employed	77	108	122	40·3	58·4
Employed labour force	1,325	1,198	1,284	−9·6	−3·1
Wales					
Employees in employment	1,033	863	988	−16·5	−4·4
Self-employed	124	148	155	19·4	25·0
Employed labour force	1,157	1,011	1,172	−12·6	1·3
Scotland					
Employees in employment	2,102	1,886	1,956	−10·3	−6·9
Self-employed	160	194	214	21·3	33·8
Employed labour force	2,262	2,080	2,225	−8·0	−1·6
Great Britain					
Employees in employment	22,638	21,316	21,353	−5·8	−5·7
Self-employed	1,842	2,801	3,091	52·1	67·8
Employed labour force	24,480	24,117	24,967	−1·5	2·0

* Employed labour force includes people on government employment and training programmes and unpaid family workers.
Sources: Department of Employment, *Labour Force Survey*, 1987; *Quarterly Labour Force Bulletin*, March 1993.

employed labour force in Great Britain. Four regions, the south east (+ 4·3 per cent), East Anglia (+ 18·2 per cent), the south west (+ 7·3 per cent), and the east midlands (+ 2·8 per cent) all recorded increases, however. All others showed declines, ranging from 5 per cent in Yorkshire and Humberside, through to the west midlands (− 5·1 per cent), Scotland (− 8 per cent), the north (− 9·6 per cent), the north west (− 12·1 per cent), and Wales (− 12·6 per cent).

The five years from 1987 to 1992 produced significant shifts in the regional balance. Overall, the employed labour force grew by 850,000 between the summer of 1987 and the autumn of 1992, an increase of 3·5 per cent. The south east emerges as the biggest, indeed the only, casualty over this period, with its employed labour force declining by 434,000 or 5·1 per cent. In all other regions there were rises, with no discernible regional pattern. Wales, up 15·9 per cent between 1987 and 1992, showed the biggest increase, followed by the south west (14·6 per cent), the east midlands (10·2 per cent), Yorkshire and Humberside (8·9 per cent), the north west (7·4 per cent), the north (7·2 per cent), Scotland (7 per cent), East Anglia (5·1 per cent) and the west midlands (1·3 per cent).

The experience of the west midlands was an interesting one. For much of the post-war period, due to the strength of its manufacturing industry, the west midlands was, in terms of prosperity and employment, an honorary member of the South. Indeed, cities such as Coventry, with their high manufacturing wages and low unemployment, numbered among the most prosperous in the country. All this changed abruptly in the 1980–81 recession, when the west midlands was severely hit by the manufacturing slump. The employed labour force in the area fell by 11 per cent from 1979 to 1983, compared with a national average fall of 7 per cent.

The area's performance improved in the mid-1980s, rising employment apparently explained by the area's traditional strengths – a skilled and adaptable labour force and a convenient central location – reasserting themselves after the shock of the recession. Additionally, the region's central position may have rendered it particularly suitable for the expansion of distribution and other service-sector activities. A third explanation comes from the fact that, in 1984, the west midlands acquired assisted area status within what remained of regional policy, both because of the severity of the earlier manufacturing downturn and, arguably, the area's electoral importance. However, the west midlands suffered greatly in the 1990–92 recession and, in terms of its employed labour force, showed only a marginal increase over the 1987–92 period, with only the south east turning in a worse performance. It is hard to escape the conclusion that the west midlands lost its traditional vitality in the 1980–81 recession, and may never regain it.

SELF-EMPLOYMENT

Two very important labour-market trends in the 1980s were the rapid growth of self-employment and the increasing importance of part-time work – the development of the so-called flexible workforce. The Conservative Government has actively encouraged the growth in self-employment, both directly through schemes such as the Enterprise Allowance – which provides a weekly allowance for the first year for unemployed people starting up their own businesses, and indirectly through reductions in taxation levels. Lower rates of income tax may have had the effect of bringing activity into the official economy from the black economy, as the relative advantages of not declaring income and running the risk of being caught, against those of paying tax, have shifted.

Nationalized industries such as British Coal and the British Steel Corporation (privatized in November 1988) have run extensive programmes of encouraging former employees to set up on their own alongside large-scale redundancy schemes. The more enlightened private-sector employers have also done this, from which, it might be thought, some of the fastest growth rates for self-employment would have been in those areas where there has been the biggest proportionate shake-out in manufacturing employment.

Self-employment cannot, however, expand in a vacuum. Most self-employed people are involved in the services sector, which, as described above, relies for its expansion on both local and external demand. The same factors which limited the growth of employment in services in the traditional industrial regions have also hampered the growth in self-employment. Table 7.6 showed that national growth in self-employment from 1979 to 1992 was impressive at 67·8 per cent, albeit from a fairly low base. But within this there was a range for self-employment growth in the regions, running from just 25 per cent in Wales to 139 per cent in the south west. Growth rates for the south east, East Anglia and the east and west midlands ranged between 65 and 91·5 per cent. In the North, with the exception of a strong 82 per cent expansion in Yorkshire and Humberside, self-employment grew at a slower rate.

One suggestion has been that this is due to an uneven distribution around the country of entrepreneurial ability and willingness to take risks. Clearly the problems of adjusting to self-employment are more difficult for someone who has spent thirty years in a steelworks or twenty years down a mine than for a magazine journalist who decides to set up as a freelance. In earlier periods of history, entrepreneurs came from all parts of the country and Scotland's poor performance in the 1980s would appear to suggest either that something radical has changed in the national character, or that other factors were at work. Typically, those who are most willing to become entrepreneurs have already worked in a small firm, usually in a service industry, and own their own property. With a greater proportion of people fitting into both of these categories, the South was the ideal breeding ground for the self-employment element of the 'enterprise culture' of the Thatcher years.

Anne Green of the Institute for Employment Research in Warwick, in her paper 'The Geography of Economic Activity', used 1991 Census of Population data to shed more light on, among other things, regional differences in self-employment. She found that the highest rates of self-employment were in rural areas. For example, the rate among males in Powys was 33 per cent, reflecting the importance of farming. The lowest rates were in areas traditionally dominated by heavy industries, the old shipyard and steel towns, in Scotland and the north. Between

Table 7.7   Male self-employment by district, 1991

Rank	Top 15	%	Bottom 15	%
1	Isles of Scilly	42·8	Clydebank	6·7
2	Radnorshire	38·5	Inverclyde	7·0
3	Ceredigion	34·8	Motherwell	7·3
4	Leominster	33·4	Dunfermline	7·6
5	Montgomeryshire	33·2	Middlesbrough	7·7
6	North Cornwall	33·2	Easington	7·7
7	Carmarthen	32·8	Glasgow City	7·8
8	South Shropshire	32·3	Wansbeck	7·8
9	Dwyfor	32·3	Scunthorpe	8·0
10	Torridge	32·1	South Tyneside	8·0
11	West Somerset	31·8	Knowsley	8·3
12	West Devon	31·4	Langbaurgh-on-Tees	8·3
13	Eden	31·1	Hartlepool	8·3
14	Meirionnydd	30·6	Barrow-in-Furness	8·3
15	South Hams	30·5	Stockton-on-Tees	8·4

Source: A. Green, 'The Geography of Economic Activity', p. 8.

the previous Census in 1981 and the latest in 1991, there was a general increase in male self-employment, but the fastest rises were in the south east – in Kent, Hertfordshire, Essex, Surrey and Bedfordshire.

Overall, however, while North–South variations in the growth of self-employment were important, the key factor in determining what proportion of the workforce is self-employed is whether an area is predominantly rural or mainly industrial, as Table 7.7 shows.

Apart from this, the evidence suggests that more basic economic factors, such as the local demand for services and the fact that the employment structure of the South prior to the 1980s was one which could adjust more easily to self-employment, were of greater importance than regional differences in the supply of able entrepreneurs. Government inducements to the unemployed to set up in business on their own undoubtedly helped to foster self-employment growth, although there is evidence (such as the University of Durham study quoted in Chapter Two) that in many cases the new entrepreneurs were encouraged to launch themselves without adequate preparation or back-up.

Moving up the scale slightly from individual self-employment, how did the 'enterprise culture' manifest itself in the growth of small and medium-sized businesses? A major study, *The State of British Enterprise* by the Small Business Research Centre of the University of Cambridge found that, as with self-employment, urban–rural differences were important. However, there were also significant disparities between North and South. The study, carried out in 1991, found that most northern small businesses were relatively old, with a third set up before 1970, while the South had a higher proportion of new, young firms, particularly in service industries. This may not, however, be a big advantage for the South. Other research has shown that small firms are most vulnerable in their first ten years. Northern small and medium-sized enterprises tended to be engaged in manufacturing, while southern firms were predominantly in business services. Partly because of this, northern firms tended to employ unskilled, semi-skilled and skilled manual workers, while those in the South employed higher proportions of white-collar clerical and administrative staff, higher professionals and technologists, as well as managers. Overall, however, the growth of employment in such enterprises did not differ significantly between North and South and, at the time the survey was carried out, in the summer of 1991, northern firms were more ambitious in their expansion plans.

PART-TIMERS

Part-time work has always constituted an important element of labour supply in Britain. Traditionally associated only with women, it has spread across the sexes. Not all part-time employment is the main source of income for the individual concerned. The autumn 1992 Labour Force Survey showed that 970,000 people in Britain had a second job, up from 700,000 in 1984. This figure probably understates the true number of second jobs, in that many are likely to be in the black economy and thus not disclosed.

By the end of 1992 there were 5·64 million part-time workers in Britain – nearly a third of the number of full-time workers.

Table 7.8 Female part-time employment

	Dec 1979 (000)	Dec 1987 (000)	Sept 1992 (000)	Change 1979–87 (%)	Change 1987–92 (%)
South East	1,296·9	1,420·1	1,371	9·5	−3.5
East Anglia	123·7	165·1	172	33·5	4·2
South West	290·8	328·4	430	12·9	30·9
West Midlands	383·2	414·8	387	8·2	−6·7
East Midlands	269·1	308·7	341	14·7	10·5
Yorks & Humberside	366·1	408·8	445	11·7	8·9
North West	475·4	513·2	518	8·0	0·9
North	210·6	236·7	245	12·4	3·5
Wales	168·5	182·3	213	8·2	16·8
Scotland	333·5	389·4	416	16·8	6·8
Great Britain	3,917·8	4,367·5	4,539	11.5	3.9

Sources: Department of Employment, *Employment Gazette*, Historical Supplement No. 1, February 1987, table 1.5; Department of Employment, *Employment Gazette*, May 1988, table 1.5; Department of Employment, *Employment Gazette*, February 1993, table 1.5.

Of the part-time total, 4·54 million were women and 1·1 million men. The growth of part-time employment, up by 17 per cent among employees and 24·8 per cent among the self-employed since 1984, has sparked a debate about the quality and magnitude of employment growth in Britain. Part-time employment continued to grow during the 1990–92 recession, even as the number of full-time jobs was falling sharply. There have been specific examples – the retailer Burton in early 1993 was one – of employers replacing full-time employees with part-timers. Much part-time work is relatively poorly paid and unskilled. Some of it is temporary in nature. In terms of hours and income, a part-time job is not the same as a full-time one. Analyses which have been conducted on the basis of converting part-time jobs to their full-time equivalent, typically by assuming that two part-time jobs are equivalent to a full-time one, showed, even before the 1990–92 recession, that the labour market was rather less buoyant than the raw employment figures suggested.

Against this, it can be argued that the availability of part-time work has itself stimulated additional growth in the labour force. Married women with families who would have found it difficult if not impossible to accept a full-time position have been drawn into the labour market by the availability of part-time employment.

Figures for the growth in female part-time employment by region are given in Table 7.8. Corresponding data for male part-timers are not available because, until recently, it was not considered important enough to warrant separate attention. The intriguing thing about the regional statistics for female part-timers is that, with the exception of East Anglia's very strong growth in the 1979–87 period, and that in the south west from 1987 to 1992, no strong regional biases are evident. Thus, taking the period as a whole, Scotland recorded above average growth, as did the east midlands, East Anglia and the south west. But the south east was below average.

Here again, it is necessary to look a little deeper into the data. Professor Alan Townsend of the University of Durham, in a detailed regional analysis of part-time employment over an earlier period, 1971–81, found important differences in the role of part-time work between different parts of the country.

In particular, he found, in regions where overall employment growth was slowest, there was a greater tendency for part-time jobs to act as a substitute for full-time work:

Important as it is, much of the growth of part-time jobs (indeed probably the majority) represents substitution for jobs which would otherwise have grown in the full-time sector, providing on average higher hourly incomes. Variable levels of substitution of part-time for full-time workers as between different areas could be a source of variation in the growth of part-time employment. (1986, p. 238)

In other words, in areas of generally strong employment growth, part-time work may have represented genuine additional jobs, while in slow growth areas it merely took the place of full-time work. In the 1980s, particularly in the North, it was a fairly common situation for the male head of household to be unemployed, with the family income, or at least the supplement to social security benefits, coming from the wife with her part-time job. The quality of employment has suffered. More recently, this

Table 7.9   Activity rates, by region, autumn 1992

	Employment* (%)	Unemployment* (%)	Activity Rate* (%)
South East	58·4	6·6	65·0
East Anglia	58·7	5·6	64·3
South West	56·7	5·7	62·5
East Midlands	59·1	5·3	64·4
West Midlands	55·7	7·4	63·1
Yorks & Humberside	56·8	6·0	62·8
North West	54·8	6·2	61·0
North	53·1	7·1	60·1
Wales	51·2	6·1	57·3
Scotland	55·8	6·3	62·1
Great Britain	56·6	6·4	63·0

* Figures are percentages of all those aged 16 and over in each region. Employment includes self-employment.
Source: Department of Employment, *Labour Force Survey – Quarterly Bulletin*, March 1993, table 11.

type of analysis can be extended to areas such as the south west, where the growth of full-time employment was previously strong.

ACTIVITY RATES

This chapter has shown that the recession of 1990–92 has produced a sharp narrowing of regional differences in unemployment rates. It has also shown that, particularly in the early 1990s, the South has done worse in terms of overall employment (and self-employment) than the North, and that this is largely explained by the difficulties of the south east. To complete the picture, one final measure is needed. This is the activity rate – the proportion of the population of working age in each region which is in work, or actively seeking work. As Table 7.9 shows, significant regional variations remain in activity rates. In the South, a higher proportion of those who could work (defined as people aged 16 and over), are in employment or self-employment than in the North. This suggests that, in spite of the South's difficulties in the 1990–92 recession, the North has not yet closed

Table 7.10   Increase in male economic inactivity rates, 1981–91

Rank	Top 10	% point change	Bottom 10	% point change
1	West Glamorgan	8·8	Surrey	1·7
2	Mid Glamorgan	8·0	Northamptonshire	1·8
3	Merseyside	7·8	Wiltshire	2·1
4	Dyfed	7·5	East Sussex	2·2
5	Strathclyde	7·5	West Sussex	2·3
6	Tyne & Wear	7·4	Oxfordshire	2·4
7	Cleveland	7·2	Bedfordshire	2·4
8	Durham	7·1	Hertfordshire	2·4
9	South Yorkshire	6·6	Buckinghamshire	2·5
10	Gwent	6·2	Berkshire	2·5

Source: A. Green, 'The Geography of Economic Activity', p. 7.

the employment gap. The position of Wales and the north, with low employment rates, stands out. Overall, the south east had the highest activity rate in the autumn of 1992, although with an unemployment rate that was, on this measure, above the national average. In general, southern regions had higher activity rates than those in the north. These comparisons could be affected by the fact that a proportion of the elderly move to retirement areas. However, the south east, with a plethora of retirement resorts on the South Coast, has traditionally been a net gainer from such moves.

Anne Green's analysis of the 1991 Census of Population provides further insight on this topic. Between the 1981 and 1991 censuses, economic activity among men declined on a national basis. In 1991, male economic activity ranged from under 80 per cent in Mid-Glamorgan and West Glamorgan, to more than 90 per cent in the Shetland Islands, Northampton-shire, Wiltshire, Berkshire, Bedfordshire and Buckinghamshire. Wales, in particular, had high levels of inactivity among men. Of seventeen local authority districts where the male inactivity rate exceeded 20 per cent, twelve were in South Wales. The other districts above 20 per cent were in Glasgow, Liverpool and Manchester. According to Green:

In all counties/regions there was a decline in male economic activity rates (and an increase in male economic inactivity rates) over the decade. The increase in economic inactivity rates ranged from under two percentage points in Surrey and Northamptonshire to at least eight percentage points in West Glamorgan and Mid Glamorgan. A North–South divide is evident, with increases in economic inactivity rates tending to be lowest in southern England and highest in Wales, north east England, Merseyside and west central Scotland. (1992, p. 2)

Such results are not, perhaps, surprising. It has long been the case that for, say, redundant steelworkers or miners in their fifties, there is no real alternative to the job they have just lost except, perhaps, for low-grade service-sector occupations such as stacking supermarket shelves. Declining economic activity among men reflects such unpalatable choices, as well as the corrosive effect of high unemployment rates sustained over a very long period. Southerners, even after the pain of the 1990–92 recession, still have a big advantage in this area. High unemployment is a relatively recent phenomenon and, as such, is not yet ingrained in the attitudes of southern regions. An unemployment culture could easily develop, but it will take time. Because of this, while many of the statistics indeed point to a levelling out of employment (and unemployment) differences between regions, activity rates, and changes in them, show that below the surface there remain significant North–South disparities. Some parts of the South, plainly, are rapidly developing an unemployment culture. One thinks of inner London, or south-coast towns such as Brighton. But, for the most part, the South's problems can be regarded, optimistically perhaps, as temporary. Later in the book I shall examine whether this optimism is justified.

8

THE HOUSING MARKET

For a man's house is his castle. (Sir Edward Coke
(1552–1634), *Institutes*, 'Commentary upon Littleton')

There was a time when the level of house prices, together with changes and regional variations in that level, would have been of no concern to the majority of the population of Britain. At the time of the First World War owner-occupiers comprised only one tenth of all households. By the end of the Second World War the share had increased, but it was still only up to a quarter. The rapid development of the property-owning democracy, to the point where two thirds of residential properties are owner-occupied, is thus a comparatively recent phenomenon, given an additional boost in the 1980s by the Conservative Government's policy of selling council houses to their tenants at prices below market value.

The growth of owner-occupation, at first at the expense of the private rented sector – which earlier in the century acted as the main source of housing – and latterly at the expense of the public sector, has been encouraged in other ways. The tax system, in offering reliefs on mortgage interest payments, has provided an important subsidy for home-ownership. So ingrained in the expectations of the British public has the system of mortgage interest relief become and so politically sensitive were suggestions of its abolition that even a reforming Conservative Chancellor of the Exchequer, Nigel Lawson, did not feel able to scrap it, even if he had been allowed to by Margaret Thatcher. Lawson did, however, later reveal that he had resisted pressure from Thatcher to raise the ceiling for mortgage interest relief from £30,000. And both he and a subsequent Chancellor, Norman Lamont (the latter under John Major), successfully restricted the scope of the tax relief, of which more later.

Property-ownership was also encouraged by the almost universal belief that housing represented one of the safest and best-performing forms of investment in Britain during the economic and financial turbulence of the 1970s and 1980s. The general belief was that house prices only went upwards, although this apparent iron law proved to be fairly flexible during and after the recession of the early 1980s, when house prices in many parts of the North and Midlands fell back under the impact of rising unemployment and falling housing demand. It was shattered completely, as we will see, in the 1990–92 recession.

It was not necessarily the case, in spite of rising housing prices, that residential property always provided a sound investment. Calculations by Peter Spencer (1988), then with the securities firm Credit Suisse First Boston, suggested that, after allowing for spending on house improvements, maintenance, mortgage interest and local authority rates, the net money return on property averaged 8.4 per cent a year during the 1970s. But over the period 1980–87 – before the onset of the last great price surge in the boom, and the subsequent recession – the return was marginally negative, at minus 0.9 per cent a year – high mortgage rates, maintenance costs and local authority rates offsetting rising house prices. In those parts of the country that hardly participated in the house price booms of the 1980s, the return was significantly negative.

Even so, it is doubtful whether even the most financially astute of home owners calculated the full return on their investment in housing. A house, it is argued, is the only investment which provides a roof over one's head. And the obsession, once the preserve of the middle classes but now entirely classless, was with one aspect of the housing equation – prices.

THE GREAT HOUSING BOOM

There is nothing new, or particularly unusual, about sharp regional differences in house prices. Housing market pressures – which spill out in rising, falling or stable prices – reflect local or regional prosperity, employment and social factors such as how early couples get married and whether or not, on marrying, it is conventional to set up a marital home immediately or live with parents. It is unlikely that all these factors will correspond exactly between localities and regions, hence differences in house prices. Such differences will also reflect the supply of housing – by their nature, housing shortages will tend to be reflected in rising prices.

In the 1980s, compared with earlier periods, the main development was the emergence of clear and widening house price differences between North and South. The labour and housing markets were inextricably linked. The recession and the sharply rising unemployment which affected the North more than the South in the first half of the 1980s was fully reflected in property price differentials. Thus, even by 1985 average house prices in Greater London were double those in the north, then the region with the lowest prices in the country. Table 8.1 shows the longstanding nature of such differences. If we take the example of Greater London and the north, average prices in the former were 1·75 times those in the latter in 1970; 1·55 times in 1975; 1·75 again in 1980; 1·94 in 1985 and 1·92 in 1990. The 1990–92 recession narrowed the gap significantly. Even so, with Greater London prices 1·59 times those in the north at the end of 1992, the difference remained larger than in the mid-1970s.

There have been three house price booms in Britain since 1970 – in the early 1970s, at the end of the 1970s and from the mid-1980s until the end of the decade. By 1988, house prices in Britain were ten times their 1970 level on average, while the general level of prices for all goods and services in the economy was less than six times its 1970 level. In each of these booms, the first burst of rising house prices came in London and the south east. In the first two, prices slowed after their initial burst in

Table 8.1 House prices by region (£)

	1970	1975	1980	1985	1990	1992*
North	3,942	9,601	17,710	22,786	43,655	48,624
Yorks & Humberside	3,634	9,085	17,689	23,338	47,231	54,699
East Midlands	3,966	9,989	18,928	25,539	52,620	56,527
East Anglia	4,515	11,528	22,808	31,661	61,427	59,961
Greater London	6,882	14,918	30,968	44,301	83,821	77,466
South East (excluding Greater London)	6,223	14,664	29,832	40,487	80,525	75,189
South West	4,879	12,096	25,293	32,948	65,378	64,330
West Midlands	4,490	10,866	21,663	25,855	54,694	58,405
North West	4,184	9,771	20,092	25,126	50,005	58,169
Wales	4,434	10,083	19,363	25,005	46,464	49,502
Scotland	5,002	11,139	21,754	26,941	41,744	52,274
Northern Ireland	4,387	10,023	23,656	23,012	31,849	39,240
United Kingdom	4,975	11,787	23,596	31,103	59,785	62,265

* Average house prices at mortgage-completion stage.
Sources: Building Societies Association and Department of the Environment, '5 per cent Sample of Mortgage Completions', *BSA Bulletin*, April 1988, table 18; Council of Mortgage Lenders, *Housing Finance*, February 1993, table 17.

London and the south east but carried on rising in other parts of the country. This 'catching up' in the rest of the country never went far enough to eliminate house price differentials between the south east and elsewhere, but it had the effect of restricting the gap.

The house price boom which commenced in the mid-1980s lasted until the end of the decade, and was at its most powerful in 1987–8. Indeed, the Treasury's desire to limit the scope of mortage tax relief, against prime ministerial pressure, provided the last, frenzied burst of the boom. Nigel Lawson, then Chancellor of the Exchequer, knew that Margaret Thatcher would not permit a wholesale dismantling of the tax relief. There was, however, an anomaly in the system. Mortgage tax relief was tied to individual tax units rather than to properties. Thus, an unmarried couple jointly buying a house or flat together were entitled to two sets of the £30,000 tax relief. But a married couple, then a single tax unit, could only obtain one amount of relief. The Treasury could argue that the system operated as a tax on marriage, or an inducement for 'living in sin'. Thatcher, presented with this argument, accepted the case for tying the relief to households, rather than to the number of individual tax units in the household.

As so often, a perfectly logical tax change produced unexpected results. The Treasury wanted an immediate restriction of the relief to households, to take effect at midnight on Budget day, 15 March 1988. The Inland Revenue, however, objected. To introduce the restriction without adequate notice would, tax officials said, produce chaos and protest. House purchases that were already under way would be scrapped because the buyers had been operating on the basis of the old tax arrangements. And, from the time the Chancellor sat down after completing his Budget, there would be an unseemly rush to try and complete purchases. The banks and building societies would be unable to cope, and it would be left to the tax authorities to adjudicate, with great difficulty, on whether transactions had been completed before or after midnight on 15 March.

The compromise was that the restriction would be announced in the Budget but not take effect until 1 August, four and a half months later. But the Inland Revenue officials who thought this would lead to an orderly housing market were wrong. What followed was a free-for-all. Estate agents saw a unique opportunity to market properties to single people, on the argument that, if buyers did not act quickly, they would miss out on many thousands of pounds of tax relief over the lifetime of their mortgage. Some London estate agents operated informal 'dating' services for single home-buyers, putting them together with others in the same position for the joint purpose of taking advantage of the Inland Revenue's largesse. And what were the risks? With house prices rising strongly, buyers could expect to trade themselves out of trouble within a couple of years. There was no need to regard their house-purchase arrangement as permanent.

Later, the Treasury announced another restriction on the availability of mortgage interest relief. In March 1991 Norman Lamont restricted the relief to the basic (25 per cent) rate of income tax. Previously, higher rate taxpayers had been eligible for relief at 40 per cent. This time, the move probably helped damp down an already depressed housing market. In March 1993, Lamont announced that the relief would only be available, from March 1994, at a 20 per cent rate.

The summer of 1988 saw the final, dramatic spurt in house prices. In the south east excluding Greater London, prices rose by 15 per cent in the July–September period. For 1988 as a whole, prices rose by 30 per cent. In some parts of London and the south east prices were rising at a 50 per cent rate during the last desperate drive to lock in to mortage tax relief under the old arrangements. But it was also during 1988, as we shall see, that sharply rising house prices became an important element in the general concern over increasing inflationary pressures in the economy and led to the dramatic rise in interest rates that was to turn the boom into a slump.

As before, the lead in the house price boom of the mid-1980s was provided by London and the south east, soon spreading to East Anglia, the south west and the east midlands. But even before house prices started 'booming', steadily rising house prices in the South had ensured a widening gap relative to the North. Table 8.2 gives percentage increases in house prices for different periods and shows this effect at work.

I shall turn to the question of the impact of the early 1990s recession on house prices in the South in more detail below. An intriguing aspect of Table 8.2, however, is that taking the 1970–92 period as a whole (or for that matter the boom period 1985–90), the strongest rises did not follow a well-defined regional pattern. Over the whole period prices rose by more than 1,400 per cent in Yorkshire and Humberside (in other words, prices at the end of the period were 15 times their level at the beginning), followed by the east midlands (1,325 per cent); the north west (1,290 per cent); East Anglia (1,228 per cent); the south west (1,218 per cent); west midlands (1,200 per cent); the north (1,133 per cent); the south east excluding Greater London (1,108 per cent); Greater London (1,026 per cent); Wales (1,016 per cent); Scotland (945 per cent); and Northern Ireland (794 per cent).

Many of the regions caught up with house price increases in the south east in the first half of the 1970s, less so in the late

Table 8.2   Regional house price changes,* 1970–92

	1970–75	1975–80	1980–85	1985–90	1990–92	1970–92
North	143·6	84·5	28·7	91·6	11.4	1,133·5
Yorks &						
Humberside	150·0	94·7	31·9	102·4	15·8	1,405·2
East Midlands	151·9	89·5	34·9	106·0	7·4	1,325·3
East Anglia	155·3	97·8	38·8	94·0	−2·4	1,228·0
Greater London	116·7	107·6	43·1	89·2	−7·6	1,025·6
South East (ex-						
cluding Greater						
London)	135·6	100·0	35·7	98·9	−6·4	1,108·2
South West	147·9	109·1	30·3	98·4	−1·6	1,218·5
West Midlands	142·0	99·4	19·4	111·5	6·8	1,200·8
North West	133·5	105·6	25·1	99·0	16·3	1,290·3
Wales	127·4	92·0	29·1	85·8	6·5	1,016·4
Scotland	122·7	95·3	23·8	54·9	25·2	945·1
Northern Ireland	128·5	136·0	−2.7	38·4	23·2	794·5
United Kingdom	136·9	100·2	31.8	92·2	4·1	1,151·6

* Percentage changes in each period.
Sources: Building Societies Association (Council of Mortgage Lenders)/
Department of the Environment data.

1970s and, ultimately, in the 1980s and early 1990s. For the period as a whole, Yorkshire and Humberside, the east midlands, north west, East Anglia, south west and west midlands recorded house price increases above the national average. The notable omissions from this list are the south east and Greater London. Even so, because these areas began with a significant price advantage, the absolute price gap increased.

There was a substantial house price gap in favour of the south east in 1970, but this narrowed in the mid-1970s. Subsequently, the gap grew wider, to the point where – in 1987 – house prices in London and the south east were between two and two and a half times those in the North. According to the Halifax Building Society in 1988: 'The gap between average house prices in London and the rest of the country is wider than it has been in living memory.' Alongside this growing price gap there was also evidence of the spreading out of south eastern prosperity, as reflected in house prices, to the south west and East Anglia. In both these areas, house prices moved up steadily relative to the national average over the period.

Table 8.3   Relative house prices* by region, 1970–92

	1970	1975	1980	1985	1990	1992
North	79·2	81·5	75·1	73·3	73·0	78·1
Yorks & Humberside	73·0	77·1	75·0	75·0	79·0	87·8
East Midlands	79·7	84·7	80·2	82·1	88·0	90·8
East Anglia	90·8	97·8	96·7	101·8	102·7	96·3
Greater London	138·3	126·6	131·2	142·4	140·2	124·4
South East (excluding						
Greater London)	127·5	124·4	126·4	130·2	134·7	120·8
South West	98·1	102·6	107·2	105·9	109·4	103·3
West Midlands	90·3	92·2	91·8	83·1	91·5	93·8
North West	84·1	82·9	85·2	80·8	83·6	93·4
Wales	89·1	85·5	82·1	80·4	77·7	79·5
Scotland	100·5	94·5	92·2	86·6	69·8	84·0
Northern Ireland	88·2	85·0	100·3	74·0	53·3	63·0
United Kingdom	100	100	100	100	100	100

* Index numbers, UK average = 100.
Sources: Derived from Building Societies Association (Council of Mortgage Lenders)/Department of the Environment survey data in Table 8.1.

Part of this, of course, was due to the self-contained economic success of these regions, compared with the North. However, a major factor has been the 'ripple effect' of high house prices spreading out from the south east. During 1988, the ripple effect appeared to have become still more important, contributing to the boom conditions in areas outside the south east but within commuting distance of London.

The Nationwide Building Society, for one, had little doubt about the importance of this effect. Its survey covering the period to mid-1988 came up with an annual change in prices in East Anglia of no less than 37 per cent, with strong increases too in the outer commuting areas of the south east, up 28 per cent, and the south west, up 27 per cent.

Brian Whitfield, a general manager at the society, commented: 'With the average price of a three bedroomed semi in London now nearly £110,000, people are clearly having to look further afield for affordable homes, and are pushing up prices in the rest of the country. How far this ripple effect can spread really depends on how long people are prepared to spend commuting to and from work.'

Halifax data for the same period showed even more buoyancy in East Anglia, with prices up by 48 per cent, followed by the south west, up 38 per cent. Its view was that the ripple effect had already spread to the west midlands, producing a 35 per cent rise in prices, and was due to move further north and west.

This was indeed evident by 1990 when, indeed, the housing boom had ended in the south east but continued in the North. As noted earlier, most home owners do not trouble themselves with complex calculations of the true return on owning their house. But another calculation, which includes only house prices and commuting costs, is a common one. The period since the Second World War has been one in which people chose to move out of Greater London, in search of greenery, less overcrowding and the mythical English village.

The population of the capital, which stabilized in the mid-1980s after decades of decline, had shifted to the surrounding towns and villages in the thirty years after the Second World War. As this shift progressed, so the range of commuting satellites around London moved further away from the centre. Traditional commuting counties such as the easily accessible parts of Kent, Surrey, Sussex, Berkshire, Buckinghamshire, Hertfordshire and Essex were, by the 1980s, no longer offering the same sort of trade-off between lower house prices and higher commuting costs as in the past. Nor, in the case of the popular commuting towns, could they be said to offer as significant advantages in terms of greenery and lack of congestion.

The age of the long-distance commuter was born, with the tentacles of London stretching out far into the southern half of Britain, and in some cases beyond. Suffolk, Cambridgeshire, Bedfordshire, Northamptonshire, Leicestershire, Northamptonshire, Oxfordshire, Wiltshire, Hampshire, Dorset and Avon all became, to a greater or lesser extent, commuting counties. There were commuters to London from Leeds and Cardiff, even more from Bristol and Bath. Two-hour journeys became commonplace. It may not have been efficient, or particularly pleasant, but it was certainly prevalent.

Anyone with any doubts about the inefficiencies of an over-concentration of economic activity in the South in general and the south east in particular need to have looked no further than the evidence on commuting. There must have been something wrong with a situation in which large numbers of productive, intelligent people spent four hours a day travelling to and from work, often where there was no strong reason, other than inertia, for their jobs to be located in the south east.

Commuters provide income and spending power for the areas where they live, but their contribution to the local economy is less than if they both lived and worked in the same town. Towns which come to qualify, to a greater or lesser extent, as dormitory towns lose out both economically and socially, because a large proportion of their population is, for much of the time, up in London at work. As Table 8.4 shows, the recession has not killed the phenomenon of the long-distance commuter, particularly into London. But the fall in house prices in London and the south east, together with higher British Rail fares on long-distance routes, significantly reduced the financial incentive for doing so.

THE HOUSING SLUMP

Seldom can there have been a turnaround as dramatic as that of the housing market in the south east, and other parts of the South, in the early 1990s. In the spring of 1989 there was still a mood of wild-eyed optimism about housing, in spite of very high interest rates (bank base rates were then 14 per cent). In the first three months of 1989, according to figures from the Nationwide Building Society, average house prices in the outer south east were 27·9 per cent up on a year earlier. In East Anglia at that time, prices were rising by 30·4 per cent a year, in the south west by 34·1 per cent, and in the east midlands by an astonishing 54·4 per cent. This was a powerful boom. Anyone who suggested at that time that house prices could fall stood very little chance of being listened to. Not that there were many such warnings around. The main concern among economists was the lack of response in the housing market, and the economy in general, to high interest rates – the Government's main weapon of macro-economic control. As 1989 progressed, activity in the housing

Table 8.4 Regional commuting patterns, autumn 1992

	Employees resident in region (000)	Employees travelling in to work (000)	Inward commuters as percentage of resident employees
South East	7,976	153	1·9
Greater London	2,947	628	18·5
Rest of South East	5,029	280	6·0
East Anglia	959	59	6·1
South West	2,122	60	2·8
East Midlands	1,864	75	4·2
West Midlands	2,250	90	4·0
Yorks & Humberside	2,176	76	3·5
North West	2,687	75	2·8
North	1,249	43	3·4
Wales	1,155	24	2·2
Scotland	2,185	18	0·8

Source: Department of Employment, *Labour Force Survey – Quarterly Bulletin*, March 1993, p. 13.

market in the South slowed. So too did the hitherto relentless rise in house prices. But few saw this as anything other than a pause after a long, steep climb. The idea that prices could actually fall, and fall substantially, was given short shrift. After all, such warnings had proved to be wrong in the past.

A year later, in the spring of 1990, the atmosphere had changed dramatically. House prices in many parts of the South were now falling. On the Nationwide's figures, prices in the outer south east in the first three months of 1990 were 12·3 per cent *down* on a year earlier. In East Anglia, the fall was even larger, at 18·4 per cent. In the south west there was an 8 per cent fall. Prices were also lower in Greater London (down 4·9 per cent), and the outer metropolitan area (11·7 per cent lower). Interest rates had moved yet higher, with base rates raised to 15 per cent in October 1989. And, with inflation climbing, there seemed little prospect of an early reduction. For aggressive buyers in the boom years, the rule of thumb had been to work out what mortgage you could afford, and then add a few thousand more. Now, the cost of servicing these enormous mortgages began to sink in. The City, which had over-expanded before and after the Big Bang, now began to come back down to earth, partly as a delayed result of the October 1987 stock market crash. The City's newly rich began to see that, in a more austere environment, they could no longer rely on huge bonuses to cover shortfalls in their mortgage bills. Unemployment, falling consistently from the middle of 1986, began to rise in March 1990, with London and the south east leading the way. Crucially, however, the sharp downturn in house prices and housing turnover was at that time very largely a phenomenon of the three boom regions, the south east, East Anglia and the south west, as Table 8.5 shows.

The boom–bust cycle of house prices (and housing turnover) in the South was evidence of the power of the speculative motive, and of sentiment, in driving the market. People were buying in the expectation of short-term capital gain. A common phenomenon was for builders or private individuals to buy houses left vacant by the death of their elderly owners, redecorate them, and sell them on for a large profit a few months later. Housing took on many of the features of a pure financial market, with wild price swings and demand, very strong one month, disappearing the next. Once the realization sunk in that prices had started to fall, the speculators extricated themselves as quickly as they could.

Demand dried up dramatically. In 1988, the peak year for housing turnover (assisted by the Treasury's mismanagement of the mortgage tax relief change), the building societies provided 1·21 million new mortgages. In every year from 1984 to 1988, the number of new building society mortgages comfortably exceeded one million. And this was not the full extent of mortgage demand. In 1988, for example, the banks provided 312,000, and other mortgage lenders (notably the so-called central lenders, who obtained their funds exclusively from the wholesale money markets) provided several thousand more. There was also a fashion for foreign-currency mortgages among some highly paid individuals. In 1989, the number of new building society mortgages fell by 29 per cent to 858,000, and further, to 721,000 in 1990, 643,000 in 1991 and just 531,000 in 1992. The number of housing transactions in 1992, in other words, was only 44 per cent of the 1988 peak level, and less than half of the 1984–8 average.

The effect, on prices and turnover, was not, however, uniform between regions. Well after transactions shuddered to a halt in the South, they continued to be relatively strong in the North. In the spring of 1990, house prices were still rising strongly in the north (where they continued to climb for another two years), Yorkshire and Humberside, the north west, Wales, Scotland, Northern Ireland and, to a lesser extent, the west midlands. Just as the South had left the North behind when house prices began to boom in the second half of the 1980s, so the North now began to close the gap. Falling house prices in the South contrasted markedly with the rises in the North. It was two nations again, but with the North, for once, enjoying the advantages. Scotland and Northern Ireland, in true tortoise and hare fashion, had no housing boom to speak of in the late 1980s. But prices continued to rise in the early 1990s.

The scale of the house price falls in the formerly booming regions of the South is worth emphasizing. If we take the first quarter of 1989 as a base, average house prices in East Anglia fell by a total of 35 per cent over the following four years; those in the outer south east dropped by 34 per cent; in the outer metropolitan area by 29 per cent; in Greater London by 30 per cent; in the south west by 24 per cent; and in the east midlands by 22 per cent.

The phenomenon of persistently falling house prices, with particularly heavy falls in some regions, was new. But was it harmful? After all, the regions where prices fell the most had been those which had enjoyed the biggest house price boom in the late 1980s. And the falls, while dramatic, did not go far enough to wipe out the gains. Perhaps it was not so surprising, after such a powerful boom, that prices had fallen back. After all, as noted above, in the late 1980s the housing market took on many of the characteristics of a market in financial assets, subject to sharp swings in sentiment, and in prices.

The answer is that it mattered a great deal to some people. I described above the situation in the summer of 1988, where many people bought properties to take advantage of multiple

Table 8.5   House price changes, 1987–93*

	1987	1988	1989	1990	1991	1992	1993
North	6·8	−2·0	30·5	18·3	7·3	2·8	−5·4
Yorks &							
Humberside	9·9	1·5	52·5	7·1	−14·9	4·2	−8·9
North West	7·8	3·8	35·2	25·7	4·3	−1·9	−3·9
East Midlands	13·7	8·6	54·4	0·9	−11·7	−4·3	−8·0
West Midlands	12·1	15·7	48·2	6·1	−7·2	−0·3	−6·7
East Anglia	18·8	30·4	30·4	−18·4	−6·7	−5·7	−9·5
Outer South East	20·8	22·5	27·9	−12·3	−13·0	−6·5	−7·5
Outer Met. Area	27·8	17·3	20·4	−11·7	−10·6	−6·2	−4·6
Greater London	28·1	14·2	15·6	−4·9	−15·6	−7·5	−6·2
South West	16·1	19·9	34·1	−8·0	−8·6	−7·1	−2·8
Wales	7·1	4·7	49·5	7·2	−10·3	−0·7	0
Scotland	5·6	−3·3	16·8	12·5	5·0	6·1	4·2
Northern Ireland	0·3	−0·2	1·1	7·3	1·6	3·0	10·2
United Kingdom	14·7	10·3	32·0	0·1	−8·7	−4·0	−4·5

* Percentage changes on a year earlier. All first quarter data.
Source: Nationwide Building Society, 'House Prices, First Quarter of 1993', p. 7. Figures are 'mix-adjusted', to take account of different types and sizes of house in different regions.

tax relief on mortgage interest in the expectation that, within a couple of years, they would be able to trade themselves out of these arrangements at a profit. It was also the case, in an era where 100 per cent mortgages became the norm, that many people over-stretched themselves, being unprepared for a prolonged period of very high interest rates, and for falling house prices. During the boom, equity withdrawal provided solid support for consumer spending. A simple example is the best way to illustrate how equity withdrawal worked. Suppose, as a result of rising house prices, a property I bought in 1980 for £20,000 on a 100 per cent mortgage was worth £60,000 by 1988. I have £40,000 of equity in the house. I now want to buy a house for £80,000 and, to do so, I persuade the building society to give me another 80 per cent mortgage. The full £40,000 of equity in the original property is thus mine to use for non-housing expenditure. All well and good, except for a government attempting to rein back demand in the economy.

In the early 1990s, however, equity withdrawal was replaced

as a source of concern by the situation of negative equity. Again, an example will serve to illustrate the general point. Suppose, as a highly paid first-time buyer, I purchase a property in East Anglia in 1988–9 for £100,000, using a 100 per cent mortgage. By early 1993 my mortgage is still £100,000 (even on repayment mortgages, very little capital is paid off in the early years). But the value of my house has fallen to £65,000. I therefore have negative equity of £35,000. In other words, if I sell my house I would still be left to find £35,000 to pay off the building society. Unless I have a sudden windfall I am stuck. And plenty of people were stuck. The Bank of England estimated that in early 1993 some 1·7 million households were caught in this negative equity trap – more than 15 per cent of all households with mortgages. And, because the house price falls were sharpest in the South, it follows that the problem of negative equity was greatest in southern regions, as Table 8.6 shows.

As an economic problem, negative equity is more serious than equity withdrawal. It implies that a large proportion of the population are prevented from moving in response to job opportunities in other areas. Such people can either wait until house prices recover, to the point where they will be able to sell up and cover their mortgage in doing so. In some areas, plainly, this meant a very long wait. Or they could attempt to accumulate sufficient savings to pay off the building society even if they sold their property at a large loss. Both routes were followed.

High interest rates and falling house prices had another effect. Mortgage repossessions (or possessions as they are called by the mortgage lenders) increased sharply. Home-buyers who encountered difficulties with their monthly mortgage payments were forced, and in some cases volunteered, to give back their property to the lender (even if this meant, for those in negative equity, not clearing their debt). Some repossessions were due to 'normal' factors such as family break-up, but their sharp increase during the housing slump and the general economic recession suggests that high interest rates and unemployment were dominant factors.

The fact that people encountered problems in meeting their mortgage payments during a period of high unemployment was

Table 8.6 Negative equity,* December 1992

Great Britain	25%
Scotland	6%
North	10%
North West	10%
Yorks & Humberside	10%
Wales	14%
West Midlands	12%
East Midlands	32%
East Anglia	26%
South West	33%
Outer South East	40%
Greater London	40%

* Extent among recent (1988 to 1991) home-buyers as at December 1992. The figures show the percentage of recent home-buyers affected in each region.
Source: Joseph Rowntree Foundation, quoted in White Horse Mortgage Services, 'Mortgage Arrears Analyses – Fourth Quarter 1992'.

not new. Double-income households suffered because of the loss of one of the two incomes. In single-earner families, the social security system provided temporary refuge, in that mortgage interest payments were met for the first six months of unemployment (leading to a few well-publicized examples where the government was left to pick up the bill on individual mortgages stretching to several hundred thousand pounds). What was striking about the 1990–92 recession, however, was the extent of the problem. There were several reasons for this. One was the extent to which people had taken out very large mortgages during the boom years. With hindsight, it is easy to see the damage that was caused by the over-generous lending policies of the 1980s. In 1980, as Table 8.7 shows, repossessions were comparatively rare, and the situation of people getting more than twelve months into arrears on their mortgage was so unusual that the statistics were not even collected. The main reason for this was the stricter lending controls applied by the building societies, during a period in which mortgages were still effectively rationed. Thus, 100 per cent mortgages were not generally available. Most first-time buyers had to struggle to accumulate enough savings to put down deposits equivalent to 10 or 20 per cent of the purchase price of the property. During the mortgage free-for-all of the 1980s, when competition between the building societies, banks and other lenders for market share was intense, many of the old prudential constraints disappeared. Any lender turning away a borrower knew that he or she could simply go to a neighbouring bank or building society to obtain the necessary mortgage.

Thus, people took on mortgages that gave them little or no room for manoeuvre in the event of a reduction in income, unemployment, or an unexpected rise in interest rates. Another factor was the change in attitudes towards keeping up to date with mortgage payments. Often people chose to go into arrears while maintaining their expenditure on other things. By the time the building society chose to act on arrears, the debt build-up (often mortgage arrears went alongside large outstanding credit card and other bills), was too large to be manageable. For the lenders, arrears and repossessions were an uncomfortable lesson that made them determined to be more cautious next time. Indeed, one common complaint in 1992 and 1993 was that the lenders' refusal to accept market valuations of house prices acted as a significant drag on recovery. Repossessed houses, sold off, usually at very low prices at auction, were often in a sad state of repair. Some were stripped of all internal fittings, including lights and bathroom equipment, by their former owners.

In December 1991, as part of a deal between the Government and the mortgage lenders, the Chancellor, Norman Lamont, announced an eight-month suspension of stamp duty on house purchases up to £250,000 in value. In return, the building societies and banks agreed to go easy on repossessions. This explains why, in Table 8.7, repossessions fell in 1992, in spite of a big rise in mortgage arrears. The danger in this situation, plainly, was that if people thought they were safe from having their houses repossessed, they would feel less obligation to persist with regular mortgage payments.

The housing slump of the early 1990s was long and deep. It is no exaggeration to say that it transformed attitudes to house purchase, particularly in the South. Renting re-emerged as a viable alternative to buying a property. And the legacy, in

Table 8.7 Mortgage arrears and repossessions

	1980	1987	1988	1989	1990	1991	1992
Repossessions	3,480	26,390	18,510	15,810	43,890	75,540	68,540
6–12 months arrears	15,530	55,490	42,810	66,800	123,110	183,610	205,010
More than 12 months arrears	—	14,960	10,280	13,840	36,100	91,740	147,040

Source: Council of Mortgage Lenders, *Housing Finance*, February 1993, table 11, p. 27.

negative equity and in mortgage arrears, would take a very long time to unwind. The Bank of England suggested that, even assuming a respectable recovery in house prices, the problem of negative equity would take until beyond the middle of the 1990s to disappear.

HOUSE PRICES AND INCOME

For analysts of the housing market, the key long-term relationship has been that between house prices and income. During house price booms, the ratio of house prices to income gets stretched higher, falling back when house price increases subside. Overall, however, it is a relationship which, apart from in the Barber boom of the early 1970s and the Lawson boom of the late 1980s, had been relatively stable over time, as Table 8.8 illustrates.

There are two ways in which house prices and incomes can be related. The first is when house prices are bid up in areas where incomes are high and growing rapidly and where, for one reason or another, the supply of new housing is restricted. The second link comes from the other direction, whereby high house prices act to push up wage rates, as employers in areas where housing costs are high are forced to pay extra wages and salaries to attract employees.

It seems that, whichever of these factors began the process, both were at work in the late 1980s in determining recent house price movements and their regional pattern. Faster growth in

Table 8.8 House prices and income (ratio of house prices to average earnings)

1953	3·73	1967	3·29	1981	3·47
1954	3·44	1968	3·25	1982	3·19
1955	3·22	1969	3·21	1983	3·21
1956	3·10	1970	3·08	1984	3·42
1957	3·05	1971	3·00	1985	3·55
1958	2·93	1972	3·46	1986	3·52
1959	2·88	1973	4·17	1987	3·78
1960	2·83	1974	4·41	1988	3·84
1961	2·92	1975	3·56	1989	4·56
1962	3·00	1976	3·30	1990	4·18
1963	3·16	1977	3·23	1991	3·50
1964	3·18	1978	3·24	1992	3·13
1965	3·24	1979	3·65	1993	2·85
1966	3·19	1980	3·84		

Source: Nationwide Building Society. All first-quarter figures.

incomes may have provided the initial spur for rising house prices, but there is also something of a wage/house price cycle at work, whereby higher prices also lead to greater wage demands, and so on around the cycle.

In London in particular, and the south east in general, sizeable salary supplements, to take account of higher house prices, became commonplace. Once they were available only to employees working in central London. Now, for banks and other institutions, supplements are paid in areas stretching far out into commuter country.

Until around 1980, observing the ratio of house prices to income provided a fairly accurate method of predicting future house price movements. The high ratios of 1973 indicated that borrowers were becoming increasingly stretched and suggested that the top of that particular house price cycle was near, as indeed it was. However, there was an important change in the 1980s which affected the relationship between house prices and incomes.

In the early 1980s, as touched upon above, as part of the general liberalization of the financial system by the Conservative Government, a freeing-up which included the abolition of exchange controls and the removal of the old 'corset' on the banking system which restricted the growth of their lending, the banks entered the house mortgage market in a big way. Building societies, the traditional providers of home loans, were also allowed new freedoms, in particular the freedom to raise funds on the wholesale money markets in order to provide mortgages.

Coupled with this was the general belief that house prices could do only one thing, that is, move upwards, and at a fairly rapid rate. Thus, borrowers could opt for mortgages that were both larger and very much easier to obtain than ever before. There was a great incentive to obtain the maximum possible mortgage, in order to purchase a rapidly appreciating asset. The supply of mortgage finance, which acted as a constraint on house prices in the past, no longer appeared to do so.

On the Nationwide figures, the ratio of house prices to average earnings stood at a record high in 1989. As regional house price differentials grew wider, so people argued that this acted as the great equalizer in the country. Those who live in the South may enjoy higher incomes, it was argued, but they also had to pay more for their housing. Add in the burden of commuting, and its costs, and living in the North had its own, possibly greater, attractions.

The Reward Group, which prepares regional cost-of-living comparisons for use by companies in setting salary levels, publishes a 'quality of life' index based on average managerial salaries and living costs in different areas. Its 1988 league table on this basis ran in almost exactly the opposite direction from the other measures of regional performance, with the north having the highest quality of life, followed by Yorkshire and Humberside, the north west, the east midlands, Scotland, the west midlands, East Anglia, the south west, the south east and, right at the bottom, Greater London.

'Those who live in the north or Yorkshire and Humberside will doubtless envy the pay levels in the south east, but when they take the cost of living into account, they will realize that there are no finer places to live at the moment,' the Staffordshire-based Reward Group concluded.

It was, of course, the case that in areas where house prices moved ahead of the growth in incomes – and the price/income ratio increased – the burden of house purchase, in particular for first-time buyers, rose. Nationwide data for mid-1988 showed a wide regional variation in the price/income ratio. For first-time buyers, it ranged from 1·98 in the north to 3·28 in East Anglia, with the highest ratios in the South and the lowest in the North.

For those fortunate enough to be in reasonably well-salaried jobs, as in the Reward survey, the combination of a relatively good income and low housing costs is indeed an attractive one. The South, and the south east in particular, had to pay the price for an over-concentration of activity in one part of the country. This represented one of a number of types of congestion cost resulting from the distribution of population, income and economic activity in Britain. These costs were borne by individuals, by the companies that employed them and ultimately by the economy as a whole.

Research by Olympia Bover, John Muellbauer and Anthony Murphy, published in the *Oxford Bulletin of Economics and Statistics*, suggested that the effect of high house prices in the south east was to push up wages, not just within the region but for the economy as a whole. National wage settlements are still important for large sections of British industry, and pay trends for the whole economy tend to take their lead from the area with the most buoyant labour market. In the past, for manufacturing industry at least, this was usually the west midlands. In the late 1980s, across a wide range of goods and services, the pace was set by the south east.

The Muellbauer–Bover–Murphy research suggested that the widening North–South gap in house prices in the first half of the 1980s had the effect of pushing up average real wages in the whole economy by 4·4 per cent over the 1984–8 period. The relationships in the Treasury's model of the economy would suggest that the effect of this would be to reduce employment. Overall, a 4·4 per cent addition to real wages may have cut employment by 2 to 3 per cent, or roughly 450,000 to 650,000. Thus, the regional differences in house prices that evolved in the first half of the 1980s could have pushed unemployment up by some half a million. The subsequent widening of the North–South house price gap was accompanied, from mid-1986 to the spring of 1990, by a sharp fall in unemployment. With monetary policy highly accommodating over the period of the unemployment fall – in other words, credit conditions did not act to restrain the economy – the effects of regional house price differences showed through in an overheated economy and higher inflation, as discussed in Chapter Six. In the reverse situation of falling house prices in the early 1990s, wage pressures subsided considerably. The Confederation of British Industry reported that pay settlements, which were running at between 3 and 4 per cent, were at their lowest since the 1960s. This was confirmed by the official average earnings data. In 1993, average earnings were rising by less than 4 per cent a year, their lowest rate of increase since the 1960s. Although the recession and sharply rising unemployment were the main factors in explaining this deceleration in pay rises, the weakness of house prices was an important additional factor. At the same time, the house price slump pushed the ratio of house prices to earnings down sharply. Its level in the first quarter of 1993, 2·85, was the lowest since 1960, prompting widespread suggestions that prices, particularly in the South, had fallen too far and were due for a recovery. Both the Halifax and Nationwide showed prices starting to rise in the spring of 1993.

HOUSING AND WEALTH

The disparity in gains from rising house prices can be measured in various ways. One is to calculate the owner-occupiers' gain on the equity he has in his house – that is, after subtracting the amount that is owed on the mortgage. Another involves simply calculating gains over a period according to the change in the average house price in the region over that period. Either method showed, as might be expected, that the South enjoyed a very considerable advantage in this area, particularly in the 1980s.

Chris Hamnett of the Open University, in a paper presented

to the Institute of British Geographers conference in January 1988, calculated that on the second of the two measurements outlined above, the average capital appreciation experienced by house buyers in London over the previous four years was 6·4 times that in the north and 5·3 times the level in Yorkshire and Humberside.

The conclusion was that 'This has major implications for regional variations in personal-wealth ownership and it has enabled many home owners in London and the south east to gain far more out of house price inflation than they would have been able to save out of earned income' (1988, p. 8).

The gains were starkly distributed in favour of the south east during the 1980s house price boom, but even taking earlier starting dates such as the mid-1970s or 1970, capital appreciation in London was roughly two and a half to three times the level in, for example, Yorkshire and Humberside.

It may be thought that such gains, while perhaps a source of quiet comfort to southern owner-occupiers during dark moments, are of little practical significance. After all, people have to have somewhere to live. Can they ever capitalize on the potential gains they have tied up in bricks and mortar? The answer, as Chris Hamnett pointed out, is that they probably can.

If owners in London and the south east move out of the region they can either release some of their accumulated equity for general consumption or they can purchase a higher standard of housing than would have been possible on the basis of income. Alternatively, the beneficiaries of their estates stand to inherit a far larger sum of money. (1988, pp. 9–10)

For a period at the end of the 1980s, property owners in the south east appeared to have the freedom of the rest of the country. The calculations were straightforward enough. People in the south east approaching retirement could hope to sell up, buy a property in the North for half the price or less, and use the rest as a sizeable nest-egg. For those tied to London by their job, there was always the possibility of using some of the equity in their property to buy a second home outside the south east.

But the secret, as is now clear, was in the timing. Selling up in the south east to move North in 1988 or 1989 achieved the maximum gain. But those who left it later found themselves trying to sell in a falling market in the South, and buy in a rising market in the North.

Estimates by John Muellbauer and Anthony Murphy, in their paper 'UK House Prices and Migration: Economic and Investment Implications', suggested that the south east suffered a net loss of population of 100,000 in 1988, mainly as a result of people cashing in on high house prices.

It may be thought that this process represents a sort of surrogate regional policy, in that it implies some reversal of the shift of population towards the South. However, apart from the fact that only a minority of southerners were likely to take up such an option – and some of those who decide to uproot may take the view that other low-cost housing areas in Europe such as Spain and Portugal offered a more attractive proposition – such moves had to be seen as a second best solution for the regions. If the North continued to lose its best talent to the South and got in return jaded southerners preparing for retirement, it would appear to be still getting the worst end of the deal. And it is still the case that most of those leaving the south east opt for other parts of the South.

Those who remained in the South still realize some of the capital gains on their house by moving to smaller properties as they grow older and the children leave home. As importantly and interestingly, they can pass on those capital gains to their children. This aspect of the house price boom, and the regional disparities which accompanied it, came to the fore in the late 1980s.

A study by Joanne Curley for the merchant bank Morgan Grenfell, *Housing Inheritance and Wealth,* came to some remarkable conclusions about the potential for a sharp growth in inherited wealth arising directly from the housing market. By implication, that wealth will be most heavily concentrated in those parts of the country where house prices are high and rising strongly.

The basis of the analysis was that the fruits of the enormous post-war expansion of owner-occupation had yet to be gathered in. This is because the sharp increase in home-ownership during the prosperity of the 1950s and 1960s was concentrated among those of working age in general, and young couples setting up home in particular. By 1970, nearly 70 per cent of households where the head was in the 30–39 age group owned their own homes, and 60 per cent of those where the relevant age range was 40–49. Among pensioners, only a quarter were owner-occupiers. By the mid-1980s, as those original post-war home buyers had grown older, the highest rates of owner-occupation were still among those of working age, ranging from 50–60 per cent in the 25–29 and 60–64 age brackets, to over 70 per cent for those households where the head was 30–39. There was also a significant increase in the proportion of retired people owning their own property – which was virtually double the 1970 proportion at just below 50 per cent.

The really interesting aspects of this situation would begin to unwind in the 1990s, according to the Morgan Grenfell analysis. Not only will the proportion of retired householders who are owner-occupiers continue to increase – to reach 60 per cent of all retired households by the end of the century – but, bluntly, they will die and pass on their properties to their children. As long as there has been property ownership, there has been inheritance. The difference in the future is likely to be both the scale of that inheritance and the larger number of beneficiaries.

The Morgan Grenfell paper suggested that in 1987 around 155,000 residential properties would be passed on by parents to their children. At an average house price for the whole country of £44,000, this implied total property market inheritance of nearly £7 billion, equivalent to about 3 per cent of all post-tax personal income. This would mainly accrue to those in the 40–60 age range – in which range they would be most likely to have parents dying and passing on properties. And it is clear from our earlier regional comparisons of house prices that the average value of properties passed on in Greater London and the south east could well have been three times that in the North.

Consider for a moment the position of those receiving these bounties. They were already likely to be home owners and substantial beneficiaries, in their own right, of the house price boom. They were in the period of their careers when wages and salaries were at a peak, and family responsibilities will be diminishing as their children reach working age and depart the family home. Thus, their inheritance was unlikely to be mainly used in a glorious consumption binge. Rather, it would either have been ploughed back into the housing market – as they traded up to better properties – or invested in other ways.

The essential point was that such a wealth build-up would be likely to have enormous cumulative effects. Inherited wealth that is re-invested in the housing market will have the effect of pushing up house prices in those areas where the proceeds from inheritance are greatest. It could have been expected, therefore, to produce a further widening of the house price gap in favour of the South. In the early 1990s, however, the inheritance effect was swamped by other, more powerful, factors, notably very high interest rates. Wealth that was invested in other ways, in particular in the financial markets, could still be passed on again to the inheriting children's children. This process of accumulated personal wealth, deriving mainly from gains in the housing market, was expected to be a major influence on the regional distribution of prosperity in the coming years. By the end of the century, on Morgan Grenfell's calculations, annual inherited wealth would be worth nearly £25 billion a year, on the assumption that house prices rose by an average of 8 per cent a year.

In principle, this analysis still applies, although the size of the pool of potential inherited wealth, and its uneven regional distribution, has changed considerably since the late 1980s. With price levels in the South still above those in the North, even after the traumas of 1990–92, future gains will still tend to accrue disproportionately to southerners. Home-ownership, mixed blessing though it may have been, was more prevalent in southern regions. In the south west, 74 per cent of properties were owner-occupied in 1990, and in the south east excluding Greater London this figure was 75 per cent. But in the north the proportion of owner-occupiers was only 60 per cent, and in Scotland just 51 per cent.

Much will depend on the extent of the recovery in the housing market. There are many reasons, as explained in this chapter, why there may never again be a housing boom on the scale of the late 1980s. The housing market cannot realistically be expected to be the powerful engine of spending and economic activity that it was in the 1980s. Both lenders and borrowers are imbued with caution, although future generations of building-society managers and home-buyers may see things differently, so 'never' is perhaps too strong a term. Figures for the early months of 1993 suggested, tentatively, that the slump in house prices was coming to an end and that the south east was leading a fragile recovery. Mortgage rates, more than 15 per cent as recently as 1990, had fallen to less than 8 per cent. On the Nationwide's figures, average prices in London in the first quarter of 1993 were 2·6 per cent up on the previous quarter, although they were still well down on a year earlier. In the outer south east, prices were up by 1·4 per cent in the quarter. Four years earlier, such increases would have been regarded as paltry. It was testimony to the severity of the slump that home-owners in the south east now saw them as a cause for celebration. The speculative bubble that had pushed house prices so high, before bursting so dramatically, was not, however, about to reappear. And that, perhaps, was the most desirable outcome of a highly undesirable recession.

9

RELUCTANT MIGRANTS

> I grew up in the thirties with an unemployed father.
> He did not riot – he got on his bike and looked for
> work and he kept on looking until he had found it.
> (Norman Tebbit, then Secretary of State for Employ-
> ment, in a speech to the Conservative Party Confer-
> ence, 15 October 1981)

When work is more plentiful in some regions than others and
unemployment consequently lower, the solution would appear
to be straightforward enough. If the unemployed were to move
to areas where the jobs are, then one important aspect of
longstanding North–South differences would go with them,
as unemployment rates around the country were equalized.
The problems of congestion in the South would be exacerbated
in the process, but if that is what the market dictates, so be
it.

There has been a convergence of unemployment rates between
regions, as described in Chapters Six and Seven. There has also,
as I shall detail in this chapter, been a steady population flow
from North to South. However, migration has been a minor
factor, compared with the major factor of the 1990–92 recession,
in evening-out regional unemployment differences. Where it has
been important, and where it will continue to act as a disadvantage for the North, is in the extent to which migratory flows
have deprived the regions of many of their most skilled and
educated people.

The role of the market mechanism in stimulating flows of

people between regions is an interesting one. On the face of it, higher wages and better job prospects in the South should have produced much larger movements in the 1980s than in fact occurred. The Conservative Government elected in 1979 certainly had in mind the idea that, in general, workers should be prepared to move to where work was available, rather than expecting government-inspired moves to take work to the workers. This was evident in Norman Tebbit's famous 'bike' speech of 1981. Margaret Thatcher, in addition, in a little-noticed speech to the Welsh Conservative Party Conference not long after she became Prime Minister, stated explicitly that the unemployed should be prepared to move to other regions to find jobs.

Out was going one important strand of regional policy, where industry was directed to the regions, often against its will, because that was there the workers were. In the new era, the workers would have to move to the work. It happened in the United States, so why not in Britain?

The preceding chapters on the housing and labour markets provide many of the reasons why migration between the regions has never been on a sufficient scale to equalize unemployment, and there are others. The labour market has been providing a clear signal in terms of employment prospects (although the signal has been by no means as clear in relative wage rates) for people to move from North to South. But the message from the housing market has been almost exactly the opposite. High house prices in the South, and in the south east in particular, made the prospect of moving daunting if not impossible for northerners. The great housing slump has made properties in the South more affordable for northerners (although a substantial gap remains). But this has occurred at a time when, because of the 1990–92 recession's greater impact on southern unemployment, the employment incentives to migrate have all but disappeared.

Meanwhile, even in the boom years, there were enough predictions of an imminent backlash from high property prices in the South, whereby firms are seen to be under increasing pressure to move to the North because high housing costs, together with

other costs associated with congestion, would make it highly advantageous for them to do so. If this was going to happen, why
should northern workers have moved when, by the time they
decided to do so, they might have found the work for which
they were uprooting themselves passing them heading northwards on the opposite side of the M1?

THE MIGRANTS

These conflicting market signals notwithstanding, it is a fact – as
Table 9.1 illustrates – that significant shifts in population have
occurred. In the ten years 1971–81, the population of Britain
increased by 168,762, according to national censuses taken at
either end of the period. Within this, there were falls in all the
regions making up the North, with the exception of Wales. The
north dropped by 44,214; Yorkshire and Humberside by 2,443;
the north west by 190,546; and Scotland by 98,228. The population of Wales increased by 59,296. In the South, there were
large population gains for East Anglia, up 195,518 (or nearly
12 per cent); the east midlands, up 174,000; the south west,
up 246,115. The population of the west midlands rose marginally, by 28,237, but the south east suffered a substantial fall,
of 199,678.

Three strands emerge for the 1971–81 period when Table 9.1 is
examined in a little more detail. The first is that, in spite of the
south east's population loss, there is a net gain for the South in
population, by 444,192 in all. The North, meanwhile, lost
276,135 (the difference between the two numbers giving the
overall population gain of Britain). There is, therefore, an overall
population movement from North to South. The second observation is that, within the South, there was a move from the south
east, and in particular from Greater London, to neighbouring
regions. Thus, part of the big population gains of the south west
and East Anglia, for example, reflected net outward migration
from the south east. The third point is that, in all areas, there
was a shift from urban to rural areas, with the big conurbations
suffering the largest population losses. Thus, Greater London
lost population, while the rest of the south east gained, and a

similar picture can be seen to have occurred in the north, with Tyne and Wear losing, as well as Yorkshire and Humberside, the west midlands and the north west. Urban–rural shifts in population and prosperity have been an important feature of modern Britain.

These strands continued in the 1980s. Between 1981 and 1991, again using census information, there was very little change in the overall population of Britain – just 8,767. Again, however, there were falls in all regions of the North except Wales, with the north down 79,400; Yorkshire and Humberside 57,000; the north west 259,600; and Scotland 168,583. The gain for Wales was 21,400. This time, all regions of the South gained population except for the west midlands (which suffered a 49,200 fall). East Anglia was up by 154,500; the south west by 273,000; the east midlands by 111,700; and even the south east up 62,000.

In the latter period, the net population gain for the South, 552,000, was even greater than between 1971 and 1981. The North's loss, 543,200, was thus also correspondingly greater. Rural population gain, at the expense of urban areas, was even more pronounced in the 1981–91 period. Greater London, for example, saw its population fall by 302,600 while the rest of the south east had a net gain of more than 364,000. This was partly, as discussed in Chapter Seven, because the fashion for a semi-rural existence, coupled with high London house prices, encouraged people to look further afield for places to live. East Anglia became a popular location for highly paid City workers just as, in earlier generations, Essex had been a favoured location. But it was also linked in with the housing boom. With some exceptions, such as the London docklands, most of the new developments by builders were out of town. And, with mortgages freely available, finance was rarely a problem. Some of the population losses for urban areas over the 1981–91 period were staggering. Thus, Merseyside suffered a drop of nearly 133,000, or 9 per cent, while for West Yorkshire, Greater Manchester, the West Midlands Metropolitan County and Tyne and Wear there were falls of more than 5 per cent.

In Table 9.2, these population shifts are split between natural

Table 9.1   Regional population change, 1971–91

	Population 1971 (000)	Population 1981 (000)	Population 1991 (000)	Annual Change (%) 1971–81	1981–91
Great Britain	53,978	54,147	54,156	0·03	0·00
England & Wales	48,750	49,016	49,194	0·05	0·04
England	46,019	46,226	46,382	0·05	0·03
North	3,142	3,098	3,019	−0·14	−0.26
Tyne & Wear	1,212	1,143	1,090	−0·58	−0·48
Remainder	1,931	1,955	1,923	0·13	−0·13
Yorks & Humberside	4,856	4,854	4,797	−0·01	−0·12
South Yorkshire	1,323	1,302	1,254	−0·16	−0·37
West Yorkshire	2,067	2,037	1,992	−0·15	−0.23
Remainder	1,466	1,514	1,551	0·33	0·24
East Midlands	3,633	3,808	3,919	0·47	0·29
East Anglia	1,669	1,864	2,019	1·12	0·80
South East	16,391	16,732	16,780	−0·12	0·04
Greater London	7,452	6,696	6,394	−1·07	−0·46
Outer Met. Area	5,153	5,379	5,447	0·43	0·13
Outer South East	4,326	4,656	4,953	0·74	0·62
South West	4,081	4,324	4,600	0·59	0·61
West Midlands	5,110	5,138	5,089	0·06	−0·10
W.M. Met. County	2,793	2,646	2,511	−0·54	−0·52
Remainder	2,316	2,492	2,578	0·74	0·34
North West	6,597	6,406	6,147	−0·29	−0·41
Greater Manchester	2,729	2,595	2,455	−0·51	−0·55
Merseyside	1,656	1,513	1,381	−0·91	−0·91
Remainder	2,211	2,298	2,311	0·39	0·05
Wales	2,731	2,790	2,812	0·22	0·08
Scotland	5,229	5,131	4,962	−0·19	−0.33

Source: Office of Population, Censuses and Surveys, *National Monitor*, December 1992, table B, p. 9.

changes and migration flows. On this basis, the flow away from Merseyside was equivalent to more than 10 per cent of the population, only partly offset by a natural population increase. Again, the figures support the contention, not only that the North–South shift in population was very largely due to deliberate decisions to migrate, but also that, within this, there was a powerful urban–rural migration taking place.

Migration is a complex process. Work is one reason why

Table 9.2 Population change and migration, 1981–91

	Population change 1981–91 (%)	Due to: Births/deaths (%)	Migration (%)
Great Britain	− 0·4	1·7	− 2·1
England & Wales	− 0·1	1·8	− 1·9
England	− 0·1	1·8	− 2·0
North	− 3·1	0·6	− 3·7
Tyne & Wear	− 5·4	0·3	− 5·7
Remainder	− 1·7	0·8	− 2·5
Yorks & Humberside	− 1·7	1·3	− 3·0
South Yorkshire	− 4·1	1·0	− 5·1
West Yorkshire	− 2·7	2·1	− 4·1
Remainder	1·9	0·5	1·4
East Midlands	2·4	2·0	0·4
East Anglia	7·3	1·6	5·7
South East	− 0·1	2·7	− 2·7
Greater London	− 4·9	3·6	− 8·5
Outer Met. Area	1·0	3·4	− 2·4
Outer South East	5·6	0·5	5·1
South West	5·5	− 0·2	5·7
West Midlands	− 1·2	2·7	− 3·9
W.M. Met. County	− 5·5	3·2	− 8·7
Remainder	3·3	2·1	1·2
North West	− 4·3	1·3	− 5·6
Greater Manchester	− 5·5	1·9	− 7·3
Merseyside	− 9·1	1·2	− 10·3
Remainder	0·2	0·8	− 0·6
Wales	0·6	0·9	− 0·2
Scotland	− 3·4	0·5	− 4·0

Source: Office of Population, Censuses and Surveys, *National Monitor*, December 1992, table C, p. 10.

people move, but there are others – proximity to family, love of a particular area, and so on. There is a well-established migratory flow from London and the south east to retirement towns in the south west. In the same way, many retired people leave the industrial towns of the Midlands and the North for resorts and retirement areas. Detailed figures for inter-regional population movements, derived mainly from the records of general practitioners and other health-service sources, show that at any given time there are migration flows into even the most depressed regions and out of even the most economically successful.

The fact that there is a net migration flow from North to South, albeit not one that is large enough on its own to equalize unemployment rates, suggests that some people are responding to the signals from the labour market. But is there a typical migrant? The evidence suggests that those who are most likely to move in search of work fall into certain categories. Migrants tend to be young, and the most mobile among the population are those in their twenties. They are generally well-educated and are predominantly in professional and other non-manual jobs. Council-house tenants are not usually to be found among the migrants, while owner-occupiers and young people previously living with parents or occupying short-let private-sector accommodation are much more likely to move between regions to find work. The incentives to move are clearly stronger for the unemployed, but people who are in employment tend to be more mobile than those who are out of work, and among manual workers skilled workers are more mobile than the unskilled.

All of which indicates that it is not possible to lump all workers and potential workers together and conclude that migration from regions where there is high unemployment and poor employment prospects, to those where the jobs position is far more favourable, is unequivocally good. There is a cost to the donor region of losing people and a consequent gain to the recipient region.

In particular, there is a danger that if migration did increase in importance, the effect could be to add to the vicious circle of economic deprivation that affected many northern areas for much of the 1980s. If those who move are the best educated, the most skilled and the potential entrepreneurs, the average quality of the remaining workforce suffers, reducing the attractiveness of the area as an industrial location. Thus, while migration may act to alleviate local unemployment problems, and this is good in the short-term, its long-term effects may be highly damaging. Michael Campbell, of the Leeds Metropolitan University's Policy Research Unit, interviewed on the Channel 4 *High Interest* programme 'Closing the Watford Gap', in 1993, made just this point. Even in the context of an improved economic outlook

Table 9.3 Employment and population growth by county, 1981–91

	Top 15			Bottom 15	
	Employment Growth (%)	Population Growth* (%)		Employment Growth (%)	Population Growth* (%)
Powys	30·0	7·9	Notts	1·3	2·8
Northants	29·2	10·7	Herts	1·0	1·9
Bucks	27·2	12·9	Strathclyde	0·5	− 4·2
Clwyd	25·6	6·2	Central Sc.	0·2	− 0·2
Cambridge	24·7	12·9	Northumb.	− 0·3	2·4
W. Sussex	22·7	6·6	Gtr. Manch.	− 0·6	− 1·1
Suffolk	22·4	6·8	Durham	− 2·1	− 2·3
Oxfordshire	21·4	7·2	Fife	− 2·2	2·0
Shropshire	20·4	7·9	Gtr. London	− 3·1	− 1·1
Grampian	18·4	5·1	Cleveland	− 3·4	− 3·2
Berkshire	18·2	9·1	Tyne & Wear	− 4·9	− 2·3
Cornwall	17·4	10·1	W. Midlands	− 5·1	− 2·5
Wiltshire	16·0	7·8	W. Glam.	− 8·3	− 2·4
Dorset	15·1	11·3	S. Yorks	− 8·8	− 1·3
Gwynedd	14·7	5·5	Merseyside	− 14.1	− 5·5

* Population figures are not directly comparable with those in Tables 9.1 and 9.2.
Source: PA Cambridge Economic Consultants/Department of Land Economy, Cambridge, *Cambridge Economic Review*, Vol. 2, Autumn 1992, table 3.A.1, p. 33.

for Yorkshire and Humberside, skill shortages would hold back the region. He said:

The growth of the Yorkshire and Humberside economy in the 1990s may well be one of the most rapid in the UK. But it will be severely constrained by serious skill shortages at a number of levels. The region has relatively low proportions of people with degree qualifications or equivalent, relatively lower proportions of people with A level or equivalent and a relatively high proportion of people with no qualification at all. So there will be severe skill shortages as this growth proceeds.

There is, as the county statistics in Table 9.3 show, a clear link between growth in employment and population changes. The relationship is not one-to-one – supporting my earlier point that migration flows are not sufficient, on their own, to even out unemployment. But the link is clearly there. This, indeed, is the meat of regional economic differences. Strong growth in employment in any one area acts as a magnet for people from other areas. In contrast, the cycle of employment and population decline is one that has condemned many regions to a second-rate economic performance. Merseyside stands out as perhaps the most dramatic example of this.

MIGRATION AND RECESSION

One of the reasons for the sharp disparities in regional unemployment rates during the 1980s was that the 1979–81 recession, the deepest since the 1930s, had the effect of discouraging workers to move to where there was work. Evidence presented by the Department of Employment to the National Economic Development Council in 1986 showed that the geographical mobility of labour was down by around a quarter in the first half of the 1980s, compared with the late 1970s.

The fact that all regions experienced higher unemployment in the 1980s than at any time since the inter-war years – even though some regions were far higher than others – appears to have had a general discouraging effect on people's willingness to consider moving to another region. The reasons for this are quite straightforward. The existence of significant levels of unemployment in the South in the early 1980s suggested to potential migrants that those jobs that were available, even in the prosperous areas, would soon be snapped up by the existing pool of unemployed there. Why move a long distance, leaving family and friends, when the likelihood was that all that would happen was that one would remain unemployed, but in a different region? Why be unhappy elsewhere when you can perfectly well be unhappy, but perhaps more comfortable, by staying at home? The lower an individual's level of skills, the more such preoccupations are likely to have been the determining factor.

Research by Christopher Pissarides and Jonathan Wadsworth of the London School of Economics, who compared 1976–7 and 1983–4, showed that higher overall unemployment in the latter period did have a depressing effect on labour mobility. The work also suggested that it is not enough for unemployment rates to be different between regions for migration to occur. A more powerful effect on migration, certainly in the earlier period, was the fact that there were sharp differences in advertised job vacancies between regions.

This helps to explain why migration was relatively muted in the first half of the 1980s. An effect of the recession was to produce a condition approaching stagnation for much of the labour market, at least until employment began to pick up again in 1983. When fewer jobs were being advertised, because employers were cutting back on their workforces and because labour-market turnover was depressed, the scope for significant migration was restricted. However, there was a significant increase in migration in the second half of the decade, before the 1990–92 recession knocked it back sharply once more.

Even in the good times, according to the Department of Employment's evidence, the majority of people would be unwilling to move long distances for job reasons. The vast majority of changes of job do not involve moving house, and the majority of house moves are not for job reasons. Less than a third of house moves involve a distance of more than five or six miles.

'There are many factors which discourage employees moving house to areas of new work,' the Department of Employment said in its submission to the National Economic Development Council:

People in one area may lack information and simply not know of available jobs in another. Looking for work, finding a job and then moving house can involve substantial costs. Sometimes these costs may be borne by the employer but they could deter individuals from moving, especially unemployed people who may have limited resources. Regional pay differences may be insufficient (perhaps because of national agreements) to suggest to people that a move to another region might be worthwhile.

A more general point is that many people are not prepared to leave their home town, family, friends and a social situation which they know, to look for or take work in a new and strange area. Surveys of employers and employees suggest that those prepared to consider moving with their employers see three main problems. These are children's education; spouse's employment, clearly important where a second income is seen as essential; and housing. Research indicates that the non-availability and/or cost of housing is a significant if not decisive barrier to geographical mobility. (1986, p. 3)

It is worth dwelling for a moment on some of the non-economic reasons for people's unwillingness to migrate to other regions, touched on above. Economists who have studied the employment mismatches between North and South have, as might be expected, come up with economic solutions to the problem. These typically involve, as we shall see below, reform of the housing market and clearer signals in the labour market. But just as you can lead a horse to water but not make it drink, so it is possible that, for a variety of social and other reasons, a significant proportion of people would not move, even when the clearest incentive to do so was placed before them.

David Coleman, a special adviser to Nicholas Ridley when he was Secretary of State for Environment, embraced this point in a talk to a 1987 Institute of Economic Affairs conference on North and South:

When one comes to consider inequalities on a large geographical scale, it is necessary to abandon the more readily measurable variables and see if people behave differently because of what I am rather reluctant to call their 'culture'. Surveys of long standing show that there are differences in the kind of diet preferred in the North and the South and in smoking and drinking habits. Furthermore, this cannot just be explained away on grounds of class and income. Social class 1 men in Warrington and Wigan smoke more and drink more than their professional counterparts in Weybridge and Wokingham. But – much more important – it is also alleged that people of all ages are, for example, more reluctant to travel to work or contemplate moving home to work in the North than in the South, irrespective of the problem of finding rented accommodation. Maybe it is not surprising that areas with a long history of out-migration where social life is unleavened by outsiders should have a different view of the world. (1987, p. 8)

This is worth bearing in mind as we come to consider two areas where there is a fair degree of consensus among students of the

North–South divide. The first is in the way in which the operation of the housing market acts as a barrier to migration and thus has the effect of, at best, preserving, at worst exacerbating, regional differences. The second concerns the labour market and the question of whether wider regional differences in one particular area – that of wages – would have the effect of reducing imbalances in the regional concentration of employment and economic activity in general.

MOBILITY AND OWNER-OCCUPIERS

How does the housing market in Britain obstruct the regional mobility of labour? Let us first take the situation of an owner-occupier in the North, perhaps unemployed or fearing redundancy, or at the very least observing better job opportunities in the South. If he lived in an average-priced property in, say, Yorkshire and Humberside, he could have obtained £37,831 for selling his existing house in 1988. If the job he wished to move to was in Greater London, the same average-priced house would have cost £97,269 – nearly £60,000 more – or in the rest of the south east £88,706 – £51,000 more – or in East Anglia £75,350 – £37,500 more. In each case, the additional mortgage he would have to find would be at least as much as the value of his existing property and, unless the job he could move to was very highly paid, the extra cost of the mortgage would appear to present an insurmountable barrier to mobility.

Even if our potential migrant lives rather grandly in Yorkshire and Humberside and had a detached house – with an average value in mid-1988 of £55,865 according to the Halifax – he would still have to take out a larger mortgage just to afford a flat or maisonette in Greater London (average price £72,874). Taking the south east as a whole, he could just about afford the average price of a flat or maisonette (£55,564), while in East Anglia his money would buy him a terraced house (£53,090) or a flat or maisonette (£47,304).

The situation has improved as a result of the housing slump of the early 1990s, but a significant gap persists. During 1992, for example, the average house price in Yorkshire and Humberside was £54,699, compared with £75,189 in the south east excluding Greater London, and £77,446 in Greater London itself. But even if the job incentive to head south exists, house prices represent a significant barrier.

The choice facing our potential migrant is a stark one. Either he has to pay a lot extra, and probably he could not afford to do so, to live in the style to which he has become accustomed. Or he is forced to trade down in the housing market by moving to a smaller property. The luxury of this choice, it should be remembered, is only available to a minority of owner-occupiers in the North. Those already living in smaller houses, flats or maisonettes face only a substantially higher mortgage if they want to move South.

With this type of barrier facing individuals, companies attempting to recruit skilled labour in the South, and in the south east especially, faced difficulties in the boom years. In 1988, the situation was serious enough for the Confederation of British Industry to assemble a report cataloguing some of the problems. John Caff, the organization's executive director of economic and international affairs, said: 'Throughout the South and East of England firms are struggling to attract new recruits simply because of the high price of housing and the lack of rented accommodation. The UK's ability to compete is suffering as a result.'

One company, Rediffusion Simulation, based in Crawley, a town of low unemployment and high house prices, reported a typical difficulty. 'Having expanded our workforce by 700 in three years in an area of low unemployment, many of our staff have come from outside the Crawley area,' its personnel manager John Skipper (quoted by the CBI) said. 'Often a new employee will stay in Crawley from Monday to Friday, travelling back to his family at the weekend. On top of that he has to look for properties in a very difficult area. Many people find the pressures insurmountable, give up their job and move back to their original home.'

Rediffusion's response was to link up with a housing trust in order to provide temporary accommodation for new employees and their families while they found housing. But this left open the problem of the property price divide. Other attempted solutions have been more dramatic. With the property boom in London's docklands, building firms set up barges floating in the Thames as temporary accommodation for construction workers imported from other regions. Airport workers at Gatwick, another area of very high house prices, were reported to have been using their cars as sleeping accommodation.

The deterrent effects of high house prices were and are powerful. Other companies in the CBI report told of some of the effects. 'The housing market is seriously affecting our ability to recruit the right people and will ultimately affect our ability to meet our business commitments,' said one. 'Personnel recruited from the north of England experience particular financial difficulties relocating to this area; and often positions are not accepted purely on a housing basis,' said another. 'First-appointment graduates would not be able to pull together the necessary deposit without many years of working.'

The Department of Employment, in its October 1986 submission to the National Economic Development Council, said that one way in which the effects of high house prices in the south east could be eased for young people was if groups of them bought properties together, thereby gaining a toehold in the housing market but spreading the cost. Until the March 1988 Budget, each buyer was entitled to tax relief on mortgage interest on loans of up to £30,000, irrespective of the number of different loans required for the purchase of a single property. But the Chancellor of the Exchequer, Nigel Lawson, announced that this facility was to be withdrawn from 1 August 1988, ostensibly to remove what had been a tax penalty on marriage – couples 'living in sin' were able to claim two sets of tax relief. An important side effect of this move may have been to raise the barriers for young people wishing to work in areas of high house prices.

If high house prices are sometimes thought to be just a London phenomenon, other evidence suggested that it stretched out well into the south east, and probably into the South in general. 'We particularly experience problems in recruiting when it involves relocating to the Luton area a prospective candidate who owns property in the Midlands, or the north west, and also to some extent, Wales or south west England,' another company said in the CBI report.

The anecdotal evidence of house price effects on mobility tallies with what would instinctively be expected. Incomes Data Services reported the case of one company in the South which mounted a recruitment drive on high-unemployment Merseyside. While most people were unwilling to attempt to cross the housing divide, the firm eventually succeeded in recruiting a few workers. But once they were in an area of high employment opportunity, those workers who had moved down felt no obligation to stay with the original recruiting firm and were soon lured to rival firms. The company which initially launched the long-distance recruitment drive ended up with little to show for its efforts.

Ultimately, however, high house prices acted to the South's disadvantage, by presenting employers with, as it appeared in the boom years, the prospect of permanent labour shortages. Christopher Haskins, the Chairman of Northern Foods, interviewed on the Channel Four *High Interest* programme 'Closing the Watford Gap' made the following points:

We have a big dairy in the south east of England, we have bakeries in the south east of England. Now, two or three years ago when unemployment was low we just couldn't get people to man those and there were questions whether they would be viable, whether we'd have to move these activities right out of the south east and do it somewhere else. Now with the recession, with high unemployment, we don't have a problem I'm afraid in getting high-quality staff to do those jobs in those two factories at the present time.

Haskins' second point is slightly more encouraging for southerners. To the extent that the combination of labour shortages and high housing costs were encouraging employers to relocate out of the South in the boom years, this pressure all but disappeared as a result of the recession.

COUNCIL TENANTS AND JOB MOBILITY

The house price divide, as we have seen, has a serious effect on people's ability to move to areas where there are jobs. But owner-occupiers as a whole represent the most mobile section of the population. The really serious immobility comes with council tenants. Owner-occupiers are five times more likely to move for reasons of work than council tenants. As a result, although the division is less appropriate than it was, non-manual workers are seen as more mobile, because they tend to own their own homes. Manual workers, a large proportion of whom are council tenants, are rendered immobile because of their housing situation. Research by Dr Barry McCormick of Southampton University suggests that manual workers in the United States are eighteen times more mobile between regions (states) than their British counterparts.

Why is this? One reason, according to McCormick, is that US manual workers tend to be educated to a higher level than British workers, and may therefore be more capable of getting information on opportunities available elsewhere in the country and responding to that information. But a more powerful reason appears to be associated with the housing system.

A council tenancy is something that has to be queued for, often for many years, and is therefore not given up easily. Council-house rents have been brought up towards market levels under the Conservative Government, but a substantial advantage remains of living in council rather than private rented accommodation. Given that the demand for council accommodation almost invariably exceeds its available supply, it is difficult for local councils in prosperous areas to allow incoming workers to jump the queue. The main hope for a council tenant in, say, Merseyside, was the unlikely one of securing an exchange with a tenant in the South, or qualifying under the National Mobility Scheme, under which local authorities are required to let 1 per cent of those council properties becoming vacant to outsiders. The scheme, however, merely scratched at the surface of the problem. As Barry McCormick said at the Institute of Economic Affairs' North–South conference in 1987:

What has gone wrong with the council system, then, that has reproduced the Poor Law in the twentieth century from the point of view of mobility? I think what is a primary problem is that local authorities have no incentives within their set-ups to let to non-locals, especially if

their local voters do not wish to migrate to other areas. There is no
incentive for them to try to build in the pressures through their
political system to generate mobility opportunities. It is interesting
that both political parties over a period of thirty years have been
prepared to allow this situation to continue, and it is interesting to
speculate on why that is. I suspect it has been advantageous for both
of the major old parties not to centralize more the allocation and
administration decisions of the council-housing system. For the
Labour Party, it was concerned – one suspects – that centralization of
council building decisions could well have led to less council housing
being built in Labour constituencies in the North and more council
housing perhaps being built where the jobs were in the Conservative
constituencies in the South. From the Tory point of view, it would
have been unattractive – one suspects – to have more council housing
being built where it made more sense against the jobs in the South,
because there is a lot of pressure in Conservative areas not to build
council housing. (1987, p. 8)

It may have been that in a different era, and under a different
political philosophy, the solution to the problem would have
been framed in terms of massive extra provision of council
housing in the South. In the 1980s, the exact opposite has
occurred, with the number of new council houses completed
averaging only 50,000 a year, a third of the level in the 1970s
and a quarter of that in the 1960s. And the dispersion of new
council house-building has been fairly even, suggesting that
there has been no conscious effort to build where the jobs are.
Rates of council house-building per head of population in the
South in the 1980s have been similar to the UK average, and
those in the south east below average.

Professor Patrick Minford of Liverpool University widened
the debate on the effects of council-house tenancy on mobility
by bringing in the question of state benefits. In a series of books
and papers, summarized in a presentation at the Centre for
Economic Policy Research in September 1987, he argued that
reforms in the housing market need to be backed up with
radical changes in the system of state benefits if they are to
work.

In Professor Minford's model of the interaction of the housing
and labour markets, disparities in regional unemployment and

real wages among non-manual owner-occupiers are eliminated quite effectively by the working of the markets. High and rising house prices in the South are, in his view, 'a testimony to the effectiveness of the market mechanism, which keeps down non-manual unemployment and generates new businesses employing non-manual workers in the North'.

The situation for manual worker council tenants is, however, rather different. If they become unemployed they are typically eligible for benefits which may not be much below their normal pay when in work. A shift in business activity from North to South has the effect of raising wages in the South relative to the North. But, in Professor Minford's view, there is a limit to the ability of firms to reduce wages in the North, a limit established by the available level of state benefits. Wages cannot fall below benefit levels without serious effects on people's willingness to work. Therefore, instead of greater employment in the North at lower wages, there is an increase in unemployment and little adjustment in wage levels. The council tenants in the North themselves do not have enough incentive to embrace the considerably higher housing costs entailed in moving to where the work is, because wage levels do not fall sufficiently relative to the South.

This analysis, while useful, probably overstates the role of state benefits. There are other reasons why wages are slow to adjust, or, in economists' jargon, are 'sticky downwards'. These are associated with national wage bargaining and the fact that absolute reductions in wages are perceived as draconian and are rare. It is more difficult to adjust relative wages between regions at a time of relatively low inflation than it is during periods when prices are rising rapidly. In the latter case, everyone can be awarded what appear to be generous pay rises, but it is easier to establish differentials between regions.

Alongside the policy of reducing council house-building across the country, Mrs Thatcher's Conservative Government pursued a policy of privatizing the state's stock of housing. Around a fifth of the council housing stock was sold to tenants, at substantial discounts to market prices. In some regions, notably Scotland, the take-up was low. The proportion of council houses sold has been highest in the south east, East Anglia and the south west. Nevertheless a substantial number of former council tenants in the North have become owner-occupiers and this, the majority of research indicates, should provide a boost to labour mobility.

Two points should be made on this, however. The first is that owner-occupation does not give the former council tenant in the North a magic key to mobility and a ticket to a job in the South. All it does is bring him up to the position of the owner-occupier in the North who, as we discussed earlier in this chapter, often faces an insurmountable gulf between northern and southern house prices. Secondly, it may take time before the former tenant even gets to this position. Council properties are rarely sold on immediately after they have been bought by their former tenants from local authorities. The process of 'privatization' takes time, involving first changes to the property to distinguish it from houses still under council control – witness the outbreak of Georgian-style front doors and new windows on council estates. Former council properties also become more saleable the greater the proportion of houses on an estate which have been taken into private ownership, and this too takes time.

The effects of the Conservatives' other main reform in the housing market – the revival of the private rented sector – has also been largely ineffective, although one effect of the housing recession of the early 1990s was that many people in the South who were unable to sell their homes, but were required to move for career reasons, rented them out instead. Conservative reforms included the 1980 Housing Act, which introduced innovations designed to strengthen the position of landlords and thereby encourage the private rented sector. The main measures were the introduction of 'shorthold' tenancies of between one and five years, at the end of which the landlord would have the right of repossession; and new assured tenancies under which approved landlords would be permitted to build for rent and charge market rents for the properties, such rentals escaping the jurisdiction of the various Rent Acts.

The effects of these measures were minimal. Six years after its introduction there were only just over 600 assured tenancies in existence, and the Government extended the scheme to properties which were substantially improved by their landlords. Even so, the revival of the private rented sector was slow in coming. Therefore, the re-elected Conservative Government of 1987 introduced a Housing Bill under which all new lettings – as opposed to only new or substantially improved properties – could be at market rents. Part of the aim was to encourage the conversion of existing empty properties, and spare rooms in owner-occupied houses, into rentals, as the then Minister for Housing, William Waldegrave, explained in November 1987: 'In England there are well over half a million empty properties in the private sector. There are also spare rooms that could be let in peoples' homes if encouragement is given. The Housing Bill will ensure that the level of rents for such accommodation encourages landlords to bring it into use.'

Further encouragement was given in 1988 by the extension of the Business Expansion Scheme – under which individuals could obtain tax relief on their investments in approved companies – to residential property developments built specifically for rent. Thus potential large-scale landlords, already provided with a significant carrot in the form of higher rents, were also to be able to offer their backers the prospect of a highly tax-efficient investment.

But the new age of the lodger, and of the private tenant in general, was slow to develop. Even with these incentives, landlords' memories may be slow to forget the years of regulation, and the danger of a future return to regulation, as Martin Ricketts of the University of Buckingham pointed out in a 1987 paper. New landlords, he said, are unlikely to be attracted into the business of providing rented accommodation 'until they are confident that the new higher rent levels will last. This confidence is unlikely to be established quickly. After more than seventy years of regulation or control the fear that intervention will be re-imposed by some future government is sure to feature prominently.'

A bigger difficulty may come with the potential tenants for these new unregulated lettings. As we noted in the previous chapter, owner-occupiers make up the majority of households in Britain. Their owner-occupation, or at least the process of buying their property, is subsidized through the system of mortgage interest relief. And the attractions of home-ownership were enhanced by the belief that house prices would continue to rise, conferring not only an advantage upon home-ownership, but also a potentially serious penalty both for remaining in or opting for the private rented sector. It may be, of course, that the experience of the early 1990s has changed all this, although anecdotal evidence suggests that those who opted for rented accommodation as an alternative to house purchase still saw owner-occupation as their ultimate goal.

For council tenants, the attractions of the private rented sector are similarly difficult to see, unless council rents were to be lifted to levels which truly reflected market rents. Even then, the council tenant on Merseyside would still face a formidable rental barrier if he or she wanted to move to the South.

The best hope for the private rented sector thus lies not in some sudden switch by existing owner-occupiers and council tenants to private rented accommodation, but in new households – probably those who would formerly have gone for council houses but who will in future be less able to do so because of the reduced supply of new public housing. Rent deregulation will therefore have some effect, as will the greater role given to housing associations by the Conservative Government, although it is likely to be one that works through slowly and over a long period. The philosophy behind the encouragement of the private rented sector is that by increasing housing supply and choice in those parts of the country where work is more freely available, a significant barrier to mobility will be removed. But it may be that the increased availability of accommodation is marginal and the effects on the most important housing barrier – house prices and rent levels – turn out to be negligible.

REGIONAL MIGRATION AND WAGES

I have concentrated mainly in this chapter on the barriers to mobility thrown up by the operation of the housing market. But it has been assumed that the labour market provides clear incentives for people to move from North to South, both because they will then have a better chance of finding work and because that work will be better paid. As we discussed above, differences in job opportunities between regions have traditionally offered a strong incentive in favour of migration, but that effect is less powerful during recessions and higher than average unemployment in all regions.

The picture for wage incentives is rather cloudier. We know that income levels are higher in the south east than in the rest of the country and that, taking the South as a whole, incomes are somewhat higher than in the North. What is not clear, however, is whether these income differences necessarily show through in advertised job vacancies and, perhaps more to the point, whether they represent sufficient additional income for it to be worthwhile for someone in the North to attempt to scale the dizzy heights of the housing market in the South.

Evidence assembled by the Treasury towards the end of 1986 suggested that regional differentials in wages were, in many cases, small or non-existent – mainly because of the process of national wage bargaining – and ministers began a campaign to attempt to correct this. The 1988 nurses' pay award, for example, included a strong regional element. The Treasury's evidence showed that around 60 per cent of non-manual workers and 70 per cent of manual workers had their pay rates determined by collective bargaining. For manual workers affected by collective bargaining, half had their pay determined solely by national agreements, and 80 per cent in a way which included a component from a national agreement. In the case of non-manual workers, 75 per cent of those affected by collective bargaining had their pay set nationally, and 85 per cent included a national agreement component. The 1992 *New Earnings Survey*, published by the Department of Employment, showed that in April 1992, average gross weekly earnings for manual workers ranged from £237.20 in Wales to £268.40 in the south east. For non-manuals the range was £296.30 in Wales to £378.90 in the south east. An incentive exists, but not one that is large enough to overcome the housing barrier.

Significantly, and in spite of the decline in trade-union membership – down from nearly 13.5 million in 1979 to under 9 million in 1992 – the Treasury found that the influence of national and company-wide bargaining had increased. Almost all public sector and nationalized industry workers had their pay fixed nationally at rates which were uniform throughout the country, except for London weighting allowances. 'Regional variation in earnings outside London is relatively small and much smaller than regional variations in labour-market pressure, as measured by relative unemployment rates,' the Treasury concluded.

The picture has changed to some extent since the Treasury assembled its evidence. Weighting allowances, once confined to central London, increasingly spread out into the south east and in some cases beyond, and have grown in size. The majority of jobs on national newspapers, for example, as well as senior Civil Service posts, head-office jobs with large companies and the majority of senior positions in the financial services industry, are based in London and the south east – usually with salary differences which more than reflect regional variations in living costs.

However, if the Treasury's evidence still broadly holds for the majority of employees, as one suspects it does, then this provides an additional reason why migration flows, even in the South's boom years, were not stronger.

REVERSING THE FLOW

The analysis outlined above needs to be borne in mind when one considers what many see as the 'market' solution to the North–South divide. This comes about as a result of the upward pressure on firms' costs resulting from their location in the South. Their overheads – rent, rates, etc. – are high because of congestion and high land prices in the South. Their labour costs are boosted by the need to pay their workers sufficiently to compensate for high housing costs. The workers themselves can see the financial attractions of selling up in the South and buying cheaper housing in the North. At some stage, it is argued, the two things will come together and there will be a significant outflow of firms and their employees from the South to the North.

Olympia Bover, John Muellbauer and Anthony Murphy, in their Centre for Economic Policy Research paper 'Housing, Wages and UK Labour Markets' concluded that a sharp outflow from the south east would occur when it was generally perceived that house prices in the region were at a peak relative to the rest of the country:

As the house price/earnings differential approaches a peak, outward migration from the south east increases. At the same time, the credit constraint for potential migrants to the south east reaches a maximum. Also by this time additional new housing in the south east will have been built. This situation cannot persist and speculative expectations are reversed: the result is a rapid fall, as in 1973–5, of the south east's premium in the house price/earnings differential. The rapidity of the fall is likely to be influenced by the initial reluctance of households outside the south east to invest in an expensive asset with a lower or negative prospective rate of return compared with their present housing. The peak and early part of this post-peak phase is likely to be a particularly uncomfortable one for firms in the south east trying to hold on to or hire workers and, unless labour demand in the south east is slackening, is likely to be associated with strong wage pressure there. 1973, for example, saw the largest net outflow of people from the south east, with further large outflows in 1974 and 1975.

The unforeseen difficulty, however, was that people who wanted to migrate from the South would be prevented from doing so by the difficulty of selling their house, or by the negative equity trap described in Chapter Eight. Professor Patrick Minford of Liverpool University, for one, regarded high house prices and wages in the south east as 'the Liverpool unemployed's best friend'. On high house prices in the South, he said: 'Let them rip! We should not worry about rising house and land prices in the South. This is evidence that markets are working, driving business to the North.'

There are several points to be made on this. If the process does work in this way, it is not necessarily a very desirable form of adjustment. It implies that firms will only have the incentive to move when wage pressures increase. And yet, presumably, companies would be prepared to absorb these higher wages for some time before considering anything as drastic as relocating to another region. Meanwhile, rising wages in the south east could well be taken by the Government to suggest that the economy is overheating and action needs to be taken to cool it down – action which would impose itself not just upon the south east but upon the whole country. This indeed was the case at the end of the 1980s. A general recession is a poor time for people and companies to migrate.

The evidence on regional wage variations also suggests that, for a significant proportion of the workforce – those affected by national wage and salary bargaining – the savings to their companies involved in moving may be minimal. To the extent that incomes in the South have been hit by the recession, as has certainly been the case in financial services, this point is reinforced. Consider too the situation of the individual employee whose company is relocating in the North. The incentive for him to do so is provided by the prospect of a substantial net gain from selling up in the South and buying in the North – giving him the opportunity either of a large overall withdrawal of equity (for those who had not bought recently) from the housing market or moving to a larger and more luxurious house – and the fact that he will have a guaranteed job when he moves there. But he also has to decide whether he intends to stay with the company in the long term, or whether, at some stage, he may want to get back in to the higher-priced housing market in the South. In the latter case there is no problem as long as house price differences between South and North have peaked, as Muellbauer, Bover and Murphy suggested. In this case the profit on the property transaction would cover the price difference involved in moving back. But peaks in house prices, in the south east in particular, had been falsely called on many occasions. And it would have taken a brave individual who decided that this was the right time to take the plunge. Most companies who have relocated lock, stock and barrel have experienced a significant cost in terms of lost employees – those who did not wish to make the move, both for economic and social reasons.

Finally, it was not necessarily the case that high housing

costs, upward pressure on wages and congestion in the south east benefited the North. There is a large body of academic literature which shows that companies, in considering sites to relocate in, will settle for the nearest suitable place. The process of searching for a new location is not one in which all places start off as equal. A firm in central London deciding that it needs to move will conduct its search in ever widening circles, spreading first out further into the south east and then into East Anglia, the east midlands and the south west. Unless attractive carrots are placed before them, they may not get beyond the South in choosing a new site.

A survey of corporate relocations compiled by Black Horse Relocation showed this process at work in 1987, when the incentives to relocate from the south east were considerable. The majority of moves, 54 per cent, were from London to elsewhere in the South, and there were no recorded moves from London to the North. According to the Black Horse report, moves from London out into the South may have been the first stage in a process which will eventually push more firms into the North. But it may be a very long process and one which requires first that the existing flow of business activity to the South is reversed. Of the 23 per cent of all company relocations originating in the South in 1987, 10 per cent were from South to North, the remainder being from southern locations to elsewhere in the South. At the same time, 23 per cent of all moves originated in the North, 14 per cent to the South or London, and the remaining 9 per cent to other locations in the North. Stripping these figures down we can see that 10 per cent of company moves were from South to North, but this was outweighed by the 14 per cent from North to South (including London). Subsequently, corporate relocations as a whole fell sharply in the recession.

A similar process is at work for individuals. Unless they have family ties with particular regions or are masochistic about long-distance commuting, they will tend to move to the nearest place which offers a significant advantage in terms of lower housing costs. This has been the driving force behind the migration from London and the south east to the south west, East Anglia and the east midlands. It has not developed to the extent that regions in the North have been significant beneficiaries.

The point was a vital one, often missed in the debate. It was usually assumed that high cost pressures in areas of the South would automatically benefit the North. But it was always more likely that there would first be a lengthy 'filling in' process in the South itself, whereby the direction of economic activity is towards lower-cost areas there, and only after this has been completed would the North benefit. The evidence in favour of this hypothesis is strong and it is implicit in the statistics for regional migration, together with the outward spread of London house price levels and London weighting allowances in the 1980s, and the pattern of relocation activity by companies.

10

THE CONGESTED SOUTH

What's good for the British economy is to allow development to take place where it wants to: directing development anywhere would be bad for the British economy, there is absolutely no doubt about that. Indeed, the whole planning process is a brake upon economic revival. (Nicholas Ridley, when Secretary of State for the Environment, BBC Radio, May 1988)

There is a very solid testimony to the long-term shift in activity and population from the North to the South, solid enough to be constructed in bricks and mortar. As population has shifted from North to South, so available land in the latter has come under pressure for building purposes. This process slowed during the housing slump and general recession of 1990–92 but, as Table 10.1 shows, the Government's own regional planning guidance assumes a substantial rise in the number of homes in the south east over the fifteen-year period from 1991 until 2006. In the 1980s, house-building per head of population in the South, driven by the private sector, ran at virtually twice the level of the North. Over the 1988–90 period, for example, private-sector house-building in East Anglia averaged 5·6 a year per 1,000 population, while in the south east excluding Greater London the rate was 4·1. This compared with 2·5 in the north and 2·3 in the north west. London's outward development has proceeded in several phases. In the nineteenth century, when the capital's population grew from one million to four million,

Table 10.1   Additional dwellings, 1981–2006

	1981–91	1991–2006
Bedfordshire	28,000	37,000
Berkshire	45,400	40,000
Buckinghamshire	45,700	49,000
East Sussex	34,200	35,000
Essex	80,100	80,000
Hampshire	84,700	92,000
Hertfordshire	45,000	50,000
Isle of Wight	4,300	8,000
Kent	65,200	87,000
Oxfordshire	29,400	37,000
Surrey	42,100	36,000
West Sussex	35,800	44,000
South East (excluding London)	547,900	595,000
Greater London	170,000	260,000
Total South East Region	717,900	855,000

Sources: SERPLAN, 'Housing Land Supply and Structure Plan Provisions in the South East', June 1988; Department of the Environment, *Consultation Draft: Regional Planning Guidance for the South East*, March 1993, table 1, p. 17.

the process of suburbanization was established. Until the London County Council was set up in 1889, distinctions were still drawn between the 'real' London at the centre, and the sprawling urban mass that had claimed previously separate towns and villages. In the inter-war years, as Gavin Weightman and Steve Humphries record in *The Making of Modern London, 1914–39*, this outward development of the capital accelerated:

Once you have an eye for inter-war architecture, which is often deceptively 'classical', you begin to understand that in the inter-war years London was not the ailing capital of a declining nation: it was a boom town. Great new office blocks were built; West End squares were completely restructured; massive new hotels arose along Park Lane; and on the outskirts of the Edwardian capital, modern factories multiplied as a vast new industrial belt arose. The built-up area of Greater London actually *doubled* in this period, as semi-detached suburbia spread out over the countryside and market gardens that had ringed the Victorian city, and the population rose to over eight million from around six million in just twenty-five years. (1984, pp. 8–9)

In the post-war period, this process continued. London's tentacles reached further out, and there was infill building in existing suburban areas. In the 1980s, the boom produced two distinct trends. The fashion for a semi-rural existence meant that London's effective population – people working in the capital – was spread even further out from the centre, producing a series of battles between the developers and the planners. There was also the attempted reclamation, for housing purposes, of inner-London areas, of which Docklands was the most notable example. Not that the economic success of the south east in the 1980s, and the pressure on available building land, should be regarded purely, or even mainly, as linked to London's spread. It was a characteristic of the 1980s that the south east, East Anglia and parts of the south west developed economic structures that were, in their time, far more successful and vibrant than that of the capital. The high-technology Thames Valley/M4 corridor was a notable example.

The Department of the Environment, in its March 1993 draft regional planning guidance for the south east, from which Table 10.1 is partly derived, projected an increase in the population of the south east from 17·5 million in 1991 to 18·6 million in 2011. The number of households, it said, would increase at a rather faster rate than this, from seven million in 1991 to eight million in 2011, for several reasons, including greater longevity and the tendency for divorced people to remain single rather than re-marry. It was vital, the guidance said, for the south east to remain competitive in Europe, and one key element of this was the provision of adequate housing. Certainly, while the south east's particular difficulties in the 1990–92 recession were recognized, the Government had no intention of presiding over a longer-term decline for the south east:

It is the Government's priority to promote the recovery of the national economy, and therefore a key priority is to maintain and develop the south east's economic performance. All parts of the UK stand to benefit from a strengthening of the position of London as one of the world's great cities and financial centres, and of the south east as one of the most competitive regions in Europe. Sustaining and enhancing the attractions of the south east, for inward investment from outside the

Table 10.2 Population density, by region, 1990 (persons per sq. km.)

South East	641
Greater London	4,302
East Anglia	164
South West	196
East Midlands	257
West Midlands	401
The South	362
Yorks & Humberside	321
North West	870
North	199
Wales	139
Scotland	66
Northern Ireland	118
The North	160

Source: Central Statistical Office, *Regional Trends 27*, 1992, table 15.1, pp. 163–73.

European Community and for the location of international groups' headquarters, is a matter of national interest. With the opening of the Channel Tunnel and the development of the Single Market, it is imperative that if the south east is to spearhead the UK's economic development and help maintain the UK's success in inward investment, the planning system must, within the necessary constraints, facilitate new developments for industry and commerce. (Department of the Environment, 1993a, p. 7)

The South, as Table 10.2 shows, has more than twice as many people for a given land area as the North. This is the product of the long-term North-to-South shift in population, although the south east is still not as densely populated as the north west which, while relatively small in size (only just over a quarter of the size of the south east) has two large conurbations in Greater Manchester and Merseyside. East Anglia, which has been a magnet for migrants in the past twenty years, remains predominantly rural and has the lowest population density in the South.

In the mid-1980s, Conservative backbench MPs formed a grouping called Sane Planning, to lobby against excessive development in the South. Under the leadership of Jerry Wiggin, it became an influential grouping with a membership of nearly

100. Even for Conservative MPs, who in general might be expected to be more sympathetic to the needs of the property developers, the political case for lobbying against development was a strong one. The MP who can successfully prevent the march of the bulldozers and the arrival of intruders is one who can expect to be rewarded by his constituency. Indeed, as we saw in Chapter Three, such was the political map of Britain that any such opposition in southern England had to come from within the Conservative Party.

Michael Heseltine, who held Cabinet posts as Environment Secretary and Defence Secretary under Mrs Thatcher, until the Westland affair cut short his Cabinet career (he returned, first as Environment Secretary and then President of the Board of Trade under John Major), quickly became a gamekeeper turned poacher in campaigning against excessive development in the South. In March 1988, he wrote to Nicholas Ridley, who was at that time Secretary of State for the Environment, saying:

Wherever I drive in Southern England today, the place is being torn up or torn apart. The pull of Europe and the completion of the Channel Tunnel, both of which I strongly support, intensify the pressure. And, as you know, we now face a new threat posed by the rash of urban villages which developers seek to impose on green-field sites against the planning policies of central and local government.

There is no solace in the argument that those urban intrusions will channel inevitable development in a more coordinated way than would otherwise proliferate along the urban fringe or by speculative infill of every village. The truth is we shall get both, with an explosion of congestion in the areas concerned and a burgeoning cost on the public purse – which will have to cope with the consequent demand for educational and other services. Indeed, already porta-cabin classrooms testify to the gap between demand and public provision. (1988a)

The response was not sympathetic. Heseltine was accused of applying double standards in his criticism of the planning process, in that when he had been Secretary of State, it was alleged, he had presided over a far looser planning regime. 'When he was Secretary of State there was net immigration into the south east and his exhortation to planning authorities was that they should grant planning permission in every conceivable case except where the factors were overwhelmingly against it,' Ridley said. 'Now I've withdrawn his guidance which was totally boom or bust and said we must be much more cautious and we must locate the development in the right places and we must make sure we don't overdo it' (BBC, 1988).

The other criticism of Heseltine and others who lobbied against development in the South was that they had discovered the virtues of directing development to the North not out of any fellow feeling for Northerners but simply to protect their own areas against the bulldozers. In other words it was self-interest, and not necessarily enlightened self-interest. In the new acronym, it was said, he was a 'nimby', as were others like him, in that his view of development was 'not in my back yard'.

Lord Northfield, the chairman of Consortium Developments, a group of ten house-building companies that came together for the purposes of attempting to secure development permission, principally in the south east, accused Heseltine of a form of blackmail:

We all know the word 'blackmail' – I do not accuse him of that. But I do accuse him of 'greenmail' – a near relative. He wants to greenmail out of the south east the sons and daughters of people already living there, many of the extra households that are expected in the 1990s. What does he propose to do – put them in trucks and forcibly bus them out of the region?

As it turned out, the Secretary of State for the Environment, Nicholas Ridley, while temperamentally opposed to the planning process – as the quotation at the head of this chapter testifies – had been something of a nimby himself. He cut short an interview on television news in June 1988 when pressed on the question of why he had earlier opposed new building on land near his home. Ridley, interviewed by ITN, refused to say why he had three times objected to a farmer's application to build on a meadow behind his Queen Anne rectory home in the Cotswolds.

There was more at stake on this issue, however, than

arguments between and embarrassments for senior Conservative politicians. If Britain's economic future was indeed going to be one in which an even greater proportion of activity and population was to be based in the South, the inevitable result would be greater pressure on available land and housing. Was it appropriate that the question of greater housing availability should be settled in a series of bitter battles – often in the forum of a public inquiry – between local planners and the developers, with the Secretary of State as the final arbiter? Was it right that the Government should accept that, whatever the costs in terms of greater congestion, no attempt should be made to halt or reverse the shift to the South?

THE PRESSURES ON THE SOUTH

There are broadly three reasons why demand for housing increases. Changes in population, in themselves, will directly affect the need for housing. With rising prosperity, people tend to want larger housing for a given size of household, and they may also decide to stretch themselves to a second home. In the latter case, this will not always involve a weekend retreat in some idyllic spot. The tendency grew in the 1980s, with longer working hours in the City and in other occupations in the capital, for people to take on a flat in central London, retaining the family home in the commuting areas of the outer south east. Other social factors also influence the demand for housing. In the past, and indeed for much of the post-war period, it was commonplace for newlyweds to move in with one set of parents until they could afford a deposit on a home or had worked their way to the top of the council-housing queue. By the 1980s this had become comparatively rare. Young people who used to live with their parents until marrying, now set up home on their own at the earliest opportunity, which often arrives soon after they start full-time work.

In the South, as the Department of the Environment's projections show, these factors are expected to work to produce an increase in housing demand. Indeed, to the extent that the housing slump slowed the process, there may be an element of

Table 10.3   Residential planning applications and consents, 1992

	Planning consents	% of national total	Planning applications	% of national total
South East	31,000	31·0	43,858	29·6
East Anglia	3,243	3·2	5,170	3·5
South West	10,357	10·4	12,641	8·5
East Midlands	7,436	7·4	10,950	7·4
West Midlands	9,172	9·2	14,245	9·6
Yorks & Humberside	6,482	6·5	12,855	8·7
North West	10,306	10·3	17,820	12·0
North	4,382	4·4	6,953	4·7
Wales	6,566	6·6	7,424	5·0
Scotland	11,096	11·1	16,431	11·1
Great Britain	100,040	100·0	148,347	100.0

Source: The House Builders Federation, *Housing Market Report*, February 1993, table 15, p. 19.

catching-up in store, particularly among first-time house buyers, who delayed their entry into the property market until prices, and the level of mortgage rates, had settled down.

The recession left house-builders, particularly in the South, with stocks of unsold properties, but it did not remove their appetite for new building, as Table 10.3 shows.

The detailed figures for applications and consents to build new homes show that, even in the depressed conditions of 1992, when the South was hit particularly hard, around 30 per cent of prospective house-building in Britain was in the south east. The South as a whole had 61 per cent of residential planning consents, while builders had put in 59 per cent of planning applications. The statistics give the lie to suggestions that the housing slump had killed off pressure for new building in the South.

The figures contained in Table 10.4 were calculated by the Department of the Environment on the basis of population projections by the Office of Population, Censuses and Surveys and using assumptions about internal migration, marriage rates and past trends on the proportion of people in each age group who are heads of household. They show clearly that, in 1991,

Table 10.4 Household projections for England

	1991 (000)	2001 (000)	2011 (000)	Increase (%) 1991–2001	Increase (%) 1991–2011
South East	7,000	7,594	8,072	8·5	15·3
Greater London	2,774	2,896	3,002	4·4	8·2
Rest of South East	4,226	4,698	5,071	11·2	20·0
East Anglia	821	935	1,029	13·9	25·3
South West	1,882	2,107	2,295	12·0	21·9
East Midlands	1,602	1,784	1,931	11·4	20·5
West Midlands	2,045	2,187	2,289	6·9	11·9
Yorks & Humberside	1,982	2,123	2,234	7·1	12·7
North West	2,493	2,615	2,707	4·9	8·6
North	1,210	1,259	1,295	4·0	7·0
England	19,035	20,604	21,852	8·2	14·8

Source: Department of the Environment, *Housing Projections to 2011.*

the Government did not believe that migration flows would reverse themselves and that there would be a shift of population and therefore economic activity back to the North. In fact, the projections showed the shift to the South continuing until well into the twenty-first century. For the ten years 1991–2001, projected growth in household numbers was above the national average in the south east, East Anglia, the south west and east midlands, and below it elsewhere. On a twenty-year view, 1991–2011, the fastest growth rates were expected to be in the rest of the south east (excluding London), East Anglia, the south west and east midlands. Of the 2·82 million increase in the number of households expected between 1991 and 2001, 1·07 million were forecast to be in the south east and 413,000 in the south west. In other words, these two regions accounted for well over half the projected household growth in England.

How was the south east to find space for more than a million new homes? Even though a large proportion of them would be single-person households, this issue of making available new land for housing was one which caused friction between the planners and the builders. The developers produced evidence, based on work carried out at the Department of Environmental Studies at the University of London, to show that the built-on area of the south east had risen from 11·9 to 15·7 per cent of the total area between 1954 and 1981. The built-on area was projected to rise to 17 per cent by 2001.

If one accepts these figures, some of the worries about overcrowding in the south east look to have been overstated. If more than 80 per cent of the land is free of building, it may be thought, then overcrowding cannot be that bad. Population density in the south east, while nearly three times the UK average, is not as high as in the north west, which includes the Greater Manchester and Merseyside conurbations. Surely a million more homes could be squeezed in without doing too much harm? But the tight population density of Manchester, Liverpool and the whole north west region should not necessarily be regarded as the way forward for the south east. The crowded north west was a product of the largely unfettered development of the nineteenth century.

To the developers, worries that the south east was being concreted over were just hysteria, stirred up by a few politicians. But to people living in the region, any sign of encroachment upon their living and breathing space was unacceptable. And the rationale for this opposition may not have been purely concerned with the environment, at least according to Samuel Brittan, principal economic commentator for the *Financial Times*: 'One would have to have been born yesterday to believe that the opposition of south-eastern activists to fresh development stems entirely from the noble love of rural vistas,' he wrote in 1988. 'Some surely reflects a very human desire to maximise the scarcity value of their existing residence.'

Housing in the south east represents the classic dilemma of Britain's unbalanced, North–South economy. If housing is restricted, the effect is to push up house prices in the south east further, potentially adding to wage pressures, with no guarantee, as we discussed in preceding chapters, that the market will work in a way that redirects activity away from the region. Allowing development, on the other hand, is an implicit recognition that the shift towards the South will continue and that the Government is a willing participant in this process. And, while the current generation of housing development may leave the south east with enough green space in between the concrete, this may not be true indefinitely.

Housing was not, of course, the only source of pressure on land in the south east. With the completion of the M25, industrial and commercial demand for sites close to the motorway increased strongly. Planning proposals for large, out-of-town shopping centres were submitted all around the orbital motorway. One, Lakeside in Thurrock, Essex, which described itself as the largest such centre in Europe, began operations just as consumer spending in the south east was turning down with the onset of recession.

Planning for housing in the south east is rather like a grand-scale monopoly game in which no one wants to accumulate the most property. On the basis of forecasts for the growth in the number of households handed down by the Department of Environment and agreed after consultation with the London and South East Regional Planning Conference (SERPLAN), the counties bargain over how many houses should be built on their patch. In general, the planning officers who are seen locally to have emerged as the winners are those who come out of the process having agreed to the fewest number of new houses for their area.

In the late 1980s, the Department of the Environment, in the person of Nicholas Ridley, the Secretary of State, fought battles with a number of counties over the provision of housing land. Berkshire, in particular, targeted for extra building because of the economic success of the M4 corridor, put up a strong fight against Whitehall's insistence that it increase its planned provision for housing, and succeeded in winning a compromise. The pressure, however, remained.

Sir Gerard Vaughan, the Conservative MP for Reading East, quoted in the *Guardian* on 18 May 1988, painted a grim picture of new developments in the over-stretched South:

We have thousands of unhappy people who have moved into new houses on these huge estates. They find they have got no proper schools, no shops, many of the roads are unmade and there is no proper health cover. We are afraid these new developments would make life intolerable for everybody in the area. We see a disaster course ahead.

For environmentalists, the Government's housing projections were bad enough. Worse was the fact that the developers did not regard them as adequate and, moreover, were not content with building on land already available for housing purposes, or in the relatively underdeveloped parts of the south east. The developers argued that, if the Department of the Environment's new projections for households were correct, and even allowing for a faster than expected rate of new building in the 1980s, insufficient additional dwellings were being allowed for by central government and the counties. But David Astor, chairman of the Council for the Protection of Rural England, writing in the *Guardian* on 8 March 1991, made the environmentalists' point:

The House Builders Federation . . . claims provision is needed for at least 750,000 new homes (by 2001), and says even this would not meet market demand. Where the new houses should go is just as controversial. Everyone agrees that a prime candidate for investment and revitalization is the East Thames corridor, but the building industry argues that the Department of the Environment should also follow market preferences by allowing more development to the west of London, even allowing green-belt land to accommodate demand. The prospect of reliving the conflicts of the 1980s, when the lack of planning control fuelled endless inappropriate housing developments in the countryside, cannot be appealing to Mr Heseltine (the Environment Secretary); yet that is precisely what will happen unless the quid pro quo for encouraging necessary development in the east is strong restraint in parts of Hampshire and Berkshire, where environmental capacity has already been breached.

Nor did the housing recession produce a scaling-down of housing plans for the south east. Michael Howard, Heseltine's successor as Environment Secretary, announced in March 1993 that the south east should continue to plan for 57,000 new homes a year, over the period from 1991 to 2011. Such an increase, he claimed, represented a 'realistic' response to the needs of the region, and could be accommodated without damaging the quality of the environment. Others disagreed strongly.

WHERE TO BUILD?

As pressure has grown for additional housing in the south east, the Government has been faced with a headache. On the one hand, as the Department of the Environment noted in its 1993 draft regional planning guidance, an adequate supply of housing was necessary to ensure the economic success of the south east, and of the country as a whole. But there was equally strong pressure in the opposite direction, which increased as public interest in environmental issues grew. This was the need to preserve the green belt, and to prevent encroachment upon it. The policy followed, therefore, was two-pronged. Developers were forced to hop over the green belt to areas beyond it, even if some of them were green fields. In addition, development was encouraged on reclaimed urban sites, notably in London's inner cities and most notably of all in the London docklands.

The docklands, or Docklands as it came to be known, was effectively abandoned as a commercial port area with the switch to containerization in the 1960s and 1970s. It had also, it appeared, been abandoned as an area of any economic significance. Most former dock workers had long since moved away from the area to Essex, and most of their former housing had been demolished. But with the establishment of an enterprise zone in the Isle of Dogs in the early 1980s and the encouragement of housing development in the area, Docklands became, by the mid-1980s, a place transformed, with an extraordinary concentration of construction activity in the area. High-cost housing was built on former derelict sites, in place of the old, run-down housing that had existed in the area.

A new Docklands Light Railway was constructed to carry the new Docklands dwellers to their highly paid jobs in the City and the West End. A massive new office development, designed to draw firms away from their City locations, was built at Canary Wharf, in the heart of Docklands. Docklands, when in the making, stood ready to beam out as Mrs Thatcher's proudest monument, living testimony to the fact that private capital could revitalize an area of dereliction and populate it with the sort of people and companies who had done best during the

Thatcher years. And the more that additional housing could be provided in areas like Docklands, the more that complaining Conservative MPs in the South would get off the Environment Secretary's back.

But Docklands, having held out so much promise, was not a success. Reliance on private capital to build new homes and offices was fine, but what about the infrastructure? The Docklands Light Railway, which began with a reputation for unreliability that it struggled to shrug off, did not even run into the heart of the City, a shortcoming that was rectified only when it was too late. Road links to Docklands were woefully inadequate, producing traffic jams and unacceptably long journey times. Normally, the process of building the infrastructure went hand in hand with the construction of new homes and offices, or better still preceded it. It was only when the failure of the Docklands dream was realized, most notably when the giant Canary Wharf project, having failed to attract enough tenants, went into administration, effectively bankrupt, that the infrastructure effort was stepped up, with the proposed extension of the underground Jubilee Line to Canary Wharf, and the building of fast new road links, including a tunnel under Limehouse. The prices of flats and houses in Docklands fell further and faster than anywhere else, as did the rents on Docklands offices. The twin disadvantages of inadequate infrastructure and a recession that hit the City of London hard (from which Docklands could have expected the lion's share of both residential and commercial occupants) brought Docklands to its knees.

Even so, the idea of reclaiming derelict or underdeveloped land to the east of London, to preserve space and the quality of life in the rest of the commuter belt, persisted. In March 1993 Michael Howard, the Environment Secretary, revived plans for the development of the so-called East Thames corridor, stretching along the river beyond Docklands, which was under-developed and economically backward compared with the fast-growing and increasingly congested area to the west of London.

According to Howard:

Development will continue to take place throughout the south east and there is capacity to meet development needs in the short term, whilst recognizing the important environmental constraints. However, in the medium and longer term the opportunities in the eastern part of the region, particularly the East Thames corridor, will have an increasingly important part to play as London and the south east responds to improving transport connections to the European market. Nevertheless, one of my key objectives will be to raise the environmental quality of the corridor – to safeguard its internationally important wildlife habitat and to make the most of its landscape for the enjoyment of everyone. (1993b)

The expanding service and high-technology industries had been drawn to the western part of the south east, the so-called Western Crescent and M4 corridor, the Department of the Environment said, reflecting its comparative advantages 'in terms of environmental quality, transport communications and labour supply, but also negative investor perceptions of the East Thames corridor'. As a result, the department said in a special report on the East Thames corridor:

This pattern of investment has led to a significant economic imbalance between the eastern and western parts of the south east. While large parts of the east cry out for regeneration and increased economic activity, areas of the west have suffered from overheating with the attendant problems of skills shortages, pressures on the transport systems, high land values and increasing pressure to encroach into environmentally sensitive areas. The present recession may bring only temporary respite from these problems. (1993c, p. 1)

The vision set out by Howard was of an area of vibrant development, with perhaps 87,000 new homes by 2006 (and 112,000 by 2015), utilizing the river and revitalizing an area which the prosperity of the south east had largely by-passed. It included the forlorn, abandoned areas of 'railway sidings, disused docks, industrial land, old gasworks and power stations, and marshland' of London's old riverside commercial strip, east of the capital, together with the development of a broad area straddling either side of the Thames running down through Thurrock, Dartford, Tilbury, Gravesend, Northfleet, Gillingham and Sittingbourne. The task was a considerable one. Providing the necessary infrastructure was one thing, persuading people and companies to move to these unfashionable areas would be another.

Even with such developments, moreover, there remained a large and growing number of people who did not want to be slotted into reclaimed inner-city sites or live on the marshes on the edge of the Thames. Prosperity in the south east had brought with it an increasing demand for a semi-rural existence – housing that was within reach and within sight of green fields, but with the amenities of most urban locations. It has been over such developments that most of the planning battles have been fought.

NEW TOWNS AND VILLAGES

It was with a view to satisfying the demand for housing in semi-rural locations, as described above, that the developers turned their attention in the 1980s to the creation of new, free-standing towns and villages. Consortium Developments, a group of builders consisting of Barratt Developments, Beazer Homes, Bovis, Ideal Homes, Laing, Y. J. Lovell, McCarthy & Stone, Tarmac, Wilcon Homes and Wimpey, launched its scheme for 'small country new towns' in the south east.

'The country town is one of the most familiar and attractive features of English life,' Consortium Developments' publicity literature said.

At its most typical it presents to the inhabitant and the visitor a sense of positive balance between city and village. It is large enough to sustain many social and commercial facilities, but not so big that it overpowers the natural environment. It is small enough to offer a real sense of identity and quality of life, but not so small that it denies access to a wide range of people and their families. (1988, p. 12)

Behind the flowery prose, the hard facts were that the group would seek to acquire areas of land on which planning permission could be obtained. This land would be distributed among those builders and developers willing to pay a market price for it. Non-housing and non-commercial projects, such as community centres, health and educational facilities, would be provided from the difference between the original purchase price of the land and the price at which it was sold on to the builders for development. Each town would contain around 5,000 homes in an area of something over one square mile. It would house between 12,000 and 15,000 people and it would take about ten years to develop.

Was this the pattern for new housing in the south east in the twenty-first century? Apart from fulfilling an obvious housing demand, the plan had the considerable advantage, from the point of view of the Conservative Government, that the building of the towns did not necessarily involve any additional public expenditure. In its statement of intent, Consortium Developments said it would 'By its own financial investment seek to assure the comprehensive development of the town including housing, employment, education, health, shopping, community and recreation facilities.' The land and buildings for public services would be provided 'at no cost to the public purse'.

The first test for the concept of these small country new towns was at a site called Tillingham Hall in Essex, within the Metropolitan Green Belt and not far from the M25. In August 1985, a planning application for the site was rejected by Thurrock Urban District Council and, following an appeal to the Department of the Environment, the rejection was upheld by the Secretary of State in February 1987. Consortium Developments' mistake was to propose a development in the Green Belt, apparently still regarded as sacrosanct by the Environment Department. But the idea had clearly struck a chord. In its rejection, the Department of the Environment said: 'Well-conceived schemes of this kind, in appropriate locations, may have a part to play in meeting the demand for new housing, especially when the development meets most or all of the local infrastructure costs and the need for community facilities' (1988c, p. 11).

The Town and Country Planning Association, originally set up in 1899 as the Garden City Association and responsible for the development of Letchworth and Welwyn Garden City, took matters a stage further by proposing twelve new garden cities in the south east, to take pressure off the Green Belt and allow

open spaces to be maintained within existing towns and cities in
the region. In a speech to the Association's annual meeting in
May 1988, its director David Hall said:

The communities of the south east are suffering from ad hoc house-
building. But the solution to housing need is not to cram people into
the inner cities, but to rediscover the need for garden cities. Garden
cities can provide the right balance of housing, jobs and recreation,
combining all the advantages of town and country. And they can be
used to take pressure off existing towns and villages, off the Green Belt
and other attractive country areas – many of which have already taken
far more development than should ever have been allowed.

The strategy should therefore prescribe 'no-go' and 'go' areas
where development will and will not be permitted. In the south east, the
'go' areas should be such as to allow for at least a dozen garden cities
beyond the Green Belt, with an average size of 75,000–100,000 population, but with some smaller and others larger. (1988, p. 2)

Such a solution was a little too radical even for the tastes of
Nicholas Ridley at the Department of the Environment. It was
clear, however, that the proposals for new free-standing developments by Consortium Developments and others had a major
influence on Government thinking. In July 1988, the Department
of the Environment issued a discussion paper, *Housing in Rural
Areas: Village Housing and New Villages*. The paper, while not
solely directed at housing in the south east, was clearly relevant
to the debate over where to build in the region. The concept of
new settlements had a long history in Britain, it said, and could
continue to do so in the future. Already, 11·1 per cent of the
population in England and Wales lived in settlements of fewer
than 2,000 people, and 16 per cent in small towns and villages of
less than 5,000 people.

The Department's preference was for villages of between 200
and 1,000 homes, roughly 500 to 2,500 people – smaller than the
new country towns proposed by the developers and a fraction of
the size of garden cities. Villages of this size, it suggested, would
be capable of supporting facilities such as a primary school,
doctor's surgery, bank, post office, one or more pubs
and a range of shops. Such new settlements, it suggested, with
the due proviso that the Green Belt and Areas of Outstanding

Natural Beauty would be protected, were infinitely preferable to the engulfing of existing villages in suburban development, ribbon development stretching out along country roads or haphazard scattered building in the countryside.

The official stamp of approval for new village settlements emerged from the recognition that, however much housing is created in the inner cities, the probability of a continuing shift in population from urban to rural areas had to be embraced in the planning process. In the ten years to 1981, population in over a third of mainly rural districts expanded by more than 10 per cent. Population in towns and cities of 100,000 people or more fell by 4 per cent over the same period. The urban–rural shift accelerated in the 1980s, as I noted in Chapter Nine.

There was also a recognition that much of this urban–rural movement had damaged existing villages and small country towns, according to the discussion paper. The process of organic growth:

Should not be confined to dense 'infilling', since the character of many villages derives partly from the mixture of closely built cottages, larger houses in gardens, paddocks and incidental open space. It would be a mistake to pack new development in too tightly when there is no need to do so and when there are better alternatives available, including new settlements. In some parts of the country, villages have tended to develop over the centuries in a linear pattern but that could too easily revert to the ribbon development of the inter-war years, which nobody wants to see. (1988c, p. 11)

The main difficulty with these smaller village developments, apart from the likelihood that local opposition to a village of 1,000 houses would probably be as powerful as to a small town of 5,000 dwellings, could be expected to come with the Government's insistence that the cost to the public purse should be minimal. According to the discussion paper:

One of the main reasons that is sometimes advanced against either the expansion of existing villages or the creation of new ones is the concern about the associated infrastructure costs or the overloading of existing facilities – roads, drainage, water, etc. New developments of this kind would generally be expected to meet the costs of such provision. (1988d, pp. 12–13)

The developers' rationale for proposing larger settlements was that they could be seen to be acting in a public-spirited way by providing amenities for the community. The larger the proposed town or village the more, up to a point, there are economies of scale to be derived from the provision of amenities, and the greater the willingness of the developers to set aside parcels of land in the area to be developed for, for example, low-cost housing. Such costs would be lower in a smaller village, but they would also be spread over fewer new houses, implying either that the cost of new housing in the new villages would be higher, or the builders' profits substantially reduced.

Even so, the Department of the Environment's initiative pointed the way to a rash of planning applications for new village settlements, particularly in the south east, and an eventual scattering of such developments – with names intended to convey the flavour of the well-established, authentic English village, but never quite achieving it – across the countryside. The housing slump of the early 1990s put a brake on this process, but only temporarily. Even in the depressed market conditions of 1992, planning consents were given for nearly 1,200 housing schemes, of various sizes, in the south east.

Whether or not new settlements specifically established as villages could be prevented from growing up into towns was a matter for future planners. But one possibility raised by the Department of the Environment's 'new villages' proposal was that the Secretary of State, when considering future planning appeals, would have the additional option, besides those of upholding or overturning the verdict of a local planning inquiry on a new, larger development: that of simply scaling the size of that development down to fit in with the village concept.

It would be wrong, however, to give the impression that everything went the developers' way. In fact, two well-publicized cases, one in the late 1980s and the other in the early 1990s, showed that in the right circumstances developments could be prevented.

Foxley Wood

In the late 1980s a new town was proposed at a place called Bramshill and a development there christened Foxley Wood in north east Hampshire. The proposal, again by Consortium Developments, was for a town of 4,800 homes on what it described as 'one of the best sites for a new community in Southern England'. The new housing, according to the proposal, would be spread across all price ranges, with 400 units of social housing for rent and shared ownership, and there would also be two primary schools, a library, two community halls, a leisure centre, an entertainment hall, a health centre for six general practitioners and a serviced site for a church, fire station and secondary school. The developers also pledged themselves to providing a 44-acre nature reserve, over 250 acres of woodland and a water park. £11 million would be spent on road improvements, including a by-pass for the nearby village of Eversley.

It sounded as if the developers were pulling out all the stops, and indeed they were. The site itself, consisting of disused gravel workings, could not be regarded as beautiful even in the eye of the most anti-building beholder. Unlike the earlier application for Tillingham Hall in Essex, rejected by both a planning inquiry and the Secretary of State, Foxley Wood did not threaten the Green Belt. 'This site is not in the Green Belt, we are recycling brown land and the whole site is surrounded by an established tree screen,' said Andrew Bennett, Consortium Developments' executive director.

The developers appeared to have everything on their side. The site they were planning to develop was as unsightly as most abandoned industrial locations, and the construction of a new town could be seen, if anything, to enhance the landscape. The project itself, with due provision for an extensive, privately provided infrastructure, appeared to be a model of its kind, and one against which future large-scale planning applications would be judged by the Department of the Environment. When the planning inquiry began at Fleet in Hampshire on 1 June 1988, the developers also discovered that they had the weight of the

Department of Trade and Industry, and its then Secretary of State, Lord Young of Graffham, on their side.

In what was a first for the Department of Trade and Industry, a submission in favour of the scheme was given to the inquiry. Never before had the DTI intervened in support of a housing proposal, and the move was justified on the grounds that, with an important concentration of Britain's high-technology industries located within striking distance of the proposed Foxley Wood development, a failure to provide adequate housing in the area would lead to the loss of such jobs to Europe. But contained in the DTI's submission was a more general plea for additional housing in the south east. 'It would therefore be a mistake to interfere with market forces, by putting protective barriers around the south east and other desirable areas in the hope that this would open up opportunities elsewhere,' it said. 'The DTI is concerned that in certain areas of the south east, economic growth may stand to be unnecessarily restrained by restrictions on the provision of housing land' (1988b).

This intervention by the DTI, apparently made without consulting the Department of the Environment, was later the subject of an apology to Nicholas Ridley from Lord Young. The line had to be drawn somewhere and a situation in which one branch of government was lobbying for something over which another branch was supposed to be the independent arbiter appeared to represent that point.

Even so, the DTI's submission put an argument that Andrew Bennett of Consortium Developments had little difficulty in agreeing with: 'If the south east is so bloody awful, why are firms queuing up to relocate there? Listen, it's no good telling firms to go and base themselves in the North. They want the things that Silicon Valley can offer. If they can't move there, they'll go off to Geneva or Italy or Germany. They won't pick Teesside' (Rusbridger, 1988).

All this might suggest that the developers faced a relatively easy run at the planning inquiry, but this was far from the case. The local opposition was as strong as if the plan had been to concrete over acres of lush, green meadow, perhaps because it was recognized that the case against had to be a strong one in order to prevent the Environment Secretary, mindful of another government department's support of the scheme, from ruling in favour of it. Thus, while 'Save Bramshill Forest' posters appeared in the area, the main plank of the case against development was that the area was already quite congested enough and did not need any new towns.

The Council for the Protection of Rural England was undiminished in its opposition to Foxley Wood, either by the nature of the site or the style of the developers' planning application. 'We think the proposals from Consortium Developments and other consortia trying to build in the countryside are quite outrageous, that there is not a single structure plan or local plan in the south east which advocates the building of these kinds of settlements,' said Richard Bate of the CPRE.

Yet the kind of bully-boy tactics we're seeing from these large companies are absolutely outrageous. The first effort they made to build one at Tillingham Hall, in the Green Belt, no less, in Essex, was roundly thrown out. The inspector's report into that proposal was sufficient to ensure that all these schemes should be refused in the future for the simple reason that there is no regional housing crisis and therefore no need to breach policies for protecting the countryside in the way that Consortium Developments are proposing. They are simply trying to break through the planning system and propose something so extreme, so horrendous, that it makes other schemes which only a few years ago would have seemed absolutely horrific, now seem almost benign and quite acceptable. (BBC, 1988)

Tony Crowson, the chief planner for Hart District Council, which opposed the scheme, summarized the main objection:

The whole of the south east is being peppered with such schemes and inquiries in the hope that one might sneak through. There isn't a blade of grass in our area that someone hasn't got their eyes on. We bore the brunt of new development after the war and in the early sixties. There is now a feeling that another area ought to do its share. I feel someone else should have the benefits now. We have very low unemployment, plenty of jobs. Is it fair that it should all come to the south east? That's the question that's got to be addressed. (Rusbridger, 1988)

Local independent councillor David Carrow shared this view:

We would like to see the prosperity of the south east spread to the North. If they do carry out the massive development of the south east that Ridley apparently wants then the south east will choke and the North will weep. (Rusbridger, 1988)

This was not a view, however, that the developers could find any sympathy with. 'It's touching how the south east has just discovered the North,' said Andrew Bennett of Consortium Developments:

It's a wonderful dumping ground for them. 'We have all this wealth in the South and we want to share it with you poor sods in the North.' The trouble is that all these people want to live ten minutes from the M3, half an hour from Heathrow, just up the road from one of the major cities in the world. And at the same time they want to pretend they're living in the Scottish Highlands. (Rusbridger, 1988)

The planning inquiry for the Foxley Wood development finished on 20 July 1988 and the Secretary of State, Nicholas Ridley, gave the go-ahead for the development almost a year later, on 7 July 1989. This was in spite of the fact that the inspector's report had advised against the proposal. There was, however, another twist in the Foxley Wood tale. When Ridley was moved from the Department of the Environment to the Department of Trade and Industry, his successor, Chris Patten, re-examined the scheme and overturned Ridley's decision, rejecting the scheme. At the time, in the autumn of 1989, the developers were bitterly disappointed at this policy switch, and protested loudly. But, given the scale of the south east's subsequent housing recession, and the financial pressure it created on the house-building industry, the companies may have reason to be grateful to Patten.

For areas in the developers' sights, the recession came as a considerable relief. But it did not offer permanent protection against development. The pressure to slot more housing developments into the South, the new towns and villages, would reappear. The question was whether the additional planned housing in the latter part of the twentieth century would be seen as a great planning disaster in the twenty-first century.

THE MARCH OF THE MOTORWAYS

If the housing recession brought some relief to those trying to halt development in the South, there was no such luck for those seeking to stop areas falling prey to new transport links. The Channel Tunnel rail link, finally given the go-ahead in 1993, was the subject of fierce controversy in the south east, and the cause of planning blight along the potential routes. The route finally chosen, from Stratford in east London along the East Thames corridor, before crossing the river into Kent, partly reflected the strength of local protests against the other routes. Throughout the South, controversial new transport links were being proposed by the Government, and generally succeeding in making it through the planning process. At Twyford Down in Hampshire, the Government's plans for extending the M3 motorway southwards enraged environmentalists. Local groups called in the assistance of Brussels, in the person of the European Community's Environmental Commissioner, but to no avail. The road went ahead. A minor victory was achieved in 1993 at Hindhead in Surrey, when after a strong intervention by the National Trust, the Government agreed that the A3 Hindhead by-pass run in a mile-long tunnel beneath the Devil's Punchbowl, a Surrey beauty spot. This was despite the fact that the tunnel would add between £20 million and £30 million to the cost of the project. In general, however, battles between the bulldozers and protestors were won by the former.

The Department of the Environment, in its regional planning guidance for the south east, made clear that it would seek to improve the ability of the region's road network to deliver faster and more efficient movement of goods and people from all parts of Britain through the south east to Europe, and vice versa. It said:

The Government's priority for the trunk-road and motorway network in the south east is to provide efficiently for the strategic movements which pass through the region, linking it to continental Europe, to the neighbouring regions and the north, and the major intra-regional flows essential to the region's economy. The accessibility and level of service afforded by the trunk-road and motorway network also benefits local inhabitants and businesses, but its primary function is to serve longer-distance traffic. (1993a, pp. 18–19)

The south east, therefore, had the worst of both worlds in terms of congestion. Not only did it have the highest concentration of economic activity in Britain, but it was also the region that much of Britain's trade with Europe had to pass through. It differed in this respect from, for example, the Pas de Calais region of northern France, where the building of new transport links to the Channel Tunnel provided for a welcome influx of economic activity in a comparatively underdeveloped region.

Even so, the Department of the Environment could not promise enough new roads to remove the south east's congestion problems. Again, quoting from its regional planning guidance, the department said:

Transport use in the south east is greater than in other parts of the country ... High levels of transport use have led to considerable congestion in London, in many towns and on major radial routes. Congestion imposes costs on businesses, undermines economic activity, and inhibits the functioning of the transport system. It increases pollution, damages the environment and reduces the quality of life in the south east. It would be unrealistic to seek to increase the capacity of the road network to match all projected demand throughout the region. The costs would be prohibitive and the environmental impact would be unacceptable. (1993a, p. 18)

The south east seemed to be destined for road-pricing, in an effort to limit demand for road use. John MacGregor, the Transport Secretary, issued a consultative document on road-pricing in 1993. Among the options was a system of charging for drivers venturing into central London during peak hours. Pricing on other congested parts of the south east road network also looked likely, though perhaps not until the early part of the twenty-first century. The provision of roads in the south east had, as always, run hard just to maintain a given level of congestion. And the Department of the Environment's observation that future road development had to guard against an unacceptable environmental impact was the height of irony for environmentalists. To them, the impact of planned road schemes was already unacceptable.

Again, however, development was not a foregone conclusion. An example was at Oxleas Wood (not to be confused with Foxley Wood) in south east London. Oxleas Wood, a 321-acre area of ancient woodland, said to be at least 8,000 years old, was on the planners' route for a new East London River Crossing, intended to take traffic away from the congested Blackwall Tunnel. The crossing, between the Blackwall Tunnel and the Dartford Tunnel and bridge further downstream, would link the A2/M2 road from the Kent Channel ports (and the Channel Tunnel) to a new bridge across the Thames at Thames-mead, in the East Thames corridor. The six-mile road link between the A2/M2 and the new bridge would cut directly through Oxleas Wood as well as, further along the route, requiring the demolition of 240 homes.

Oxleas Wood justifiably captured the imagination of environmentalists, as a project against which the strongest stand had to be made. Visiting Brazilian Indians from the rain forest invoked the spirits against the development. The European Commissioner for the Environment was lobbied. A 10,000-signature petition was presented to John Major at 10 Downing Street. Tony Aldous, writing in the *Evening Standard*, captured the mood:

What makes a 13-year old girl, off her own bat, organize a petition that attracts 10,000 signatures? What makes those 10,000 people sign it? What makes nine ordinary (or rather extraordinary) Londoners take on the Government in the courts, and risk £100,000-plus in legal costs? And what makes one of London's financially most hard-pressed councils decide to take the case to appeal? The answer to all those questions is Oxleas Wood, a 321-acre public open space containing an 8,000-year-old woodland miraculously preserved among the suburban sprawl of Eltham, Woolwich and Bexley ... Even if you don't know that this is one of only three sizeable ancient woodlands in Greater London, and wouldn't recognize a tree of gelder rose if you saw it, just walking there among the massive oaks gives a sense of magic, majesty and mystery. (5 April 1993)

The protestors failed in court because the Department of Transport had promised to provide an open space of equal area, albeit one that had to be planted with new trees and would be subject to considerable traffic noise. This, according to Mr Justice Hutchison in the High Court in February 1993, meant that the balance was 'just in favour' of the Department of Transport. According to Friends of the Earth, quoted in the *Independent* on 20 February 1993: 'Mr Justice Hutchison has given the Government extremely wide powers to take our best open spaces and give any land they like in exchange. This judgment means the Environment Secretary can ignore the fact that unique wildlife habitats are irreplaceable.'

The protestors appeared to have lost. They could pin their hopes on an appeal, or on a Hindhead-type tunnel under the wood, which could have been built for less than half the cost of the proposed bore under the Devil's Punchbowl in Surrey. They could also hope for help from Brussels, although precedent suggested that the Government would have little trouble in heading off pressure from the European Community to change its decision.

Michael Howard, the Environment Secretary, certainly appeared determined to see the scheme through. In February 1993, after the initial High Court judgment, he was criticized in the *Daily Telegraph* for inconsistency. The Government, the writer said, was concerned to establish an international reputation for working to preserve the Brazilian rain forest while, closer to home, it allowed ancient woodlands such as Oxleas to be destroyed. Howard responded in a letter to the newspaper on 24 February 1993:

I have never, and never would, argue that the Amazonian rain forest should be declared an economic no-go zone. Indeed, I am certain that unless ways can be found for both its immediate inhabitants and the Government of Brazil to derive sustainable economic advantage from its existence, I see no way at all of preserving its unique features. This will inevitably involve striking a balance between economic development and ecological sanctity. By the same token, in the crowded and difficult circumstances of the south east of England a balance has to be struck between the economy and the environment. Sometimes this will be painful, as was the decision on Oxleas Wood ... No stretch of the imagination allows Oxleas Wood to be described as 'the last vestige' of our 'wild nature', and although it is our policy to avoid damage to ancient woodlands wherever possible, it was not possible in this case.

The congested South appeared ready to claim another victim. But Howard was promoted to the position of Home Secretary in May 1993, to be replaced by John Gummer at Environment. And, in a surprise move, the British Road Federation proposed an alternative plan that did not require the route to the new river crossing to pass through the wood. Quietly, in a parliamentary written answer in July 1993, Transport Secretary John MacGregor announced that Oxleas Wood was to be saved. Again, there was a limit to the extent that the Government would allow unpopular developments.

11

THE DECISION-MAKING DIVIDE

By seeing London, I have seen as much of life as the world can show. (Dr Johnson)

Imagine the United Kingdom as a large, oddly shaped body. The limbs of the body, way up in the North and over in the West, have often suffered from poor circulation and wasting muscle. The heart, in the old industrial areas, has had its own difficulties and is not what it was. But the head and brains in the south east, at least until the 1990–92 recession, were working overtime. The body may not have been what it once was, but it had retained its faculties. Perhaps the recession, with its harsh impact on the South, was proof that you cannot have a selective approach to good economic health.

A prime cause of long-standing southern bias in the British economy, and in British society, is the concentration of decision-making power in London and the south east. London is the seat of government and the home for a huge civil-service machine. The financial system is centred upon the City of London, although by the late 1980s there was evidence of a revival of regional financial centres, Leeds being a good example. Most company head offices are in London and the south east, spawning a vast array of support activities in administration, advertising and marketing, research and development, and financial and business services such as banking, accountancy and management consultancy. The national media, both broadcast and print, are exclusively London-based. National opinion-formers, if that is not too grand a term, see things from a south-eastern point of view, and attempt to influence national decision-makers, who are subject to the same regional bias.

The exception to this general pattern is Scotland which, since the Act of Union of 1707, has had its own legal and educational systems and, since 1885, has had its own separate Scottish Office. The Welsh Office, created in 1964, is much more recent. The majority of decisions affecting Scotland (and Wales) are taken in London although the importance of the status of Scotland and Wales should not be underestimated. During the 1980s, Nicholas Edwards and Peter Walker, as successive Secretaries of State for Wales, operated economic and industrial strategies that were much more interventionist (and, given the circumstances of Wales, more successful) than those operated in England under Mrs Thatcher. Both Wales and Scotland benefit from higher public expenditure per head than English regions with similar circumstances. Small wonder that the English regions of the North called out for similar treatment.

The south-eastern bias of decision-making in Britain has applied for a long time. In Chapter One I discussed the dominance of London in the centuries prior to the industrial revolution and the re-establishment of that position in the twentieth century. In recent years the influence, indeed the control, exerted by London and the South has grown at a time when the influence of the North has declined. This has occurred in a number of ways. Whitehall has fought to wrest control over what were formerly local decisions and has tightened its grip on local-authority finance against the town halls. The City has grown in importance as an international financial centre, and the once important regional stock exchanges in Birmingham, Manchester and Glasgow have been rendered virtually obsolete. The boom in individual shareholding was unevenly distributed in the South's favour.

The North has lost company head offices as firms have closed or merged, and the 'company town' is fast becoming a rarity as the big employers of the past have rationalized or shut down. The tradition, exemplified in towns such as Sir Titus Salt's Saltaire, near Bradford, is not necessarily dead, however. Nissan has turned Washington in Tyne and Wear into something of a company town. Even so, most corporate decisions are made in head offices in London and the home counties or, in the case of foreign-owned firms, even further afield. Television and radio, in spite of a conscious attempt to encourage regional and local broadcasting, remain dominated by London. Regional newspapers, with the exception of local advertising freesheets, have lost out to national, London-based papers. The vast majority of weekly and monthly magazines sold in Britain are produced in London.

THE CENTRALIZATION OF GOVERNMENT

As described in Chapter Three, the last serious attempt to devolve political power away from London was under the Labour Government of James Callaghan, shortly before Margaret Thatcher came to power in 1979. Referenda for limited devolution from Westminister for Scotland and Wales were held, and in both cases the devolution lobby was defeated. At the same time, a survey carried out in England showed that only 5 per cent of people were in favour of elected assemblies for the English regions.

The Conservative Government elected in 1979 made it clear that it would have no truck with devolution, although the Labour Party indicated that, if elected, it would look upon the idea more sympathetically. However, while popular support for a form of Scottish devolution increased, this was hardly the case in Wales and, in spite of Labour's efforts to stimulate the debate, barely at all in the northern regions of England. As well as rejecting devolution, the Conservative Government took a number of steps which had the effect of shifting power from local to central government. Under the general policy of attempting to control public expenditure more tightly, it introduced changes in the system of block grants available from central to local government, supplementing these with measures to limit high-spending local authorities through rate-capping. This resulted in some memorable battles between the Government and certain local authorities, notably Liverpool, but – with central government setting the rules – there was little doubt as to the eventual outcome. Rate-capping powers were used more extensively during the Government's failed three-year experiment (in England and Wales; in Scotland it was four years) with the poll tax, or Community Charge.

The Thatcher Government abolished the upper tier of local government, the metropolitan councils, removing not only the Greater London Council and the West Midlands Metropolitan Council, but also the metropolitan councils in Tyne and Wear, South Yorkshire, West Yorkshire, Greater Manchester and Merseyside. The role of councils as employers was reduced as many of their services were put out to competitive tender, again as part of a policy emanating from Whitehall and Westminster rather than the councils themselves. Similarly, their role as landlords was scaled down, very dramatically in some areas, by the policy of council-house sales – forced through against the objections of many councils.

Important though these changes were in the further centralization of political power in Britain, it should be remembered that the context in which they took place was that of an already highly centralized political system. The German academic and former director of the London School of Economics, Ralf Dahrendorf, wrote in his book *On Britain*:

Yet when all is said and done, there remains the fact that many strands do converge, if not in Westminster then in Whitehall. One may well add a number of other London addresses to the list: Smith Square (although the Labour Party has now moved and others never went there); the Bank of England and the Law Courts; Buckingham Palace of course. Britain is a highly centralized country, not just a unitary state, but one that is run from London in virtually all respects. (1982, p. 105)

Stephen Fothergill and Jill Vincent, in their book *The State of the Nation*, conducted an analysis of addresses in *Who's Who* and found that the political élite – senior politicians and civil servants – were, perhaps unsurprisingly, concentrated in London and the south east, along with the business and military élites. Within London itself, the south-western postal districts, particularly Westminster but also Kensington, Chelsea, Knightsbridge,

Belgravia, Fulham, Putney and Wimbledon, were where the élite tended to live.

Since 1970, Britain has had one prime minister from the north of England, Harold Wilson, and one from Wales, James Callaghan. Both, of course, led the Labour Party. Of the three Conservative prime ministers, Edward Heath, Prime Minister from 1970–74, is a southerner, born in Broadstairs in Kent, while Margaret Thatcher, born and brought up in Grantham in Lincolnshire, is from the east midlands. John Major, born in Carshalton, Surrey, and brought up in Worcester Park and Brixton, is a suburban south Londoner. Conservative governments will always tend to exhibit a southern bias, largely because of the regional distribution of their voting strength.

In the spring of 1993, only one member of John Major's Cabinet of twenty-two was born in the north of England. The minister, John Gummer from the Department of Agriculture, was born in Stockport in Cheshire, but represented an East Anglian constituency (Suffolk Coastal) in the House of Commons. The Scots were better represented, with six Cabinet members – Ian Lang, born in Kincardine; Norman Lamont, from Lerwick in the Shetland Islands; Malcolm Rifkind, Edinburgh-born and representing an Edinburgh constituency; Lord Mackay of Clashfern, the Lord Chancellor, born in Sutherland; John MacGregor, born in Edinburgh but representing the constituency of South Norfolk; and Virginia Bottomley, the Health Secretary who, surprisingly, was born in Dunoon. Wales had three Cabinet members – Michael Heseltine, born in Swansea; Michael Howard, from Llanelli; and David Hunt, born in north Wales.

Of the twenty MPs in the Cabinet, no less than eleven represented constituencies in London and the south east. Four came from East Anglian seats, including the Prime Minister, whose constituency was Huntingdon. Two of the remainder, Scottish Secretary Ian Lang, and Defence Secretary Malcolm Rifkind, held Scottish seats. The three others were Kenneth Clarke, Home Secretary (Rushcliffe, Nottingham, in the east midlands), Welsh Secretary David Hunt (Wirral West, in the north west) and Chancellor of the Duchy of Lancaster William Waldegrave

(Bristol West, in the south west). The remaining Cabinet member, Lord Wakeham, came from Essex. The bias of the Cabinet towards seats in the south east and East Anglia was clear. Northern England could justly claim to be grossly under-represented, by both birth and parliamentary constituency.

Virtually every MP who has written an autobiography has told of the fatal attraction of Westminster life. The company is generally good, the existence usually more interesting than the job that he or she did before. If not, why would so many generally talented people strive for years to become MPs? Set against the bustle and fun of life in Westminster, the constituency can seem like a dull and distant place. The Saturday morning surgery listening to constituents complaints and demands is something that few MPs, with hand on heart, can say that they genuinely look forward to. For ministers, who are generally much busier than backbench MPs, this is even more likely to be the case. Their impressions of the North are conditioned by flying visits to factories, schools and hospitals and, in the nature of these things, their hosts usually make a considerable effort to show their area in its most favourable light. Even for cabinets with a fair sprinkling of members born in and representing the North, the pull of Westminster and the tendency to regard what is happening in the south east as typical of the rest of the country is a danger. For those that start off with a southern bias it is doubly dangerous.

THE CIVIL SERVICE

Anthony Sampson, in his first *Anatomy of Britain*, written in 1962, said of Britain's civil service that 'of all the world's bureaucracies, the British civil servants are perhaps the most compact and self-contained'. This extends not just to the size and method of operation of the civil service but also, crucially, to the area in which it operates. Sampson wrote:

The tingling centre of the civil service, where the major decisions are taken, remains the half-mile of stone buildings from Trafalgar Square to Westminster Abbey, with high classical façades, tall cupolas, and heavy marble staircases. The propinquity is important: ideas, misgivings, suggestions can brush from one to another in Whitehall as casually and smoothly as dust on to a coat. In a walk through the park you can have a few casual encounters and at once sense the political attitude. (pp. 219-20)

Three decades on, very little has changed. The Department of the Environment's ugly headquarters over at Marsham Street is a taxi ride, or a brisk walk, away from the hub of Whitehall. Whitehall has stretched as far as the Elephant and Castle, south of the river, where the Department of Health and Social Security was located at Alexander Fleming House. This is a post-war building so unattractive that there have been demands for a preservation order to be placed upon it as an example of the Eastern European-style functionalism of the period. With the break-up of the DHSS into separate departments of health and social security in 1988, some civil servants employed there found themselves brought back into the bosom of the civil service in Whitehall. For virtually every government department, the most senior civil servants, and large numbers of less senior ones, operate in London SW1, within striking distance both of the Houses of Parliament and of each other.

Attempts have been made to reduce the southern, and in particular the south eastern, bias of the civil service. During the Second World War, the threat of air raids on London led to a shift of some government offices away from the capital, notably to seaside and other resorts such as Blackpool, Bath and Harrogate, where hotel accommodation was easily adaptable to office use. This dispersion was reversed after the war, with one or two exceptions, for example the Department for National Savings Office at Lytham St Annes. Immediately after the war, in 1946, a new office for the then Ministry of Pensions and National Insurance was established in Newcastle.

A 1963 report by Sir Gilbert Flemming for the government called for the dispersal of 20,000 civil-service jobs from London. The programme adopted did benefit the regions – the Driver and Vehicle Licensing Centre was set up at Swansea and the Inland Revenue moved some of its activities to Merseyside and

Manchester. But, as with industrial relocation, it was often the rest of the south east, for example Basingstoke, that benefited from the dispersal from London.

In July 1974, the Labour Government responded to the Hardman report of the previous year, which recommended the dispersal of 31,000 civil-service jobs from London. The report, by Sir Henry Hardman, had recommended that 12,000 of the total be relocations from London to the rest of the south east. The decision was taken by Labour to retain the Hardman total of 31,000 but for only 850 of the jobs moved to be relocated elsewhere in the south east. The remaining posts, just over 30,000, were to go to regions in other parts of the country over a ten-year period at a cost, in the first five years alone, of £20–30 million. Glasgow was to receive 7,000 jobs, mainly in the Ministry of Defence, Merseyside 3,000, Cardiff and Newport 5,400, and Teesside 3,000. In the event, Mrs Thatcher's Conservative Government, when elected in 1979, drastically cut back on its predecessor's targets. This was partly on the grounds of cost – which had escalated dramatically – and the fact that within its overall policy of reducing the size of the civil service, large-scale job moves out of London were no longer considered to be appropriate. A modest target of dispersing 5,900 civil-service jobs out of London was set. Nine years on, in 1988, the Paymaster General, Peter Brooke, told the House of Commons that even this modest target had not quite been met, with 5,560 of the dispersals having been achieved, and the remaining 340 in hand. However, in addition to these, departments had, under their own initiative, moved more than 6,000 jobs out of London.

It was this latter route that represented official policy on civil-service dispersion in the late 1980s. Under Treasury guidelines issued in March 1988, called 'Running Costs Guidance: Location of Work', departments were not given any targets for moving staff out of London and the south east to the rest of the country. Instead, it was demonstrated to them that, in some circumstances, the best way of staying within the limits on running costs imposed by the Treasury was to consider moving staff to other parts of the country.

The location of central government work influences its cost. Employment and accommodation costs differ considerably by geographical location. They are influenced by local property and labour markets, which may show marked variations within and between regions. Generally speaking, location in London and the south east imposes higher costs than location in other regions, though within any locality or region, areas of well-established office development will often tend to be more expensive than others. An important element in Government policies for evening-out the spread of employment in the regions, Scotland, Wales, Northern Ireland and inner cities, is to encourage greater market flexibility. Using running-cost disciplines as a spur to relocation fits in well with these policies. (1988a, p. 1)

While the process of moving staff was far from cheap – the Treasury estimated the direct costs to a higher executive officer with family moving from London to Cardiff as £8,000, which would have to be refunded – there would be compensating benefits. Apart from the obvious ones of lower rents and the removal of the obligation to pay London weighting allowances, departments could expect lower staff turnover in areas of higher unemployment, although the move itself could involve the loss of key staff. The Department of Employment announced plans to move staff to Runcorn in Cheshire, in line with the policy. Other moves included that of the Patent Office to Newport and the establishment of a new Land Registry in Hull.

As Table 11.1 shows, the effect of this policy had, four years later in April 1992, been to cut the number of civil-service jobs in London by 4,170, and in the south east as a whole by 6,987. East Anglia, the south west and the west midlands were net gainers, leaving an overall loss for the South of 5,657. All northern regions, with the exception of Scotland, gained civil servants, although the numbers were small, 2,301 for the North as a whole. The difference between the two figures is accounted for by a small overall decline in the size of the civil service, and by a 1,538 increase in the number of civil servants stationed outside the United Kingdom (the 'others' in the table).

The Treasury claimed a rather larger impact. Stephen Dorrell, the Financial Secretary to the Treasury, said at the end of 1992

Table 11.1   The geographical spread of the civil service

	April 1988		April 1992	
	Number employed	Percentage of total	Number employed	Percentage of total
Inner London	74,732	14·8	71,778	14·2
Intermediate London	20,444	4·0	20,131	4·0
Outer London	19,762	3·9	18,859	3·7
Total London	114,938	22·6	110,768	22·0
Rest of South East	79,482	15·7	76,666	15·2
Total South East	194,420	38·4	187,433	37·2
South West	45,467	9·0	46,112	9·1
East Anglia	13,935	2·8	14,657	2·9
East Midlands	20,298	4·0	19,702	3·9
West Midlands	30,433	6·0	30,992	6·1
The South	304,553	60·2	298,896	59·3
Yorks & Humberside	32,255	6·4	32,665	6·5
North West	51,350	10·1	53,594	10·6
North	31,772	6·3	32,376	6·4
Wales	27,186	5·4	27,583	5·5
Scotland	48,353	9·6	46,824	9·3
Northern Ireland	3,082	0·6	3,257	0·6
The North	193,998	38.3	196,299	38·9
Others	7,504	1·5	9,042	1·8
Total, non-industrial civil servants	506,055	100.0	504,237	100.0

Source: H.M. Treasury, *Civil Service Statistics* (1988, 1992), pp. 22–3, pp. 26– 7.
Totals may not sum exactly because of rounding.

that a total of 14,300 civil service jobs had been 'located or relocated' outside the south east, with a further 11,400 due to follow, and another 3,200 under review. The new policy, based on running-costs guidance, was, said Dorrell, much more effective than the old policy of centrally directed dispersal. 'This decentralized approach has resulted in the establishment outside the south east of over twice as many civil-service jobs in the last four years as in the previous eight,' he said in a Parliamentary answer on 17 December 1992.

Welcome though such moves are, the process will be a gradual one, and against the objections of many civil servants who simply do not want to be uprooted. More importantly, it is highly unlikely that the basic feature of Britain's centralized government structure will change, which is that the vast majority of senior civil servants, and their ministers, will continue to be located in Whitehall. The prospect of relocating the Department of Trade and Industry, en bloc, to Birmingham, say, or the Ministry of Defence to Manchester, does not appear to be there. The decision-makers will continue to be firmly rooted in London.

For Labour's Bryan Gould, this, along with other facets of the decision-making dominance of London and the south east, meant that: 'Overwhelmingly the decisions that matter are taken in the south east, for the south east and by the south east.' And the prospect of a shift in the role of regional offices of government departments, from that of representing Whitehall to the regions to that of representing the regions to Whitehall, seemed remote.

It is still the case that, as with industrial relocation, it is not necessarily the North which will gain from any shift from London and the south east. In April 1988, the Bank of England (a state-owned institution rather than a government department) announced that it was shifting its Registrar's Department out of the City of London. The chosen location for the 600–650 jobs that would result was not, however, Manchester or Sheffield, but Gloucester, on the argument that communications with London were better there than in the North.

And the story does not end there. As Michael Heseltine, himself a former Conservative Defence Secretary, has pointed out, a substantial majority of those employed in the armed forces are stationed in the South, and a high proportion of defence contracts go to southern factories. In a speech in April 1988 he said:

We recruit 30 per cent of service personnel from the nearly 40 per cent of the population that lives in the south east and south west. But we station 60 per cent there. On the other hand we recruit 30 per cent of service personnel from the 25 per cent of the population who live in the North (of England) and we station 8 per cent there; 14 per cent of our service recruits come from the north west. Only 1 per cent of jobs are located there.

We are actually recruiting disproportionately large numbers of young people in the north and north west to station them in southern areas already overcrowded. Study after study has pointed to the growth potential of military research laboratories or MoD procurement and contract departments. The Ministry of Defence Quality Assurance division is located at Woolwich. It should go north before the rest of the companies it monitors move south. (1988b, pp. 12–13)

The armed forces have long displayed a southern bias in their location. The Army, traditionally centred on London, initially developed Aldershot in Hampshire and, in the present century, Salisbury Plain, as alternative locations. Throughout Britain's history, the naval threat was from continental Europe and so the major bases were at Chatham, Portsmouth and Plymouth, all on the South Coast. Southern and eastern Britain have the majority of Royal Air Force establishments.

The South's advantage in this area turned into a disadvantage, however, when the end of the Cold War and government cuts in defence spending began to produce reductions in the numbers of military personnel and base closures. A study, 'The Impact of Reduced Military Expenditure on the Economy of South West England', produced by Bristol Polytechnic's Research Unit in Defence Economics, suggested the loss of 52,000 defence jobs in south west England by the year 2000, with as many again to go if jobs in supplier firms were included. According to Richard Woolhouse and Nick Mansley, writing in the *Cambridge Economic Review* in the autumn of 1992:

There is considerable divergence of opinion as to the scale and timing of the cuts. We believe that the cuts are likely to amount to less than 25 per cent in real terms by the end of the decade. If larger-scale cuts are made, however, this analysis suggests Avon, Hampshire, Devon, Fife, Wiltshire and Somerset will be amongst the areas most adversely affected. (1992, p. 31)

PRIVATE DECISION-MAKERS

The concentration of political and bureaucratic decision-making in London and the South east would be a major source of disadvantage for the North even if it was balanced by a significant proportion of private-sector decision-makers in the regions. Even as Britain's industrial golden age was beginning to look tarnished this was still the case. A study, 'The Large Manufacturing Employers of 1907', by Christine Shaw of the Business History Unit of the London School of Economics, showed that in that year around three quarters of the top 100 manufacturing employers had their head offices outside London and the south east, principally in the Midlands, Yorkshire, Lancashire and Scotland.

The modern multi-plant firm is largely an extrapolation of a phenomenon already established before the First World War, but there is none the less a strong indication . . . that the largest firms differed from those of today in other ways. The dominance of the basic industries of the Celtic fringe and the industrial north is evident, and this impression is confirmed by a study of the location of their head offices. (1983, p. 48)

By the 1930s, the dominance of London and the south east as a head-office location had increased sharply. This was due both to rapid development of the new service and light consumer goods industries in the south east and the west midlands and also to the rationalization of, for example, steel and textiles in the industrial north. The Bank of England played a direct role in the creation of the Lancashire Cotton Corporation – formed from a merger of around 100 cotton-spinning firms – and in the establishment of the English and Lancashire Steel Corporations. Leslie Hannah, the head of the LSE's Business History Unit, has estimated that between 1919 and 1930 the proportion of the head offices of Britain's fifty largest companies in London rose from less than a third to more than half.

The more recent position, as indicated in Table 11.2, derived from *The Times 1,000* largest companies by turnover, is that the dominance of London and the south east in head-office location extends well beyond the biggest 100 companies (where nearly 90 per cent are located there). Even well down the list, 50 or 60 per cent of head offices are in the south east, including London, and there is no evidence that this concentration of decision-making in the area in and around the capital is reversing itself.

A survey carried out by the Manchester Business School for Granada Television, published in October 1988, showed that among 110 southern-based chief executives and finance directors questioned, 93 per cent said that their senior staff would not consider moving to the North, in spite of lower rents, cheaper housing and, in some cases, proximity to markets. In addition, 86 per cent of those questioned thought that their careers would be hampered by a move to the North, because career opportunities were so much better in the South, while 99 per cent thought that the opening of the Channel Tunnel would make them even less likely to consider business opportunities in the North. A high proportion of the executives in the survey thought that the workforce in the North was unionized and disruptive, that there was a lack of financial services, including merchant banks, and that it was a cultural desert. Although the pattern of the recession may have changed some of these perceptions, there was no evidence of a move northwards for company head offices.

What is also striking from Table 11.2 is the very small proportion of head offices in the 'peripheral' regions of the north, Wales and Northern Ireland. In every respect, these areas can be classified as branch economies. Overall, according to the definitions of North and South used in this book, 94 out of the largest 100 firms, including UK subsidiaries of foreign firms, had head offices in the South, and 783 out of the top 1,000.

The shift to the South, and in particular London and the south east, in companies' head-office activities has resulted from changes in Britain's industrial structure. When firms were based on a single activity, and often a single plant, it was appropriate to locate the head office where that activity was carried out. As larger firms developed through the process of horizontal mergers – that is, a collection of units under the same ownership but producing the same or similar products – then it became necessary to have head offices away from at least some parts of the productive process. The further development of diversified, multi-product companies, again principally as a result of mergers, and often with large numbers of factories in different areas of the country, accentuated this development.

Table 11.2   Head office location: Britain's top 1,000 companies

	London	Rest of SE	South West	East Anglia	East Mids	West Mids	Yorks /Hum	North West	North	Wales	Scotland	Nthn Irel
1–100	73	16	1	0	1	3	3	2	0	0	1	0
101–200	50	21	6	1	2	6	6	6	2	0	5	0
201–300	39	32	1	2	2	6	6	7	2	0	3	0
301–400	29	33	2	1	6	5	7	6	1	2	7	1
401–500	29	28	1	3	6	8	11	7	1	0	6	0
501–600	27	34	2	1	6	5	8	9	2	2	4	0
601–700	24	36	4	4	6	3	5	9	3	1	5	0
701–800	38	22	3	1	7	7	9	5	0	0	7	1
801–900	24	23	3	4	7	8	9	8	4	2	8	1
901–1000	21	25	4	4	7	10	11	7	4	1	6	0
1–1000	354	270	27	21	50	61	69	66	19	8	52	3

Source: The Times 1,000 1987–88 (Times Books Ltd).

With no overriding need to be located in a specific region, firms looked for head offices which were close to the government department with which they were likely to have frequent dealings and near to their merchant banks and stockbrokers, as well as the head offices of the English clearing banks. National bodies such as the Confederation of British Industry, if close at hand, could also be useful. They looked for a location which was well served in transport links, both within Britain and, for the increasing proportion of companies with overseas factories and a high proportion of foreign trade, abroad. Inevitably too, company chairmen looked for a location for their head office which was prestigious, both for their own personal gratification and to impress customers. Only London came anywhere near to satisfying these criteria.

Doug Watts of the University of Sheffield, who has studied the effects of the regional distribution of head offices, made the point that these go well beyond their direct employment consequences. The uneven distribution of head offices 'presents two major regional problems', he said at the Institute of British Geographers' conference in January 1988:

The first is an under-representation of white-collar jobs in the north; the second is a reduced demand for business services, which results in fewer business services for local firms which need them. It is also possible that the north receives unfavourable treatment by distant head offices such as less investment or more plant closures. Whether the advantages gained by the economy as a whole from the concentration of head offices in the south is sufficient to offset the north's disadvantages is open to debate.

John McEnery, a former Under Secretary at the Department of Trade and Industry, writing in the *Financial Times* in February 1988, was more colourful in his evocation of the damage done by too high a proportion of head offices in London and the south east:

The cancer debilitating the rest of the country is the concentration of company headquarters in the London area, whether in manufacturing or service industry. It is these headquarters, themselves autonomous services, that in turn spawn the vast range of ancillary services in the south east and cause the national imbalance in service employment and in house prices.

As with many of the developments described in this book, the southern bias of head-office location has important cumulative effects. What may have begun as a fashion for a London head office becomes an irreversible trend, by which process many of the facilities required, or believed to be required, by companies, only exist in the capital, or at least within a short distance of it. Head offices generate a wide range of business activities, including demands for business services such as accountancy, and are likely to be where a large company operates its marketing and advertising functions.

Research and development activities, originally located near the factories where new products would be produced and new processes operated, are now also disproportionately concentrated in the South. Successive studies have indicated that at least half of the research establishments of the top 100 to 200 manufacturing companies are in the south east, accessible to the head office, if not always to the company's factory sites. There is a typical pattern in most large companies whereby there is a large, centralized research institution, usually in the South, and a series of smaller, on-site research units. Apart from the attractions of a location near to London, with its universities and research institutions, as well as the company's head office, research scientists have shown the same preference for being based in the South – for similar reasons – as the chief executives in the Manchester Business School survey described above. The huge science research establishments on the Berkshire Downs – Harwell and the Rutherford–Appleton Laboratory – provided a good reason for high-technoogy firms to locate in the Thames Valley.

REGIONAL TAKEOVER TARGETS

Throughout this century, the proportion of companies controlled and run from the North has declined. An important cause of this decline has been the takeover of regionally based companies, either by other British firms based in London and the south east or by foreign firms. Indeed, companies with head offices well away from London may have been more vulnerable to takeovers, because they failed to cultivate close enough links with the City.

It has been open to governments to block takeovers of regionally based firms. The Thatcher Government blocked the attempted takeover of the Royal Bank of Scotland in 1982 on regional grounds, but subsequently – in 1985 – shifted to a position, the so-called Tebbit guidelines, whereby competition alone would determine whether or not a proposed takeover would be permitted.

There have been numerous recent examples of London-based or foreign firms acquiring, or seeking to acquire, companies with head offices in the regions. The infamous Guinness takeover of Distillers was one, with Guinness's broken promise to shift its head office to Scotland perhaps the least surprising event in a quite remarkable saga. British Petroleum's acquisition of Britoil – the firm created out of the former British National Oil Corporation, was another, although in this instance the Government was able to use its special position as owner of a 'golden share' in Britoil to insist that BP move its exploration operations to Glasgow, to replace the former Britoil head office functions there.

Two takeover battles in the second half of the 1980s stand out in the history of the North's fight to retain control of at least some major companies. The first was in 1986, when the industrial conglomerate BTR bid for the St Helens-based glass manufacturer Pilkington. BTR, run by Owen Green, had become the darling of the City, with an aggressive programme of taking over and rationalizing ailing companies. It had already swallowed up Dunlop, formerly one of the country's leading tyre manufacturers, when it launched a bid for Pilkington. Pilkington, meanwhile, was a company with a long tradition of service to its local Lancashire community, having operated there since 1862, and in this was something of a relic of a bygone age of company philanthropy. The two protagonists could not have been more different: the aggressive creation of the takeover-crazy

1980s against the traditional firm which, in attitude, could virtually have been lifted out of the Victorian age. BTR, in launching its £1·2 billion takeover bid for Pilkington, said that 'nothing less than a change of culture in Pilkington is required to produce a long-term enhancement of Pilkington's perform-ance.' The local attitude to Pilkington, or 'Pilks' as it was known, was summarized in a document produced jointly by the council, trade unions and other community representatives:

Unlike most large UK companies Pilkington maintains its Headquar-ters in St Helens; its Group-wide research Headquarters is also nearby; its close relationship with the people of St Helens, and surrounding areas is, it believes, of strong mutual benefit. The energetic initiatives taken by Pilkington and the Council have convinced people that there is a future in the town.

The very qualities of BTR which appealed to the City were anathema to St Helens, and, to a certain extent, many of Pilkington's virtues were lost on the City. This was a company which, in the jargon, had not succeeded in making itself bid-proof and there seemed every possibility that Pilkington's institu-tional shareholders were prepared to give BTR the chance to run, or rationalize the company. There was strong pressure on the Government to block the takeover because of the damage that it would inflict on the local economy of St Helens. But, under the rules established in 1985, there were no grounds for referral. The BTR takeover might have done untold damage to Lancashire, but it was not an issue on which the Government felt able to act.

In the event, there was a happy ending for Pilkington. BTR withdrew its bid early in 1987, insisting that this was not be-cause of political pressure – there was no evidence of Govern-ment pressure on the company to withdraw, although even the Confederation of British Industry, normally neutral on such matters, registered its disapproval. Instead, contacts between BTR and Pilkington's institutional shareholders had revealed that, while they were not necessarily averse to the idea of a take-over, they expected a rather higher price than BTR was willing to pay.

There was a postscript to this failed bid in 1988, when Pilkington had to decide on the installation of new float glass capacity at one of two sites – at St Helens or in the south east, at Thanet, in Kent. Had the investment gone ahead at all under a Pilkington controlled by BTR, it is likely that, based on the proximity of the European market, the Channel Tunnel and many of the other factors favouring a south east location, St Helens would have lost out. As it was, Pilkington chose to invest in its home town.

The BTR–Pilkington affair may have had a happy ending for the North, but it did not represent a turning point. Indeed, the bid had demonstrated that the regional card would no longer be played by the Government in response to politically sensitive takeovers of the few remaining major northern-based companies. This was clearly shown to be the case in 1988, when Rowntree, the York-based confectionery maker, became the subject of takeover interest from two Swiss companies. Like Pilkington, Rowntree had a tradition of service to its local community and of social awareness. Early in the twentieth century the company, established in York by the brothers Henry and Joseph Rowntree in the 1850s, built a model housing development, New Earswick, for their workers, introduced a 48-hour working week and a company pension scheme and provided schoolrooms and a gymnasium for their workers. The Joseph Rowntree Memorial and Charitable Trusts continued to provide large sums for good works. This tradition, perhaps even more than that of Pilkington, cut little ice in the City, however, and Rowntree suffered from its failure to convince the City that it was running the business in the right way.

The result was that Rowntree had long been regarded as an ideal candidate for a takeover when the Swiss chocolate firm Jacobs–Suchard began to buy up shares in the company, eventually building up a 29·9 per cent stake – the maximum that is permitted before a full takeover bid has to be launched. However, it was Jacobs–Suchard's Swiss rival, the food giant Nestlé, which was the first to bid for Rowntree, offering £2·1 billion for the company.

What followed was in many ways reminiscent of Pilkington's

eventually successful attempt to escape BTR's attentions. The Government was urged to refer the bid to the Monopolies Commission, both on regional grounds and on the argument that, while British companies were fair game for Swiss predators, the nature of Swiss company structures made foreign takeovers very difficult there. The Secretary of State for Trade and Industry, Lord Young, said that there were no grounds for referring the bid, against the protests of some 150 northern MPs, including the then local Conservative MP, Conal Gregory, who had been elected on a paper-thin majority of 147 in his constituency.

In York, an impromptu meeting of the old Council of the North, which had last met in 1641, was called, this time with around fifty northern mayors as its members. The meeting, which was of publicity rather than constitutional value, was intended to demonstrate the solidarity of the North against overseas or, for that matter, southern predators. Rowntree workers marched on Parliament to the accompaniment of a brass band, creating a hundred headlines about chocolate soldiers. The local newspaper ran a 'Hands off Rowntree' campaign. But it was to be of no avail. Nestlé's original offer for Rowntree was at virtually twice the level the company's shares had been trading at before the two Swiss firms started buying. Once the two companies had built up substantial stakes it was not a question of whether Rowntree would be taken over, but which of the two would be successful. Jacobs–Suchard bid £2·3 billion but sold out to Nestlé when the latter offered £2·55 billion. At this level, even Rowntree workers queued up to sell their shares. The battle was over, and one of the last bastions of northern control of industry had fallen.

One of the dangers for the North in the concentration of head offices in London and the south east is that of creating a branch economy. When pruning is required, the branches are the first things to be cut off. And, while affected workers can lobby the company's head office, the fact that decisions are being made so far away makes it much more difficult to bring effective pressure to bear. Why, then, did the South suffer more, even in manufacturing industry, from the cutbacks of the 1990–92 recession? There are, I would suggest, four reasons. The first was the extent of the overheating in the South in the late 1980s. Company directors and senior managers, commuting to their London head offices, or trying to recruit in the south east, would have been keenly aware of the difficulties created by the boom. Thus, to the extent that they needed to shift production within the firm in a general retrenchment, they would tend to favour northern locations and cut back in the South, perhaps unaware that, in doing so, they would be helping to relieve those pressures, eventually quite dramatically. Secondly, the North had, in the first half of the 1980s, been through a dramatic period of rationalization. In many firms, those production sites that had escaped the cull had done so because they were the most efficient, a position reinforced by subsequent investment in the latest technology. Thirdly, I have already touched on the reason for service-sector redundancies in the South during the recession – because demand there fell more sharply. But in manufacturing, the downturn appears to have been disproportionately felt in certain, southern-based industries. Aerospace, for example, hit by the impact of post-Cold War defence cuts, had, like defence installations, been biased towards southern locations. Fourthly, and this is a point I shall go into in more detail in the next chapter, the North was helped by continued expansion by overseas firms. Many Japanese firms, for example, were attracted by non-congested, low-labour-cost northern locations. The London head-office factor was not significant in their decisions.

THE CITY

The experiences of both Pilkington and Rowntree illustrate the dangers to any company of distancing itself, both geographically and in philosophy, from the City. The City, which can still be defined fairly precisely as the square mile stretching from Moorgate to London Bridge, and from Holborn Viaduct to Aldgate, is the centre for financial decision-making in Britain. This has, of course, been the case for centuries. But, as the role of financial services in the economy has grown, so the City has become more important. London is the major financial centre in

Europe, forming the European leg of the global triangle which has as its other points New York and Tokyo.

One consequence of the City's growing international role is to give added weight to the argument that its interests lie beyond those of ensuring financial conditions which are of greatest benefit to the 'real' economy of Britain. Thus, as in the cases outlined above, institutional investors are likely to take an unsentimental attitude towards foreign takeovers of British companies. The City is likely to favour a stronger currency and higher interest rates than those which industry would choose. Given the huge number of foreign banks with active branches in the City, and the importance of American, Japanese and, to a lesser extent, Continental European securities houses, the divergence of interests between the City and the domestic economy is perhaps inevitable. And, since the abolition of exchange controls in 1979 by Sir Geoffrey Howe, the City has shown that it is prepared to direct capital overseas in large quantities, at the same time that under-investment has been cited as a weakness of the UK economy.

The City's short-termism, and its failure to provide capital in a way that is in the long-term interests of industry, has been widely commented upon. Professor Colin Mayer, in his inaugural City University Business School lecture in 1988, observed that 'the most efficient financial markets in the world appear to be the most deficient at funding their industries', adding that: 'The fundamental challenge that faces any institution or government that can affect the practice of finance is to encourage the emergence of closer relationships and to direct the wealth of talent that has now been concentrated in financial institutions into direct participation in corporate activities.'

Even a Conservative Chancellor of the Exchequer, Nigel Lawson, could find dangerous elements of 'short-termism' in the City's behaviour, in a speech in June 1986:

The big institutional investors nowadays increasingly react to short-term pressure on investment performance. As a consequence many British industrial managers complain that their institutional shareholders are unwilling to countenance long-term investment or a sufficient expenditure on research and development. (CBI, 1987a)

The Confederation of British Industry set up a task force, consisting of representatives from both industry and the City, to examine the apparent gulf between the producing and the financing sides of the economy. Its conclusions, published in October 1987, were that while there were problems of communication between companies and their shareholders, many of the charges about the City's failure to take a long-term view were unjustified. Two weeks after its report was published the stock market in London crashed, along with markets in other world financial centres, in perhaps the most comprehensive display of collective short-term behaviour since 1929.

A year later, in a survey published at the time of its annual conference in November 1988, CBI members expressed concern about the financial market attitudes which rendered even well-run companies liable to takeover. They called for greater government protection, particularly against foreign predators.

The combination of political, corporate and financial decision-making in London and the south east represents a major cause of the North–South divide. Regional interests are not adequately catered for and regional considerations largely absent from investment decisions. Added to this, the City and the growing financial-services industry, by being disproportionately located in the South, has direct and important consequences for the distribution of employment and wealth. As with company head offices and government departments, the City creates its own demand for business and other services. And the spending power of a generally high-earning sector of the population was particularly important in the 1980s in generating regional house price differences and in further concentrating economic activity in the South.

Andrew Leyshon and Nigel Thrift of the University of Bristol, in a 1988 paper 'The City of London: Southern Fortune or Northern Misfortune?' concluded that few of the effects of the City's expansion had leaked beyond southern England, but that there was now a possibility that other regional financial centres would begin to benefit. Edinburgh is probably the best known, but not the largest, regional financial centre. The development of existing centres in Leeds, Liverpool, Manchester and Newcastle could clearly have important implications for the North. Leeds, indeed, developed significantly as a financial centre in the late 1980s and early 1990s. The Midland Bank, in setting up a 24-hour telephone banking service, First Direct, chose Leeds as its location. Thus banking jobs were being expanded in Leeds at a time when they were being cut back in London and the south east. According to Kevin Newman, First Direct's chief executive, quoted on the Channel Four *High Interest* programme, 'Closing the Watford Gap':

The Leeds option worked out at round about two thirds of the cost of an equivalent building in Swindon. Secondly the communications. We're located very near the M62, very near the M1, and that extends the area in which we can attract staff and indeed it makes it easier for the staff to come to work.

The point about telecommunications is that it absolutely breaks any physical link between where we as a business are situated and where our customers are situated. The majority of our customers do come from the south east and the fact that we service them out of Leeds and Yorkshire really is of no consequence to them whatsoever.

The programme also quoted the example of Hammond Suddards, a Yorkshire-based firm of solicitors. ICI, the chemicals giant, used to handle litigation work in-house at its London head office. But in 1992 it put the work out to tender and Hammond Suddards won the contract. According to Barry O'Meara, ICI's deputy solicitor:

There has always been an assumption that the City of London provides the only centre of legal expertise and it's true that they can provide a breadth of knowledge that possibly you won't find elsewhere. However, the northern provincial firms have without doubt made inroads into that assumption and can provide straight commercial and corporate advice every bit as good as you'll find in London, added to which they can charge rates that are much lower than firms in London can charge and this is a matter of great interest to a company like mine which is naturally wanting to make certain that it gets the best value for money.

The role of the City in creating a powerful southern decision-making bias remains important, but the City's boom period of the 1980s was followed by a period of considerable retrenchment.

Indeed, the City's over-expansion in response to financial liberalization had been a symbol of the North–South divide of the Thatcher years. It also triggered over-building of new offices in London, a phenomenon that was to linger as a legacy of the recession.

THE MEDIA

Finally, and briefly, we can consider the role of newspapers, television and radio in promoting a southern, and in particular a south-eastern, view of Britain. Britain is unusual among countries of relatively large population in having a large and dominant national press, unlike for example the United States, France and Germany, where regional newspapers are much more important. British newspapers are concentrated both in their ownership and in the London location in which they are largely written and produced, even if they have now shifted away from Fleet Street to various points in the capital.

Some two thirds of the population of Britain read a national daily newspaper, and around 70 per cent a national Sunday paper. Readership proportions of national morning newspapers are higher in London, the rest of the south east and East Anglia, possibly because more people in these areas commute by train to work, but such proportions are more than 60 per cent in all parts of the country.

The *Guardian* sold less than 50,000 copies a day in the inter-war years, when it was the *Manchester Guardian*. The dropping of the Manchester prefix and the shifting of its editorial base to London in the early 1960s were factors in its becoming a larger-circulation national newspaper, currently selling more than 400,000 copies daily.

The combined circulation of national morning newspapers in the second half of 1992 was 14.25 million. By contrast, the combined circulation of regional morning newspapers in England such as the *Yorkshire Post*, the *Northern Echo* and the *Western Daily Press* was less than 600,000; in Wales it was 72,000 (the *Western Mail*); in Northern Ireland 43,600; and in Scotland 1.19 million, although this includes nearly 760,000 for the *Daily Record*, the Scottish version of the *Daily Mirror*. Regional morning newspapers have suffered, not only from competition from national morning newspapers and radio and television, but also from the shift from morning to evening readership in regional newspapers, and the evolution of the free newspaper. A new venture, the *North West Times*, closed in November 1988 after just seven weeks of publication. A national tabloid, the *Post*, launched in the same month by Eddie Shah and run from offices in Warrington in the north west, closed just five weeks later.

The position of regional evening newspapers is far healthier than that of their morning counterparts. The combined weekday circulation of regional evening newspapers in England reporting to the Audit Bureau of Circulations was 3.55 million in the second half of 1992, although this included many titles in the South. In Wales it was 217,000, in Northern Ireland 131,000, in the Channel Islands 40,000, and in Scotland around 400,000.

Two points need to be made about regional evening newspapers, however. The first is that they are probably not looked upon by their readers as a primary source of political and economic opinion, and the bulk of their reporting on national politics and economics comes from London-based agencies, and in particular the Press Association. In addition, most evening and morning newspapers in the regions are not independent but are owned by larger groups, many of which are publishers of national newspapers. Thus, both Associated Newspapers, publishers of the *Daily Mail*, and United Newspapers, publishers of the *Daily Express*, feature as major owners of regional newspapers. Pearson, which owns the *Financial Times*, also has a string of regional newspapers. Other prominent owners of regional newspapers include Reed International, which also publishes a wide range of national magazines, and the International Thomson Organization.

In broadcasting, while both the BBC and the Independent Broadcasting Authority have taken steps to increase regional input, notably through local radio, it is still the case that the bulk of news and current affairs coverage, on both television and radio, emanates from London. The regional television companies rely on Independent Television News for national news coverage, supplementing it with regional news and magazine programmes. Similar arrangements apply for the independent local radio stations and Independent Radio News.

On the BBC, national news coverage and most current affairs programmes, for both television and radio, come from London. Some 70 per cent of the BBC's radio output – measured according to hours of broadcasting – is local radio. But BBC national radio output dominates the statistics for listening, as opposed to broadcasting, with almost six times the number of listeners as BBC local radio. And half of national radio programmes, of all types, are produced in London.

The precise way in which the London dominance of the media displays itself is difficult to assess. When the great storm of October 1987 struck the South of England it was said that the amount of coverage it received was directly related to the fact that many journalists and broadcasters had been personally affected by it. Thus, it was argued, a similar storm in the North of England would have received far less attention. The media are criticized for their over-emphasis on reporting and analysing House of Commons debates and, in their business coverage, for concentrating too much on events in the narrow confines of the City of London, rather than the wider industrial and business scene. Certainly, there must have been considerable puzzlement in the North when, following the stock market crash of 1987, much space was devoted to reports of relatively small numbers of City redundancies, when set against the scale of earlier and continuing redundancies in industry.

The south-eastern bias of the national media, indeed, was said by many observers to have come to the fore in the 1990–92 recession. The reporting of the recession, and the intensity of the criticism of the Government even by Conservative newspapers, appeared to be linked to the fact that the downturn was most severe on journalists' own doorsteps. A sharp fall in advertising revenues hit newspapers directly, and ended abruptly the expansion of the 1980s. Two new titles, the *London Daily News* and the *Sunday Correspondent*, folded. Unlike in the early 1980s, when journalists reported the great manufacturing recession at a distance, this one was affecting them and their friends. Northerners, who were suffering far less than in the earlier recession, were often bemused by the tales of deep woe that they read in their national newspapers, particularly when they contrasted it with the reporting of, and editorial attitude to, 'their' slump. Ministers hinted that part of the blame for the length and depth of the recession could be attributed to the uniformly gloomy tone of the media.

12

DIVIDED NO MORE?

Our chief interest in the past is as a guide to the
future. (W. R. Inge, former Dean of St Paul's)

There is a great temptation, in analysing regional disparities in
Britain, to see things in black and white terms. Thus, in the
1980s, people tended to believe, either that there was an irreversible North–South divide in Britain, with the cards stacked firmly
in the South's favour, or they saw talk of a North–South
divide as part of a softening-up process by grasping northerners
and soggy liberal southerners for a return to old-style interven-
tionism, through large-scale, blanket regional assistance. The
position was complicated by the fact that such views did not
split along regional lines. Many southerners, perhaps motivated
by a wish to direct development away from their own area, took
the view that something had to be done about the North–
South divide. But a significant proportion of northerners, either
because they were happy to let the south east stew in its own
congested juice, or because they were in the business of attracting
investment to their regions and wanted to present their local
economies as vibrant and expanding, declared themselves happy
with the status quo. This view – life in the North will remain
great as long as we do not let southerners in on the secret – was
common in the economic boom years, and became even more so
when the South suffered disproportionately in the recession.

Another characteristic of the debate has been the tendency to
assume that the economic advantages enjoyed by some regions of
Britain relative to others imply that the former are inherently

superior to the latter. I hope that I have avoided that in this book. The true position, as described in Chapter 4, is that regional problems take several forms. Most of the concern in Britain has been with the difficulties faced by underdeveloped or declining regions. But this ignores the problem of congested regions which, in some ways, are more serious. It is necessary to stand back a little from the regional league tables and recognize that all three types of problem are associated with the inefficiency of wasting resources. Congestion, and consequent overheating, in the South limited the economy's ability in the 1980s to sustain a rapid rate of economic growth.

The 1990–92 recession, with its uneven impact on the South and its limited impact on, for example, Scotland, has been hailed as proof that, left to its own devices, the economy will correct regional disparities. This, however, is far too simplistic a view. The first and most important point is that even a recession as severe as that of the early 1990s cannot undo the effects of a century in which economic activity, and population, has shifted from North to South. What the recession undoubtedly did was to undo the sharp increase in North–South differences that occurred in the second half of the 1980s. And this, perhaps, was not surprising. The South had grown at an unsustainable rate in the late 1980s. Secondly, the recession was not brought about by the ebb and flow of a freely functioning economy. It was due to one of the most abrupt shifts in the direction of economic policy in the post-war period. In the spring of 1988, the Government was still pursuing a highly expansionary fiscal and monetary policy. By the autum it had slammed the brakes on hard. The South's boom and bust was due to an unstable economic policy environment. Thirdly, it is fanciful to think that the recession corrected Britain's long-standing regional problems at a stroke. Even in recession, pressure on the transport infrastructure of the south east continued to create serious delays and, as described in Chapter 10, meant that the Government had to plan for significant additions to that infrastructure, even at a substantial cost to the environment. The North did not suddenly acquire new advantages as a result of the recession. The main effect, indeed, was to produce a greater equality of misery between regions. Something similar had happened in most previous recessions, although not quite as dramatically as in 1990–92.

The pattern of North–South disparities in the late 1970s and 1980s provides a useful insight into their likely development in the 1990s. The 1980–81 period was a watershed for the British economy. The recession then was no ordinary one. It represented a catharsis for the economy – the end of overmanning, the beginning of the end of trade unionism as a major force and the end of manufacturing as a source of new employment. A process was set in train which resulted in the drastic rationalization, and in some cases the complete disappearance, of many of the old, northern-based industries. This continued for much of the 1980s, dogging the North and condemning most northern regions to low growth and high unemployment. At the same time, the liberalization of the banking and financial systems had the effect of creating lucrative business and employment opportunities in the South. The retailing revolution followed. The severe recession at the dawn of the Thatcher period, and the economic expansion that followed it, created a substantial shift away from manufacturing and primary industries, such as coal, and towards services. In doing so, it produced an economic shift in favour of the South that went well beyond trend. The 1980–81 recession did not produce a narrowing of regional differences, rather it widened them, as did the subsequent period of growth. In many ways, the entire period represented a coming-together of a number of one-off factors which could have been designed to benefit the South at the North's expense. But what set of factors, presumably different ones, will be at work in the future? And will they, as in the 1980s, widen North–South differences, or continue the pattern set in the 1990–92 recession?

The North–South shift in Britain in the 1980s in many ways resembled the move from the old industrial areas in the north-eastern United States to the sunbelt states of California, Florida and Texas. There, as in Britain, a primary cause was the decline of the traditional heavy industries of the northern states, in favour of new high-technology industries. An additional factor, more obvious in the case of the USA than in a small country such as Britain, was the better climate in the fast-growing states.

But in the USA, manufacturing industry revived in the late 1980s, helped by a lower dollar, and the economy-wide recession that began in 1990 hit the previously booming sunbelt states hardest. As this was being written in 1993, the American economy was recovering, but in states such as California the recession seemed hardest to shake off.

In the first edition of this book, I wrote:

Turning points in history are, by their nature, virtually impossible to detect at the time when they occurring. A case can be made for the reversal of relative decline in the North in Britain. It would be based on congestion in the South having reached the point where large numbers of people, given the choice, would prefer the North. If such a mood coincides with a growing belief among managers that they face over-crowding and escalating land and labour costs in the South and the solution lies with a relocation 250 miles to the north, then a significant movement in activity could indeed occur. If, at the same time, there was a realization among decision-makers in government about ... the inefficiency and potential unsustainability of an unbalanced economy, then there would be a chance of making northern revival both real and permanent (pp. 239–40)

I was sceptical, perhaps over-sceptical, about whether such a turning point had been reached. But certainly, as far as the next five years was concerned, the recommendation, to adapt stock-market terminology, should have been to 'buy' the North and 'sell' the South. And, with hindsight, one can conclude that North–South disparities will never again reach the levels that they did in the late 1980s. Let us now look at some of the factors that will increasingly come into play, pulling the economy either northwards or towards the South.

EUROPEAN INTEGRATION

Well before Britain completed her protracted negotiations with the original six European Community members, and eventually joined them in 1973, much of the opposition to membership had been based on the argument that it would leave the northern regions dangerously exposed. The idea of a golden triangle joining Birmingham (or in some versions London), Hamburg and Milan – within which growth would be concentrated – was a powerful one. The possibility that the creation of a common market would risk the further decline of already backward regions was recognized by the founding fathers of the EC. The Treaty of Rome contained, in its preamble, the hope that in strengthening economic unity, one aim would be 'to ensure their harmonious development by reducing the differences between the various regions and the backwardness of the less-favoured regions'. In 1958, per capita income in the Hamburg area was seven times that of the Italian region of Calabria.

The contribution of EC membership to Britain's regional problems of the 1970s and 1980s is hard to assess. It appears to be the case that British industry was ill-prepared for entry and, in spite of an adjustment period during which tariff barriers were brought down gradually, it has failed to recover from that poor start. In 1977, by which time most of the tariff adjustment had occurred, Britain had a visible trade deficit of £1·8 billion with the rest of the Community. The deficit narrowed in the late 1970s under the impact of rising North Sea prices and output, and in both 1979 and 1980 small trade surpluses were recorded. But by 1987 the deficit with the Community was large, at £9 billion, and rising.

The extent to which this would have occurred in the absence of membership is hard to assess. It has been the case that, as well as suffering from increased competition from France, Germany, Italy and the other EC members, Britain's regions have benefited from the Community's regional policy, notably the European Regional Development Fund, established in 1975. The Fund has spent between 4·5 and 8 per cent of the Community budget annually on regional aid and development.

Even so, the image of the golden triangle, while it has grown rather more fuzzy with the enlargement of the EC to its present twelve members, has been an enduring one. Dennis Swann, in his book *The Economics of the Common Market*, describes 'the existence of a central block of economic activity and prosperity which stretches from south-east England, Denmark and the Netherlands in the north, through central and north-east France and much of West Germany (other than certain eastern regions) to south-east France and northern Italy' (1988, p. 260).

The pull of the EC is one that exerts itself strongly on the south-eastern corner of Britain, including the south east itself, parts of the south west, most of East Anglia and the east midlands, and some of Yorkshire and Humberside. It does not exactly match the North and South of this book, but there is clearly a significant overlap. And it is a pull which operates in the same way as that which produces regional imbalances within individual countries. Favoured regions are perceived to offer significant advantages for industry, in terms of transport and communication links, availability of business services and economies of scale.

The process of integration was always intended by the European Community's designers to be a continuing one. Most of the package of measures to complete the Community's internal market were implemented by the end of 1992. The 1992 proposals, embodied in the Single European Act, mean the creation of an economy of 320 million people, with (relatively) free movement of goods, services, labour and capital, uniform technical standards for products throughout the Community, equal treatment for firms from all member countries in tendering for public-sector projects and greater harmonization of indirect taxation (notably value added tax). Another significant development was the creation of a European economic area, following an agreement in 1991 between the European Community and the members of the European Free Trade Association (EFTA), Austria, Switzerland, Norway, Sweden, Iceland and Finland. The agreement extended many of the single-market arrangements to the EFTA countries.

Integration has co-existed, not always comfortably, with enlargement. In the 1980s, three relatively poor countries of southern Europe – Spain, Portugal and Greece – became members of the EC. So too, in 1990, did the former German Democratic Republic (East Germany), thanks to the destruction of the Berlin Wall and subsequent unification with West Germany. For Britain's underdeveloped regions, this has meant that competition for EC assistance has become much tougher. In 1993, the European Commission announced that two areas of Britain would be granted so-called Objective 1 status, making them eligible for assistance from the Community's structural funds. Michael Heseltine had pressed for five areas of mainland Britain to be granted Objective 1 status – Devon and Cornwall; rural Wales; south Yorkshire; Merseyside and the Scottish Highlands and Islands. As it turned out, the Commission only accepted two, Merseyside and the Highlands and Islands. Much of Spain qualified, as did the whole of Portugal, Greece, Northern Ireland, Ireland, and East Berlin, Brandenburg, Mecklenburg, Saxony, Saxe-Anhalt and Thüringen in the former East Germany.

The Conservative Government's position, under Margaret Thatcher and to a lesser extent John Major, has been to welcome the development of the single market but to resist those aspects of integration which imply a loss of national sovereignty. Thus, in the December 1991 Maastricht negotiations, Major effectively secured British opt-outs from a series of social and employment protection provisions (the other eleven countries agreeing to a special social protocol) and monetary union, where any decision by Britain to participate would be the subject of a later vote by Parliament.

The result of this approach is that Britain has tended to operate on the fringes of the European Community. Major's attempt to put Britain at the heart of Europe, by taking sterling into the exchange rate mechanism of the European Monetary System in October 1990, ended in tears less than two years later, when the pound was ignominiously forced out of the system. The Labour Party, and Jacques Delors, the European Commission President, have pointed out that by not agreeing to joint proposals on social protection, Britain was setting itself up as a country where workers would be exploited. The Conservatives, for their part, appeared happy for Britain to be labelled the 'Taiwan of Europe'.

A report on Europe in the 1990s, *Efficiency, Stability and Equity*, prepared for the European Commission by a committee under the chairmanship of the Italian central banker Tommaso Padoa-Schioppa, focused on some of the potential dangers for the Community's problem regions. According to the report, published in 1987, around 10 per cent of the population of the

EC lived in declining industrial regions, and these were mainly situated in the north and west of the UK, the north and east of France, the north of Spain and the east of both Belgium and the Netherlands. A further 20 per cent of the population lived in what the report described as least-favoured regions, which had never been fully developed, and these included Portugal, Greece, Ireland, Northern Ireland, the south of Italy and half of Spain.

Current trends in industrial structure in favour of high-technology industries mean on the whole an aggravation of the problems of, especially, backward and peripheral regions, and sometimes the old, declining industrial regions ... There are strong tendencies for high technology industries (such as electronics and informatics) to cluster together, mostly in areas characterized by excellent transport locations and telecommunications facilities, an abundant supply of highly skilled labour, the proximity of major academic and research centres, and the proximity also of major financial centres. These industries also show a certain aversion to older industrial centres, at least those with physically less attractive environments. In the United Kingdom this is contributing to an increasingly deep north–south divide in economic fortunes, with a similar (albeit globally less problematic) trend in Germany. (1987, pp. 94–5)

The committee warned of potential conflicts between the Community's aim of boosting the efficiency and competitiveness of high-technology industries (which implies allowing them free rein to operate in those parts of Europe which they see as best suited to their purposes), and the problems for those regions left behind by this shift in the industrial structure towards high technology. This was in addition to the regional problems created by the completion of the internal market and the enlargement of the Community to twelve members (with the potential for further enlargement if, for example, Turkey is able to negotiate membership).

Such developments intensified the need for an adequate regional policy to help the less favoured areas. As part of the Maastricht agreement, additional 'cohesion' money was agreed – expenditure to help the less efficient regions. But adequately helping all the Community's needy regions – both underdeveloped and declining – would be, it was recognized, very expensive.

This was why, as described above, the selection of regions eligible for assistance had to be rationed. In 1993, for example, assistance under the Structural Funds for EC regions only amounted to 25 per cent of the Community's budget. And the budget itself was only just over 1 per cent of combined EC gross domestic product.

Assessing the impact of further European integration on North–South imbalances is far from easy. The Henley Centre, in its 1988 report *The United Markets of Europe*, observed that while the south east has the most to gain from the 1992 proposals – and in particular the potential it offers for Britain's financial-services industry – it also has the most to lose. On one view, developments in the European Community in the 1990s could lead to a levelling out of regional imbalances in Britain if the south east found it difficult to compete and lost out. But this would be more of a levelling down than a levelling out, and it would not be a vision of Europe in the 1990s to which the British Government would subscribe.

Britain's experience with membership of the European exchange rate mechanism (ERM), and indeed the Government's general approach to monetary union in Europe, offers marginally more encouragement to the North than to the South. The 23-month period of ERM membership, which was brought to an abrupt end on 'Black' Wednesday, 16 September 1992, had the effect, particularly during the last twelve months of membership, of intensifying the high interest squeeze on the indebted South, because British interest rates could not be reduced to a level appropriate for the needs of the domestic economy. Membership also imposed a high exchange rate on industry in both the North and South of the country. But membership could also be seen as providing clear advantages for the City of London. As the premier financial centre in Europe, the City had a strong claim – when sterling was in the ERM and Britain, notionally at least, was on the first step towards taking part in full monetary union – to be the home of the proposed European Monetary Institute (which would ultimately become Europe's central bank). The location in London of the central bank would reinforce the City's position, and add to the potential for further expansion of the financial services industry in the south east. Even though London's claims were challenged by member countries which had shown a greater long-term commitment to monetary integration, a compromise suggested itself. London could be the home of the operating arm of the central bank, just as the Federal Reserve Bank of New York is the operating arm of the US Federal Reserve Board. The administrative base could then be in continental Europe – Bonn, Lyon and Amsterdam were among the suggestions – just as the Federal Reserve Board has its headquarters in Washington. But Black Wednesday dealt a body blow to London's aspirations. After it, it seemed likely that Frankfurt would be the home for both the central bank's headquarters and its operating arm. Europe's leaders said that to have London as the location for the central bank, outside the system, would be ridiculous.

Sterling's departure from the ERM on 16 September 1992, and its subsequent fall from a central rate of DM2·95 to a new level of between DM2·30 and DM2·50, offered industry an immediate competitive advantage in relation to the rest of Europe. When the departure from the ERM was followed by a well-publicized decision by Hoover, the domestic electrical goods manufacturer, to close a factory in Dijon, France, and shift production to Cambuslang in Scotland, British industry appeared set for a new era of growth and rising market share. However, there were doubts about the extent to which this could be sustained. For one thing, the benefits of previous devaluations had tended to be lost in higher inflation and pay settlements. There was no guarantee that the pound would remain at its new lower level. And British industry's traditional shortcomings, in skills, research and development and the quality of investment, would surely win out in the longer term over the short-term advantage conferred by a fall in the exchange rate. As John Rhodes and Peter Tyler put it in the *Cambridge Economic Review* in autum 1992:

The UK's recent withdrawal from the ERM should ease the competitive pressures in the short term. Nevertheless, the longer-term prospects for UK manufacturing industry to the end of the century are far from bright, whether or not the UK re-enters the ERM ... The need for the United Kingdom to have a strong and vibrant manufacturing sector remains convincing and as strong as ever. There is an urgent requirement to assess how UK manufacturing can improve its performance relative to other countries. The whole of European manufacturing is facing increasing competitive pressures from the Far East and the UK has to respond to this challenge as well as strengthen its overall competitiveness in Europe ... The momentum for the strengthening of the UK's manufacturing base will require new measures from within. (1992, pp. 125–6)

In early 1993 John Major announced his commitment to enlarging Britain's manufacturing base. The March 1993 Budget contained a series of measures intended to help industry, notably in export markets. But an unpublished investigation by the Department of Trade and Industry's industrial competitiveness unit showed that British industry was well behind most other advanced economies in a range of measures of productivity, in the skills of the workforce and in the ability of management.

INWARD INVESTMENT

One substantial advantage for Britain in general, and for the North in particular, has been in the pattern of inward investment. Statistics from the Japanese Ministry of Finance show that, in the forty years 1951–91, Britain attracted investment from Japan worth $26·2 billion, out of total investment in Europe over the period of $68·6 billion. Britain's share was 38·2 per cent. A similar story emerged from figures produced by the US Department of Commerce. Cumulative inward investment in Britain from America at the end of 1991 was $68·3 billion, out of a European Community total of $188·7 billion, a 36·2 per cent share.

Several factors determine where foreign firms will tend to locate after weighing up different locations. They include the size of the market, and access to it; the availability, cost and skills base of the labour force; the political and economic environment, including political stability, the tax system and the degree of intervention; the availability of grants and other financial incentives; language (American and Japanese firms have tended to favour British locations, because of the common language in the case of the US, and because English is the most popular second language for Japan); the infrastructure, including transport and communications and also the presence of local suppliers; the quality of life – educational, cultural and leisure facilities, with golf courses said to be an important factor in Japanese location decisions; and existing inward investment, either by the firm itself or national competitors, with the 'cluster' effect important.

Within Europe, these factors often pull in opposite directions. Thus, location in the north of England cannot be said to be at the heart of the European market (or even the UK market), but it has the advantages of low labour costs, regional incentives and, depending on the choice of site, quality of life. Indeed, it has been a feature of Britain's regional development that, while domestic firms have been reluctant to relocate out of the South, foreign firms, with perhaps fewer prejudices, have opted directly for locations in the North. The north of England and south Wales have been particular beneficiaries of inward investment flows.

The impact of foreign investment is significant. Although two projects, the Nissan plant at Washington, Tyne and Wear, and Toyota in Derbyshire, have attracted much attention (partly because it is hoped that, during the 1990s, they will eliminate Britain's trade deficit on cars), the range of inward investment projects goes much wider than this. It includes the setting up by Japanese, American, French and German banks and securities houses of operations, often quite substantial ones, in the City of London. It also includes investment in retailing by foreign firms. But it is most significant, perhaps, in manufacturing. In 1991–2, for example, foreign enterprises accounted for 15 per cent of manufacturing jobs, 21 per cent of net output and 28 per cent of net capital expenditure (investment).

In 1991–2, the Invest in Britain Bureau recorded 332 inward investment projects, which created or safeguarded a total of 51,357 jobs. The regional breakdown of this investment is shown in Table 12.1.

Table 12.1   Inward investment by region

	Number of projects	Percentage of total	New or safeguarded jobs	Percentage of total
South East	28	8·4	3,365	6·6
East Anglia	9	2·7	4,681	9·1
South West	9	2·7	3,434	6·7
East Midlands	4	1·2	254	0·5
West Midlands	43	13·0	5,524	10·8
The South	93	28·0	17,258	33·7
Yorks & Humberside	15	4·5	2,407	4·7
North West	65	19·6	8,945	17·4
North	38	11·4	6,152	12·0
Wales	71	21·4	10,678	20·8
Scotland	39	11·7	4,821	9·4
Northern Ireland	11	3·3	1,096	2·1
The North	239	72·0	34,099	66·3
United Kingdom	332	100·0	51,357	100·0

Source: Invest in Britain Bureau, *Annual Report*, 1991–2, supplementary regional statistics. Totals may not sum exactly because of rounding.

The North regularly attracts the lion's share of inward invest-ment into Britain. As the table shows, more than 70 per cent of projects, and two-thirds of jobs created or safeguarded were in the North, as defined for the purpose of this book, in 1991–2. The success of Wales, as a result of an active Welsh Development Agency, was particularly notable. It was not always this way. In the past, foreign firms tended to prefer locations close to London, for example Ford at Dagenham. The pattern of recent inward investment, which is in part explained by the availability of special incentives for locating in the regions, begs the question of why, if incentives have been successful at directing foreign investment to the North, they have not done so more in the case of domestic investment. It may be that the Government has operated a double-standard in this field, allowing the agencies to pull out all the stops when the competition for inward investment is with other countries, but limiting the scope of regional investment incentives at home.

It could also be, however, that the North's success is due to foreign firms taking a longer-term view and responding to low labour costs and commercial rents. Some of the factors that have held back British companies from moving to the regions, for example a shortage of workers with appropriate skills, do not appear to have discouraged overseas companies. Nissan, for example, took the decision to train all the workers for its Washington plant from scratch. In this respect, the analysis of the effects of inward investment has moved on from the old concern that foreign-owned plants were simply established to assemble parts imported from the company's country of origin. Inward investment is now generally seen as adding to the quality of the workforce, to the quantity of investment, and to the competitiveness of the economy. The North's success in attracting inward investment is an important counterweight to other factors that have traditionally operated in the South's favour.

One question hanging over inward investment in Britain is, if the motivation has been low labour costs, will eastern Europe, with even lower costs, displace the North? The evidence so far has been that Japanese and American companies have been cautious about investing in the old eastern bloc, but this could clearly change. British industry, despite the productivity improvements of recent years, also suffers from a productivity gap relative to, for example, Germany and France. The implication, and it is something of a catch-22 for the North, is that if wage levels caught up with those of the stronger industrial countries in the EC, its advantages as a location would disappear – barring an elimination of the productivity gap which, in present circumstances, appears to be a considerable distance away.

THE CHANNEL TUNNEL

In the latter part of the nineteenth century, the great infrastructural project was the Manchester Ship Canal, which provided direct trade access to the sea for exporters. In the late twentieth century, the great project, at least in the popular imagination, is the Channel Tunnel. There are parallels between the two, except, of course, that while one was in the North, the other is in the South. The Manchester Ship Canal faced lengthy planning and construction delays. It also ran into difficulties over finance. The Channel Tunnel, first proposed under Napoleon at the beginning of the nineteenth century, finally secured a go-ahead in the late 1980s, after numerous false starts, the most recent in the 1970s. The rail-only tunnel, built by the Anglo-French Eurotunnel consortium with private finance, is scheduled to open in 1994. The high-speed rail link, running from St Pancras eastwards along the East Thames corridor, before crossing the river near Dartford and heading through Kent to the Folkestone entrance of the tunnel, will not be completed until after the year 2000. Until then, trains will operate on existing lines in Kent, from a terminus at Waterloo.

The opening of the Channel Tunnel is, of course, inextricably linked in its effects with the EC single market. Just as the latter will eliminate, or at least sharply reduce, artificial trade barriers between Britain and the rest of the Community, so the tunnel will reduce physical barriers to trade. Ideally, the two should have coincided. Eurotunnel's original plans were that the tunnel would open during 1993, but this slipped to 1994 as a result of a protracted dispute with the building contractors TML (Trans Manche Link).

There are two principal ways in which the construction and opening of the tunnel could contribute to North–South disparities. The first is in the building of the project itself and the associated infrastructure – including improved road and rail links – in the south east. The second could be that, when it is opened, the improved links with the Continent will act to increase the advantage of proximity to Europe already enjoyed by the south east. Allied to this, the North could face additional competition in servicing the different markets for goods in the South from firms in, for example, northern France.

The Government and the Eurotunnel consortium, aware of the political sensitivities involved in the tunnel project, between them sought to spread the contracts for the construction of the fixed channel link around Britain. The first major engineering contract, for example, was awarded to a firm in Glasgow. But the infrastructural improvements deemed necessary for the tunnel have been, and will continue to be, concentrated in the south east.

Brian Street, the chairman of the Confederation of British

Industry's south-eastern regional council, warned in 1987 of the dangers of a loss of business to northern France, because the French authorities were taking a more positive attitude both to the infrastructure needed along with the Tunnel, and because of their attitude towards the industrial development that would result from its opening. 'We must beware that we do not let industrial development get drawn down that hole to the Pas de Calais. We want to keep some of it here' (*The Times*, 14 December 1987). The fear was that just as the rest of the South, rather than the North, benefited from the overspill of activity from the crowded south east, so such a spreading out of growth in the future could benefit parts of the Continent.

There has been a major debate on the failure of the planners to provide for improved transport links from the south east to the North, and in particular on the delay (until 1993) in the decision to go ahead with the high-speed rail link to the tunnel. The Town and Country Planning Association set out the fears of the North in a letter to the then Transport Secretary, Paul Channon, in June 1988:

On the freight side, failure to invest in the right infrastructure will mean that the vast bulk of traffic will continue to be lorry-borne and carried by Eurotunnel shuttles through the Tunnel. If this were to happen businesses anywhere beyond London would be at a growing disadvantage with increasing delays year by year as motorway connections – particularly the M25 – get progressively clogged up. The Tunnel would have failed to live up to its economic promise, the north–south gap could become wider and the fears expressed by Kent residents about environmental damage could prove to have been well founded.

On the passenger side, travellers from London will enjoy excellent access to Paris, Brussels and other Continental cities with frequent very fast services. Regrettably, and in complete contrast, a very unambitious line is being taken regarding through passenger services from beyond London, the excuse being that there will be little demand for such services. This attitude is disappointing and at odds with that prevailing in France, where great priority is being given to extending very fast rail links to a number of provincial cities and incidentally to building TGV routes *around* Paris. The result of this will be that when the Tunnel is opened it should be possible to travel from London direct to Lyons in just five hours. We are dismayed that, as yet, nothing comparable is envisaged for Manchester–Paris or for the Yorkshire conurbations to Paris, routes similar in distance to London–Lyons.

We see no reason in principle why the businessman (or other traveller) from the north or west of London should be denied the opportunity to get into Europe by rail almost as quickly as his southern counterpart. (1988, pp. 1–2)

A similar conclusion was reached in a report entitled *The Channel Tunnel: Rail Infrastructure and the North of England*, published by the Manchester-based North of England Regional Consortium in March 1988. It examined the effects of the tunnel and the infrastructure as planned on four industries – textiles, metal manufacture, mechanical engineering and chemicals. In the case of textiles and metal manufacture, both heavily concentrated in the North, the reduction in transport costs was found to have a greater effect on imports than exports, and therefore an overall negative effect on the trade balance in these industries. Again, the main recommendation was that rail links between the North and the tunnel be improved, notably through electrification of the Midland Main Line, greater use of regional rail depots for the customs clearance of rail freight and the construction of more private sidings to encourage companies to shift from road to rail and thus accrue the advantages of the tunnel. Some progress has since been made in these areas, although the general point still stands.

It may seem illogical that a project which speeds transport links to the rest of the European Community could act to the detriment of the North. However, looked at a little more closely it is easy to see how this could indeed be the case. The essence of the argument is not the tunnel itself, but the transport links from the tunnel to the rest of the country. A company operating in the south east will be able to transport its goods to the tunnel entrance by road, ignoring the rail network until the transfer of goods at the tunnel to take them through. Meanwhile, its northern counterpart struggles to get its goods down a motorway network that becomes increasingly crowded as it approaches the south east. And the same company is unlikely to switch from road to rail for all its freight needs until it is convinced that rail investment has been adequate for its needs.

The tunnel could, therefore, operate to the disadvantage of the North in three ways. It will make it easier for firms on the Continent, benefiting from the heavy investment in road and rail links on the French side of the tunnel, to get their goods to the markets of southern England. It may increase the transport disadvantage of the North relative to the South. And, if it increases road congestion on, for example, the M25, it would make it harder for Northern firms to supply to the South.

By the early 1990s, however, the view was emerging that some of these fears were overstated. For one thing, the lengthy wrangle between Eurotunnel and its contractor TML had succeeded in giving the project a bad name, even before it was opened. Indeed, some still doubted whether the tunnel would ever open, let alone whether it would be profitable. In addition, it appeared that Eurotunnel would not be adopting an aggressive approach to pricing, dashing expectations that, by making the crossing much cheaper, the tunnel would generate a large increase in traffic. In April 1993, Christopher Garnett, Eurotunnel's commercial director, announced that car fares through the tunnel would be broadly similar to those charged by the ferry companies. Quoted in the *Independent* on 20 April 1993, he said: 'Prices would have to be broadly in line with the ferry operators. If we charged less they would simply respond by cutting prices, and if we tried to charge more we would lose business since our product is still something of an unknown in the market.' Eurotunnel said it would negotiate with hauliers over charges for freight traffic three months before the tunnel's opening. Again, however, there seemed little prospect of cheap travel. Eurotunnel's intention was to charge a premium over ferry crossings because of the time saving that traffic through the tunnel would gain.

Perhaps most importantly of all, the English Channel was not, nor would be, the main route for northern traffic to and from Europe. The east coast ports, from Humberside up to Tynemouth, represent important links to Germany, the Netherlands and Scandinavia. In the early 1990s the Humber ports were already handling four times the tunnel's eventual freight capacity. As Christopher Haskins, the chairman of Northern Foods, put it on the Channel Four programme, *High Interest*: 'Closing the Watford Gap':

Well it's a very, very small hole in the ground, the Channel Tunnel, and you can put very small tonnage through it that will be quite expensive compared with freight. And a lot of the goods we're talking about don't have to move at the pace that the Channel Tunnel is designed for. The Channel Tunnel is designed for speed, therefore for newspapers and food yes, but if I'm moving a transformer out of Sheffield, I first of all couldn't get it into the hole and, secondly, this estuary (the Humber) is a very efficient way into Europe.

AIRPORTS

Many of the arguments about the effects of the Channel Tunnel were rehearsed during the lengthy debate over whether, and where, London's third major airport would be located. The tunnel clearly had to be located in the south east for geographical regions. But the siting of a third major airport was a decision in which the location constraints were much weaker. Northern MPs saw the choice of Stansted, near Bishop's Stortford in Essex, as inevitably reinforcing the economic dominance of the South.

The decision was a potentially important one in the context of the North–South divide. A major airport provides the impetus for the development of industry in its surrounding area. A large part of the reason for the development of Britain's high-technology corridor along the London–Bristol stretch of the M4 motorway was proximity to Heathrow – the world's largest airport in terms of traffic. A similar phenomenon has occurred around Gatwick, with Crawley consistently having one of the lowest unemployment rates in Britain. In the late 1980s, the development of Stansted airport helped spur the emergence of the so-called M11 corridor from east London to Cambridge as one of the fastest-growing areas of Britain.

As importantly, the concentration of what will be Britain's three major airports in the south east added to the incentive to locate head offices and their associated support activities in or near London. An international business – and virtually every major company is now international – faces considerable disadvantages if it has its head office anywhere other than London. Its travelling executives and salesmen typically have to use feeder flights from the regional airports to the south east before they commence their international flights. Potential customers from abroad have to be ferried long distances within Britain.

A good example of the effect of airport capacity on head-office location was provided during the North Sea oil boom. American, and indeed British, oil companies had traditionally based their UK head offices in London, because of the ease of travel to, for example, the Gulf and the United States. When their UK operations became producing activities, rather than simply refining and marketing, and when that production became centred on Scotland and the North Sea, there was a case for shifting head offices to, say, Aberdeen. But this was not done. In the case of the US oil companies, senior British-based executives preferred to be in a location where there was easy access to the United States, while visitors from the company's head offices on the other side of the Atlantic would have baulked at missing out London on a trip to Britain.

The promoters of Manchester's Ringway and Glasgow's Prestwick airports argued strongly for their further development as an alternative to Stansted. Manchester, it was suggested, could have offered as comprehensive a range of flights to Europe, the United States and the Far East and serve business and private users from the whole of the industrial North. A similar role for Scotland was envisaged for Glasgow.

Northern despair over Stansted was, however, relatively short-lived. The airport was duly opened, offering convenient motorway links, an attractive, customer-friendly terminal and free parking. But, the best-laid plans of the planners did not allow for one thing – passengers did not want to use it. Despite special cheap-flight offers from the airlines using it, Stansted failed to gain acceptance among customers, instead gaining a reputation as something of a white elephant. At the same time, high-technology companies operating along the M11 corridor, and in particular around Cambridge, were among those hardest hit by the recession. A similar phenomenon occurred with a smaller-scale project, the City airport at Beckton in the London Docklands. The airport, a mere six miles from the Square Mile, also suffered from a lack of passengers, and only partly because proximity did not mean good transport links. Passengers, particularly business customers, wanted to fly in and out of the south east, but they also wanted to continue to use Heathrow and Gatwick. Indeed, the Department of the Environment's 1993 planning guidance for the south east allowed for the construction of additional runway capacity at either Heathrow or Gatwick. Meanwhile, Manchester, in submitting its unsuccessful bid to host the Olympics in the year 2000, could point to its own international airport as a powerful factor in the city's favour.

LOCAL TAXATION

At the very end of Margaret Thatcher's time as Prime Minister came a reform that she had promised since taking over: a radical shake-up of local government finance. Its key ingredient, the Community Charge or poll tax, contributed to her downfall. The Government's plans were set out in a Green Paper *Paying for Local Government* in January 1986. There were two main strands to the reforms, which passed into law after a stormy passage through both Houses of Parliament in 1988. The first was the replacement of domestic rates, which were levied according to the type and value of a property – and were unaffected by the number of occupants of that property – with a new Community Charge, set at an equal amount for each adult within the local authority. And the level at which the Community Charge was set by each local authority would depend on the services it provided and the efficiency with which it carried out those services. The underlying philosophy, for a Government which was determined to rein back local-authority spending further, was to introduce a new source of downward pressure on such spending, emanating from individuals unwilling to continue to pay high levels of Community Charge and thus voting out high-spending councils or voting with their feet and moving to other areas where the charge was lower.

The second main strand to the reform was the replacement of the existing business rates with a new uniform business rate (UBR). The intention here was to prevent local authorities from loading the financial burden on businesses in order to keep down the cost to individuals – and therefore voters – of paying for local services.

The poll tax (but not the UBR) was introduced in Scotland in April 1989, and both poll tax and UBR came into effect in England and Wales in April 1990, their coming marked by a demonstration which turned into the worst riot in central London in modern times. The poll tax was regarded as the flagship of Mrs Thatcher's third term, albeit a highly controversial and unpopular one even within the Conservative Party. In selling it, ministers used the example of the poor elderly widow living in a large house, paying the same rates as the house next door with, say, four income-earners occupying it. Critics of the charge pointed to the case of the low-paid worker with a non-working wife, paying twice the amount as a millionaire in the same local authority area.

The main criticism of the Community Charge was, therefore, on its effect on the distribution of income. As with any flat tax, unrelated to income, it was inevitably regressive in its impact, and much more so than the system of local authority rates it was designed to replace. One feature of the charge was that all those who were eligible to pay – and the exclusions included groups like prisoners and nuns – had to come up with at least 20 per cent of the charge (to reinforce local authority accountability). This was a departure from the rates, whereby large numbers of people were effectively exempt through rate relief.

The poll tax also had important regional implications. Any flat tax, uniformly applied, would benefit the South more than the North, simply because income levels are higher in the South. The important point about the community charge was, however, that it was only a flat tax within each local authority area, varying significantly between such areas. The favourite comparison was between Wandsworth, which set very low poll tax levels, and neighbouring Lambeth, where the poll tax was one of the highest in the country.

Apart from Greater London, the effect of the change from domestic rates to the poll tax was to produce a reduction in local taxation on individuals for virtually every part of the south east, and for most of the rest of the South. But the majority of households in northern England faced not only large increases but also in most cases a higher poll tax level. The Department of the Environment produced figures showing nearly four times as many gainers from the new system as losers in the south east, while gainers outnumbered losers by 2·8 to 1 in East Anglia, and by 1·8 to 1 in the south west. In the north, losers outnumbered gainers by 2·5 to 1 and in Yorkshire and Humberside by 2·3 to 1.

The poll tax therefore worsened the distribution of income between North and South. It was also expected to push up house prices even further in the south east, by removing one penalty (higher rates) previously suffered by people trading up in the housing market. The Department of the Environment predicted a 5 per cent rise in house prices, nationally, as a result of the change. This effect was, however, swamped by the effects of the housing recession.

Fortunately for the North, the poll tax was short-lived. Michael Heseltine's autumn 1990 challenge to Margaret Thatcher was two-pronged – he pledged to change policy on Europe and abolish the poll tax. In the subsequent leadership election all three candidates, Heseltine, John Major and Douglas Hurd, promised speedy reform of local government finance. When Major won, he made Heseltine Environment Secretary, with the first item on his agenda that of coming up with a poll tax replacement. As an interim measure, in the March 1991 Budget, Norman Lamont succeeded in defusing the poll tax issue by announcing a £140 across the board reduction in its level, paid for by increasing value added tax from 15 to 17·5 per cent.

Heseltine's solution was the Council Tax, a local tax that was closer to the rates than to the Community Charge. The only concession to the spirit of the poll tax was that people living alone would only pay 75 per cent of the Council Tax on their property. Unlike the poll tax, where even the poor had to pay 20 per cent, there was no minimum payment for the Council Tax. As with the old domestic rates, many people obtained full exemption or relief.

The Council Tax operated on the basis of property valuations, typically based on the market price of houses (the valuations were carried out by estate agents). Properties were placed in one of eight bands – A to H – on the basis of these valuations, and the tax varied, both from local authority to local authority and, within council areas, according to the band the property fell into. Worse still for the South, April 1991 property valuations were used to determine which band of tax a household would be faced with. This was only part of the way into the sharp price falls in the South of the early 1990s. The Council Tax was introduced in April 1993, and its impact was virtually a mirror image of the poll tax. According to an analysis conducted by the Institute for Fiscal Studies, *Right this Time? An Analysis of the First Year's Council Tax Figures*, bills compared with the poll tax increased substantially in Greater London, the rest of the south east and the south west. The north, north west, east midlands and west midlands were the biggest gainers. Smaller gains accrued to Yorkshire and Humberside and, perhaps surprisingly, East Anglia. And, while transitional relief was used to cushion the losers from some of the effects of the change to the Council Tax (as had been the case with the poll tax), the new tax was bad for the south east. Thus, the shift to one new form of local taxation in 1990, which had benefited the South, was followed by a change which more than reversed the gains, and which seemed likely to be longer-lasting.

A paradox of the Thatcher Government's reforms of local authority finance was that, while the poll tax benefited the majority of individuals in the South – and added to the attractions of living there – the uniform business rate (UBR), the second strand of the reforms, helped the North. Under the rating system, Labour councils in the North tended to set business rates high, in order to minimize the burden of the rates on households, while Conservative councils in the South did the opposite. When the decision was taken to establish a uniform business rate as an average of the existing business rates, the effect was to lower business rates in the North and raise them in the South. Woolworth, for example, calculated that it paid 40 per cent less in rates on its stores in Newcastle-upon-Tyne, and 39 per cent more on its store at St Pauls Cray, near Sidcup in Kent. The National Westminister Bank expected a 33 per cent increase at its head office in the City of London, and a 38 per cent reduction at one of its Sheffield branches. Overall, businesses in northern England were officially expected to experience a £700 million annual reduction in their rates bill. And, while some of the impact was cushioned by a phasing-in period, the change added to already high business costs in the South.

And the new system, which came into force in April 1990, penalized businesses in the South in another way. Before the system came into operation, most business premises were revalued for rating purposes. This was the first major revaluation since 1973 and increased the rateable value of properties in the South, reflecting changes in the distribution of economic activity and its impact on property values. The Confederation of British Industry calculated that the combined effect of the uniform business rate and revaluation would be to ultimately increase the rates bill for the average business by 22 to 30 per cent in the south east, 28 to 32 per cent in the south west and 19 to 25 per cent in the west midlands. In the Thames valley, the South's high-technology corridor, the CBI said increases of up to 90 per cent would eventually feed through.

Would the UBR produce a large-scale relocation from the South to the North? Probably not. Rates are small in relation to industry's wage bill – roughly 7 per cent. And the five-year phasing-in period helped limit the damage to the South. But they could be a contributory factor in location decisions, particularly for new projects.

DIVIDED NO MORE?

The 1990–92 recession was remarkable in a number of respects. It was the longest in the post-war period, and it was not due to some outside force or shock to the British economy. Its most notable characteristic, however, was that it reversed much of the widening of North–South disparities that had occurred in the Thatcher years. It was, above all, a time when the smugly successful South got its comeuppance, and retribution was severe.

It is important to put this shift into perspective. There are two aspects to North–South disparities in Britain. The first is the regional structure of the economy, and the second is concerned with changes within that broad structure. To give some examples: the recession did not suddenly produce a sharp shift in population, or in company head offices, or even in relative shares of gross domestic product, from South to North. In other words, if there was an uneven concentration of economic activity in the south east before the recession, as the figures suggest, there was still an uneven concentration after it. Despite the recession's severe impact on the South, its effect on Britain's regional economic structure was marginal. And this is not surprising for, as I described in Chapter 1, a North-to-South shift in economic activity has been taking place for around a hundred years.

The recession's main effect, indeed, has been to push the problem of regional economic disparities a long way down the political agenda. In the boom of the late 1980s, even a government temperamentally opposed to regional policy was beginning to see that things could not go on as they were. Now, the view that Britain's regional economic structure requires radical surgery has been moved to the back of Whitehall filing cabinets, to be resurrected next time it is recognized that a regionally unbalanced economy is ultimately a highly inefficient one.

What of the future? Will the North chip away further at the South's economic dominance, building on the progress it made in the 1990–92 recession? Or will the South, having had a nasty shock, recover its composure and re-establish the 1980s pattern of growth above the national average? Predicting the future of Britain's regional economic geography is more difficult in the early 1990s than for a very long time. The 1990–92 recession could have marked the beginning of a new northern renaissance, or it could just have been a temporary setback for the South.

It is useful, in assessing Britain's North–South future, to break down the South in a little more detail. In the late 1980s, well before the recession took hold, the focus – for both economic growth and population pull – had already shifted outwards from Greater London and the inner south east to the outer south east, East Anglia, the south west (or at least the eastern half of it), the east midlands and, to a lesser extent, the west midlands. There was also strong evidence of a spread of growth and prosperity to Yorkshire and Humberside and Wales, particularly south Wales. Studies by Champion and Green and others, described in detail in Chapter 5, defined a crescent-shaped area of most-rapid growth and greatest prosperity stretching around the western side of London from Sussex and Hampshire in the south to Norfolk and the Fens, but with clear indications of an outward spread to other areas.

Thus, at the end of the recession, Greater London had a serious problem. Its unemployment rate in February 1993, 11·7 per cent, was higher than in any English region except for the north (12·2 per cent), and higher too than in both Wales and Scotland. But the afterglow of 1980s growth was still evident in the zone of greatest prosperity, with Berkshire (7·6 per cent), Buckinghamshire (8·4 per cent), Hertfordshire (9·1 per cent), Oxfordshire (7·1 per cent), West Sussex (8 per cent), Cambridgeshire (8·5 per cent) and Suffolk (8 per cent), all with unemployment significantly below the national average of 10·5 per cent.

The difficulty with this position is that, if maintained, it negates a central explanation for North–South differences in Britain. London's dominant role in decision-making in Britain, and as a cultural centre, its pull for overseas visitors, and its key position as a major world financial centre – all these have contributed to the over-concentration of economic activity in the south east. But if we are now to regard London as the problem – dirty, crime-ridden, over-built, sapped by high unemployment, inadequately provided for in terms of roads and public transport, its streets crowded at night with the homeless – can the South's future really be regarded as bright?

There is a twofold answer to this. The first is concerned with the nature of big cities and people's desire to opt for a suburban or semi-rural existence. American cities such as Los Angeles and New York have had many of the problems currently associated with London for decades. But this has not prevented the regions in which they are located from continuing to prosper. And, to take unemployment as a measure of London's difficulties, there is some evidence that, because of the nature of employment in the capital, with a high proportion of demand-related service jobs, employment is quick to fall in recessions, but can rise quite sharply during upturns.

Secondly, a longer-term perspective on London's problems was provided by Simon Jenkins, the former editor of *The Times*, in the LWT London lecture, *London's Forthcoming Boom*, in November 1992. He began by summarizing current opinion, culled from newspaper headlines and reports, on the capital's plight:

London is in crisis. London is seizing up. London lacks leadership. Its economy is faltering. Homelessness is soaring. Education is collapsing. Public services are in terminal decline. Libraries are closing . . . and for good measure the theatre is dead. Crisis, crisis, crisis . . . House prices, for the first time in most people's memory, have been actually falling. Registered unemployment, albeit an unreliable indicator, is higher than ever. Figures on commercial property suggest that as much as a fifth of the central business district is available for letting. A majority of new office space east of the City would appear to be empty. Any drive along Lower and Upper Thames Street or through Tower Hill will see 'To Let' signs on all sides. Most spectacular of all, the colossal Canary Wharf development is in receivership, along with fifteen large east London commercial and residential projects: from Butler's Wharf through Tobacco Dock to Burrell's Wharf on the Isle of Dogs. It can only be a matter of time before much of this empty space is consigned to mothballs. (1992, pp. 1–2)

The idea that London was in terminal decline was, said Jenkins, almost as old as the capital itself. And the usual cause for that gloom, the grisly end of a building boom, was, far from being a new experience for London, a regular occurrence. From the 1820s and the struggles of John Nash, the developer of Regent Street and Regent's Park, together with those of Smith, Cundy and Cubitt, developers of Belgravia on behalf of the Grosvenor estate, London's building cycle had been one of boom and bust. The latest cycle was no exception. As in the nineteenth century, the developers had been allowed to build freely in the City of London and Docklands. As in previous booms, too many had rushed in, creating chronic over-supply. However, in the depths of the commercial property slump, with rents in many cases having halved, lay the seeds of the next revival. Out-migration by large companies from London, noted Jenkins, had virtually come to a halt, because the incentive for doing so had disappeared. His central conclusion was that, as in the past, London's cycle had been dramatic and painful, but it was nonsense to say that the capital would never recover:

London cannot fail to revive. Its industries are what they have always been, growth ones. Commentators in gloom mode tend to point to London's docks or cars or metal-bashing or other manufacturing. But London's economy has for hundreds of years been diverse. It largely avoided the industrial revolution, concentrating like all capital cities on government and administration, the law and money, tourism and leisure, health and education, the arts and printing. To be sure there has always been manufacturing in London, but London has not depended on it. Sure, efforts are being made to decentralize much white-collar business. Bureaucrats are moved to Croydon and Sheffield and Bootle. London's vast health industry is struggling to reduce in size, though I'll believe it when I see it. But the capital's vitality always replaces old uses with new ones . . . In no capital in the world are public administration or the professions in long-term decline . . . Tourism, and its related industries of catering, hotels and the arts are also on a long-term upward trend. (1992, pp. 15–16)

The capital's recession was, in many respects, necessary for its long-term prosperity. Without it, house prices and commercial property rentals would have moved further out of line with the rest of the country, making London an impossibly expensive location. The pressure on the available land and labour supply would not have allowed the industries of the future, necessary for London's long-term growth, to develop. The scale of the property slump could have been prevented by the operation of better controls in the boom years, but that would have been out of sympathy with the spirit of the unfettered 1980s.

What is true for London also, of course, applies to much of the rest of the South. The growth industries of the 1980s, in high technology for example, have not suddenly become commercial dinosaurs. The factors favouring the South in the late 1980s – such as European integration, the Channel Tunnel and the long-term expansion of service and high-technology industries – had not suddenly disappeared, even if their effects may have been overstated. There was also the possibility that, because the South was hit so hard in the 1990–92 recession, it would bounce back fastest. The British economy as a whole began to grow again in the first quarter of 1993, with non-oil gross domestic product rising by 0·6 per cent. The Nationwide Building Society reported a first-quarter rise in house prices in London and the south east, while the Confederation of British Industry's May 1993 regional industrial trends survey named the south east as one of the three fastest recovering regions. The others were the west midlands and Wales. John Wriglesworth, a housing analyst with the City firm UBS Ltd, predicted that London and the south east would lead the recovery in house prices, with a 10 per cent rise in 1994.

Against this has to be set the legacy of the recession. In the housing market, this included the problem of negative equity (where the value of property fell to less than the mortgage taken out to purchase it). This problem, far more severe in the South than in the North, as we have seen, would surely act as a drag on any upturn in housing activity. There was also the general problem of burnt fingers. People, particularly in the South, had taken advantage of their new freedoms and borrowed heavily in the 1980s. This was followed in the recession by a determination (in many cases a necessity) to repay debt. Borrowers would be more cautious in the future. A repeat of the borrowing binge of the 1980s was highly unlikely. Even if individuals acquired the borrowing habit again, the lenders would be more cautious about allowing them to exercise it. And what was true for individuals was also true for businesses, particularly small firms. The combination of high interest rates, a tough approach by the banks and a falling housing market, had been a lethal one. Many who had failed declared that they would never start up again. Surviving businesses would be much more cautious about expanding.

For the North, the legacies of the recession were far less problematic. And in the new era following sterling's departure from the European exchange rate mechanism the macro-economic policy combination of a low exchange rate and substantial interest-rate reductions (rates having come down from 15 per cent at their peak to 6 per cent) offered significant advantages for industry. This would tend to benefit northern regions proportionately more than the South. True, the programme of industrial rationalization was not over. Although the Government delayed a programme of thirty-one pit closures (and the loss of 30,000 mining jobs) first announced in October 1992, there seemed little prospect of the long-term survival of the mines. In 1993, the Swan Hunter shipyard on Tyneside, the last in the north east, seemed destined for closure. But there was also a rationalization programme at work in the South, notably in banking and other financial services. No longer was it the case that changes in Britain's employment structure would operate exclusively to the North's disadvantage.

PA Cambridge Economic Consultants, in conjunction with the Department of Land Economy in Cambridge, offered, in their autumn 1992 *Cambridge Economic Review*, a longer-term view of the regional economic outlook. Their report acknowledged the narrowing of North–South disparities in the recession, with this process likely to continue, in their view, into 1994. After that, however:

When the recovery takes place after 1994 some traditional regional economic differentials begin to reassert themselves, with Northern Ireland as the slowest growing region (1·6 per cent per annum) and East Anglia the fastest growing (3·3 per cent per annum). (1992, p. 19)

The key point about these projections is that differences in regional rates of growth in the recovery phase of the 1990s are expected to be considerably smaller than in the 1980s. The forecast is summarized in Table 12.2.

It is possible that this forecast understates the potential for the North to grow under the impact of an industry-friendly macro-economic policy. It is also possible that the South's hangover from the recession will last longer and cast a shadow over the whole decade. The key point, however, which I endorse, is that there will be a significant narrowing of the North–South growth gap. For this, at least, one should be grateful.

Even so, and returning to the point made earlier in this

Table 12.2 Changes in GDP by region (per cent per annum)

	1971–81	1981–91	1991–2001	1984–9	1989–94	1994–2001
South East	0·9	2·6	1·6	4·4	− 0·7	2·4
East Anglia	2·1	4·0	2·3	4·9	0·1	3·3
South West	1·9	3·3	2·0	4·4	0·3	2·7
East Midlands	1·8	3·4	2·1	4·9	0·9	2·6
West Midlands	− 0·5	2·6	1·6	4·5	− 0·6	2·3
Yorks & Humberside	0·7	2·6	1·7	4·2	0·3	2·1
North West	0·0	2·0	1·4	3·4	− 0·5	1·9
North	0·7	1·9	1·5	3·5	0·2	1·8
Wales	0·4	2·9	2·2	5·2	0·3	2·7
Scotland	0·9	2·2	1·5	3·1	0·7	1·9
Northern Ireland	0·9	2·5	1·3	3·5	0·4	1·6
United Kingdom*	0·8	2·6	1·7	4·2	− 0.1	2·3

* Excluding North Sea oil.
Source: PA Cambridge Economic Consultants and The Department of Land Economy, Cambridge, *Cambridge Economic Review*, Volume 2, autumn 1992, table 2.3, p. 19.

chapter, this growth prospect will leave the existing structure of Britain's regional economic geography largely intact. To some people this is not a problem. The over-concentration of economic activity in the south east is a fact of life in Britain. To me it is evidence that short-term changes in regional economic performance have very largely removed concern about the distribution of activity within Britain. But they have not removed the underlying problem.

The recession of the early 1990s took us back to the position of ten years earlier, at the end of the first Thatcher recession. Then, as now, growth wherever it occurred was welcome. The result in the 1980s was the emergence of very serious regional disparities and, ultimately, the destructive impact of one powerful region, the south east, coming up against capacity limits. Even with slower growth in prospect in the 1990s, there is no guarantee that history will not repeat itself.

APPENDIX: THE UNITED KINGDOM'S STANDARD REGIONS

North

Cleveland, Cumbria, Durham, Northumberland, Tyne and Wear.

Yorkshire and Humberside

Humberside, North Yorkshire, South Yorkshire, West Yorkshire.

East Midlands

Derbyshire, Leicestershire, Lincolnshire, Northamptonshire, Nottinghamshire.

East Anglia

Cambridgeshire, Norfolk, Suffolk.

South East

Bedfordshire, Berkshire, Buckinghamshire, East Sussex, Essex, Greater London, Hampshire, Hertfordshire, Isle of Wight, Kent, Oxfordshire, Surrey, West Sussex.

South West

Avon, Cornwall, Devon, Dorset, Gloucestershire, Somerset, Wiltshire.

West Midlands

County of West Midlands, Hereford and Worcester, Shropshire, Staffordshire, Warwickshire.

North West

Cheshire, Greater Manchester, Lancashire, Merseyside.

Wales

Clwyd, Dyfed, Gwent, Gwynedd, Mid Glamorgan, Powys, South Glamorgan, West Glamorgan.

Scotland

Borders, Central, Dumfries and Galloway, Fife, Grampian, Highland, Lothian, Orkney, Shetland, Strathclyde, Tayside, Western Isles.

Northern Ireland

Belfast, North Eastern Board, South Eastern Board, Southern Board, Western Board.

BIBLIOGRAPHY

Albrow, Desmond (1990), 'The Divided Loyalties of a Former York-shireman', *Daily Telegraph*, 29 August.

Aldous, Tony (1993), 'Can Alice Save this Wonderland?', *Standard*, 5 April.

Allen, S., Waton, A., Purcell, K., and Wood, S. (eds.) (1986), *The Experience of Unemployment*, Macmillan.

Armstrong, Harvey, and Taylor, Jim (1985), *Regional Economics and Policy*, Philip Allan.

Armstrong, Harvey, and Taylor, Jim (1987), *Regional Policy: The Way Forward*, Employment Institute, London.

Astor, David (1991), 'A Greenprint for the Future – The Future of the South East is at Stake', *Guardian*, 8 March.

Atkinson, Rodney (1988), 'A Return to the Regions', Bow Group Educational Briefing, London.

Audit Bureau of Circulations (1988), *Circulation Review*, June.

Audit Bureau of Circulations (1993), *Circulation Review*, April.

Bank of England (1988), 'Regional Labour Markets in Great Britain', *Quarterly Bulletin*, August.

Banks-Smith, Nancy (1992), 'Granadaland', *Guardian*, 29 December.

Beaumont, Philip B. and Harris, R. I. D. (1988), 'The North–South Divide in Britain: The Case of Trade Union Recognition', Paper prepared for EMRU Labour Economics Study Group, Swansea.

Black Horse Relocation, *Corporate Relocations within Great Britain*.

Blackaby, Frank (ed.) (1978a), *British Economic Policy*, National Institute of Economic and Social Research.

Blackaby, Frank (ed.) (1987b), *De-industrialisation*, National Institute of Economic and Social Research.

Bover, O., Muellbauer, J., and Murphy, A. (1988), 'Housing, Wages and UK Labour Markets', Centre for Economic Policy Research, Discussion Paper No. 268, July.

Bover, O., Muellbauer, J., and Murphy, A. (1989), 'Housing, Wages and UK Labour Markets', *Oxford Bulletin of Economics and Statistics*, 51(2), 97–136.

Briggs, Asa (1968), *Victorian Cities*, Penguin.

Bristol Polytechnic Research Unit in Defence Economics (1992), 'The Impact of Reduced Military Expenditure on the Economy of South West England', Bristol Polytechnic.

British Broadcasting Corporation (1988), 'File on Four', BBC Radio, 17 May.

British Broadcasting Corporation (1990), *The Great North? A Special Report for BBC North East* by Fred Robinson, February.

British Road Federation (1988), 'The Cost of Congestion'.

Brittan, Samuel (1988), 'Inflation, New Jobs and the Poll Tax', *Financial Times*, 21 April.

Building Societies Association (1988), *BSA Bulletin*, April.

Business Mazagine (1987), 'Across the North–South Divide', September.

Butler, D., and Kavanagh, D. (1988), *The British General Election of 1987*, Macmillan.

Butler, D., and Kavanagh, D. (1992), *The British General Election of 1992*, Macmillan.

Cambridge Econometrics and Northern Ireland Economic Research Centre (1987), *Regional Economic Prospects*, October.

Central Statistical Office (1975), *Regional Statistics 11*, HMSO.

Central Statistical Office (1987), *Regional Trends 22*, HMSO.

Central Statistical Office (1988), *Regional Trends 23*, HMSO.

Central Statistical Office (1992a), *Regional Trends 27*, HMSO.

Central Statistical Office (1992b), *Economic Trends, Annual Supplement*, 1992 edition, HMSO.

Central Statistical Office (1992c), 'Regional Accounts Part 1', *Economic Trends*, December 1992 edition, HMSO.

CES Ltd (1988), *Beyond the North–South Divide*, Black Horse Relocation.

Champion, Tony, and Green, Anne (1985), 'In Search of Britain's Booming Towns', Dicussion Paper 72, Centre for Urban and Regional Development, University of Newcastle upon Tyne.

Champion, Tony, and Green, Anne (1988a), *Local Prosperity and the North–South Divide*, Institute for Employment Research, University of Warwick, January.

Champion, Tony, and Green, Anne (1988b), *Local Prosperity and the North–South Divide*, summary paper presented to Institute of British Geographers' conference, Loughborough University, 6 January.

Champion, Tony, and Green, Anne (1990), *The Spread of Prosperity and the North–South Divide: Local Economic Performance in Britain during the Late Eighties*, Booming Towns, Gosforth and Kenilworth.

Coleman, David (1987), transcript of talk to Institute of Economic Affairs' conference on North and South, May.

Confederation of British Industry (1987a), *Investing for Britain's Future: Report of the City/Industry Task Force*, October.

Confederation of British Industry (1987b), *Rates Reform: Lifting the Burden on Business*, November.

Confederation of British Industry (1988), *Companies and the Housing Market*, April.

Confederation of British Industry/Business Strategies Ltd (1992), *Regional Trends Survey*, November.

Confederation of British Industry/Business Strategies Ltd (1993), *Regional Trends Survey*, May.

Consortium Developments (1988), *The Report on the Plan for Small Country New Towns*, May.

Council of Mortgage Lenders (1993), *Housing Finance – the Quarterly Economics Journal of the Council of Mortgage Lenders*, February.

Curley, Joanne (1987), *Housing Inheritance and Wealth*, Morgan Grenfell, November.

Dahrendorf, Ralf (1982), *On Britain*, BBC.

Department of Employment (1986), 'Geographical Mobility and Housing', Paper to the National Economic Development Council, 24 October.

Department of Employment (1987), *Employment Gazette*, Historical Supplement No. 1, February.

Department of Employment (1988), *Preliminary Results from the 1987 Labour Force Survey*, 16 February.

Department of Employment (1992), *New Earnings Survey 1992, Part A*, HMSO.

Department of Employment (1993a), 'Labour Force Trends in the Regions, 1984–92', *Employment Gazette*, March.

Department of Employment (1993b), *Labour Force Survey – Quarterly Bulletin*, March.

Department of Employment (1993c), '1991 Census of Employment' and 'Revised Employment Estimates for September 1989 to December 1992', *Employment Gazette*, April.

Department of the Environment (1988a), 'New Estimates of Households to 2001', press release, 15 February.

Department of the Environment (1988b), 'Housing in Rural Areas, A Statement by the Secretary of State for the Environment', 5 July.

Department of the Environment (1988c), *Housing in Rural Areas, Village Housing and New Villages*, July.

Department of the Environment (1991), *Household Projections to 2011*.

Department of the Environment (1993a), *Consultation Draft: Regional Planning Guidance for the South East*, March.

Department of the Environment (1993b), *The East Thames Corridor – the Government's Approach*, March.

Department of the Environment (1993c), *East Thames Corridor – A Study of Development Capacity and Potential*, March.

Department of Trade and Industry (1983), *Regional Industrial Development*, White Paper, Cmnd. 9111, HMSO.

Department of Trade and Industry (1984), 'Regional Industrial Policy', press release, 28 November.

Department of Trade and Industry (1988a), *DTI – The Department for Enterprise*, White Paper Cmnd. 278, HMSO, January.

Department of Trade and Industry (1988b), 'Submission to Foxley Wood Planning Enquiry', June.

Disraeli, Benjamin (1982a), *Coningsby, or, The New Generation*, Oxford University Press. (First published 1844.)

Disraeli, Benjamin (1982b), *Sybil*, Oxford University Press. (First published 1845.)

Dyson, John (1991), *The Northern Playground: Britain's Most Prosperous Area*, BWD Rensburg.

Engels, Friedrich (1973), *The Condition of the Working Class in England in 1844*, Lawrence and Wishart. (First published 1845.)

Finegold, David, and Soskice, David (1988), 'The Failure of Training in Britain: Analysis and Prescription', *Oxford Review of Economic Policy*, 4 (3), pp. 21–53.

Fothergill, Stephen, and Vincent, Jill (1985), *The State of the Nation*, Pan.

Gaskell, Elizabeth (1970), *North and South*, Penguin. (First published 1854–5.)

Goddard, J. B., and Coombes, M. G (1987), 'The North–South Divide: Local Perspectives', paper to Institute of Economic Affairs conference on North and South, May.

Gould, Bryan (1988), speech to the Association of District Councils conference, Blackpool, 1 July.

Green, Anne (1992), 'The Geography of Economic Activity', Institute for Employment Research, University of Warwick.

Green, Anne, Owen, David, and Winnett, Colin (1993), 'Local Unemployment Dynamics in Great Britain, 1978–91', paper presented to the EMRU Labour Economics Study Group Meeting, Department of Employment, London, 19 March.

Halifax Building Society (1988), *Regional Bulletin*, Nos. 18 and 19.

Hall, David (1988), speech to Town and Country Planning Association Annual Council Meeting, 26 May.

Hamnett, Chris (1988), 'The Owner-Occupied Housing Market in Britain: A North–South Divide?', paper given at Institute of British Geographers conference, January.

Heath, A., Jowell, R., and Curtice, J. (1985), *How Britain Votes*, Pergamon Press.

Helm, Dieter, and Smith, Stephen (1987), 'Decentralization and Local Government', *Oxford Review of Economic Policy*, 3 (2), i–xxi.

Henley Centre (1988a), *The United Markets of Europe*, June.

Henley Centre (1988b), *The Channel Tunnel: Rail Infrastructure and the North of England*, March.

Heseltine, Michael (1988a), letter to Nicholas Ridley, published in the *Independent*, 14 March.

Heseltine, Michael (1988b), 'Congestion in the South: The Subsidised Market', speech to Blackpool and West Lancashire Chamber of Commerce and Industry, 11 April.

Hetherington, Peter (1991), 'Children of the Giro Economy', *Guardian*, 18 September.

Hill, Christopher (1969), *Reformation to Industrial Revolution*, Penguin.

H. M. Treasury (1986), 'Regional Pay Variations', paper presented to the National Economic Development Council, 25 November.

H. M. Treasury (1988a), 'Running Costs Guidance: Location of Work', March.

H. M. Treasury (1988b), *Civil Service Statistics*.

H. M. Treasury (1992a), *Civil Service Statistics*.

H. M. Treasury (1992b), 'Financial Secretary Reports on Progress of Civil Service Relocation', press release, 16 December.

Hobsbawm, Eric (1969), *Industry and Empire*, Penguin.

House Builders Federation (1993), *Housing Market Report*, March.

Howard, Michael (1993a), 'Consistent Policy on Oxleas Wood', *Daily Telegraph*, 24 February.

Howard, Michael (1993b), 'Task Force Proposed to Boost East Thames Corridor', Department of the Environment press release, 24 March.

Howard, R. S. (1968), 'New Information on the Movement of Industry', *Board of Trade Journal*, 13 September, 695–7.

Institute for Fiscal Studies (1993), *Right this Time? An Analysis of the First Year's Council Tax Figures*, April.

Invest in Britain Bureau (1992), *Annual Report* 1991–2.

Jack, Ian (1990), 'So Farewell Then, Land of Miracles', *Independent*, 24 November.

Jenkins, Lin (1988), 'Industrial North "worst for men's blood pressure"', *Daily Telegraph*, 25 May.

Jenkins, Simon (1992), 'The LWT London Lecture: London's Forthcoming Boom', November.

Johnman, Lewis (1986), 'The Large Manufacturing Companies of 1935', *Business History*, 28 (2), April, 226–45.

Johnson, Christopher (1991), *The Economy Under Mrs Thatcher*, Penguin.

Johnston, R. J., and Pattie, C. J. (1987), 'A Dividing Nation? An Initial Exploration of the Changing Electoral Geography of Great Britain, 1979–87', *Environment and Planning*, 19, 1001–13.

Johnston, R. J. and Pattie, C. J. (1988), 'Voting in Britain since 1979: A Growing North–South Divide?', paper presented to Institute of British Geographers conference, January.

Johnston, R. J., and Pattie, C. J. (1992a), 'Is the Seesaw Tipping Back? The End of Thatcherism and Changing Voting Patterns in Great Britain 1979–92', *Environment and Planning* 24, 1491–1505.

Johnston, R. J., and Pattie, C. J. (1992b), 'Unemployment, the Poll Tax, and the British General Election of 1992', *Environment and Planning (Government and Policy)* 10, 467–83.

Johnston R. J., Pattie, C. J., and Allsop, J. G. (1988), *A Nation Dividing?*, Longman.

Johnston, R. J., Pattie, C. J., and Russell, A. T. (1993), 'Dealignment, Spatial Polarisation and Economic Voting: An Exploration of Recent Trends in British Voting Behaviour', *European Journal of Political Research*, 23, 67–90.

Lamont, Norman (1992), 'Britain and the Exchange Rate Mechanism – Chancellor's Speech to the European Policy Forum', H. M. Treasury, 10 July.

Law, Christopher M. (1980), *British Regional Development Since World War I*, David & Charles.

Lawson, Nigel (1984), 'The British Experiment – the 5th Mais Lecture', H. M. Treasury, 18 June.

Lawson, Nigel (1992), *The View from No. 11: The Memoirs of a Tory Radical*, Bantam Press.

Lewis, J. R. (1987), 'The Urban and Regional Consequences of the Financial Services Revolution in the UK', paper to the twenty-seventh European Congress of the Regional Science Association, Athens, August.

Leyshon, Andrew, and Thrift, Nigel (1988), 'The City of London: Southern Fortune or Northern Misfortune?', University of Bristol.

Lipsey, David (1981), 'Is the North–South Divide a Great British Myth?' *Sunday Times*, 13 September.

McAllister, Ian, and Rose, Richard (1984), *The Nationwide Competition for Votes*, Frances Pinter.

McCormick, Barry (1987), transcript of talk to Institute of Economic Affairs conference on North and South, May.

McEnery, John (1981), *Manufacturing Two Nations*, Institute of Economic Affairs.

McEnery, John (1988), 'Closing Britain's Economic Divide', *Financial Times*, 8 February.

MacInnes, John (1987), 'The North–South Divide: Regional Employment Change in Britain, 1975–87', Centre for Urban and Regional Research, Discussion Paper No. 34, University of Glasgow.

Manchester Business School (1988), 'Survey of Business Leaders' Opinions', commissioned by Granada Television, October.

Marcus, Steven (1974), *Engels, Manchester and the Working Class*, Weidenfeld and Nicolson.

Market and Opinion Research International (1986), *Survey on 'Modern Man'*, MORI, London.

Market and Opinion Research International (1992), *British Public Opinion*, March, MORI, London.

Martin, Ron (1988), 'The Political Economy of Britain's North–South Divide', revised transcript of paper delivered to Institute of British Geographers annual conference, Loughborough University, January 5–8.

Martin, Ron, and Tyler, Peter (1991), 'The Regional Policy Legacy of the Thatcher Years', University of Cambridge Department of Land Economy, Discussion Paper 36.

Mathias, Peter (1983), *The First Industrial Nation* (second edition), Methuen.

Matthews, R. C. O., Feinstein, C. H., and Odling-Smee, J. C. (1982), *British Economic Growth, 1856–1973*, Oxford University Press.

Mayer, Colin (1988), City University Business School Inaugural Lecture.

Messinger, Gary S. (1985), *Manchester in the Victorian Age*, Manchester University Press.

Miller, W. L. (1977), *Electoral Dynamics*, Macmillan.

Minford, Patrick (1987a), *Centres and Peripheries: A Policy Perspective*, University of Liverpool.

Minford, Patrick (1987b), Summary of talk on 'How Housing and Labour Market Distortions Reinforce the North–South Divide', Centre for Economic Policy Research, 25 September.

Minford, Patrick, Peel, Michael, and Ashton, Paul (1987), *The Housing Morass*, Institute of Economic Affairs.

Mintel (1988), *Regional Lifestyles*, August.

Mintel (1992), *Regional Lifestyles*, November.

Mitchell, Austin (1987), 'Beyond Socialism', *Political Quarterly*, 58, 389–403.

Moore, B., Rhodes, J., and Tyler, P. (1986), *The Effects of Government Regional Economic Policy*, Department of Trade and Industry, HMSO.

Morrill, John (1984), 'The Stuarts', in Kenneth O. Morgan (ed.), *The Oxford Illustrated History of Britain*, Oxford University Press.

Muellbauer, John, and Murphy, Anthony (1988), 'UK House Prices and Migration: Economic and Investment Implications', Shearson Lehman.

Naisbitt, John (1984), *Megatrends*, Futura.

National Westminster Bank (1993), *Economic and Financial Outlook*, April.

Nationwide Building Society (1988a), press notice on second quarter of 1988 house-price survey, 4 July.

Nationwide Building Society (1988b), 'House Prices, Third Quarter of 1988'.

Nationwide Building Society (1988c), 'House Prices, Second Quarter of 1988'.

Nationwide Building Society (1993), 'House Prices, First Quarter of 1993', April.

Northern Echo (1992), 'Health – The Hirsute North–South Parting', 22 February.

Northern Ireland Economic Research Centre/Oxford Economic Forecasting (1992), *Regional Economic Outlook*, August.

Northfield, Lord (1988), 'Michael Heseltine Accused', Consortium Developments press release, 31 May.

Office of Population, Censuses and Surveys (1992), '1991 Census, Great Britain', *OPCS Monitor*, December.

Orwell, George (1959), *The Road to Wigan Pier*, Secker and Warburg. (First published 1937.)

Orwell, George (1968), *Collected Essays, Journalism and Letters of George Orwell*, Secker and Warburg.

PA Cambridge Economic Consultants/Department of Land Economy, University of Cambridge (1992), *Cambridge Economic Review*, 2, November.

Pacione, M. (ed.) (1985), *Progress in Industrial Geography*, Croom Helm.

Padoa-Schioppa, Tommaso (1987), *Efficiency, Stability and Equity: A*

Strategy for the Evolution of the Economic System of the European Community, Oxford University Press.

Pattie, C. J., Johnston, RJ., and Fieldhouse, E. (1993), 'Plus ça Change? The Changing Electoral Geography of Great Britain, 1979–92', in D. Denver, P. Norris, D. Broughton and C. Rallings (eds.), *British Parties and Elections Yearbook 1993*, Harvester Wheatsheaf.

Peck, Francis, and Townsend, Alan (1984), 'Contrasting Experience of Recession and Spatial Restructuring: British Shipbuilders, Plessey and Metal Box', *Regional Studies* 18 (4), 319–38.

Pissarides C. A., and Wadsworth, J. (1987), 'Unemployment and the Inter-regional Mobility of Labour', Centre for Labour Economics Discussion Paper No. 296, London School of Economics, November.

Pliatsky, Leo (1982), *Getting and Spending*, Basil Blackwell.

Pollard, Sidney (1983), *The Development of the British Economy, 1914–80* (third edition), Edward Arnold.

Prest, A. R., and Coppock, D. J. (1982), *The UK Economy*, Weidenfeld and Nicolson.

Priestley, J. B. (1984), *English Journey* (Jubilee edition), Heinemann. (First published 1934.)

Randall, Colin (1990), 'North–South Twinning is Marred by Squabble', *Daily Telegraph*, 24 March.

Reward Group (1988), *Cost of Living, Regional Comparisons*, February.

Rhodes, J., and Tyler, P. (1992), 'Manufacturing in Europe', *Cambridge Economic Review*, vol. 2, Department of Land Economy, Cambridge/PA Cambridge Economic Consultants.

Ricketts, Martin (1987), 'Property Market Rigidities and the North–South Divide'. Paper presented to Institute of Economic Affairs conference on North and South, May.

Rollins Julian (1990), 'Scots Girls Inch Ahead in 30-something C Cups: Bra Sizes', *Today*, 19 June.

Rostow, W. W. (1960), *The Process of Economic Growth*, Clarendon Press.

Rubinstein, W. D. (1988), 'Social Class, Social Attitudes and British Business Life', *Oxford Review of Economic Policy* 4 (1), 51–8.

Rusbridger, Alan (1988), 'Village Ripe for Development Haunted by Neighbour's Fate', *Guardian*, 30 May.

St Helens (1988), 'Pilkington's only option', Metropolitan Borough of St Helens.

Sampson, Anthony (1962), *The Anatomy of Britain*, Hodder.

SERPLAN (London and South East Regional Planning Conference) (1988a) *Annual Report*, 1987–8.

SERPLAN (1988b), 'South East England in the 1990s: A Regional Statement'.

SERPLAN (1988c), 'Housing Land Supply and Structure Plan Provisions in the South East', June.

Shaw, Christine (1983), 'The Large Manufacturing Employers of 1907' *Business History* 25 (1) March, 42–60.

Sinfield, Adrian (1981), *What Unemployment Means*, Martin Robertson.

Small Business Research Centre, University of Cambridge (1992), *The State of British Enterprise: Growth, Innovation and Competitive Advantage in Small and Medium-sized Firms*.

Small Business Research Programme, Economic and Social Research Council.

Smith, David (1987), *The Rise and Fall of Monetarism*, Penguin.

Smith, David (1989), *North and South* (first edition), Pelican.

Smith, David (1992a), *From Boom to Bust*, Penguin.

Smith, David (1992b), *Small Business in Britain: A Review of the ESRC*

Smith, Les (1991), 'Giro Blues', *Guardian*, 9 October.

Spencer, Peter (1988), 'The Community Charge and its Likely Effects on the UK Economy', Credit Suisse First Boston, June.

Stewart, Ian (1988), *A North/South Divide? Some Reflections on Regional Policy*, Conservative Research Department, March.

Stilwell, Frank J. B. (1972), *Regional Economic Policy*, Macmillan.

Sunday Times (1987a), 'The Nonsense of North–South', 11 January.

Sunday Times (1987b), Letters, 18 January.

Swann, Dennis (1988), *The Economics of the Common Market* (sixth edition), Penguin.

Taylor, M., and Thrift, N. (eds.) (1986), *Multinationals and the Restructuring of the World Economy*, Croom Helm.

Taylor, P. J., and Johnston, R. J. (1979), *Geography of Elections*, Penguin.

Thatcher, Margaret (1980), speech to Welsh Conservative Party Conference, Conservative Central Office, 20 July.

The Times (1987), *The Times 1,000, 1987–88*, Times Books.

Today/TV-am (1990), 'British Male Survey', *Today*, 5 November.

Toulson, Leslie (1987), 'Horrible Secret of Northern Baldies', *Sun*, 16 July.

Town and Country Planning Association (1987), *North–South Divide: A New Deal for Britain's Regions*, November.

Town and Country Planning Association (1988), Letter to Paul Channon, Transport Secretary, 23 June.

Townsend, Alan (1986), 'Spatial Aspects of the Growth of Part-time Employment in Britain', *Regional Studies*, 20 (4), 313–29.

Townsend, Peter, Davidson, Nick, and Whitehead, Margaret (1988), *Inequalities in Health: The Black Report and The Health Divide*, Penguin.

Townsend, P., Phillimore, P., and Beattie, A. (1986), 'Inequalities in Health in the Northern Region: An Interim Report', Northern Regional Health Authority/Bristol University.

Trevelyan, G. M. (1944), *English Social History*, Longmans, Green.

Waldegrave, William (1987), speech to the East Surrey Conservative Women's Committee, Conservative Central Office, 27 November.

Watts, H. D. (1988a), 'Non-financial Head Offices: A Northern Perspective', paper presented to Institute of British Geographers conference, January.

Watts, H. D. (1988b), 'Regional Industrial Change', *Geographical Magazine*, January.

Weightman, Gavin, and Humphries, Steve (1984), *The Making of Modern London*, 1914–39, Sidgwick and Jackson.

White Horse Mortgage Services (1993), 'Mortgage Arrears Analyses – Fourth Quarter 1992'.

Wight, Robin (1987), 'The Cost of Anti-southern Prejudice', *The Times*, 23 June.

Willsher, Kim (1987), 'Travel South to Stay Young', *Daily Express*, 24 April.

Woffinden, Bob (1988), 'Life Swapping', *The Listener*, 5 May.

Woolhouse, Richard, and Mansley, Nick (1992), 'The Prospects for the Counties in the 1990s', *Cambridge Economic Review*, vol. 2, 25–33, Department of Land Economy, Cambridge/PA Cambridge Economic Consultants.

Yusuf, Nilgin (1991), 'Northern Comfort', *Guardian*, 28 January.

INDEX

READ MORE IN PENGUIN

In every corner of the world, on every subject under the sun, Penguin represents quality and variety – the very best in publishing today.

For complete information about books available from Penguin – including Puffins, Penguin Classics and Arkana – and how to order them, write to us at the appropriate address below. Please note that for copyright reasons the selection of books varies from country to country.

In the United Kingdom: Please write to *Dept. JC, Penguin Books Ltd, FREEPOST, West Drayton, Middlesex UB7 0BR*

If you have any difficulty in obtaining a title, please send your order with the correct money, plus ten per cent for postage and packaging, to *PO Box No. 11, West Drayton, Middlesex UB7 0BR*

In the United States: Please write to *Penguin USA Inc., 375 Hudson Street, New York, NY 10014*

In Canada: Please write to *Penguin Books Canada Ltd, 10 Alcorn Avenue, Suite 300, Toronto, Ontario M4V 3B2*

In Australia: Please write to *Penguin Books Australia Ltd, 487 Maroondah Highway, Ringwood, Victoria 3134*

In New Zealand: Please write to *Penguin Books (NZ) Ltd, 182–190 Wairau Road, Private Bag, Takapuna, Auckland 9*

In India: Please write to *Penguin Books India Pvt Ltd, 706 Eros Apartments, 56 Nehru Place, New Delhi 110 019*

In the Netherlands: Please write to *Penguin Books Netherlands B.V., Keizersgracht 231 NL–1016 DV Amsterdam*

In Germany: Please write to *Penguin Books Deutschland GmbH, Friedrichstrasse 10–12, W–6000 Frankfurt/Main 1*

In Spain: Please write to *Penguin Books S. A., C. San Bernardo 117-6° E–28015 Madrid*

In Italy: Please write to *Penguin Italia s.r.l., Via Felice Casati 20, I–20124 Milano*

In France: Please write to *Penguin France S. A., 17 rue Lejeune, F–31000 Toulouse*

In Japan: Please write to *Penguin Books Japan, Ishikiribashi Building, 2–5–4, Suido, Tokyo 112*

In Greece: Please write to *Penguin Hellas Ltd, Dimocritou 3, GR–106 71 Athens*

In South Africa: Please write to *Longman Penguin Southern Africa (Pty) Ltd, Private Bag X08, Bertsham 2013*